Parents Killing Children

Parents Killing Children: Crossing the Invisible Line explores hidden forms of violence within the family. This socio-legal study addresses the interactions between the family and the state, focusing on six parent perpetrators and the ways in which child endangerment is concealed within society.

Drawing on symbolic interactionism, mythology and a modelling of case study data, this book puts forward a unique conceptualisation of representation and risk, both on familial and state levels. The failure of the state to intervene and neutralise volatile perpetrators also sheds light on the socio-legal status of children – society's most vulnerable – and the book concludes by discussing means by which the underlying social conditions and maladies symptomatic of child abuse and killing should be addressed.

Janice Sim is a Lecturer at Griffith University School of Criminology and Criminal Justice and a Griffith University Law Futures Centre Associate Member. She convenes Introduction to Maritime Law at the Griffith Law School. Janice completed her doctorate at the Faculty of Law at the University of Sydney and was a post-doctorate Fellow. She has an eclectic range of research interests in, but not limited to, filicide, child protection, intervention, representation, vulnerable populations, piracy and maritime law and security.

Parents Killing Children

Crossing the Invisible Line

Janice Sim

Routledge
Taylor & Francis Group
LONDON AND NEW YORK

First published 2019
by Routledge
2 Park Square, Milton Park, Abingdon, Oxon OX14 4RN

and by Routledge
52 Vanderbilt Avenue, New York, NY 10017, USA

First issued in paperback 2020

Routledge is an imprint of the Taylor & Francis Group, an informa business

British Library Cataloguing-in-Publication Data
A catalogue record for this book is available from the British Library

Library of Congress Cataloging-in-Publication Data
A catalog record has been requested for this book

ISBN 13: 978-0-367-58550-1 (pbk)
ISBN 13: 978-1-4724-7074-4 (hbk)

Typeset in Galliard
by Florence Production Ltd, Stoodleigh, Devon, UK

To my family,
thank you.

And
for the children whose voices
go unheard.
In the shadows, they remain
invisible.

Contents

Figures

Table of cases

Case judgments that have been de-identified in accordance with the book's privacy undertaking are excluded from this list.

Table of legal instruments

Preface

This book retells the stories of six parent perpetrators of filicide. Set in New South Wales, Australia, these six filicide cases present the book's central themes on representation and intervention. In these stories, state intervention is a tragic and passive force in the lives of the deceased children. These are stories of parents who portray themselves and are portrayed by others as loving, compliant and caring towards their children, and who were never thought of as dangerous prior to their crime. The book takes the reader through the lives of these parents and ultimately, to their final breaking points. Each analysis re-examines the confluence of events that led to the failure of state workers to neutralise the danger to the child. The stories reveal certain risks of harm to the child that may have been manifested if not for the fact that they are often masked by the parent's outward loving demeanour towards the child. At its very heart, the book unmasks the complex symbolisms of parental love.

This is also a book about forms of hidden violence in the family. Drawing on symbolic interactionism and mythology, the book unpacks the nature of representation to be multi-layered and symbolically weaved and embedded within, and structured along, deep social and cultural beliefs. In its conclusion, an understanding on risk is reached, that risk cannot be detached from representation. A nuanced understanding of risk must be contextualised within the social conditions and social maladies that are symptomatic of child killing.

Abbreviations

CAR	Commonwealth Arbitration Reports (Australia)
CLR	Commonwealth Law Reports (Australia)
Cr.App.R.	Criminal Appeal Reports (England and Wales)
CRNZ	Criminal Reports of New Zealand
CYP Act	*Children and Young Persons (Care and Protection) Act 1998* (NSW)
FamCA	Family Court of Australia
FLC	Australian Family Law Cases
FLR	Family Law Reports (England and Wales)
NSWADT	New South Wales Administrative Decisions Tribunal
NSWCCA	New South Wales Court of Criminal Appeal
NSWIRComm	Industrial Relations Commission of New South Wales
NSWSC	New South Wales Supreme Court
SASC	South Australia Supreme Court
UNCROC	*United Nations Convention on the Rights of the Child*

Introduction[1]

Child killing is a terrible event that challenges the existing framework of child protection and its policies. Yet it is often difficult to obtain a holistic understanding of the social influences leading to the death of a child. Child killing is of course a most serious crime and is dealt with, after the event, under the criminal law in all criminal jurisdictions of Australia and in most jurisdictions internationally. Problematic behaviours and events leading up to filicide are often dealt with by human and social services, but without the recognition that they may be indicators of intent to kill a child. The primary purpose of this book is to provide a nuanced and critical understanding of some of the social influences that impact on risk of filicide; to examine the meaning of social and legal representations of the child, parent, family and state in the context of child killing; and to explore the interactions between the social and the law in this context.

A variety of sources using qualitative methodology and methods have been drawn upon to explore instances of filicide. Data sources are taken from coronial and prosecution files of filicide cases, government reports and other secondary sources, including news media and published biographies and autobiographies. These are essentially documentary narratives, which focus on the interactions between the perpetrator, state agents and the child. To interpret these narratives in a meaningful and interactive way, the narratives are written up as case studies, and are interpreted and analysed. Modelling is used to assist this process, with different representations constructed from different individual perspectives drawn together in order to map the social interactions between key stakeholders prior to the death of the child. This then allows for a meaningful interrogation of representation in a way that sheds light on the construction of risk. The modelling analysis provides critical theorising on the nature of representation. This critical frame of enquiry questions the given form and vitality of representations about risk, the perpetrator(s) and the social interaction between the state and family, all of which emerge from the case studies. The significance of symbols in creating meaning through social interaction aligns with symbolic interaction theory.

1 This chapter introduces the conceptual development of the book in terms of critical theorising, literature review and methodological development.

Hence, symbolic interactionism is used as an overarching theoretical framework. An influential factor in the choice of symbolic interactionism is its focus on the law, labelling and representation.

The originality of this research emerges from its interactionist method of enquiry and its theorising on meanings and symbols in relation to the parent, the child and the state. Its research method, utilising information in the form of case studies, involves examining closely social interaction, representations and symbols. The data is modelled to show the significance of representation and symbols and to investigate the consequences of representation and reaction that produce risk. In Chapter 6, new understandings of interactive risk are suggested that may enable the repositioning of the child away from endangerment. The parent and the state represent key stakeholders in the child's life and have a strong influence over the factors of endangerment. This study seeks to enrich understandings of the different socio-legal factors in a child's life that endanger the child and bring about death. These factors emerge as a result of looking holistically at the conditions that produce death. The most insightful way to theorise about these conditions producing endangerment and death is to employ a symbolic interactionist train of enquiry that allows for an interactive methodology that looks at social interaction and processes of decision-making and meaning-making of symbols and representations.

The book's symbolic interactionist method developed out of a research interest in tracing the perpetrator's experience through the criminal justice system that did not stop short at self-accounts. It gradually became clear that a wider net needed to be cast over data sources in order to develop a richer understanding of the influences that construct perpetrator representation. This interest in perpetrator representation soon developed into an exploratory interest in factors around child endangerment. From the coronial files it became clear that the background information provided by the coronial method needed to be extended to include prosecution files, which would provide a fuller account of what happened to the perpetrators and how they were dealt with in the criminal justice system. From data from coronial and prosecution files, certain representations and symbols about the parent, child and state emerged clearly. The data also showed that the interaction between the different stakeholders was crucial to the outcome of the child, i.e. whether he or she lived or died. Essentially, this is a study about social and symbolic interactions between parent, child and state, which influence the developmental safety pathways of a child's life. Interactionists argue that social life is patterned by symbolic indicators.[2] This theorising justifies the use of coronial and prosecution files and trial observation, the purpose of which is to develop a richer conceptualisation of the meanings of representation around these key symbols. Sourcing a range of data sources is also in alignment with symbolic interactionist theory because these different data sources represent different stages in the decision-making process, which has its foundations in interactionism.

2 David Downes and Paul Rock, *Understanding Deviance* (Oxford University Press, 4th ed, 2003) 183.

The research interest led to the case study data, which arose from a selective symbolic interaction method requiring more data sources to enrich understandings with regard to interaction and symbolic appreciation. Representation became significant when questions regarding the creation of meanings through symbols emerged,[3] leading to a new understanding of risk that relied on representation. The choice of an interactive case study method and symbolic interactionist theory enriches this understanding process in ways that previous research has not. Additionally, as the fieldwork progressed, it became clear to me that the research data that was emerging from the cases was pointing to symbolic indicators of violence, which were not detected by the authorities. This observation led to a deeper and more critical enquiry into the symbols of child endangerment, which over time grew into observable conditions of risk that arose from the case study data and the interpretive modelling of this data. Looking back on the interactive process of research enquiry, symbolic interactionism provided the interactive and developmental method that gave birth to the eventual conceptualisation of representation and the centrality through which representation informs and constructs meanings of child endangerment and risk.

Purpose

The purpose of this introduction is to demonstrate that symbolic interactionism theory and the interactive method when applied to a study of social interactions can make inroads into understanding specific research themes on representation, symbols and violence within child killing. The data sources relied upon – coronial and prosecutorial files, media narratives, case law, biographies and autobiographies – enhance the interactionist method and approach to conceptualising social interaction in meaningful ways that contribute to understandings as to the purpose, vitality and form of symbolic indications in social life.[4] In this book, these include symbols of the state, the parent and the child. Understanding the purpose of interactional relationships within these contexts is important if insights are to be gained into the phenomenon of filicide, particularly where the symbol of the child is representative of, and central to, constructions around rights and protections in the international and national human rights and law discourses.

The use of definitions is important in symbolic interactionist theory and for contextualising the discussions to follow. In particular, definitions are important to the extent that they influence representation and vice versa. Similarly, when examining the development of symbols it is analytically dangerous to take definitions out of their representative context, which would distort their intended meaning. Additionally, it is necessary to acknowledge the 'dark figure of crime', the amount of crime that is undetected or unreported, at the outset and note

3 Marcel Hénaff, 'Lévi-Strauss and the Question of Symbolism' in Boris Wiseman (ed) *The Cambridge Companion to Lévi-Strauss* (Cambridge, 2009) 189–190.

4 Norman Denzin, *Symbolic Interactionism and Cultural Studies: The Politics of Interpretation* (Blackwell, 1992) 22–25.

that the nine case studies in this book are not representative of all child killings in New South Wales.[5] The following section attempts to provide context by defining the key descriptors used throughout the book.

Definitions

Child killing in Western societies generally refers to child homicide, which is defined as the death of a child under the age of 18 whose case has been referred to the Coroner's Court as a suspected homicide, and where the subsequent investigation by the coroner or police reveals that the death was caused by another person.[6] The term 'infanticide' is used to refer broadly to the killing of a child by its mother within the first 12 months of life,[7] and the term 'neonaticide' refers to killing of a child within the first 24 hours post-birth.[8] 'Filicide' refers to the killing of a child by a parent or parent-substitute, such as a stepfather or stepmother.[9] Alder and Polk point out that filicide, for millennia, has been a 'method of eliminating devalued or unwanted children such as those lacking a socially acceptable father, deformed infants, infants possessing an undesirable physical characteristic such as the wrong skin colour or sex, and those conceived by rape'.[10] For the purposes of this book, the term 'child killing' is used to refer to both filicide and infanticide. The term 'child homicide' is rarely used, because 'homicide' is a term specific to the legal and criminological discourses and defined by the criminal law in each Australian state and territory.[11] The book takes the broader view that child killing is a term that is culturally sensitive, particularly in

5 Nor is the broader original sample of 40 coronial cases representative of child killing in New South Wales for this time period. The search parameters to the National Coronial Information System discussed in the following sections were formulated with a specific focus on assault and homicide. It did not pick up child deaths as a consequence of parental neglect or maltreatment that may have been coded as natural death or accidental death at the point of data entry into the system, save for the case study of Hannah Bromley, which was identified in the public domain in 2009. As pointed out by Alder and Polk and also Wilczynski, there are many reasons why certain child deaths go undetected as homicide and thus it is probable that the true incidence of child killing is underestimated: Christine Alder and Ken Polk, *Child Victims of Homicide* (Cambridge University Press, 2001) 19–21; Ania Wilczynski, *Child Homicide* (Oxford University Press, 1997), 23–36. For the 'dark figure of crime', see Hennessey Hayes and Time Prenzler, *Introduction to Crime and Criminology* (Pearson, 2nd ed, 2009) 35.

6 Alder and Polk, ibid 18.

7 Ibid 4.

8 Phillip Resnick, 'Murder of the Newborn: A Psychiatric Review of Neonaticide' (1970) 126(10) *American Journal of Psychiatry* 1414–1420, 1415–1416.

9 Wilczynski, above n 5, 8.

10 Alder and Polk, above n 5.

11 Marie Virueda and Jason Payne, *Homicide in Australia 2007–2008 National Homicide Monitoring Program (NHMP) Annual Report* (Australian Institute of Criminology Monitoring Reports No. 13, 2010) 3.

certain cultures and periods of time where the practice was widespread and its criminality was less than clear.

Themes

Unlike the pre-existing literature on filicide, this book looks particularly at the relationship between risk and representation, which are used as dynamic tools for risk analysis and policy developments in child protection. These terms are discussed and defined in Chapters 4 and 7.

A key theme emerging from the analysis is misrepresentation, which sits alongside other interactive themes such as meaning-making (discussed in Chapters 4 and 5), masking (defined in Chapter 2), labelling (discussed in Chapters 2 and 5), dysfunctional intervention (discussed in Chapter 6) and symbolic violence (discussed and defined in Chapter 2). All these themes can be conceptualised under the broad umbrella of symbolic interactionism theory, which, as noted, has been chosen as the underlying theory for the book. As such, it merits a brief introduction. This is followed by an exposition of the combination of case study and case law method used in the book. Following this, there is a lengthier theoretical discussion on the choice and significance of symbolic interactionism. There is then a short discussion on the existing literature on filicide and, finally, an explanation of the structure of the book.

Symbolic interaction theory

Symbolic interactionism is an interactive and multifaceted theory that combines sociological and criminological analyses in order to gain an understanding of criminal behaviour.[12] As will be discussed below, this theory moves beyond studying social interactions between individuals. It also explains the interactions between individuals, symbols, the law, the process of meaning-making, and understandings regarding the interplay of these interactive forces. In other words, symbolic interactionist theory is grounded in, and embodies, an aspect of social theory.[13] It can be an interactive methodology as well as an interactive theory, as will be explained below.

First, a brief discussion on the connection between the interactionist method and symbolic interactionism theory is needed to demonstrate their connection in this book, which is built on the interaction between method and theory. In this

12 Downes and Rock, above n 2, 178–182. See also Stanley Cohen, 'Criminology and the Sociology of Deviance in Britain' in Paul Rock and Mary McIntosh (eds), *Deviance and Social Control* (Tavistock, 1974) 2–7; and John Kitsuse, 'Societal Reaction to Deviant Behavior: Problems of Theory and Method' (1962) *Social Problems* 247–256.

13 Downes and Rock, above n 2, 180. See also Howard Becker, *Tricks of the Trade: How to Think about Your Research While You're Doing It* (University of Chicago Press, 1998) 53.

book, the method is built on the study of different social and legal interactions between the state and the parent, and the state and the family. At the heart of the book is a study of filicidal violence. By utilising multiple data sources, the book replicates symbolic interactionism theory by placing emphasis on the study of symbolic indicators of violence. Some of these indicators will be argued to be crucial to the production of understandings that mask violence. This can only be theorised using a method that involves representing these symbols and demonstrating the connection between social actors and the system.[14] Such a method can only be interactionistic in the sense that it is able to represent these interactions under study. From this perspective, the method embodies the theory, and this provides the foundational groundwork for the book to make its conclusions as regards the riskiness of certain representations, symbols and interactions.

The following section now discusses the choice of a case study method and the process of formulation of this research. It conceptualises for the reader the processual decision-making as to the research questions and method interaction with the choice of data sources, both of which are shaped by symbolic interactionism.

Mind and method: why a case study method?

The combination of case study and case law[15]

The method used in this book is a case study method. This section maps the development of this method, but it is first necessary to differentiate the meaning of case study method in the sociological and criminological discourses from the legal meaning of case law. In the social sciences, case study is a formal research strategy or method that describes and illuminates the development of the subject topic, which can include a set of decisions, individuals, organisations, institutions or events.[16] Robert Yin provides the following definition of 'case study': 'The essence of a case study, the central tendency among all types of case study, is that it tries to illuminate a *decision* or set of decisions: why they were taken, how they were implemented, and with what result.'[17] Yin argues that case study is a 'comprehensive research strategy' that investigates contemporary phenomena within real-life contexts, particularly where the boundaries between the phenomenon and context are not clearly evident.[18] The following sections are devoted to explaining the process of data collection and my reasons for using the case study methodology. 'Case law' is a legal term that generally refers to judicial

14 Ibid 194.
15 Case law is not used in this book as a critical narrative any more than in terms of lawyers' submissions and case judgments, which are but one form of representation.
16 Robert K Yin, *Case Study Research: Design and Methods* (Sage, 3rd ed, 2003) 12.
17 Ibid.
18 Ibid 13.

determinations and legal decisions made in disputed cases that are heard in a court of law.[19] The combination of case law and legislation is essentially what constitutes the legal research methodology in an Australian legal context.[20] This book uses a combination of the social science case study research strategy and legal research methods to analyse the data. The social science method is used for data collection and to construct the case studies, and the legal research method is used to provide corroboration, triangulation and enhancement of the data arising from the social science method of data collection. This method allowed me to draw out specific sociological and criminological themes from the fieldwork data and from the case judgments, which were sourced from case law available in the public domain.

This said, the legal narrative and pronouncements did not offer a sufficiently comprehensive understanding of child killing beyond perpetrator motives and legal representation of the deviant parent. What was sought was a fuller picture of child killing that takes into account understandings as to interactions between key symbols such as the state, the parent and the child. It can be said that the legal narration reflected the expressive role of the law, but did not adequately provide insights into the facilitative aspects of law, such as interactions between state agents and the family.[21]

The present study[22]

At the beginning, the aim was to explore the broad theme of self-perception within labelling theory. The initial research reflected a contemporary perspective grounded in theory about how filicide perpetrators perceive themselves, and how their experiences in the criminal justice system have shaped their lives. The intention was to interview mothers and fathers, as well as parent-substitutes such as stepmothers and stepfathers, who had killed their children, or children in their care, to test my hypothesis, which was that the site of primary deviance in labelling theory begins with the perpetrator. Labelling theory within criminological discourse is usually applied to theft, prostitution, drug-taking, mental illness, alcoholism, sexual deviance and juvenile delinquency, but its limits are

19 William Twining and David Miers, *How to Do Things with Rules: A Primer of Interpretation* (Cambridge University Press, 5th ed, 2010) ch 9. These cases make up a larger body of law called the common law in Commonwealth countries.

20 Terry Hutchinson, *Researching and Writing in Law* (Lawbook, 2nd ed, 2006) 36–37.

21 Bronwen Morgan and Karen Yeung, *An Introduction to Law and Regulation* (Cambridge University Press, 2009) 5–6.

22 The key influences for the shift from an initial interest in self-representation to a broader interest in representation and risk are the practical considerations of access, the emerging nature of the data as revealed by the data files, the type of documentary narratives, and the committed focus to interrogating state intervention at depth.

rarely specified.[23] The project wanted to uncover whether labels were used against these perpetrators either by themselves (through funnelling into his or her circumstances and through the imposition of self-labels leading to the primary act of deviance) or through partners or members of society that may have led them to believe and become the label (applied).

There were, however, significant challenges to such a task, such as the theory of secondary deviance in labelling theory. Secondary deviance follows from the imposition of the formal label by the criminal justice system for the initial act of killing.[24] In cases such as theft and drug-taking, this means greater opportunities for criminal recidivism after the imposition of the label on the perpetrator by the criminal justice system. Yet in most cases of filicide, practically speaking, it is unlikely that the perpetrators will have an opportunity to reoffend following a conviction for murder or manslaughter, especially for female filicide perpetrators, as they may most likely be past their childbearing years. From this perspective, the study challenged the labelling proposition of secondary deviance in filicide cases. Alternatively, it was next hypothesised that there might be no secondary deviance in filicide crimes, which implies that negative criminal labelling can be productive.

Another aim was to undertake a study of the labelling process at the point where perpetrators are subject to formal intervention by the police and judicial authorities. The intention here was to study the effects of publicly imposed labels and social and judicial responses to the killing and consequences of societal reaction. The intention was to investigate the positive and negative impact of labelling on the perpetrators, as well as to trace the ramifications of having been labelled to the subsequent impact of their reintegration (if any) into society. The purpose of this approach was to challenge the labelling proposition that negative labelling produces secondary deviance, and to provide an in-depth exploration of the relationship between the initial labelling and the disadvantages of such labelling, if any. Additionally, the purpose is to follow up on any subsequent effects and impacts of labelling on the perpetrator's psyche and mental construction, or reconstruction, of his or her Self and 'Other'. In particular, the focus was to be on theories regarding female filicidal perpetrators and the reasons for the different perception of the nature of their crimes compared to those of male perpetrators.[25] As such, the idea was to examine female and male filicide perpetrators in terms of differing social reactions and socio-legal labels for the same act of killing.

23 Edwin M Lemert, *Social Pathology: A Systematic Approach to the Theory of Sociopathic Behaviour* (McGraw-Hill, 1951) 236–443; Thomas J Scheff, *Being Mentally Ill: A Sociological Theory* (Aldine De Gruyter, 3rd ed, 1984), ch 5, ch 9; and John Braithwaite, *Crime, Shame and Reintegration* (Cambridge University Press, 16th ed, 2006) 20.

24 Lemert, ibid 75–76.

25 Wilczynski, above n 5, ch 5; and Alder and Polk, above n 5, ch 4, ch 5.

Limitations

There were obvious challenges to this initial conceptualisation of the project, such as the availability and sufficiency of data to support rigorous testing of the hypothesis and labelling theory. These limitations, however, were addressed in a revised plan for the book by the subsequent pursuit of Director of Public Prosecution ('DPP') files and triangulation of the case study data wherever possible. This said, there were still concerns regarding access to the data. Faced with this data 'minefield', I visited the New South Wales Department of Corrective Services to discuss options for data access. A number of concerns were raised as to: human ethics clearance from Corrective Services, in addition to the human ethics clearance from the University of Sydney; the indeterminate parameters of the study; and the impact of the research on the offenders. It was pointed out that there were only two cases in New South Wales in which the perpetrators were charged with the crime of infanticide under section 22A of the *Crimes Act 1900* (NSW) in 2001 and 2002,[26] and Corrective Services would not be able to assist me with ascertaining a sample population. There were concerns about communicating with the incarcerated population, such as identification of the perpetrators and the method of physical communication.[27] It was pointed out that this process could be dangerous for the offenders because of the nature of their incarceration and their custodial environment, as it could appear to other offenders that these persons were receiving special treatment from the prison wardens if they were seen receiving envelopes or other documents.

There were also genuine concerns regarding the proposed interview method involving filicide perpetrators, such as the danger of raising past traumas and the impact on offenders' welfare and rehabilitation prospects. If the study proceeded, there would need to be a psychologist or counselling referral within reach in case the interviewed offenders needed to be debriefed. As the researcher, I had concerns about the veracity of offenders' verbal accounts and memories of the event. Although this criticism could be countered by arguing that the interview represented their life stories, there was the challenge of making the right call regarding issues such as fact versus representation and injustices, if they arose. There was also the option to access post-release offenders. Having considered these challenges, and the time constraint of three years for the completion of the book, I decided to pare down the original project to reflect only core themes, but I knew this had to be done in a way that would not compromise options for data access.

26 *R v Cooper* [2001] NSWSC 769; and *R v Pope* [2002] NSWSC 397. The perpetrators in similar types of cases were dealt as murder or manslaughter.

27 Snowball sampling could not be used because Corrective Services officers were concerned it might portray the wrong impression to the offenders, that there was some benefit in the project such as the chance of an appeal or opportunities for publicity.

The initial research focus was revised to incorporate only the themes of representation and social interactive symbols. The challenge with regard to the veracity of perpetrator accounts was addressed by employing an interactive method involving multiple data sources, which would allow for corroboration and triangulation of the data. To counter concerns regarding life stories, offender trauma and time constraints, a decision was made not to interview offenders. The study as finally envisaged presented a clearer framework within which the project could reasonably be achieved.

From the original research, the focus narrowed to the core themes of self-perception, or self-representation; social and legal representations; and the interaction between the state and the family, that is, state intervention. The new research questions would be built around these identified themes. By this time, secondary data materials were sourced from the public domain, such as from the New South Wales State Library and various online search engines, criminology, legal and sociological databases (e.g. Factiva), and stories (including autobiographies and biographies) of alleged and convicted child killers, such as Lindy Chamberlain, Kathleen Folbigg and Myra Hindley.[28] The secondary data sources were crucial in informing some of the key themes around the nature of child killing, such as the sensitive environment of their incarceration, personal motivations and circumstances, and the 'shock and awe' nature of media representation of such killings. From researching past newspapers from the year 2000 onwards, a list of child killers who were possibly still incarcerated was accumulated. The next step was to formulate research questions and the research strategy, including the fieldwork options for data access. The core themes pointed to a necessarily theoretical grounding in symbolic interactionism, which provided the analytical framework for critiquing some of the symbols associated with child killing, such as the parent, the child and the state. The research questions too were formulated with these considerations in mind.

The research questions

The new approach focused on representation and risk in relation to state intervention. In particular, it was observed that the data files were revealing representations of risk that were not identified by the authorities and state agents responsible for the safety of the child. This observation led to a desire for a closer examination of the nature of risk representations and conditions from

28 Lindy Chamberlain, *Through My Eyes: The Autobiography of Lindy Chamberlain-Creighton* (East Street Publications, rev ed, 2004); Jean Ritchie, *Myra Hindley: Inside the Mind of a Murderess* (Bay Books, 1988); Mathew Benns, *When the Bough Breaks: The True Story of Child Killer Kathleen Folbigg* (Bantam, 2003); Joe Karam, *David and Goliath: The Bain Family Murders* (Reed Books, 1997); Carolyn Harris Johnson, *Come With Daddy: Child Murder-Suicide After Family Breakdown* (University of Western Australia Press, 2005); Ann Jones, *Women Who Kill* (Holt, Rinehart & Winston, 1980).

which they emerge, and the following four research questions were developed to drive the study:

1. How does perpetrator representation connect with the conditions of child endangerment and risk?
2. How do interactions, symbolic and social, between representations and symbols exacerbate risk?
3. How can risk be assessed in a more significant manner when looking at the interactions of key representations and symbols?
4. Can the repositioning of the child and the child's visibility defuse endangerment? If so, how?

Using symbolic interactionism, the research questions were framed around social interactions, particularly between the state, the family, the parent and the child. This position accords with the thinking of Thomas Scheff, who argues:

> The original labelling theory was also oriented toward the formal labelling process, court hearings, and psychiatric examinations. Labelling (and non-labelling) in these contexts were crude and overt. But in the family . . . labelling is covert. It depends on innuendo, manner, unstated implications, and especially emotion. To detect it, one must interpret words and actions *in context*. (Emphasis added)[29]

Scheff's argument supports the relevance of studying labelling theory outside of the formal context of the court, and as my fieldwork progressed I developed a special interest in how informal labelling by others and self-labelling take place in the home. Scheff's argument suggests that self-labelling can have a powerful influence on criminal behaviour. In addition, little is known about the sociological effects of self-labelling and how this shapes the perception of, and interactions with, other people.

A more detailed discussion of the theorising and its limitations is now needed in order to show how symbolic interactionist theory influenced the development of the book's interactive method. The focus on key symbols and representations in child killing necessarily meant that there was a heightened need for reliance on an interactionist method, and on an investigation of the influence of symbols over this interaction and its impact on representation. An interactionist method and theory in tandem would provide the foundation for this to happen.

Symbolic interactionism[30]

From the beginning, it was clear that a theory with interactive influences had to be used, because of the focus on representation and state intervention. The

29 Scheff, above n 23, 158.
30 Howard Becker, *Outsiders* (Free Press of Glencoe, 1963) 9.

research questions indicated that the study included interactions between symbols and understandings of social and legal actions around representation and misrepresentation in the socio-legal contexts of the family, the criminal justice system and the media, and self-representation. A theory that discussed social interaction and particular symbols, and allowed for the management of case study data in a meaningful and interactive way, was needed. Symbolic interactionism would satisfy all of these requirements, as it is an interactive theory that uses interactive methodology,[31] and it is a single theory that can defend its position effectively. The alternate school of thought is that symbolic interactionism is an umbrella theory that encompasses many other social, interactive and critical theories, such as labelling theory, representation theory, critical social theory and differential association theory. I chose to side with the school of thought that symbolic interactionism is a broad theory. But what exactly is symbolic interactionism?

The theory developed out of the University of Chicago's sociology department. Key proponents of the theory were Edwin Sutherland,[32] Howard Becker,[33] Edwin Lemert[34] and Erving Goffman.[35] They viewed social life as a complicated process that can be studied and observed.[36] They sought to understand behaviour in its particular and situated forms, and advocated an analysis that grasped the meanings that animated and shaped social activity.[37] Social processes include the meaning employed by social actors themselves for the audience and observers, and the actors' perspectives on themselves, their acts and their environments.[38] Downes and Rock explain that social situations are a 'blend of activity, history and material props' whose meanings are derivative from shared symbols; and these are created by people who experience them within 'sets of changing resources, opportunities, contexts and constraints'.[39]

In choosing symbolic interactionism to address the research questions, it became clear that the predominant focus of the study must be the process of social interaction that shapes the perpetrator's perspective of himself or herself, and the perpetrator's interactions with other individuals around him or her. On the macro level, when examining state intervention, the theory supplements a socially interactive framework within which the interaction between the state and the family can be studied, such as the interaction between social workers and the parent, or a third party's observation as to risk and their subsequent interaction

31 Downes and Rock, above n 2, 194.
32 Edwin Sutherland, *White Collar Crime* (Holt, Rinehart & Winston, 1961).
33 Becker, above n 30.
34 Edwin Lemert, *Social Pathology: A Systematic Approach to the Theory of Sociopathic Behaviour* (McGraw-Hill, 1951).
35 Erving Goffman, *Asylums* (Anchor Books, 1961); *The Presentation of Self in Everyday Life* (Penguin, first published 1959, 1990 ed).
36 Downes and Rock, above n 2, 179.
37 Ibid.
38 Ibid.
39 Ibid.

with state agents, or the processing of information as to understandings about risk representations. Within this social frame are deeply shared and embedded symbols that represent strong social influences. As will be illustrated in Chapters 4 and 5, there are social forces that shape the meanings of these symbols, some of which are individuals, emotional and physical distance, and degrees of formalisation within social relationships. This study of shared symbols paves the way for symbolic interactionism, which provides an interactive methodological framework within which an investigation of social meanings and representations is made possible.

Pertinent to this end is the theoretical exposition of labels using labelling theory, which is a component of symbolic interactionism. It seems straightforward that in order to address the research question on self-labelling and representation, symbolic interactionism would broadly provide the theoretical basis for examining the representations made by the social actors. For example, Chapters 4 and 5 rely heavily on Goffman's conceptualisation of social roles;[40] in particular, the models in Chapter 4 extend Goffman's analysis on the evolving representation of the social actor. As Downes and Rock point out:

> [T]he internal gyrations of the self would be virtually impossible without language. Words have the power to fold back on the speaker with a special force: people cannot see themselves, but they can hear themselves speak and it may well be that their hearing is not too dissimilar to the hearing of others. Speaking, they can become their own stimulus: they are able to act and then react to themselves.[41]

Interactionists hold that life is patterned by symbolic indications; people continuously interpret themselves, their settings and their partners.[42] This makes symbolic interactionism the best theory for the book, because of its focus on social interaction, interpretation and meaning-making. The focus on the process of legitimation of certain representations and symbols in the criminal justice system, as well as the significance of the criterion of safety placed on the child following developments in the law on child protection in the late nineteenth century, justifies the use of this method. Embedded within the legal framework of rights are the symbols of the child and the mother, which have developed prominence with the advent of human rights and feminist challenges to patriarchy. The discussion of patriarchy sits within the symbolic interactionism framework of enquiry alongside feminist and critical social theories such as those of Gerda Lerner and Pierre Bourdieu, because of the way they pursue active enquiries into the processes of dominant symbols and understandings about these particular social symbols and representation.

40 Erving Goffman, *Frame Analysis* (Harvard University Press, 1974) 1.
41 Downes and Rock, above n 2, 182.
42 Ibid 183.

Criticisms

Symbolic interactionism theory is not without criticisms. One criticism, raised by Downes and Rock, is that symbolic interactionism does not provide an in-depth analysis of power differentials, which are assumed to be as they are. In other words, symbolic interactionists 'faithfully reflect central properties of social order' in their bid to 'capture the authentic workings of symbolic process'.[43] Having said this, this does not diminish its theoretical utility. As stated, I have chosen in this book to use symbolic interactionism in conjunction with critical social and feminist theories in order to illuminate the key themes of patriarchal dysfunction and male violence and their representations, which are essentially about power differentials. The system of patriarchy discussed in the context of the case studies in this book regards the male's assumed right and reassertion of his belief in his right to control, authority and ownership over his family as pivotal to understanding the male's perception of his wife and children, and his subsequent disempowerment. The book uses the feminist theory of Lerner and the critical social theory of Bourdieu to interrogate the dominant representation of the father archetype in mythology and the law.

The second criticism is that perpetrators are presented by symbolic interactionism as innocent and passive targets, and the effects of labelling are indeterminate, contingent and variable, lacking predictable outcomes in individual cases.[44] While acknowledging this idea, the position of the book is that the potential of labelling is not fully understood. Braithwaite, for instance, has argued that labelling can have a positive effect if it is done in a collective, supportive environment, such as reintegrative shaming.[45] As such, it is believed that symbolic interactionism provides a broad theoretical core into which other theories can be injected. The interactive framework it provides supports the interrogation of the social and interactive forces and symbols, such as between the state and the family, and between the parent and the child, as well as meanings of violence in the home. Alongside this theory, the book discusses feminist theories with regard to masculinities and the system of patriarchy. Additionally, as will be shown in the chapters to follow, symbolic interactionism is a resonant theme, not just a recurrent one. This is demonstrated by the analysis on representation.

From my perspective, symbolic interactionism applies to the research questions in the way that it actively and interactively explains social processes of understanding, knowledge, and social and symbolic constructions of representations. Downes and Rock stress the significance of symbolic interactionism as an interactive methodology:

43 Ibid 196.
44 Ibid 199.
45 Braithwaite, above n 23, ch 4.

> [I]nteractionism defines research itself as emergent and exploratory. Knowledge about the social world is built up little by little in an active process of enquiry that continually transforms an original problem and the questions that can be asked about it.[46]

The interactiveness of the methodology is evidenced in the way the data are interpreted in Chapters 4 and 5 and, within this interpretation, the exploration of different levels of interactionism. As will be explained in the following section, the book's method relies on documentary narrative. This is a narrative that is informed by different understandings and interactions around the subject matter. The coronial data, for example, are interactive because they deal with the perspectives of key stakeholders, such as family members, the police, the Coroner and state agencies. This questioning of the data then leads to the next phase of active enquiry, which looks at the interaction between the suspect or perpetrator and the criminal justice system and state agents, such as the police and social workers. The process of interactive enquiry in the symbolic interactionist methodology leads from one data source to another, and this is shown to be a dynamic process in which symbols and meanings about representation are constantly being interpreted and questioned.[47]

Literature review

This is a selective literature review[48] designed to identify examples of various research purposes and methods. The review is organised around groups of research questions and methods of filicide.

46 Ibid 194.

47 Denzin, above n 4, 24, 27. See also Peter Berger and Thomas Luckmann, *The Social Construction of Reality: A Treatise in the Sociology of Knowledge* (Doubleday, 1966) 39, 43–61.

48 Josephine Stanton and Alexander Simpson, 'Filicide: A Review' (2002) 25 *International Journal of Law and Philosophy* 1–14; Robert Silverman and Leslie Kennedy, 'Women Who Kill Their Children' (1988) 3(2) *Violence and Victims* 113–127; Jeffrey Alder, '"I Loved Joe, But I Had to Shoot Him": Homicide by Women in Turn-of-the-Century Chicago' (2003) 92(3–4) *Journal of Criminal Law and Criminology* 867–898; Mensah Adinkrah, 'Maternal Infanticides in Fiji' (2000) 24(12) *Child Abuse and Neglect* 1543–1555; Wendy Bacon and Robyn Lansdowne, 'Women Homicide Offenders and Police Interrogation' in Mark Findlay, Sandra J Egger and Jeff Sutton (eds), *Issues in Criminal Justice Administration* (George Allen & Unwin, 1983) 53–82; Kate Cavanagh, R Emerson Dobash and Russell Dobash, 'The Murder of Children by Fathers in the Context of Child Abuse' (2007) 31 *Child Abuse and Neglect* 731–746; Jacques Marleau, Bernard Poulin, Thierry Webanck, Renée Roy and Line Laporte, 'Paternal Filicide: A Study of 10 Men' (1999) 44 *Canadian Journal of Psychiatry* 57–63; Dominique Bourget and Pierre Gagné, 'Paternal Filicide in Québec' (2005) 33 *Journal of the American Academy of Psychiatry and Law* 354–360; John Campion, James Cravens and Fred Covan, 'A Study of Filicidal Men' (1988) 145(9) *American Journal of Psychiatry* 1141–1144; Susan Friedman, Sarah Horwitz and Phillip Resnick, 'Child Murder by Mothers: A Critical

Classification type studies

The early research on the purpose of child killing attempted to pinpoint the perpetrator motives behind filicidal killings. For instance, seminal studies such as Resnick's[49] and d'Orban's[50] posited an understanding of perpetrator motive and suggest a model of classification.[51] Wilczynski's study[52] went down a similar path but differed in terms of its socio-legal orientation. Indeed much of the literature focused very broadly on biological pathology, such as post-partum depression for female perpetrators,[53] and provided superficial analyses regarding

---

Analysis of the Current State of Knowledge and a Research Agenda' (2005) 162(9) *American Journal of Psychiatry* 1578–1587; Margaret Spinelli, 'Maternal Infanticide Associated With Mental Illness: Prevention and the Promise of Saved Lives' (2004) 161 *American Journal of Psychiatry* 1548–1557; Suresh de Silva and Kim Oates, 'Child Homicide: The Extreme of Child Abuse' (1993) 158 *Medical Journal of Australia* 300–301; Martha Smithey, 'Infant Homicide: Victim/Offender Relationship and Causes of Death' (1998) 13(3) *Journal of Family Violence* 285–297; John Emery, Enid Gilbert and Frederick Zugibe, 'Three Crib Deaths, a Babyminder and Probable Infanticide' (1988) 28(3) *Medicine, Science and Law* 205–211; David Kaplun, 'The Murdered Child and His Killers' (1976) 133(7) *American Journal of Psychiatry* 809–813; D Hargrave and D P Warner, 'A Study of Child Homicide Over Two Decades' (1992) 32(3) *Medicine, Science and the Law* 247–250; Steven Myers, 'The Child Slayer' (1967) 17 *Archives of General Psychiatry* 211–213; Arshad Husain and Anasseril Daniel, 'A Comparative Study of Filicidal and Abusive Mothers' (1984) 29 *Canadian Journal of Psychiatry* 596–598; and Olav Nielssen, Matthew Large, Bruce Westmore and Steven Lackersteen, 'Child Homicide in New South Wales from 1991 to 2005' (2009) 190(1) *Medical Journal of Australia* 7–11.

49 Phillip J Resnick, 'Child Murder by Parents: A Psychiatric Review of Filicide' (1969) 126(3) *American Journal of Psychiatry* 325–334, 325; Phillip J Resnick, 'Murder of the Newborn: A Psychiatric Review of Neonaticide' (1970) 126(10) *American Journal of Psychiatry* 1414–1420, 1415–1416; P D Scott, 'Parents Who Kill Their Children' (1973) 13(2) *Medicine, Science, and the Law* 120–126; and 'Fatal Battered Baby Cases' (1973) 13(3) *Medicine, Science and the Law* 197–206.

50 P T d'Orban, 'Women Who Kill Their Children' (1979) 134 *British Journal of Psychiatry* 560–571, 560–561.

51 Resnick proposed that filicide could be classified into five categories: altruistic filicide, acutely psychotic filicide, unwanted child filicide, accidental filicide and spouse revenge filicide, which is also described as 'retaliated killings' by d'Orban, above n 50, and Wilczynski, above n 5. See also Edward Stern, 'The Medea Complex: The Mother's Homicidal Wishes to Her Child' (1948) 94 *Journal of Mental Science* 321–331. D'Orban proposed six categories: d'Orban, above n 50, 561–570.

52 Wilczynski's study obtained quantitative and qualitative data from three general samples: 65 cases from the Director of Public Prosecutions in London; 47 English reported cases from the English Criminal Appeal Reports between 1980 and 1990; two Australian studies and quantitative filicide data from the Home Office in England between 1982 and 1989.

53 Susan Ayres, 'Newfound Religion: Mothers, God, and Infanticide' (2006) *Fordham Urban Law Journal* 336–356, 337; Christine Anne Gardner, 'Postpartum Depression Defense: Are Mothers Getting Away With Murder?' (1990) 24 *New England Law Review* 953–989, 966; J Butterfield, 'Blue Mourning: Postpartum Psychosis and the Criminal Insanity Defense, Waking to the Reality of Women Who Kill Their Children' (2006) 39 *John Marshall Law Review* 515–537, 522; Michelle Oberman,

observable factors of risk and relationship statuses, particularly in studies done on male perpetrators.[54]

Socio-legal studies

Another research method utilised in the literature was psychologically based analysis, which did not consider the variety of social interactions and symbolic indicators of risk and violence. Two socio-legal studies on child killing, those of Wilczynski and of Alder and Polk, superficially discussed representation but lacked an in-depth interrogation of its meanings. They also shed little light on the development of applied labels and particular symbols of parenthood, such as the 'mad', 'bad' and 'sad' mothers and fathers.

Wilczynski's study merits some discussion in that her ideas overlap with this book's research focus on representation, labels, symbols and risk. Wilczynski argued that filicidal male and female perpetrators are perceived and treated differently by the criminal justice system. Wilczynski also pointed out that the dichotomous labels of 'good' and 'bad' are reflected in the court judgments and the sentences received by the offenders.[55] Since women offenders are more likely than men to be perceived as 'good' parents, and more likely than men to be diagnosed as suffering from a mental disorder at the time of the crime, they were more likely to receive non-custodial sentences.[56]

Additionally, Wilczynski found that female filicide offenders were more readily and more likely to be labelled as mentally ill in comparison to male filicide perpetrators.[57] In particular, it was one of Wilczynski's findings that filicidal women labelled as 'mad' often distanced themselves from the crime such that the perception of the crime became that the crime was not committed by the offender herself but by 'a disordered and alien part of her being' or the 'Other'.[58] When describing the killing, women tended to use linguistically distancing phrases to separate their 'real' selves from the killing, and the use of such phrases often led to the imposition of non-custodial sentences.[59] The same does not apply to male filicidal perpetrators.

'Understanding Infanticide in Context: Mothers Who Kill 1870–1930 and Today' (2002) 92 *Journal of Criminal Law & Criminology* 707–736, 714, and 'Mothers Who Kill: Coming to Terms with Modern American Infanticide' (2004) 8 *DePaul Journal of Health Care Law* 3–107, 45–51; and Jayne Huckerby, 'Women Who Kill Their Children: Case Study and Conclusions Concerning the Differences in the Fall From Maternal Grace by Khoua Her and Andrea Yates' (2003) 10 *Duke Journal of Gender Law & Policy* 149–172, 147.

54 Marleau *et al*, above n 48, 57–63; Bourget and Gagne, above n 48, 354–360; Wilczynski, above n 9; and Alder and Polk, above n 5, ch 5.

55 Wilczynski, above n 5, 130.

56 Ibid 121–125.

57 Ibid.

58 Ibid 139.

59 Ibid 139–146.

In general, Wilczynski concluded that female and male filicidal perpetrators were judged in courts according to their conformity to gender stereotypes, which had greater impact on women offenders than men in terms of treatment by the criminal justice and legal system.[60] It is important to highlight that Wilczynski's findings on the sentences received by filicide perpetrators cannot be generalised to represent the sentencing of filicide perpetrators in other jurisdictions. In Quebec, for instance, a study by Marleau *et al.*,[61] in comparison, found that female filicide perpetrators of low socioeconomic status (often coupled with a criminal and substance abuse history) tended to be sent to prison and receive harsher sentences.[62] Out of Wilczynski's study emerged a particular form of representation of filicidal perpetrators. However, this does not adequately explain why and how such stereotypes emerge, or the contexts in which they do so. Least of all does it consider the social interactions that produce the phenomenon.

Wilczynski argued that women's crimes and the images of criminal women are often pathologised and polarised into two extremes, the 'mad' or the 'bad', the 'Madonna' or the 'whore'.[63] This dichotomy is more pronounced for filicidal women, as the filicidal woman stands in direct contradiction to conventional notions of motherhood and femininity. In Wilczynski's examination, almost any type of case where there is a perceived psychiatric, emotional, personality or mental problem can be interpreted by psychiatrists, lawyers and judges, if they so choose, as severe mental illness, which falls within the ambit of the *Infanticide Act*.[64] 'Bad' women, according to Wilczynski, are often seen as 'monsters' and viewed as 'ruthless, selfish, cold, callous, neglectful of their children or domestic responsibilities, violent or promiscuous'.[65] These two categories often simplify the social and economic circumstances surrounding filicide and filicidal 'women's position of helplessness and powerlessness in society'.[66] The 'mad' or 'bad' phenomenon is one of the central themes of this book. However, this is used in what is hopefully an insightful way, aiming to 'unpeel' representation to reveal the roots from which such labels emerge.

Wilcyznski argues that filicidal male perpetrators tend to receive harsher punishments, including custodial sentences or the most coercive forms of

60 Wilczynski, above n 5, 121–130.

61 Marleau *et al*, above n 48.

62 By comparison, Wilczynski found that more female filicide offenders received non-custodial and treatment oriented sentences as a result of pleading a medical disposition, above n 5, 118, 120, 144.

63 Ania Wilczynski, 'Images of Women Who Kill Their Infants: The Mad and the Bad' (1991) 2(2) *Women and Criminal Justice* 71–88, 73. See also Huckerby, above n 53; and Ania Wilczynski, 'Mad or Bad? Child Killers, Gender and the Courts' (1997) 37(3) *British Journal of Criminology* 419–435.

64 Ibid 76.

65 Ibid 78; and Wilczynski, above n 5, 131.

66 Susan S M Edwards, 'Neither Bad nor Mad: The Female Violent Offender Reassessed' (1986) 9(1) *Women's Studies International Forum* 79–87, 82, 86.

psychiatric disposal.[67] In terms of images in male filicides, the expectations of a 'good' father, according to Wilczynski, are more modest than those of a 'good' mother since it is assumed that for women to have 'sole or primary care of children is perfectly "natural", and not requiring any great sacrifice'.[68] By comparison, it is praiseworthy and altruistic for men to carry out the primary child-care role.[69] Wilczynski's discussion on the images of female filicide perpetrators is lengthier than that on male perpetrators, as she argues that the distinctions made between 'good' and 'bad' mothers have a greater impact on sentencing than between 'good' and 'bad' fathers.[70] Her study confirms earlier studies that female filicidal perpetrators are more likely to be labelled mentally ill compared to male perpetrators, who tend to be constructed and labelled as 'bad'.[71] Wilczynski proceeds to consider various factors, such as social work intervention, the presence of a family, psychiatric pleas, remorse and standards of parenting, including the application of good and bad labels, which she argues affected the sentencing of the perpetrators in her sample.[72] The labels discussed here are no more than superficial observations as to their social value. And, even though Wilczynski discusses a host of risk factors, these were not considered in terms of the interactions that produce them. While the study is useful in terms of what it has to offer – a forensic analysis of child killing – it offers little to the researcher who is looking for richer understandings with regard to symbols, meaning and social representation, and particularly the interactions that produce and embed stereotypes.

A study by Alder and Polk[73] deals with representation to a limited extent. The study explores the complexity surrounding the killing and the varied contexts in both male- and female-perpetrated violence. They argue that understandings of child homicide need to include the meaning and experience of being a man or woman in everyday life, and the structural situations of both victims and perpetrators.[74] They identify the presence of depression in the majority of filicidal perpetrators.[75] Additionally, their study challenges common perceptions about why men and women kill, and they argue that male and female perpetrators kill for different motivations which are grounded in a variety of social and situational factors, such as family breakdown, feelings of powerlessness and economic stress.[76] Their analysis of gender factors presents different observations in relation to male

67 Wilczynski, above n 5, 119.
68 Ibid 130.
69 Ibid.
70 Ibid 132.
71 Ibid 136.
72 Ibid 130–146.
73 Drawn from case study data arising from the Office of the Coroner for the State of Victoria between the years of 1985 and 1995: Alder and Polk, above n 5, 18.
74 Ibid 4, ch 8.
75 Ibid 149.
76 Ibid 155.

and female filicide perpetrators. Among male perpetrators they observed that themes of control and possession, including emotions of anger and possessive jealousy, threat of separation and stretched economic resources, are likely to feature in filicidal killings.[77] By comparison, bio-social and economic factors, such as cultural conflict and social isolation, marital or relationship separation (including retaliatory killings), feelings of insecurity and powerlessness, altruistic feelings for the children, domestic violence and psychiatric disturbances, are likely to feature in female filicidal perpetrator killings.[78] Yet, like the Wilczynski study, this study touches on social interactions without looking at the interactive conditions that produce them. Having said this, this study offers a far richer understanding of the complexity of child killing than others. This book is different from the studies just discussed in that it offers a still richer and more holistic theoretical position with regard to symbolic interactionism. Additionally, the current literature appears narrow in terms of focus and theory, with little said about the social interactions of risk and the impact of dysfunctional interaction on the child.

This brief survey of the literature has been intended to show the reader why this book opens up new possibilities for method. Compared to the studies mentioned, the method used in the book aims to be more insightful in terms of the questions asked about representation and intervention. I am attempting to get to the more subtle causes of child killing, the ways they are concealed and made visible, and the social interactions producing risks for the child. Child killing is seen, then, as a visible multimodal interactive phenomenon. The interactive research method, involving narrative analysis, observation and content analysis, aims to place child killing at the centre of social relations in the family and the community. This approach is, it is intended, more holistically connected with theory and, more importantly, sees child killing as a product of subtle, but not obscure, interactions involving state intervention. Symbolic interactionism provides the framework for this analysis and opens up possibilities in which more informed and interactive methods can be applied to the phenomenon in order to understand the relationships,[79] representations, symbols and interactions that engender child killing.

Taking a step back from the studies summarily discussed here, it seems clear that there is a need for a more enriched understanding on the interactions that produce risk of harm to the child. This book's engagement with symbolic interactionism, unlike earlier studies, does this more meaningfully by having an interactionist method, which represents the data interactively to make sense of the way social interactions function to produce risky representations for the child. This is a more convincing method when interrogating questions on risk and the meanings of key symbols of child killing, such as those involving

77 Ibid ch 5.
78 Ibid ch 4.
79 Downes and Rock, above n 2, ch 7.

the parent and child. To contextualise the key symbols in child killing, a brief canvassing of its history and cultural representations is explored in the following section.

Review of various cultural representations

> Infanticide has from time immemorial been the accepted procedure for disposing not only of deformed or sickly infants, but of all such newborns as might strain the resources of the individual family or the larger community.[80]

The killing of children is by no means a new phenomenon. Throughout the history of human civilisation, child killing has been and continues to be practised around the world among diverse cultures. While child killing is not frowned upon in some parts of the world among certain societies, it is considered immoral in others. The anthropologies of child killing divide between concerns for utility and concerns for morality. Those who seek to explore child killing represent generalised distortions about, for example, 'primitive' tribal societies, against Judeo-Christian concerns for the sanctity of the child. Even when it is conceded that the destruction of the newborn may be out of concern for surviving children, the venal nature of the act is paramount in the critique. The other school of thought, which looks at the reasons behind child killing, accepts the cultural relativity of this amoral behaviour and seeks to explain child killing in terms of various social factors, such as population control; survival of the community unit; protection of the relative worth of pre-existing children; maintenance of the reputation of unmarried mothers; mercy killing and gender-specific killing. Mythologised child destruction also has at its foundation the pre-eminence of the child (or the foetus) within religious morality, along with controlling the errant mother. The position and subsequent treatment of the mother posited in the family unit is central in most, if not all, discourses on child killing across cultures.

The utility versus morality polemic takes a practical view of the realities of survival of the family unit, and this has been so among a range of societies. Early ethnographic records inform us of the practices of child killing among these societies. In the Ayoreo society, for instance, peoples who occupy the border area of Bolivia and Paraguay, women would bury unwanted infants at the time of birth when social circumstances at the time were poor.[81] Child killing in this context is a method of survival, a way to keep the family status quo intact and within manageable limits. Among the stories of the women of the Yanomamo tribe, newborns would be killed if there was already an older sibling to compete with for food and shelter.[82] Australian Aborigines too would practise this method

80 W Langer, 'Infanticide: A Historical Survey' (1974) *History of Childhood Quarterly*, 1(3), 353–366, 353.

81 Martin Daly and Margo Wilson, *Homicide* (Aldine De Gruyter, 1988).

82 A Napoleon and N A Chagnon, *Yanomamo: The Fierce People* (Holt, Rinehart & Winston, 1983) 27.

of family preservation. The Kurnai tribe, for example, had a practice of leaving behind newborn infants as a result of their wandering nomadic lifestyle and where there were already several children to feed.[83] The survival of the family unit is but one among the umbrella of utility 'reasons' for child killing.

Belief in the survival or preservation of the family lineage is another utility practice that seeks justification for gender-specific killings, in particular, female infanticide practised in China and India,[84] and historically in other societies such as the Aymara Indians of South America,[85] the Yanomamo, Mataco, Trobriand Islanders and Tikopia,[86] and in Japan[87], where female children more so than male children were routinely killed at birth because of parental and cultural preference for sons over daughters. In a patrilineal familial system, only sons can carry on the family name and thus are preferred over daughters. A daughter is usually if not almost always married out and away from the family to take on another family's (her husband's) surname; this act of marriage is considered as a loss or an economic liability to her family, whereas there is a belief that a son will carry on to have children of his own, thereby preserving the family's name, lineage and reputation. Among tribal patrifocal societies, men articulate a preference for sons due to a need for warriors, as their strength is prized in inter-communal conflicts and warfare.[88]

Child killing is culturally relative and, even though the above examples posit that the behaviour takes place under the utility umbrella, in reality, there are other cultural and social factors that overlap and find their place as another justification for the continuation and promulgation of this practice. The overlapping reasons for child killing, such as population control[89] (the utility of

83 Lorimar Fison and A W Howitt, *Kamilaroi and Kurnai* (Aboriginal Studies Press, 1880/1967) 190. This said, a reading of Fison and Howitt's ethnographic narration of the Kurnai lifestyle reflects their marked contempt for this native practice, perhaps stemming from their 'civilised' perspective.

84 J Lee and W Feng, 'Malthusian Models and Chinese Realities: The Chinese Demographic System 1700–2000' (1999) 25(2) *Population and Development Review* 33–65, 47; S Krishnaswamy, 'A Note on Female Infanticide: An Anthropological Inquiry' (1984) 45(3) *Indian Journal of Social Work* 297–302.

85 See Daly and Wilson, above n 81.

86 Ibid 53.

87 M Jackson (ed), *Infanticide: Historical Perspectives on Child Murder and Concealment, 1550–2000* (Ashgate, 2002) 9.

88 Daly and Wilson, above n 81, 55. Daly and Wilson postulate that a son's reproductive potential is seen as a financial asset for the family. In other words, a son is perceived as having more social utility to the family and to the larger community than a daughter. However, W T Divale and M Harris, 'Population, Warfare and the Male Supremacist Complex' (1976) 78(3) *American Anthropologist* 521–538 offer an alternate explanation; they say that warfare (the elimination of males) and infanticide (of females) are harmonising elements that balance and regulate population growth in horticultural studies. This explanation is partial at best as it applies only to societies where warfare is the sole channel in the resolution of disputes.

89 Aristotle, *Politics*. Book 7 (Aeterna Press, 2015) section 1335b.

maintaining the status quo), gender-specific killings (the utility of sons) and the survival of the family unit (the utility of pre-existing children), demonstrate the complexity inherent in the dynamics of child killing. The discussion that follows here and in Chapter 3 will look at some mythologised and Western representations of child killing. These representations are diametrically contrasted to child destruction by 'primitive' tribal societies, and the (Western) generalised perception of this 'uncivilised' practice. Two pre-eminent social reasons emerge from the anthropologies of child killing: the maintenance of the reputation of unmarried mothers and mercy killings or 'altruistic killing'.[90] These 'reasons' tend to fall under the branch of morality following the advent of the Judeo-Christian church, which brought to the fore a religious fervour in controlling what was perceived to be the errant mother.

The morality dimension of infanticide emerged when leaders of the Christian faith took on a more proactive role in seeing to the moral and social conduct, and salvation, of individuals. Prior to this, child killing belonged to the realm of the pagans, societies such as the Greeks who saw the need for population control and to those who dabbled in superstitions. In the pre-modern era, superstitions abounded that deformed children were omens or harbingers of the future, the product of a consortium with animals or demons, a representation of animal–human coition or even types of miraculous 'sacred animals'.[91] The nature of mythologised child destruction leans towards elucidating the human quality of mercy. The rationale is that a sick or deformed child would have to struggle for his or her existence and has little chance of developing into a strong human being and a useful member of society. In killing the sick or deformed child, the element of mercy is exercised and this act inclines one to question the feelings of compassion, protectiveness and humaneness in murder, feelings that are only exhibited in the parent. Mercy is a human instinct that is so basic that it stands on its own as one of the categories of motives in child homicide literature.[92] Ancient Greek mythology also contains stories of infant exposure (for example, the myth of Medea discussed in Chapter 3); these stories, arguably, reveal and reflect the religious and moral traditions of cultures that created them, and a recurring underlying theme in mythologies of child destruction is the representation and magnitude of human frailty and human mercy.

Human mercy, however, was not shown towards those thought to be witches during the medieval period of the witch trials where there existed a sharp divide between good and evil, a pervasive belief in the manifestation of God and the Devil in human lives. During the Christian epoch, a deformed child came to be regarded as a changeling or a demonical child of the Devil himself. Belief in the Devil in medieval times had a profound influence on the social lives of Christian

90 Coined by Resnick, above n 51.

91 Kathryn L Moseley, 'The History of Infanticide in Western Society' (1986) 1(5) *Issues in Law and Medicine* 345–361.

92 Resnick, above n 51.

believers. Stigma was attached to the mother of the deformed child because she was thought to be a witch who had consorted with the Devil or other demons or animals.[93] The representation of the Devil arose in connection with the actions of the mothers who deposed that they were led astray. What emerged most starkly from these witch trial sagas was the preponderance of female deviance. The gender specificity of witch trials spoke volumes about men seeking to exert power and impose control over the errant, disorderly, deviant female. The traditionally defined feminine space, such as the home, kitchen and nursery, is posited next to culturally defined female occupations and juxtaposed against their direct opposites, such as feeding (poisoning), child-rearing (infanticide), healing (harming) and birth (death).[94] The symbol of the witch was the stereotypical opposite of the good wife. The representation of child killing in the context of the witch trials flies in the face of the traditionally carved out role for mothers as being caring, nurturing and loving. It is not surprising that child destruction became socially and negatively constructed as an act that deserved the church's condemnation because of its iniquitous nature and strong symbolic association with the Devil.

Further to the dichotomous labelling of mothers – the good (God) versus evil (Devil) – this deeply embedded symbol has culturally transcended over time and evolved within contemporary labelling discourse as representative of the traditional (good) verses mad/bad (deviant) mother. On the one hand, child killing by the mother became represented as the antithesis of the female nature.[95] For most women, male authority, power and control pervaded beyond physical reality and intruded into the realm of birth, the social construction of post-birth and its repercussion resulted in the medicalisation of women's experiences of birth.

The influence of the church and the law

The external reality of early Western civilisation was that child killing and child abandonment were prevalent, harshly prosecuted, severely condemned by the church, and acts of sheer desperation. This condemnation originated with Emperor Constantine the Great around AD 318, with his decree that the killing of children was a serious matter. In AD 374, the Christian emperor Valentinian took the bold

93 Mark Jackson, *Newborn Child Murder: Women, Illegitimacy, and the Courts in Eighteenth Century England* (Manchester University Press, 1996). In a study of the depositions of 124 individuals accused of witchcraft in Suffolk in 1645, it was found that child murder and harm to children were common accusations in many of these witch trials, with approximately 20 per cent of the Suffolk 'witches' accused of harming or killing children in their capacity as mothers who were instructed by the Devil.

94 Jackson, above n 93, 71.

95 Hillary Marland, 'Getting Away with Murder? Puerperal Insanity, Infanticide and the Defence Plea' in M Jackson (ed) *Infanticide: Historical Perspectives on Child Murder and Concealment, 1550–2000* (Ashgate, 2002).

step and ruled that the killing of an infant was a crime punishable by death under Roman law. In AD 418, at a time when the church strongly disapproved of illegitimate children, St. Augustine ruled against child killing on the grounds that an infant killed was deprived of the opportunity of salvation. The church took the view that an unbaptised infant was a soul condemned to eternal punishment because ensoulment took place only at conception or 40 days thereafter, and so, unbaptised children were treated in association with the Devil.[96]

So strong was this Christian message that it led to an increase in the number of children being abandoned.[97] Later Christian emperors Valens and Gratian continued to condemn infanticide as a pagan practice and saw to the establishment of foundling hospitals in Europe for the first time during the eighth century. Early representations of child killing in the West were affixed with a cloth of religiosity and stigma. There was no doubt child killing was viewed by the church as a serious moral problem. The church, being the prevailing public authority in medieval and early modern times, embraced its purview and jurisdiction under formal canon law to severely punish this act. Not surprisingly, the punishment of death fell mostly on unfortunate women, and sometimes on both parents. The Canterbury church records, *ex officio* Act books which contained disciplinary records, showed successful infanticide prosecutions.[98] Although the information derived from the church records was incomplete and inconclusive, what little can be gleaned from these accounts of prosecution depicted the church's prevailing and condemning moral stance on what was considered a public and venal sin.

The prevalence of killing children in the first 24 months of life (infanticide) in England[99] gave rise to burial clubs, a practice also known as 'baby farming',[100] whereby women enrolled their infants, paid a fee to have the child die of starvation and then collected a small token by way of benefit.[101] Child killing was largely carried out by the mothers of the children involved in isolation with no witnesses and was usually undetectable until infant victims were discovered killed or left to die by unknown persons.[102] This took place amidst social maladies ranging

96 Barbara A Kellum, 'Infanticide in England in the Later Middle Ages' (1994) 1(3) *History of Childhood Quarterly* 367–388.

97 Robert Bluglass, 'Infanticide' (1990) 2(8) *The Psychiatrist* 139–141.

98 R H Helmholz, 'Infanticide in the Province of Canterbury in the Fifteenth Century' 2 (1975) *History of Childhood Quarterly* 379–390, 380.

99 Langer, above n 80; Kellum, above n 96; Helmholz, above n 98; Catherine Damme, 'The Worth of an Infant Under Law' (1978) 22 *Medical History* 1–24; P C Hoffer and N E H Hull, *Murdering Mothers: infanticide in England and New England 1558–1803* (New York University Press, 1981); Jackson, above n 87.

100 For example, the baby farming trial of Alice Mitchell in 1907 in Western Australia, her case prompted the *State Children Act* of 1907, which set out to eradicate baby farming.

101 Langer, above n 80.

102 J R Dickinson and J A Sharpe, 'Infanticide in Early Modern England: The Court of Great Sessions at Chester, 1650–1800' in M Jackson (ed) *Infanticide: Historical Perspectives on Child Murder and Concealment, 1550–2000* (Ashgate, 2002).

from poverty to warfare, religious and political persecutions, economic hardship, promiscuity (hence stigma), bigamy, lack of family controls, survival and widespread social change and unrest. Furthermore, the stigma of having an unbaptised child and the stigma affixed to an unmarried woman with a child weighed heavily on the psyche of the female perpetrators involved.

Foundling hospitals, which were originally set up as places of refuge for abandoned children, became overfilled with infants, mostly left by unwed mothers.[103] The plight of unmarried women was unduly harsh. Many of the unmarried women under the age of 26 were living-in servants who were powerless and vulnerable to seduction and rape, and were also often working-class women of marginal status.[104] Pregnancy for these women was catastrophic because their good character and reputation held economic and social values to them – in terms of moving upwards to acquire greater social and financial status or affecting their future marriage prospects.[105] The wanton abandonment of children in the hospitals[106] came to be described as 'legalised infanticide'.[107] The ecclesiastical church tried to warn parents of the dangers of overlaying, a commonly used phrase at the time that referred to the smothering of an infant in bed by its (allegedly drunken) parents, in order to control the overwhelming number of suffocated children found, and to impress upon the masses, the church directly associated overlaying with a failure of being a good Samaritan.[108] Despite the church's efforts, society continued to disregard the lives of children and the rights of women. Those found responsible for the deaths of their children were punished brutally by methods such as burial alive, drowning, decapitation and hanging.[109] Yet, these measures proved ineffective in the eighteenth and nineteenth centuries across Europe.

Legislation was introduced in 1623 to control the proliferation of child deaths. The law was targeted at women, or more appropriately unmarried women, for concealment of the death of a newborn child. The victims were usually if not almost always children born out of wedlock.[110] This early law (discussed in more detail in Chapter 3) was society's attempt to control errant mothers. Infanticide trials had much in common with witchcraft trials.[111] The 1623 legislation

103 Langer, above n 80, 358.
104 Arnot (2002) argues that this lack of social, economic and moral space was the primary force that drove women to child murder.
105 K O'Donovan, 'The Medicalisation of Infanticide' (1984) *Criminal Law Review* 259–264.
106 Langer, above n 80.
107 Ibid 359.
108 Damme, above n 99; Kellum, above n 96.
109 Langer, above n 80; Hoffer and Hull, above n 99.
110 O'Donovan, above n 105; D Seaborne, 'Child Killing in English Law' (1937) 1(3) *Modern Law Review* 203–233.
111 J Geyer-Kordesch, 'Infanticide and the Erotic Plot: A Feminist Reading of Eighteenth-Century Crime' in M Jackson (ed) *Infanticide: Historical Perspectives on Child Murder and Concealment, 1550–2000* (Ashgate, 2002).

established a specific female form of criminality based on the precedence of female deviance during the 'witch burning' era. The social implication of the law meant that women would forever be associated with the stigma of having a child out of wedlock, and marriage and the family unit were legally consecrated as the acceptable benchmark within which pregnancy was allowed. Outside of the legal space, an unmarried woman had to fend for herself.[112] The law stigmatised the errant mother, who was delivered as a scapegoat as a warning to the rest of society, warning them that women are expected to conform and behave in accordance with the traditional stereotype – nurturing and faithful – or else risk being ostracised and punished.[113] The *Lord Ellenborough Act* of 1803 was later passed to repeal the 1623 legislation. Like its predecessor, the Ellenborough Act continued to impact on unmarried women and illegitimate children.

The development of puerperal psychosis

Women, throughout history and until the feminist movement, have been largely regarded as operating from a position of powerlessness, perceived as victims of their social circumstances, biological whims and mental pathology; or, where they may have had social and financial status, they often paid deference to male authority. Madness, since early days, has been associated with a woman's mental state in relation to witchcraft, childbirth and child murder. Although men were not exempted from pleading insanity to a charge of murder, the direct association between men and madness was never really cemented in the law, because men were held out to be rational; they constantly held positions of authority, including as head of the household, a familial arrangement that had been in place since the Roman Empire, where a father possessed the absolute right (*patria potestas*) under the law to dispose of all his descendants as he pleased. The errant woman, on the other hand, had difficulty finding cultural and societal acceptance, especially so when she does not fit the female stereotype. The shame was worse still if she was unmarried and carried a child. From the fifteenth century onwards, marital status increasingly became the benchmark differentiating those charged with murder from those charged with child destruction. Married women charged with murder could claim temporary insanity, while single women, who were tried

112 D Rabin, 'Bodies of Evidence, States of Mind: Infanticide, Emotion and Sensibility in Eighteenth-Century England' in M Jackson (ed) *Infanticide: Historical Perspectives on Child Murder and Concealment, 1550–2000* (Ashgate, 2002) 75.

113 J Sharpe and J R Dickinson, 'Infanticide in Early Modern England: The Court of Great Sessions at Chester 1650–1800' in M Jackson (ed) *Infanticide Historical Perspectives on Child Murder and Concealment, 1550–2000* (Ashgate, 2002) 35–51. Jackson, above n 93, stipulated that as many as 40 per cent of women accused of the crime in England were found guilty and hanged following the passing of this Act in the seventeenth century. What is pertinent from Dickinson and Sharpe's research was the fact that the majority of those accused of the crime under the 1623 legislation were spinsters; men were seldom involved.

under the 1623 legislation for child destruction, often pleaded that the baby was born dead.[114] The import of marital status and its effect in a legal trial can only be one of social significance – having a child out of wedlock was the epitome of the errant deviant woman.

There had been a handful of recorded cases[115] where the mother killed her child in a fit of madness.[116] A common thread that runs through these cases is the trial's ability to educe often complex and emotional circumstances from both the perpetrator and the public audience. Many infanticide trials were (as they still are) fraught with emotions, which elicited sympathy from the court.[117] The power of emotions surrounding the complexity of child killing, which was perceived as going against the grain of traditional womanhood, cannot be downplayed. If anything, the emotional pandemonium is another possible explanation why the death sentence fell out of public favour. By the end of the eighteenth century, the law needed a new approach.

At that time, a new legal and medical direction towards regulating child destruction seemed inevitable and forthcoming. It was one prominent physician, anatomist, man-midwife and surgeon William Hunter,[118] who first elaborated on the relationship between insanity and shame of pregnancy felt by single women. He argued that disturbances of the mind such as physical and mental distress associated with the process of childbirth explained women's irrational concealment of birth.[119] Hunter argued that it was shame and the panic of pregnancy that drove one of his patients out of her senses to commit suicide.[120] He contended that women who gave birth to a child out of wedlock were often overwhelmed with distress, terror, despair, agitation and conflict such that their state of mind was unbalanced to the extent that what is irrational conduct would appear natural to them.[121] Hunter's analysis was significant at the time in that it introduced for the first time the states of mind in childbirth that directly impacted on the acts of child destruction and concealment. Doing so, he transformed the errant

114 Rabin, above n 112.

115 B Westman, 'The Female Felon in the Fourteenth Century England' (1974) *Viator V*, 9–11; or B Hannawalt, 'The Female Felon in Fourteenth-Century England' (1975) *Viator* 5m, 253–268, at 260–261; and more generally, Kellum, above n 96, 372–373.

116 Mary Dixon, *Old Bailey Sessions Papers*, July 1735, 145; *Warwick Advertiser*, 11 May 1867, 2; *The Lancet* 1 (1848) 318–319; Anonymous, 'Chelmsford – Friday, March 10. Charge of Murder – Acquittal on the Ground of Puerperal Insanity' (1848) *Journal of Psychological Medicine* 1, 478–483; see Hilary Marland, 'Under the Shadow of Maternity: Birth, Death and Puerperal Insanity in Victorian Britain' (2012) 23(1) *History of Psychiatry* 78–90.

117 Rabin, above n 112.

118 W Hunter, 'On the Uncertainty of the Signs of Murder, in the Case of Bastard Children' (1784) 6 *Medical Observations and Inquiries* 266–290.

119 Jackson, above n 87.

120 Hunter, above n 118, 271–279, 279.

121 Ibid 278.

deviant woman into a passive victim of her mental and biological pathology, which invariably meant that her criminal and moral responsibilities under the law were reduced. This deterministic approach to infanticide was to be forever welded into the law.

The *Infanticide Act* of 1922 was introduced in a time of social upheaval.[122] The disturbance of the mind was further medicalised with the observations of a medical superintendent, John Stanley Hopwood, at the State Criminal Lunatic Asylum in Broadmoor in 1927.[123] Based on his observations, he developed the diagnoses of puerperal and lactational insanity. According to Hopwood, the presence of puerperal insanity within the initial 24 hours of giving birth was uncommon because the mother was too physically weak to carry out the task of killing. However, the presence of lactational insanity in the months post-birth was a matter to be treated with serious care, because mothers who tended to be unfit to undertake nursing of their children could not withstand the strain of lactation, with the result that insanity developed; and it is in cases of lactational insanity that child murder occurs most frequently.[124] For this reason, lactational insanity became directly associated with infanticide and later found its way into the law as a mitigating factor in child killing.

The next legislative change, the *Infanticide Act* of 1938, became the pre-eminent legislation on infanticide in New South Wales, Victoria and Western Australia and in some other countries such as Tasmania, New Zealand, Canada, and the United Kingdom (with the exception of the United States). The 1938 legislation reformed the 1922 Act in two directions. First, it refined the definition of 'newly born' to 'under the age of 12 months' and second, it introduced the phrase 'effect of lactation' to the wording of the law.[125] The jury now had the option to either return a verdict of manslaughter or a verdict of not guilty by reason of insanity, or a verdict of concealment of birth.[126] The significance of this law was that a medical condition associated with childbirth mitigated criminal responsibility.[127] At this point, it is relevant to point out that

122 *Infanticide Act 1922* section 1(1); and O'Donovan, above n 105, 261.

123 J S Hopwood, 'Child Murder and Insanity' (1927) 73 *Journal of Mental Science* 95–108. See also K J Kramer and W D Watson, 'The Insanities of Reproduction' (2006) 15 *Social and Legal Studies* 237–255.

124 Hopwood, above n 123, 96–97.

125 *Infanticide Act 1938* (UK).

126 *Infanticide Act 1938* section 1(3); and *Crimes Act 1900* (New South Wales) section 22A. See also O'Donoghue (1927) 20 Cr. App. R. 132; and in the *Times*, 22 July 1936 at p. 13. For some like O'Donovan, above n 105, and Seaborne, n 110, the law was not as a result of nineteenth-century medical theory about the effects of childbirth but of judicial effort to avoid passing death sentences that were not going to be carried out. O'Donovan in particular presents several criticisms in response to the development of the 1938 legislation, arguing the lack of consistency in the application of the law to a woman who has given birth within the first 12 months but not to the killing of older children.

127 Kramer and Watson, above n 123, 242.

it is madness rather than the deviance of the mother that has found determination in the law. The tide of legislative changes and the medical import of madness into the law on infanticide have since placed child killing as a hotly contentious social and deeply cultural issue. The primitive forces that drive child killing appeared to be divided into two strands of thought – the utility argument and the morality influence. A more recent interpretation of the understandings behind child killing seeks to locate child killing in our social and cultural milieus where there are a number of social dynamics that seem to dictate the necessities (utility) of this heinous or merciful taking (morality) of infant life. These understandings also find justification as part of the utility and morality polemic as they themselves are not devoid of the underlying strength of either strand of thought. However, what seems to emerge most strikingly from these layers of understanding across time and culture is the representation of the deviant mother. She is portrayed as both the bringer and destructor of life; not easily subsumed under the control and influence of the church, she rises time and again from the shadows of men to exalt in the preservation and sustenance of her subtle power amidst the patriarchal structure of human society. The 'heroine' in every scenario finds little room to manoeuvre, caught between society's expectations of the archetypal nurturing mother and the pressure to maintain a constant status in order to survive. This is still the position of the woman who kills her children in contemporary times.

As elucidated, the cultural representation of child killing has always been one dictated by necessity and survival of the family; it is a dichotomous creation of good and evil juxtaposed in a single identity. This dichotomy is not removed from the law. Instead, the law is one of concessions and transformation, acknowledging the rigidity of motherhood and making allowances for deviance, thus converting a fictional representation of madness into a reality that is, and has been since its introduction, a sombre reflection of the male gaze.

Method

Coronial files

This book's method developed as the fieldwork progressed. The utility of having different data sources meant that it was possible to employ three key methods of analysis: narrative analysis, content analysis and observational analysis; these complement each other and they fit within the symbolic interactionist framework. The coronial and prosecutorial files provided the data for narrative analysis, the case judgements and media reports provided the data for content analysis and the 'live' fieldwork observation phase provided the data for observational analysis. This three-pronged approach allowed me to gain multiple angles on the analysis of risk and representation, and to better illuminate key representations and symbols as they emerged from the case studies.

The research began with an examination of coronial files. The advantage of using coronial files is that the recorded data is closest to the point of origin of recorded information on homicide.[128] Arguably, this means that the data will be original and raw and pertinent to the circumstances of the crime. In addition, the raw recorded data would contain the bare facts of the case, such as the social circumstances at the time of the crime, background information, the conditions in which the death was situated, the social climate of the perpetrators at the time of the killing and representations made by the perpetrators and witnesses immediately following the killing or when speaking to the police at the scene of the crime. In addition, there would be information relating to relationship status, recorded history of domestic abuse and violence, and previous records of abuse and violence towards the child, all of which were relevant to my research questions. According to Alder and Polk, coronial files are:

> considerably better for research purposes than, for example, homicides derived from either court files or prosecutions or prison files of convictions of criminal homicide, since there are a great number of factors which contribute to the attrition of cases as one moves deeper into the criminal justice system.[129]

Using coronial files as a source of information not only indicates the size, nature and boundaries of the filicide sample; with the knowledge of these files and the types of information that arose from them, the focus on the theme of representation could be streamlined. On the flip side, recorded information was sometimes scant and depended on the diligence and perspective(s) of the officer writing down the information. A typical coronial file will contain the following documents (if they have been made available): police report of death to the coroner; autopsy report; toxicology reports; death certificate; police charge sheet; police brief of evidence if a coronial inquest has been called, which includes police statements from the relevant parties; post-mortem photographic evidence; police charge sheet and summary of the alleged crime if the perpetrator(s) have been charged and arrested; coronial inquest judgment; and transcript of coronial inquest hearing. The coronial inquest is an especially valuable document because it examines issues such as the circumstances of the death and whether the death could have been prevented. The inquest also reviews the participation of state agencies and their role in the death of the child, a process that is not reviewed by the criminal court.

To assist with sifting through and reading the information in these files, data templates were created.[130] The data templates helped to structure the flow of information, and streamlined the note-taking process by providing a strategy for coping with the arduous task of manual data collection.

The University's human ethics approval for this book was granted on the basis of the original research proposal, which included access to coronial files,

128 Alder and Polk, above n 5, 18.
129 Ibid 18.
130 See the Appendix.

DPP files, face-to-face interviews, and post-release offenders in person.[131] (At that stage, the intention to pursue face-to-face interviews was still intact.) The problems pointed out by Corrective Services were addressed in the ethics application. Based on the University's approval, human ethics approval by the Coroner's Office to access its records was sought. On 3 April 2008, approval was granted by the New South Wales State Coroner to access filicide files from the Coroner's Office.[132] The approval was given on the basis that all parties would be de-identified, including the deceased, next of kin, family and alleged offenders. On 11 April 2008, a request was put to the manager at the National Coroners Information System (NCIS) requesting access to filicide files based on the following search parameters:

- Age of deceased child: under 18 years.
- Location: New South Wales.
- Timeframe: 1 July 2000[133] to 1 April 2008.
- Classification of death at the point of record entry or death coded as: 'assault' and/or 'homicide' and/or 'murder' and/or 'manslaughter' and/or 'fatal abuse' and/or 'interpersonal violence', but excluding deaths classified as 'accidental'
- Medical cause of death coded as: 'suspicious' and/or 'unnatural'.

These search parameters were arrived at based on a view that the research questions needed to explore the applicability of the theory of labelling in homicide studies, because this was an area where there was a paucity of research. As discussed in the literature review, little research has been done on the effects of self-labelling in homicide. Additionally, the practicality of the search parameters meant a manageable sample of cases within the timeframe of the book.

A total of 64 coronial matters from the NCIS were received. Out of this total, 40 were relevant matters consisting of parent perpetrators and 24 were irrelevant because they did not involve parents. One year was spent retrieving data from the 40 relevant matters at the Glebe and Westmead Coroner's Courts in New South Wales. A register of these cases was developed to reflect the characteristics of each case.[134] This register was categorised in such a way that allowed the filtering of collected information and it was used to develop a broad perspective of the demographics of the cases. The categorisation in the register pertained to the perpetrator's marital status and ethnicity; classification of the case by motive;

131 The University's human ethics approval was obtained on 6 December 2007, 2 December 2008 and 27 January 2010.

132 The Coroner's Court ethics approval was obtained on 3 April 2008.

133 Prior to 2000, case files were held at the New South Wales State Archive and so one needed knowledge of the name of the deceased, date of death and/or other specific detail to be able to identify those files.

134 See Tables A.1–A.4 in the Appendix, which summarise the various characteristics of these 40 relevant files.

the types of information available from each file, such as report of death or transcript of coronial hearing; a summary of the facts, which included codification of the nature of violence or family conflict (e.g. domestic violence, child abuse or violence resulting from mental illness); and the nature of the state intervention (police, courts, housing, community services, etc.). The register was later pivotal in directing the specific focus to the selected handful of cases used in this book.

During this process, it came to my attention that a number of coronial cases proceeded to court. In matters where perpetrators were charged with an indictable offence, the coronial jurisdiction immediately ceased and the file would be transferred to the DPP under section 19 of the now repealed *Coroners Act 1980* (NSW).[135] In some cases where the alleged perpetrators were eventually not charged because of insufficient evidence following police investigations, a coronial inquest was held. In deaths concerning children, the State Coroner has jurisdiction to hold an inquest if it appears that the deceased was a child within the meaning of section 24 of the *Coroners Act 2009* (NSW) (then section 13AB of the *Coroners Act 1980* (NSW)). A 'child' within the meaning of this section includes a child in care, a child about whom a risk of harm report has been made in the preceding three years prior to the death (under the *Children and Young Persons (Care and Protection) Act 1998*), and a child whose death is due to abuse, neglect or suspicious circumstances. A copy of the file would also be forwarded to the New South Wales Child Death Review Team ('CDRT').

This thorough process of review in place for suspicious deaths of children and deaths resulting from abuse and neglect meant that I did not have to approach CDRT because many of its reports following investigations are available online and also the CDRT was undergoing a transitional period, so I felt that this avenue of enquiry would add another layer of bureaucracy and delay. Following Justice Wood's 2008 Inquiry into Child Protection Services in New South Wales ('Wood Inquiry'), the CDRT transferred from the New South Wales Commission for Children and Young People to the New South Wales Ombudsman. The option to seek access from Legal Aid and the Public Defenders' Office were open, but they were not as easily accessible as the Office of the DPP, as the DPP had the consolidated files. With the elimination of these options, I decided that, after looking at the emerging data, the next step was to pursue the cases that proceeded to the DPP.

The progression from one data source to another, from coronial to DPP, was necessary in order to gain a fuller understanding of the interactions that produced risk and failures of state intervention. As pointed out above, the interactionist method reflects symbolic interactionism in theory. Multiple data sources mean that more interactions could be examined, sources that related to meaning-making of different social and legal symbols and representations and the decision-making processes in relation to providing protection for the child.

135 The equivalent section to section 19 under the repealed *Coroners Act 1980* (NSW) is section 78 of the *Coroners Act 2009* (NSW).

Data analysis

While analysing the emerging data from the coronial files, two prominent types of data emerged. The first was the court cases, which did not represent the whole story. The second was the stories told about the death of the child, which were mainly represented by parties' police statements.[136] It then became clear that a smaller selection of stories had to be done in order to examine them in depth. I discuss below the process of selection of the different stories which were to become my case studies. I believed that this method allowed a richer perspective than talking with the perpetrator in each case, which represented only one player in a nest of complex key factors in a family history. Additionally, it became apparent that stories associated with the death of the children were more relevant to the purpose of the book and likely to yield valuable insights. As a number of the coronial cases had well-documented and recorded stories from the coronial investigations, a decision was made to reconstruct the stories around the deaths of the children from police statements. As a precaution, before delving head first into the DPP files I requested two files as a 'pilot' to see what types of data would emerge, and how much could be extracted from them.[137] This was a successful exercise because it paved the way for the data collection process and allowed further refinement of the field templates.[138]

DPP files

Approaching the DPP reaffirmed the commitment to follow through with the official account of filicide perpetrators and their systematic engagement with the criminal justice system and the media following the death of the child. After examining the coronial records, I decided to go further and access police and prosecutorial records as well. Contact was made with the deputy solicitor at the DPP, who, after much persuasion, allowed access on the condition of an undertaking not to identify and reveal the identities of any of the parties in the files, and not to provide any subsequent academic publications to the DPP. With the DPP's approval to access gained, a list of 12 cases was submitted to the DPP based on a non-randomised selection of cases. Because the DPP files contained

136 The use of police information can be problematic, but this does not render it an invalid data source to the extent that it documents parties' representations and perceptions of the killing and the perpetrator. Bacon and Landsdowne's research, for example, highlights grave concerns with the standard of police interrogation and their techniques: Bacon and Lansdowne, above n 48, 53–82, 73–76. In this book, police record of interviews and investigation reports act as a form of representation, without necessarily recording truth, by giving voice to the interviewee and documenting police opinion on the interviewee's voice and behaviours.

137 Yin, above n 16, 78–81.

138 See the Appendix (Table A.3).

the police brief, which includes police statements, a decision was made that it was unnecessary to approach police records for the same material.

The selection of the 12 cases was based on a range of factors that represented complex characteristics in the familial context of conflict, such as substance abuse; mental illness; the presence of state and non-state intervention, including extended family support or non-support; relationship status, whether single, married or de facto; evidence of child abuse; domestic violence; and type of family conflict and/or breakdown, such as divorce, marital separation or child residence (previously known as 'custody' in legal terminology) battle. Out of these factors, priority was given to cases in which external intervention was a factor. A conscious choice to select cases that presented different scenarios in terms of the conflict dynamics, family relationships and background was made. In this selection, the one factor that was not a priority in my decisions was gender. In the 12 cases chosen, six had female alleged perpetrators, four had male alleged perpetrators, and two had both male and female alleged perpetrators.

Finally the list of 12 cases was presented to the DPP and access to seven files was obtained, six of which are presented in Chapter 1. In two of the remaining five cases access was not granted because the original suspects were not prosecuted. They consisted of a female suspect in one case and joint male and female suspects in the other. The remaining three non-accessible cases involved a female alleged perpetrator, a male alleged perpetrator, and male and female alleged perpetrators respectively. They were ongoing matters at the time, so access to the files could not be given. Concerning the seven accessed files, I decided not to include one of them as a case study, because it contained little relevant information, and by that time there was a wealth of other information on the other cases. The seventh case is, however, referenced in Chapter 5 (*R v Jester*[139]), and discussed at some length as a comparison to the case study of Jack Drummond. In another one of the accessed files, the suspects were not prosecuted and the case reverted to the Coroner's Court for a coronial inquest, so its DPP file information was not forthcoming. In the end, DPP files were obtained for six cases (all of which are described in Chapter 1).

DPP files provided the opportunity to collect important data from various perspectives on the killing and the perpetrator, which the coronial records did not have. This data was central to the core theme of representation. Typically, a DPP file would, with privileged communications removed, contain police statements and their brief of evidence, photographic materials, case judgments, Crown submissions and information from the coronial records. The police statements formed the bulk of the manual note-taking. The information and themes emerging from these statements became the core data for the purposes of theorising and illustrating the theme of representation.

139 Supreme Court, New South Wales, 2004, Supreme Court No. J1. Parties in this case have been de-identified to comply with the privacy undertaking with the DPP.

The final nine stories

To the six DPP files, five coronial files from the original coronial sample of 40 cases were added, but only two of the five coronial files, those of Mark and Libby and Paul and Isabel, have been written up as short studies for the book (in Chapter 2). They are also published as short studies in an article that was accepted for publication by the *University of Tasmania Law Review*[140] (and is the basis of Chapter 6 in this book). The two short stories – those of Mark and Libby and Paul and Isabel – were child-murder suicide cases in which the male perpetrators murdered the children and then attempted suicide. There was a total of nine case studies, but this number was reduced to six stories presented in some depth for the book (Chapter 1), and gender was not a factor in placing them here.[141] Even though all of the stories help to illustrate the book's themes, the stories in Chapter 1 are especially important because they cut to the core of the arguments being developed throughout the book.

The following section describes the 'live' fieldwork stage in which I attended and observed these three ongoing child homicide trials in New South Wales.

Trial observation phase

The above discussion was centred on the process of data collection with regard to the development of narrative analysis. When the Bromley, Steppenwolf and Sheng cases were about to go on trial in the public domain, the opportunity to hear the voice of the perpetrator became an option to enrich the ongoing narrative analysis. This phase of my research provided material for the observational analysis, which enriched the research method in an interactive sense[142] by bringing the voice to 'life' and providing an interactive framework that informed the analysis of the case studies and theorising of representation in the chapters to follow. This phase and two others – content analysis of media reports and case judgments – form the three-pronged interactive method, and, importantly, they complement each other. A decision was thus made that these cases should be observed in court. The purpose of this was to explore the reality of the development of the official account and perpetrator representations in court.

Media representation

The media is a powerful and socially interactive force in the aftermath of a child

140 Janice Sim, 'Loving Fathers? Implications of State Intervention' (2009) 28(2) *University of Tasmania Law Review* 242–264.

141 The broader representation of gender arising from the 40 coronial cases is discussed below.

142 The observation analysis impacted on the way the models presented the concept of representation in Chapters 4 and 5, and built into the overall analysis of the case studies and the theorising on representation.

killing.[143] The decision to discuss media representation in the book was based on the trial observation stage and the initial research phase, which involved locating secondary sources of material to build a sample for the initial research proposal. It was not a new data source as such, but a decision to use the media data to employ content analysis meant that it would complement the content analysis of the case judgments as well as the observation and narrative analyses discussed above. Additionally, media analysis extended the scope of the case studies because of its examination of media publicity arising as a result of the trials. This examination completed the social interactionist pathway of the perpetrator from the conception of the killing to its conclusion, and the creation and development of dominant representations and symbols pre-killing and in the aftermath.

A decision was made that media representation was important to the meanings of perpetrator action and motives, particularly where these meanings were legitimated by the court, and the processes of meaning-making was seen as significant to the tenets of symbolic interactionism. Of interest also was the impact of media representation on perpetrator representation. During the trial observation phase, the presence of the media at the courts and the regular summarised reporting of the judicial narrative in the news were key factors with respect to the interactions between the media and the stakeholders in the court cases. Data from the DPP files also contained a handful of media reports, which led me to the realisation that when looking at the broad picture of representation the angle of media reporting is crucial to the research question, the symbolic interactionist perspective and the theme of representation. Using the data from the coronial and DPP files, it was possible to research and retrieve from the public domain more media reporting on the cases, most of which were not contained in the accessed files. Particularly for the three court cases that relied heavily on the media reporting, the media sources that provided content analysis became crucial to the development of the discussion on media representation in Chapter 5, including media representation in the fieldwork that also harks back to the utility of symbolic interactionism and the focus on the social audience as the determinant of certain representations and meanings regarding deviant episodes and behaviour.

Limitations with analytical style

Narrative analysis

Unlike other studies in this field, as mentioned above, this research focuses on a handful of selected cases in order to understand forms of representation in child killing. This technical conceptualisation of the case studies as 'stories' creates

143 Wilczynski, above n 5, 132–135. See also Moira Peelo, Brian Francis, Keith Soothhill, Jayn Pearson and Elizabeth Ackerley, 'Newspaper Reporting and the Public Construction of Homicide' (2004) 44 *British Journal of Criminology* 256–274, 256–257.

distance between the researcher and the sensitivity and painful nature of the data.[144] The researcher's role in shaping, and representing, the outcome of the data analysis is central to narrative analysis and shows the difficulties of this approach as well. There must also be a process of reflection for the researcher, which Bourdieu calls 'self-reflexivity'.[145] As much as my intention was to let the voices of the perpetrators and the deceased children surface from the data, it could not be achieved for various practical reasons, such as word constraint; the sensitive and private nature of some of the accounts; the lack of a voice for the child in many if not all of the cases; and the nature of the medium, being police statements, in which the perpetrators' voices were reflected and recorded. The option to pursue face-to-face interviews with some of these perpetrators was available, but I was uncertain what end this would serve in enhancing the 'stories', bearing in mind two influential factors for the perpetrators: their distance from the killing and, most importantly, the passage of time, which might have an impact on their recollection, particularly of painful and traumatic memories, and possibly lead to memory lapses.

Content analysis

The stories eventually contained only information that was central to, and reflected, the core themes. In terms of content analysis, the main challenge was the de-identification of the parties. Coding was necessary to achieve de-identification, and this included de-identification of references from secondary sources that were obtained in the public domain. A consistent coding system was therefore developed. Throughout the book, all the sources of data materials that were used in the writing-up of the narratives, such as court documents (including case law, media reports and police documents) and self-made notes, were coded to comply with the privacy and ethical undertakings.[146]

Observational analysis

The other challenge was the process of data collection, particularly where it concerned the fieldwork observation phase. The DPP imposed a condition that restricted approaching and speaking with the alleged perpetrators at the trials; however, it was possible to liaise with the Crown Prosecutor and the DPP team. Every effort to contact the defence lawyers in these cases was made, but to no avail. Understandably, there were difficulties given the adversarial nature of the criminal justice system, and possibly concerns that a researcher might compromise an ongoing trial.

144 Pierre Bourdieu, *Homo Academicvs* (Peter Collier trans, Stanford University Press, 1988) xiv [trans of: Les Editions de Minuit (first published 1984)].

145 Pierre Bourdieu, *Pascalian Meditations* (Richard Nice trans, Stanford University Press, 2000) ch 1 [trans of: *Méditations pascaliennes* (first published 1997)].

146 The system of coding in this book is explained in the following section.

The coding system

As noted, a coding and referencing system for the data analysis was needed to de-identify the parties. The process is explained here for the reader as it was necessary to have a consistent naming system for the modelling in Chapters 4 and 5; this should also allow the reader to get a sense of the person behind the 'voice'. First, pseudonyms for all the parties in all the files were created. Next, a naming system for the type of document and the date the document was made was needed. For judgments, the case name was replaced by the pseudonym, such as '*R v Melanie Drummond*', followed by the hierarchy of the court, the Australian state or territory where the case was heard, the year of the case, and a case file reference number. As the actual legal citation for the case could not be given, it had to be referenced as such. This applied to the transcripts of the coronial inquests too. For newspapers and magazines, the article was given a report number, followed by the newspaper title, then the Australian state or territory where known (for newspapers), and finally the actual date of the article. Police statements were given a report number and then the pseudonym of the maker of the statement; this is followed by the actual location and actual date of the statement made, and finally, the place at which the statement was made, such as 'police station A'. Undated notes were noted and, for purposes of coding, an approximate date in line with the rest of the data was given to maintain a consistent referencing system. For specialised government publications such as those of the New South Wales Ombudsman, the agency producing the documents had to be de-identified because the reports would identify the deceased. This was also done for reports in which the name of the deceased could be published due to a court order, because other factors could possibly identify the case. Such was the format of the coding system developed; this was also the format that was used for recording the research process, such as the use of bibliographic cards.[147]

Broad representation of the study

To place the representation of gender, relationship status and state involvement in the context of the research questions, it is necessary to provide a broad breakdown of the original coronial sample of 40 cases. In particular, I look at the original coronial sample in order to show the relevance and importance of examining the interactions between the state and the family. This breakdown of the cases shows that the majority of the child deaths, as a result of abuse, neglect, murder or other suspicious circumstances, were at the time of death known to the state,[148] or that one or both of the parents had previously been

147 Hutchinson, above n 20, 24–25.

148 This is in line with the following reports. New South Wales Ombudsman, *Report of Reviewable Deaths in 2005 Volume 2: Child Deaths* (New South Wales Ombudsman, 2006) 7. Out of the 117 reviewable child deaths in 2005, 33 children died as a result of abuse or neglect or suspicious circumstances, out of which 25 children were

involved with a professional (social or medical) agency. The observation that there was a strong presence of state intervention in these cases of children's death further strengthens the research theme on state intervention and the need to closely examine its implications.

More than half of the cases (62.5 per cent) involved incidents of violence either between partners or between parent and child, and 75 per cent were known to the state at the time of death. More than half of these incidents of violence involved male perpetrators. Among the female perpetrator cohort (40 per cent), a number of them (43.6 per cent) killed as a result of mental illness and half were caught up in a state of dysfunction where there were apparent risks to the safety of the child as a result of strife, abuse or violence perpetrated by one or both parents. At the time of the killing, in most cases, the family could be described as conforming to a nuclear family model such that there had been one male role model and one female role model in the children's lives, whether they were the biological or de facto parent or de facto partner. Only in a handful of cases (5 per cent) was the nuclear model incomplete, consisting of a single-parent household. The relevance of this data is further discussed in Chapter 6, where I argue that the data supports my contention that many of these cases reveal a deeply ingrained family structure built on patriarchy. This observation[149] then informs my argument that, in the majority of child killings in this study, the male's assumed right of ownership and control of his family has, in his view, unjustly and unfairly collapsed.

The observations made in Chapters 4 and 5 all emerged from the data sources. The reader will notice that the stories within the case studies are built around the perspectives of the different parties who have been involved in the conflict and who have relationships with the perpetrator and/or victims, or both. The perspectival format of the case studies is designed to reveal the nature and processes of representation and representing, and it reproduces a framework that utilises the same types of data construction, that is, official recorded accounts or 'stories'. The case study format also allows the voices of the parties to 'surface' from the data, which was one of the reasons for using this format. The other reason is to avoid disempowering the actors. Even though each case study has

known to child protection services within three years of their deaths. In the period December 2002 to December 2003, 103 out of 137 reviewable child death cases, where information was available, were of children where there had been a risk of harm report to DOCS for the child and/or a sibling, within three years preceding their deaths: New South Wales Ombudsman, *Reviewable Deaths Annual Report 2003–4: An overview* (New South Wales Ombudsman, 2004) 1. In 2006, 123 child deaths were reviewable, out of which 114 children were known to DOCS. Eighty-one out of the 114 children known to DOCS were the subject of a risk of harm report to DOCS in the three years preceding their deaths: New South Wales Ombudsman, *Report of Reviewable Deaths in 2006 Volume 2: Child Deaths* (New South Wales Ombudsman, 2007) I, 13–19.

149 These observations are based on coronial data in the 40 relevant filicide cases.

been written up in a consistent format, each case relies on different forms of data. For example, the coronial data generally gives an insight into the social background of the conflict and the deceased child, whereas the DPP data usually provides insight into the perpetrator's background and motivations. The types of data that emerged, such as police statements and police reports of death, are different in their contents even though they are presented using the same forms. That is to say, each police report is different because it discusses the story in a different way. This is because they have been written up, and recorded, by different persons. As a result, they reveal the conflict, perpetrator, third parties and deceased in different ways, and therefore the data in each case study is presented differently. As explained before, conscious choices as to what data to include and exclude were made. Only data that were relevant, necessary, significant and illustrative of the themes of the book were included. Because of the way the data emerged, the initial interest in representation and labelling was preserved in spite of my not pursuing face-to-face interviews.

It was possible to achieve all of the above because of the focus on only a handful of case studies that grew out of non-random sampling. This method provided coverage of the types of cases in the original coronial sample. Even though the sample was not representative, this selectiveness provided fuller accounts than a quantitative study could do. The richness of the stories meant that the research could provide a comprehensive understanding of some of the deeper underlying issues posed in the research questions.

Justifying the case study methodology

Robert Yin[150] highlights the two main aims of case study methodology: first, the case study as an empirical enquiry that investigates a contemporary phenomenon within its real-life context, especially when the boundaries between phenomenon and context are not clearly evident; and second, the case study as an enquiry in which there are more variables of interest than data points, relying on multiple sources of evidence with the data converging in a triangulating fashion, and benefitting from prior development of theoretical propositions to guide data collection and analysis.[151] Yin further states that case studies can be based on any mix of quantitative and qualitative evidence, and are best used to answer 'why' and 'how' types of research questions.[152] Given that the majority of my research questions are 'how' questions, it seems reasonable that the case study methodology is the best option for this project.

Yin points out that there are at least five different applications for case study methodology – this book satisfies at least three of them. The five applications are: first, to explain presumed causal links in real-life interventions that are too

150 Yin, above n 16, 13–14.
151 Ibid.
152 Ibid 7.

complex for survey or experimental strategies; second, to describe an intervention and the real-life context in which it has occurred; third, to illustrate certain topics within an evaluation in a descriptive mode; fourth, to explore those situations in which the intervention being evaluated has no clear, single set of outcomes; and fifth, as a meta-evaluation.[153] The first, second and fourth of these are applicable to my study because the real-life interventions are state intervention and self-labelling and representation. It could be argued that the third application is also relevant, because labelling and representation are presented in a descriptive mode, and thus the case study strategy is a method that should sufficiently illustrate these topics.

The nature of my research sources and evidence – being documentation, direct observation and archival records[154] – further justifies the use of the case study methodology. Documentation, in this book, consists of secondary materials from the public domain, such as biographies and autobiographies, ombudsman reports, case judgments, newspaper articles, magazines and government publications and reports. Direct observation refers to my trial observation phase, where (echoing Yin[155]) much of the material covered was selective and required reflexivity on my part. Archival records refer to the coronial and DPP files, regarding which accessibility was an issue due to privacy reasons.[156] As the case studies have been written up using various sources and types of documents, the facts have been suitably corroborated, which is the most important use of the documents.[157] The documentary and qualitative nature of these narratives can be seen as a product of interaction between, for example, the perpetrator and state agents. The focus on these interactions around the killing of the child prompts an interactive analysis that would reconstruct stories as well as contexts from which the critical enquiry into representation and risk can arise.

Data analysis

The method of analysis, as indicated in the discussions above, is interactive and enhances the data each of the styles above elicited. Data analysis proceeded using the field templates. As the data was categorised in accordance with the categories in the field templates, it was easier to find what was relevant to reconstructing the 'story' around the killing. For instance, information pertaining to background facts and context were considered important in order to situate the killing against possible conditions of dysfunctionality. This made up the general framework of my enquiry. It was then pertinent to examine if there were any dysfunctional factors in the case that may impact on the safety of the child, such as substance abuse, mental illness, residence disputes and dysfunctional intervention. The

153 Ibid 15.
154 Ibid 86.
155 Ibid.
156 Ibid.
157 Ibid 87.

term 'dysfunctional factors' can be defined as a set of basic conditions in which the safety of the child is not met; this is further discussed in Chapter 6, which examines the theoretical conceptualisation of the meaning and applicability of a 'state of dysfunction'. The next stage of analysis was to extract the stories of the parties as related to the perpetrator or conflict. This depended on the availability and richness of the data arising from the police statements, but sometimes there were additional pieces of data such as perpetrator self-written statements.

First, a determination as to which parties to include in the case study had to be made. As explained, this was usually determined by what was offered in the extensive police statements. The stories had to be comprehensive in such a way that related to the general framework of enquiry concerning the background of the perpetrator and the killing, and the party's understandings of the perpetrator and the family. Second, a choice had to be made regarding the way the story emerged. For example, there were sometimes pieces of data that were irrelevant to the general framework, such as the perpetrator's hobbies, and these had to be excluded from the writing up. Once pieces of data required to fit into the general framework were identified, the next challenge was putting the stories together in a meaningful way for the data to be interpreted. It made sense that one way to 'read' the data was to write the stories up chronologically. After the stories were written up, attention focused on the forcefulness of certain representations made by the perpetrators and key individuals in the killings. The next step was to examine closely what these representations were, and how they impacted on the interplay and interactions of the various social forces happening at the time of the killing, such as external intervention by family members and state agents, including police officers, social workers and courts.

The general framework created is in line with Yin's strategy regarding analysing case study evidence. He argues that there is a need for an analytical strategy,[158] and this must be informed by one's core themes. He also points out three general strategies: first, relying on theoretical propositions; second, thinking about rival explanations; and third, developing a case description.[159] The steps outlined above point to the utilisation of the first and third of these strategies for analysing the data. The first is my reliance on symbolic interactionist theory, especially labelling theory, and the second is my reliance on the case descriptions around the killing and the perpetrator, which make up the overall 'story'. This is also corroborated by the objective facts contained in the case judgments of the judicial narratives. The advantage of merging the case judgments,[160] being case

158 Yin, above n 16, 109.

159 Yin, above n 16, 109–115.

160 Writing case judgments into the case studies was done at the end of the case studies. This was done to provide the reader with a sense of conclusion and allow for the interrogation of core socio-criminological themes of labelling and representation in the legal framework of case law method. Last, a decision was made that to omit case law would be to the detriment of a more enriched understanding of the official processes of labelling. This train of enquiry is also grounded in symbolic

law, into the case study is that doing so informs the development of the theoretical conceptualisation of representation based on the interactive method and theorising.

Having introduced the book, its theoretical framing and methodology and methods, this chapter now concludes with a brief overview of the structure of the book.

Book structure

This book consists of seven chapters. Chapter 1 presents the case study data, which consists of six main case studies. The case studies are generally constructed using the following format, which is discussed in greater detail in Chapter 1. The background to the case is stated first; this usually comprises coronial and DPP file data. Second, the stories of the perpetrator and the killing are told from the perspectives of other parties involved in the conflict or with the perpetrator. Third, the legal representations of the perpetrators, where available, are presented. Fourth, the judicial narrative – the case judgment where the matter has proceeded to trial or sentencing in court – is discussed. In the alternative, the coronial narrative, where it is available, usually in the coronial inquest, is discussed. This particular format emphasises, and brings out, the strengths of the symbolic interactionist methodology in the sense that selected voices of the key stakeholders are given priority. This format also allows for an interactionist analysis of the social influences that inform the representations of the parties, which is the research focus of the book.

Chapter 2 analyses certain forms of violence that appear 'invisible' to state agents and surrounding actors in the conflict. The chapter tries to identify the nature of filicidal violence and how it expresses itself in a variety of ways, some physically evident, others surreptitious and symbolically complex. The argument pursued is that, viewed through Bourdieu's symbolic violence theory, these expressions of violence elude detection because they are so embedded in dominant representations, such as the loving parent representation, that they are not recognised as violence. Also introduced in this chapter is the dramaturgical device of masking, which is used in the book as a sub-theme to explain perpetrator social transformations and representation.

Chapter 3 describes a broader framework of myth within which filicidal representations have been played out through storytelling. Utilising storytelling

---

interactionism. Merging case law and case study methods has a twofold purpose. First, the use of case law illustrates the objective standard by which the perpetrator is judged. Second, the facts presented in the case judgments allow comparisons as to parties' representation, and allows observations to be made about the nature of the judicial narrative and the representation, and voices, arising from it. This method also traces the point of entry of the perpetrator's entrance into the criminal justice system, and the development and formulation of the official account of the 'story' that is eventually presented to the public through media reporting.

and mythology, the chapter argues for the relevance of mythological filicidal representations in modern-day narratives around perpetrator description and construction, particularly in the judicial narratives. It also considers the socio-legal field that shapes these representations and produces, in many cases, an ideological consonance with traditional patriarchal beliefs on women and children. The argument is that these representations are structured along, and deeply embedded within, deep social and cultural beliefs. The intent is to tease out the development and attachment of certain meanings relating to the attributes of parents that are given to legal archetypes of the parent in both myth and law. The chapter also touches on the symbolism and power of these representations, which are derived from the realm of mythology. The argument pursued is that characteristics of filicide perpetrators have been drawn from mythology into the law.

Chapter 4 presents a theoretical conceptualisation of representation. The chapter presents a model of representation that is used to explain and interpret the case study data in a meaningful way. The chapter argues that there is a framework within which representation can be understood and analysed in such a way that charts the risk of child endangerment. The chapter then explains how modelling is used to understand the broader structural framework – first-, second- and third-degree representation – by which the concept of representation is framed, and makes an observation that these are the same types of social framings that are used to frame individual social representations. Within this analysis, the chapter discusses the various styles of representation by the perpetrator and of the event of killing: self-representation; perpetrator representation of killing; event representation by third parties; and the context of representation. Here it is argued that the perceptions of the parties in the case study provide insight into the perpetrator's background and motives, and also provide insight into the nature of the risks to the child. From this, the chapter argues that there are varying degrees of relationship that structure and give meaning to understandings of risk.

Chapter 5 discusses the critical social theories relevant to representation as a theoretical conceptualisation. The chapter explains the importance of the construction of meanings pertaining to images, symbol, risk and representation. The purpose of representation is seen here as social governance. The chapter further argues that the loving parent representation is an important enduring symbol of parenthood. Chapters 4 and 5 in fact inform each other. The analytical themes of parental ownership, dysfunctional intervention, the loving parent representation and the use of masking are highlighted in both these chapters as important indicators of potential risks of child endangerment.

Chapter 6 examines the nature and implications of state intervention. This chapter argues that state intervention has a masculine representation in that its response of meeting violence with violence, particularly in the context of domestic violence, parallels the responses of the male perpetrators in the case studies. The chapter begins with a theoretical conceptualisation of the 'state of dysfunction'. This is followed by a discussion of the idea that the loving parent representation is misleading and deceptive, particularly in the way it is used by male perpetrators as an invisible cloak over the state of dysfunction to mask the risks of child endangerment.

Chapter 7 brings the disparate threads together and consolidates the book. This chapter addresses the central relationships between representation, state intervention and risk. Based on the exploration of these themes in the preceding chapters, this chapter argues that the prominence and visibility of the child, which are lacking in the case studies, must be situated within the broader national and international contexts of children's rights. The conclusion reached is that there is a need for policy makers and state agents to better understand the inextricability of representation in constructions of risk, which must depend on holistic assessments rather than the current assessments based on forensic and procedural analysis. This holistic understanding not only sits within the framework of human rights and child protection, but challenges state agents to recognise hidden representations and symbols of violence for what they really are. The argument raised is that social interaction produces labels, symbols, representation and risk, and places child killing at the centre of social relations between state, family and community. The analysis here highlights a need to situate the child in a place of prominence and visibility in the family and the community, and within current structures of actionable rights and protections. The chapter then reconnects with the research questions through an examination of the interactive conditions of risk in which child endangerment and false, and distorted, representations develop. It argues for a more holistic and realistic makeover of risk assessment through the consideration of symbolic and social interactive processes and key representations and symbols. Finally, the recentring of the child's role is discussed in light of national and international contexts of children's rights and protections, and by which child endangerment and risk of harm may be defused.

1 Introducing the six filicide cases

Introduction

The following stories are written in a way that draws out socio-criminological themes pertaining to theoretical conceptualisations of: masking as a dramaturgical device (discussed in Chapter 2); the criminological theory of labelling (discussed in Chapter 5); representations (perpetrator, judicial and media) (discussed in Chapters 4 and 5); and parental ownership in the social and symbolic sense (discussed in Chapters 2, 3 and 6). The six stories are based on written accounts of events and written statements of persons whose identities have been changed.

The thread that runs through the themes is symbolic interactionist theory, which links these social processes through a focus on symbolic and social indications in which people make meaning of each other, themselves, and their family and environment.[1] These interactions are between the individual actor and his or her family and community members; between the parent and the child; and between the family and the state. Using case study methodology, the 'story' can be presented from multiple perspectives, and this reflects the social processes and meaning-making within it. Of particular significance is its ability to tease out these complex interactions illustrating the perspectival nature of representation, which informs the modelling and theorising of representation in Chapters 4 and 5. Some of these complex interactions also provide insight into the 'hidden' expressions of violence towards the child and the conditions of dysfunctionality affecting child safety in the family. Additionally, this method allows the reader to grasp the decision-making processes associated with the actors in the case, which is crucial when looking at the broader role of state agents and their interactions with the family.

The stories are written in a way that retains the first-person narrative to preserve the voice of the individual as far as possible. Some narratives may contradict each other. Where there is a dispute with regard to the corroboration of certain facts, the disputed statement or incident is referenced as conflicting. This is difficult and challenging, as 'truth' in its limited sense in the context of

1 David Downes and Paul Rock, *Understanding Deviance* (Oxford University Press, 4th ed, 2003) 183.

these stories is largely a legal, subjective and objectively indefinable concept; this difficulty is pointed out in Chapters 3 and 4 in the discussion on representation. The veracity of each person's account is presented with the intention of showing that 'truth' and 'fact' are not the same. In the subjective sense, each person's account is taken to represent the truth of his or her belief.

The stories are told from evolving perspectives. Family members, and sometimes the perpetrators themselves, give inside contextual insight into the unfolding conflict. Representations from the court where the presiding judge's comments pertain to perpetrator motive and sentencing lend an objective 'flair' to the story. The media's representation is included where its reconstruction and interpretation of the killing and of the perpetrator are relevant to the interpretation of shared symbols and the processes of social life. The media is also seen as a pivotal social force in giving 'voice' to the perpetrator, the community and, sometimes, the deceased. Government and coronial reports are sometimes provided where they explain the agency's position in respect of their alleged failures to protect the child. Each of these stories ends with my concluding remarks, which draw out the themes in the book. The themes discussed in the following chapters, and through which the stories are presented, are: masking, dysfunctional intervention, patriarchal ownership, judicial and media narratives, symbolic violence, meaning-making, representation and risk. The stories have been pared down, with many of the accounts given by the perpetrators and family members stripped of raw emotions, which were very powerful because they were first-hand experiences of the conflict. Nevertheless, they have been written in such a way as to give primacy to the leading voices in the stories and to stay true, as far as possible, to their original content.

Recounting the 'voice'

The recounting of the voice is the central focus of this chapter, because of the book's interest in representation. Each person's account is written in such a way as to provide different points of representation, such as from the perspectives of the perpetrator(s), the child (deceased) and external observers, including family members and social workers. The purpose of focusing on the 'voice' is to be 'true' to the data by representing it as closely as possible; this became an exercise of retelling the accounts as 'stories'. The retelling of the 'stories' then revealed the significance of certain contextual features that impact on representation, as discussed in Chapters 4 and 5. These features include emotional proximity, physical space, distance and time. These features are the same cultural and social framings that shape the representation around the style of the 'story'. For example, storytelling by the perpetrators, family members and community workers reveals different aspects of representation. Risk, for instance, takes the final form of risk of harm reports. Objective representations as to fact, for instance, are represented by government reports and the 'voice' of the judicial narrative. In these stories, the reader may well notice that the child is rarely heard, seen or represented prior to the killing. In some brief instances their lives are represented in the coronial, judicial and media narratives, but their voices are rarely heard. This key observation, although not within the analytical themes, is discussed in depth in Chapter 7, which looks at the issue of children's rights and representation.

One obvious conclusion is that representations, such as the perpetrator representation of self and events or a risk of harm to the child representation, are shaped, and given meaning, through the eyes of the observer. This sets the stage for discussions on the nature of representation in the chapters to follow. The broader message to take away from the stories you are about to read is this: these are very tragic stories of children whose deaths could have been, very possibly, prevented by an intervention. Children are society's most vulnerable and they deserve to be heard, seen and protected. The fact that the children's voices are silent and their presences nearly invisible is a reflection of a reality for some, in which children's lives matter little.

Horace Faulkner

Summary: *Horace Faulkner's story is about the repercussions, and nature, of vengeful domestic violence. At the heart of this violence were three young children, one girl aged 7 and two boys aged 5 and 4, who were the victims of an acrimonious separation and child residence (custody) fight between father and mother. The children were eventually drugged and drowned by their father, who, following their failed struggle for life, arranged a ritualistic setting – a scene of shock and horror – aimed to create maximum impact and to send a message to their mother. Horace's anger towards his ex-wife is physically manifested through the deaths of the children, and his treatment of the children ties in with the theme of ownership of children. Horace believed he had the right and power to dispose of his children when presented with the possibility of the children having a stepfather. Aligned with the theme of ownership is the displacement of Horace's anger onto the children, who became pawns for the expiation of his own suffering.*

In spite of the family's record of domestic violence with various support agencies, there were no real concerns for the safety and well-being of the children because Horace had always appeared as a loving, doting and protective father. Paradoxically, it was Horace's desire to save the children from his broken marriage that gave him a reason to wear the mask of the altruistic loving parent in order to murder them. This particular representation, as the loving parent, masked the risk of violence to the children and concealed from the public gaze the true nature of the dysfunction in the home, and in Horace himself.

Background

Since childhood Horace had been a disturbed individual. His parents separated when he was young. He became traumatised by various incidents, leading him to attempt suicide several times during his early adult years. After Horace met his wife, Melissa, at work, they got married and had three children. When the marriage failed, the contentious separation and child residence proceedings aggravated Horace's unstable disposition. When Horace heard that Melissa was seeing someone else, and after his attempts at reconciliation failed, Horace took the children's lives by drugging and drowning them when Melissa left them in his care at his unit one afternoon. He then attempted suicide. He was found by his mother, Annette, who had become increasingly concerned about his state of mind following his phone call to her the night before. Horace was arrested and charged with three counts of murder. His defence of substantial mental impairment was rejected by the jury. He was sentenced to 32 years in jail.

The scene of death

> He had deliberately set out to create a horrifying spectacle for her benefit. It was to be a scene from her worst nightmare and one that she would never forget.[2]

Walking into the unit, one was first confronted with a stuffed monkey (one of the children's toys) hanging from a noose fashioned from an electrical cord,[3] with a knife through its upper body. Its hands were severed and lying on the ground. To create the appearance of blood, there was tomato sauce on the entry and exit points of the knife, and on the floor. Further into the house lay the bodies of three children, each in separate rooms with final messages of love such as 'I love you' and 'RIP' written on their faces.[4] On the walls were messages such as: 'I'm waiting, Bethual [Melissa's boyfriend]. Come to Papa'[5] and 'I'm not to be toyed trifled with!'[6] Finally, on Horace's computer screen was the message: '[Melissa], you were forever telling me that you would take our children from me . . . I always promised you that come what may, [the children] would be with me forever together, always . . . with or without you.'[7] The post-mortem later revealed that their daughter had struggled violently against Horace's efforts to drown her; the marks on her neck and other injuries indicated the violent struggle between father and child.[8]

Family and perpetrator representations

Horace's story[9]

Horace remembered little of his father, Alan. After his parents divorced, his mother relocated the children frequently. Horace expressed a desire to live with

2 *R v Horace Faulkner*, Supreme Court, New South Wales, 2004, Supreme Court No. HF1, [18].
3 Report 'AR', taken on 25 August 2001 from the Department of Forensic Medicine in Sydney at hospital B.
4 Ibid [19], [20].
5 Ibid.
6 Ibid.
7 Ibid [22].
8 Ibid [21].
9 This account is written from Horace's point of view and has been paraphrased. It is based on report 'HF2', taken on 21 May 2002 from Dr Frank in Sydney at prison

his father, but felt that his father did not want him.[10] When he was 13, Horace was sexually assaulted at school, and appeared in court to testify against his perpetrator. The experience traumatised Horace emotionally. After this, he saw counsellors and psychiatrists irregularly. He felt angry and frustrated because he did not believe the doctors were helping him. At 19, Horace left school. He had long periods of unemployment. He attempted suicide at least three times, each attempt about two years apart. By then, Horace had a number of diagnoses: schizophrenia, paranoid psychosis, acute schizophrenia and depression. The periods between Horace's hospital admissions were disruptive in that he was sometimes homeless. He was once discharged to a halfway house. He later lost contact with his mother and began drinking heavily and gambling.

Horace became very depressed during one of his hospital admissions, where he developed a relationship with a girl, who subsequently fell pregnant. As he did not want to carry the guilt of an abortion, he wanted her to have the child. However, she went for the abortion and left him. He never fully recovered from the abortion and relationship.

His early memories of his mother were tainted with anger. Horace described Annette as a 'dominating woman', 'emotionally abusive' and an 'abusive bitch'.[11] He said he could not deal with her. Her absence in his childhood years caused Horace to grow close to his aunt Gertrude. When Horace heard that his aunt lost her child at birth, he was greatly affected and became upset and angry. These were the same feelings of anger and upset after his girlfriend's abortion. Again, Horace felt that he had lost something.

Horace described his marriage as 'a constant battle'.[12] He recalled that they embarked on a sexual relationship immediately after they met. Unknown to him, Melissa wanted to have children but did not want a husband.[13] Early in their relationship, Melissa began her provocations. Horace felt resentment and came to believe that Melissa was manipulating him to obtain welfare benefits. She incited him by telling him to prove himself and taunted him by asking if he was

---

F; report 'HF3', taken on 31 January 2001 from Dr Costello in Sydney at prison F; report 'HF4', taken on 26 November 2001 from Dr Butts in Sydney at prison F; report 'HF5', taken on 5 July 2001 from Horace Faulkner in Sydney at police station B; report 'HF6', taken on 14 November 1997 from Horace Faulkner in Sydney at solicitor's office P; and *R v Horace Faulkner*, above n 2. Some portions are written in first-person narrative to preserve Horace's voice. All identifiers have been changed to comply with the book's privacy undertaking.

10 Later, Horace went on to live with his father. However, his memory of his father is inconsistent and is challenged by Horace's father's memories of Horace.

11 Report 'HF2', taken on 21 May 2002 from Dr Frank in Sydney at prison F; report 'HF4', taken on 26 November 2001 from Dr Butts in Sydney at prison F; and report 'HF3', taken on 31 January 2001 from Dr Costello in Sydney at prison F.

12 Report 'HF2', ibid.

13 Report 'HF6', taken on 14 November 1997 from Horace Faulkner in Sydney at solicitor's office P, [8].

gay or a 'mummy's boy'.[14] Horace felt that he confided in Melissa but she did not reciprocate this intimacy and instead focused on hurting him by using his secrets against him. He said Melissa was 'building a campaign'[15] against him. He felt she was cruel to him when she became pregnant, using the pregnancy to toy with his feelings because she knew the threat of abortion would affect him.[16] When she wanted to abort their child, Annerley, his first instinct was to leave. Melissa promised to work things out and he returned, but felt that she was cold towards him. He later described her as 'not a very loving person'.[17] When Annerley was born, Horace cried with happiness. He did not want a second child, but Melissa fell pregnant again. He described Russell as a 'strange baby' and did not feel close to him.[18] Six months later, Melissa was pregnant with Joshua. By then, Horace and Melissa were constantly fighting. When Joshua was born, both were working alternate shifts and took turns to care for the children.

Horace felt that Melissa was controlling, violent and deliberately provocative in order to make him upset; for example, Melissa would phone him at work to check on him. She accused him of being unfaithful. He believed she threw things at him with the intention of injuring him, and to get him to hit her so as to incriminate himself. Once, Melissa smashed a glass on him while he was asleep. He cut his finger and she fled the house, leaving pieces of glass lying in the baby's cot. Horace lodged a police report and obtained an apprehended violence order ('AVO') against her. After that, Melissa's behaviour towards him changed, but even though she ceased to be physically violent she did not stop her verbal provocation. For example she told him, 'I've got to take the children away from you, we don't need you'[19] and called him 'a sperm donor'.[20]

Their relationship did not improve with time. As the fighting became worse, the police advised Horace to seek legal advice because Melissa was complaining to the police about him. Horace then ran into financial problems. He started to believe in Melissa's threats to take the children away from him and that she was goading him to hit her. Horace felt stressed and frustrated, and this was compounded when Melissa rang the police about his aggressive behaviour. He was 'fed up' with her threat to take the children away.[21] As a result, he took the children to Annette's home for a week because he felt he had no one to turn to. Melissa asked him to return home and said that they would 'talk'.[22] But when this promised 'talk' did not occur, Horace felt manipulated once again.

14 Report 'HF3', taken on 31 January 2001 from Dr Costello in Sydney at prison F.
15 Report 'HF2', above n 11.
16 Report 'HF6', above n 13.
17 Report 'HF3', above n 14.
18 Ibid.
19 Ibid.
20 Ibid.
21 Ibid.
22 Ibid.

Horace returned home from work one day only to realise that Melissa had taken the children to a refuge. He felt that this move was unfair, claiming that the separation was unhealthy for the children, and that Melissa did not care about the impact on the children. It was this move that caused him to formulate his first thoughts of killing the children.[23] In the following weeks, Horace and Melissa went to court over the residence of the children. Melissa told the court that Horace was 'bashing her every day' and that he 'kept her housebound'.[24] He believed that the refuge coaxed her to say these lines. The court experience destabilised him. Horace said:

> I lost it, I could not go to work, it was then I started feeling that I was going to take . . . I felt like such a failure, I did not look at it like I'm going to kill my kids. I looked at it like I don't want my kids to go through the pain and suffering and insecurity I had to go through and now I have to watch it all again.[25]

Later, the police asked Horace about his relationship with his wife and children, and about the events on the day of the killing. Horace lamented:

> My poor kids . . . I didn't say I didn't love my kids. I love my kids more than anything. I don't trust my wife . . . *My kids were going to be taken away by my wife and I told her that my kids would always be with me*. No way was I going to leave them, do that to my children. Put them through misery for the rest of their lives. To be driven insane by unreciprocated love . . . More than anything I wanted my children to have their mother and father together . . . I was molested when I was a child and I'm scared the same thing might have happened to them. *I wasn't a good husband. My children were my world. I killed my kids because I had to protect them* . . . My kids are in peace now, they don't have to go through the shit I had to. You've all been abused through your lives. I didn't kill my children for nothing. *It was so that they did not have to go through what I had to* . . . I could not stop though not once I started. I thought I can't let my children live the rest of their lives thinking their father died of a drug overdose. In one way, I feel relieved because I stopped them from feeling pain . . . There is nothing I wanted more than to be with my wife and kids . . . do you know how hard it was for me to kill my children. I took drugs to do it, otherwise I couldn't have done it. There is one thing that I am glad that I killed my kids, they won't have to suffer. I have put them out of their misery, I have saved them from pain. *For once, my wife was not in control.*[26] (Emphasis added)[27]

23 Report 'HF2', above n 11.
24 Report 'HF3', above n 11.
25 Ibid.
26 Report 'HF5', taken on 5 July 2001 from Horace Faulkner in Sydney at police station B; and *R v Horace Faulkner*, above n 2, [25].
27 The emphasis here is intended to stress the importance of Horace's proprietary attitude towards, and his perception of, Melissa and the children.

Even though they had agreed on an interim, flexible parenting schedule, Horace described his condition as suicidal and hopeless with small bouts of optimism and hope.[28] He felt that he had been the primary caregiver of the children and, when compared to Melissa, he was better able to provide for them.[29] He feared he would be totally alienated from the children if Melissa gained residence and contact rights over the children.[30] Horace became preoccupied with the notion that the children would be permanently and emotionally scarred, and that death was the better alternative for them.[31]

When Melissa tried to take the children overseas, Horace retracted his consent at the last minute and called airport security to stop them boarding the plane.[32] A Family Court hearing was scheduled to resolve this dispute. Before the hearing could take place, Horace was already feeling the pressure of going to court again.[33] Finding out about Melissa's affair with Bethual was the final straw for Horace.[34] Horace feared Bethual would become a father figure to the children and sexually abuse them. This was when he became convinced that death was the only way out.[35] Horace later said, 'What I did was a message to my wife. My anger was about her.'[36] The stabbed monkey, he said, represented Melissa. This was to demonstrate to her how angry he was with her. Horace did not think that the killings were wrong.[37] To him, it was like an abortion and he believed he was saving the children from a broken marriage.[38]

Horace felt that separating from the children after spending time with them on weekends was difficult for him. The separation brought back memories of his own feelings about his father. As such, he was determined for the children to have both parents living together. He felt he was fighting for his right to be a good father.[39] He did not want a divorce. Horace described himself as a responsible and devoted father, because he took care of the children whenever Melissa suffered depression and would leave the children unsupervised.[40]

Regarding Horace's mental situation, Melissa felt that Horace held a lot of negative emotions and repressed anger towards his parents, especially his mother,

28 Report 'HF4', taken on 26 November 2001 from Dr Butts in Sydney at prison F.
29 Report 'HF6', taken on 14 November 1997 from Horace Faulkner in Sydney at solicitor's office P, [12].
30 Ibid.
31 Report 'HF2', above n 11.
32 *R v Horace Faulkner*, above n 2, [6].
33 Report 'HF3', above n 11.
34 Report 'HF4', above n 11.
35 Ibid.
36 Report 'HF4', above n 11.
37 Report 'HF3', above n 11.
38 Ibid.
39 Report 'HF2', above n 11.
40 Report 'HF6', above n 29.

and his parents' separation. When Annette visited, Horace would physically abuse her in the presence of the children.[41] Horace told Melissa,

> you are not going to take my children away from me. I am not going to be like my father. He left us with my mother and should not have done that. My mother was abusive and my father should not have taken my sister and I with him.[42]

Melissa said that their entire relationship had been marked by communication difficulties; for example, Horace would not listen and would walk away from a conversation about their problems.[43]

Horace described himself as 'a social misfit',[44] being unable to relate to Melissa. He saw himself as a failure in the children's eyes, because he was unemployed, drinking heavily and without friends. He did not think he would one day become a father. When the children came, he desperately wanted to be a better parent than his own parents had been to him. Looking back, Horace believed his insecurities stemmed from his parents' separation and the absence of his father.

Melissa's story[45]

Melissa described Horace's attitude towards her, after he found out about the pregnancy, as 'hurtful', because he doubted the baby was his.[46] After Annerley was born, the relationship improved slightly but quickly deteriorated when Melissa became pregnant with Russell. Horace borrowed money and lost it in an investment scheme.[47] He was working nights and they frequently quarrelled

41 Report 'MK4', taken on 7 November 1997 from Melissa Kennedy in Sydney at solicitor's office K, [5].

42 Ibid. In this statement, Horace felt that his father should have taken him and his sister when his father left his mother. Horace's memory of his father here is again inconsistent with his father's version of events.

43 Report 'MK9', taken on 21 October 2003 from Melissa Kennedy in Sydney at court room P, 120.

44 Report 'HF2', above n 11.

45 This account is a condensed representation of Melissa's perspective. It is based on report 'MK1', taken on 21 August 2001 from Melissa Kennedy in Sydney at police station C; report 'MK2', taken on 6 November 1997 from Melissa Kennedy in Sydney at solicitor's office K; report 'MK3', taken on 29 October 1997 from Melissa Kennedy in Sydney at solicitor's office K; report 'MK4', taken on 7 November 1997 from Melissa Kennedy in Sydney at solicitor's office K; report 'MK5', taken on 9 December 1997 from Melissa Kennedy in Sydney at solicitor's office K; report 'PR1', taken on 20 August 2001 from police officer C in Sydney at residence H; and *R v Horace Faulkner*, above n 2. Portions are written in first-person narrative to preserve Melissa's voice.

46 Report 'MK1', taken on 21 August 2001 from Melissa Kennedy in Sydney at police station C.

47 Ibid.

violently. He would hurl verbal threats of physical harm at Melissa, throw things in her direction and become physically violent on some occasions.[48] He regularly threatened her that she was not going to keep the children. Melissa rang the police because she feared for her safety, but the police took no action. After Joshua was born, Horace threatened that he would kill the children and that Melissa would be left to take the blame. Melissa could not cope with Horace's threats and violence. She took the children and went to a women's refuge. When Horace later took similar action by taking the children to his mother's place, Melissa applied to Legal Aid to retrieve the children and took out an AVO against Horace to stop him harassing, threatening and assaulting her.[49] In spite of the numerous incidents of violence,[50] Melissa was not fearful for the safety of the children as it appeared obvious to her that Horace loved them.[51] By the time Melissa filed the application for residence and contact, she and Horace had separated and entered into an agreement for contact (previously known as 'access' in legal terminology) to the children. Horace visited the children regularly. At this time, he was unemployed and did not provide financial support for the children.

Melissa described their relationship as extremely volatile and marked by periods of separation and brief reconciliations. Horace would transform from happy to angry to violent. In spite of the AVO, Melissa allowed him back into the home. Horace again threatened that he would take the children away. But Melissa could not relocate away from Horace as the children would miss him terribly. Horace also refused to see a counsellor. Instead he spent most of his time on the Internet. The next year, he moved out and the relationship improved. Melissa wanted Horace to move back in, but Horace refused and told her that their relationship was purely physical to him.[52] Two weeks later, Melissa found out she was pregnant for the fourth time. This time, in spite of Horace's pleas to have the baby, Melissa went for the abortion.

When Melissa tried to take the children overseas to visit her parents, Horace refused to give his consent. Because of this, Melissa applied to the Family Court for a variation of the contact order, to which Horace objected; he told Melissa

48 Ibid. Once, the Department of Community Services attended the home to speak with Horace and Melissa after he broke a window with his fist during an argument: Report 'MK5', taken on 9 December 1997 from Melissa Kennedy in Sydney at solicitor's office K, [31].

49 Reports 'MK1', above n 46 and 'MK5', above n 48. Melissa felt that Horace's threats were aimed at making her suffer. He would tell her things like, 'if you break up my family, I will kill the children to make you suffer for the rest of your life': 'MK5', [38].

50 Report 'HF10', made on 22 August 2001 by senior police constable Rumpole Harris at police station M.

51 Report 'MK2', taken on 6 November 1997 from Melissa Kennedy in Sydney at solicitor's office K.

52 Ibid.

to take him to court. While this was happening, Melissa met Bethual and they commenced a relationship without Horace's knowledge. Horace eventually found out from Annette. He then interrogated Melissa aggressively about Bethual before trying to win her back. Melissa said Horace's attitude changed during this conversation:

> Horace tried to get me back . . . He became quite polite and kind, saying positive things . . . [Horace] blamed himself and we talked about why we could not make the relationship work . . . the afternoon, [Horace] played with the children. I asked him to leave. He made the children give me a kiss . . . I thought this was strange and made me feel insecure. He appeared so sad and very depressed. He said, 'I feel sad as you don't have feelings for me anymore' . . . He said he was worried the children would not love him as much and would forget him since he was going to be a part-time father. He cannot accept that someone will take his place . . . I smelt alcohol on him this time . . . Then he fell asleep. I checked the phone and found it off the hook. I then woke [Horace] up and told him he could either stay or go home . . . [Russell] wanted to go to his place . . . I did not hear from [Horace] or the children on Sunday night, as I believed he would return them on Monday.[53]

Horace told Melissa that all he ever wanted to be was to be a good father and that he could not accept that someone else would take his place.[54] On the afternoon of the killing on Sunday, Horace rang Melissa and questioned her about Bethual. Melissa tried to reassure Horace that he would still be the father of the children. Unknown to her, he had already taken drugs to self-medicate and was beside himself.[55] Horace's final words to Melissa were,

> I love the children more than you. You do not deserve to have them. Don't tell me I haven't warned you. I told you, you would never take the children away from me. You are going to be left behind and you only have yourself to blame.[56]

On Monday, Melissa rang Annette, who told her not to worry. When Melissa reached home that afternoon, the police came and informed her of the children's deaths.

53 Ibid.
54 Report 'MK9', taken on 21 October 2003 from Melissa Kennedy in Sydney in courtroom P.
55 *R v Horace Faulkner*, above n 2 [17].
56 Report 'MK1', taken on 21 August 2001 from Melissa Kennedy in Sydney at police station C; and report 'PR1', taken on 20 August 2001 from police officer C in Sydney at residence H.

Annette's story[57]

Annette believed that Melissa was 'using and abusing'[58] Horace, and was not behaving rationally after the birth of Russell. For example, when Horace did not agree with one of Melissa's demands to quit his job,[59] she took the children and left for the refuge. It was not long before Horace lost his job due to these stressors. Even though Horace was not living with Melissa, he continued to play an active role in the children's lives. When Horace moved back with Melissa, she gave him a hard time. He was not allowed to go to the gym or use the computer. A year later, Horace moved out. When Melissa aborted their fourth child, it affected Horace. After Melissa informed Annette that she was taking the children overseas, Annette visited them and learnt that the children had not been properly vaccinated, and that Melissa had lied about the court orders. Annette remembered Horace telling her that he felt Melissa was provoking him with the children. He told Annette, 'Mum, I'm not going to allow her to suck me in, and tell lies about me again as she did with the restraining order.'[60]

When Annette learnt about Melissa's new relationship, she informed Horace, who was, at the time, very concerned about keeping the family together. When Melissa told Horace she was going to continue her relationship with Bethual, Horace was in a lot of pain. Horace told Annette he was numbing the pain with alcohol. On the night the children were killed, Horace rang Annette, who described their conversation as follows:

> That night, [Horace] called me and told me that he felt he was losing his family. He said he begged [Melissa] to get the family together again. He asked her to stop seeing [Bethual] and to give marriage another chance for the sake of the children in order that they do not suffer the consequences of divorced parents. He was not himself. I was concerned about the state of his mind. He was crying. He was slurring . . . I called the intervention team, who told me to go to his place in the morning. My son had suffered psychologically from age 11. He was one of the many victims in a court case. He was never the same again. He attempted suicide on three separate occasions. I felt that after [Melissa] aborted the child, the abortion triggered a repeat episode when he tried to commit suicide after his then fiancée did the same without his consent.[61]

57 This account is based on report 'HF8', taken on 19 August 2001 from Annette Faulkner in Sydney at police station F. Portions are written in first-person narrative in order to preserve Annette's voice.

58 Ibid.

59 This was because Melissa wanted Horace to be eligible to apply for a Housing Commission house. Melissa eventually got a house under this scheme.

60 Ibid.

61 Ibid.

Alan's story[62]

Alan, Horace's father, described his marriage with Annette as 'strained',[63] but in spite of this he stayed on for the sake of the children as he wanted to play an active role in the children's lives. Their eventual separation was not amicable. Alan was constantly fighting for his right under their post-divorce agreement to see the children on weekends. This carried on until Alan obtained a court order to stop Annette from reneging on the agreement. Due to work, there were large gaps between Alan's visits, but he maintains, 'I can honestly say that I never put any obstacles in the way of the children coming to see me, my door was always open to them.'[64] Alan felt that Horace was estranged from him and that Annette tried to make Alan look bad in front of the children by using them to ask him for money even though he was paying the bills and maintenance for them. Contrary to Horace's memory of childhood, Alan remembered that Horace and his sister moved in with him,[65] leading to Annette becoming angry with Alan and creating problems for him. Alan felt she was blaming him for taking the children away from her. He said, 'I was then looking after the children full-time and tried to be a good father. We had some good times and did many things together as a family.'[66]

After Alan met his new wife, Kate, Horace moved out. Two years later, Horace attempted suicide while living with Annette. Alan felt that, even though he tried to be there for Horace, Horace withdrew from him. Alan told Horace that he would always be available and that his door would always be open to him. After Horace's third suicide attempt, Alan lost contact with him.[67]

Alan next saw Horace at Annerley's birth and remembered they had a great time:

> I honestly believed I would continue some kind of contact with Horace and expressed he was always welcome. However there was no contact . . . I was very angry that Horace never contacted me and was sick of him treating me like a doormat only when it suited him.[68]

62 This account is based on report 'HF9', taken on 18 August 2001 from Alan Faulkner in Sydney at police station F. Portions are written in first-person narrative in order to preserve Alan's voice.
63 Ibid.
64 Ibid.
65 As pointed out earlier, Horace's memory of his father is inconsistent with his father's version and memory of events in Horace's childhood. From Alan's account, it appears that Horace continued to reject his father in his adult life and continued to blame his father for leaving the family. Additionally, Horace was unhappy when his sister also decided to move in with Alan.
66 Report 'HF9', above n 62.
67 Ibid.
68 Ibid.

Alan further said:

> I would describe [Horace] as a person who was very lazy . . . He never took any responsibility for himself. I believed he continually used [Annette], her sister and myself in an effort to make us feel sorry for him when he did not get his way . . . [I]n my case, cut contact as my punishment. [Horace] can be quite irrational at times . . . This was evident following his [attempted] suicide, when he cut off counselling and medication . . . I believe that he suffers from some form of sickness . . . I honestly believed that he was fully aware of his behaviour . . . and cannot recall any time where he did things he could not recall or had no control over . . . His behaviour . . . was all in an effort to advance himself. This was evident in the way he manipulated people to get his own way . . . his [attempted] suicide . . . appeared more to be an effort to gain attention than to end his life. I strongly believed that the incident of interference against [Horace] had been used by him to gain attention . . . to make others feel sorry for him than to seek treatment.[69]

Judicial narrative[70]

At the trial, Horace was represented by the prosecutor as 'vengeful' and 'delusional' and with a 'wish', or desire, to 'punish his wife'.[71] In his statements, Horace did not deny that he feared Bethual would replace him as father to *his* children and sexually abuse *his* children.[72] The sentencing judge confirmed this representation of Horace and described the killings as 'cruel' and a 'selfish act' aimed at making Melissa responsible for the deaths.[73] The judge also acknowledged the revengeful, ritualistic and symbolic nature of the killings.[74] When looking at the aggravating factors, the judge stated that the fact that 'the victims were vulnerable children is itself a matter of aggravation', and Horace 'as their father was under a duty and in a position of trust, to care for them while they

69 Ibid.

70 This heading appears in all the case studies where the case has been discussed by a judge in the court, either at the trial or at the sentencing hearing. The data in this section normally comprises legal material, mostly case judgments; in the other case studies, the data sometimes consists of notes made by myself during the trial observation phase for the cases of Hannah Bromley and Greta Sheng, and notes made by the Crown prosecutor that formed part of the data in the DPP files. For example, in the Bromley and Steppenwolf cases, the Crown prosecutor's submissions were made available to me.

71 Report 'CR', taken from Mr Bailey on 20 October 2003 in Sydney in courtroom P; *R v Horace Faulkner*, above n 2, [38].

72 *R v Horace Faulkner*, above n 2, [25], [28]. Again, the emphasis in italics here is a reference to Horace's proprietary attitude towards the children.

73 Ibid [39], [41].

74 Ibid [50].

were absent from their mother'.[75] The judge further commented on Melissa's address to the court, in particular that Melissa should not feel guilt or be made responsible for Horace's conduct, since it was his 'abnormal reaction to her behaviour that resulted in the death of the children' and Horace 'was not going to allow [Melissa] to make decisions affecting her and the children, if they did not accord with what [Horace] wanted'.[76]

Agency responses

The Department of Community Services ('DOCS') was aware of the domestic violence history between Horace and Melissa, as there were three notifications lodged in the third year of their marriage.[77] By the fifth year, there were in total seven domestic-related offences reported to the police.[78] Once, DOCS was contacted but informed the police that it would not intervene unless the children had been mistreated.[79] DOCS' response was: 'There is no further role for DOCS. Having spoken to both parents, it is up to them to pursue the relationship counselling/assessment. Essentially, this situation appears to be one that will likely proceed through Family Court.'[80] At the trial, it was revealed that Horace visited a doctor in the month of the killing and confided his suicidal intentions, but this was not reported to DOCS.[81] The doctor then arranged for Horace to be hospitalised and even referred him to the mental health services on several occasions.

Concluding remarks

The central analytical conclusions that can be drawn from this story highlight the following themes.

- *Symbolic violence and parental ownership:* Horace's story is an illustration of the concept of parental ownership, in a symbolic and social sense. The story

75 Ibid [40].
76 Ibid [75].
77 Report 'HF7', taken on 1 April, 18 June and 10 December 1997 from the Department of Community Services in Sydney at office D. The incidents of violence were regarding Horace's psychological and physical abuse and intimidating behaviour, and the children's witnessing of the violence between them.
78 Report 'HF10', made on 22 August 2001 by senior police constable Rumpole Harris at police station M.
79 Ibid.
80 Report 'HF7', above n 77.
81 *R v Horace Faulkner*, above n 2, [36]. This also confirms Wilczynski's conclusion that most perpetrators had some contact with professional agencies prior to a killing: Ania Wilczynski, 'Prior Agency Contact and Physical Abuse in Cases of Child Homicide' (1997) 27 *British Journal of Social Work* 241–253, 243.

reveals Horace's proprietary attitude towards Melissa and the children, and his belief that he had the right to ownership and control of his family. This is further discussed in Chapters 2 and 6.

- *Masking:* Horace's case illustrates the analytical theme of masking, which is introduced in Chapter 2. Pertinent to this theme is Horace's wearing of different masks – as victim, loving father and abandoned child – throughout his life. In Chapter 5 it is argued that the final mask Horace wore was the loving father mask. The wearing of this mask is represented by his deliberate consumption of drugs, which gave him 'Dutch courage' to 'save' the children by murdering them. Additionally, Horace's statements reveal the complex layers of representation he used to represent himself, and to justify the killing to others.
- *Disempowerment:* Horace's case is illustrative of the patriarchal 'meltdown' in which his assumed right to authority and ownership of the family has, from his perspective, collapsed but that he was reasserting it by the act of killing the children. In Chapters 2, 3 and 6, Horace's story is discussed in light of his feelings of disempowerment and his belief that he had the right to use the children as pawns against Melissa, all of which stemmed from his belief in his weakened position in the family. This theme also harks back to Horace's belief in his proprietorship of his family.
- *Loving parent representation and risk:* Horace's case supports the argument that risks of child endangerment can be concealed by the loving parent representation. In spite of Horace's threats and the incidents of domestic violence between him and Melissa, the risks of harm to the children were not recognised by Melissa or Annette. This representation, which is deeply embedded and desired in Western cultures, short-circuits external intervention because it is not thought of as a risk factor and has been widely portrayed as a dominant and desirable representation.

Jubilee Soprano

Summary: *The dominant theme in this case is the failure of agencies responsible for child protection to intervene effectively to prevent and neutralise the threat of violence to Jubilee Soprano. The intervention team, consisting of medical and social workers and the police, had the opportunity to apprehend Brody Kitaro three days before he brutally murdered Jubilee. The team was fully aware of Brody's history of violence, mental illness and hospitalisations. This failure is characterised as dysfunctional. The reader may well question the effectiveness of the intervention team measured against Brody's immaculate representation as rational and functional. In order for the reader to grapple with this question, it is important to understand the unique set of offender and victim characteristics in this case.*

This and the next story involve perpetrators with mental illness. In this case the violence that threatened Jubilee and Angeline, Jubilee's mother, was masked by Brody, who had presented himself as articulate, charming and reasonable to Angeline and the intervention team. By virtue of his ability to manipulate his outward representation,

Brody managed to isolate Angeline and Jubilee from Angeline's family and was able to conceal his underlying mental illness from Angeline, his brother (Ross Kitaro) and the intervention team. The reader will also notice the vulnerable nature of Angeline as the victim of Brody's advances and as someone who, in the process, became subsumed into Brody's mask, which came to dominate the family. At the conclusion of this story, the reader may well ask: what is the power of this mask, and was it this mask that short-circuited the intervention – and, if so, how?

Background

Angeline was a friendly and talkative person who visited friends and family regularly before she met Brody, but she changed and became a different person altogether after Brody entered her life. Angeline did not know when they first met that Brody suffered from a mental illness. Two months later, at the height of his illness, the police attended Angeline's premises to find Brody out of control.[82] The police found Jubilee, Angeline's daughter, dead with multiple injuries on her body.[83] Angeline too suffered serious injuries as a result of Brody's multiple assaults.[84] Brody pleaded not guilty to the murder of Jubilee, and the rape and malicious infliction of grievous bodily harm to Angeline. He was found not guilty by reason of mental illness and committed to hospital detention under the purview of the Mental Health Review Tribunal.

Family and perpetrator representations

Angeline's parents' story[85]

Angeline's husband, Hamish Brown, died two years after they were married, leaving behind their daughter, Jubilee. Following his death, Angeline and Jubilee spent more time visiting Angeline's parents, Iris and Papadino, and stayed with them for long periods at a time. Iris believed their relationship strengthened as a result, and she sometimes visited Angeline to help with the house chores. One day they rang Angeline and heard that she was seeing Brody, one of the labourers doing the house guttering. This was the first time Angeline told Papadino that she did not know when she was going to visit them. Iris warned Angeline to be

82 Report 'C', from Mr Rudolf Hind, made on 1 November 2000 in New South Wales, Deputy of Public Prosecutions Office B.
83 *R v Brody Kitaro*, Supreme Court, New South Wales, 2000, Supreme Court No. BK1, 13, 14.
84 Ibid 15.
85 This account is extracted from report 'PS1', taken on 3 February 2000 from Papadino Soprano in Wollongong at police station S; and report 'IS1', taken on 23 February 2000 from Iris Soprano in Wollongong at police station S. The account is written from the perspective of Angeline's parents, Iris and Papadino Soprano, commenting on events prior to Jubilee's death.

careful of Brody, and they ended up quarrelling on the phone. In another phone conversation with Jubilee, Iris heard that Jubilee's bed had been moved to a different room. Iris was surprised about this and asked to visit, but Angeline refused. A few weeks later, when Iris and Papadino could not reach Angeline on the phone because the number was disconnected, they became concerned, and even more so after they received a call from the police that Angeline had tried to withdraw a large sum of money from the bank. When Rosaline, Angeline's sister, returned home that day, Papadino suggested that the family should travel and visit Angeline the following day. When the family arrived at Angeline's place, Angeline greeted them coldly, contrary to her usual warm greetings. Papadino said:

> When this occurred I was very hurt. Angeline was a loving daughter. Any time that we would greet each other we would hug and kiss. This is the same for the other members of the family. Her actions were not normal and it was strange for her to act this way. I was stunned to see my daughter in this condition.[86]

When they met Jubilee on that day, she did not acknowledge Papadino with her usual greeting at first. Instead, they chatted for a while before she grew comfortable around them. This, and the changes around Angeline's house, appeared strange to Papadino. During the visit, Papadino noticed Brody was speaking continuously. After they left, Iris and Papadino discussed Angeline's situation and were particularly concerned that Jubilee had stopped attending childcare. They decided they would visit Angeline again after Christmas. Over Christmas, Iris worried and was disturbed that Angeline and Jubilee did not contact them or send cards as they usually did. It was highly unusual for Angeline to remain so quiet. At their second visit, Papadino noticed two large bruises on Jubilee's face. They noticed Angeline was behaving 'like a cold statue'[87] and speaking in a voice unlike her own. Iris remarked to Angeline that she had 'a feeling someone is going to die',[88] but Angeline said everything was fine. They noticed the house was messy, which was unusual as Angeline normally kept the place clean. Iris noticed that Angeline had replaced the things Iris had given her. Angeline had new pets, which Brody said were for Jubilee, but Iris and Papadino knew that Angeline did not like keeping animals in the house. Brody then told Iris, 'this is not your daughter anymore. This is not your home. I protect your daughter. She does not need your protection.'[89]

86 Report 'PS1', taken on 3 February 2000 from Papadino Soprano in Wollongong at police station S, 6.

87 Report 'IS1', taken on 23 February 2000 from Iris Soprano in Wollongong at police station S, 5.

88 Ibid.

89 Report 'PS1', taken on 3 February 2000 from Papadino Soprano in Wollongong at police station S, 11; and report 'IS1', taken on 23 February 2000 from Iris Soprano in Wollongong at police station S, 7.

Later, Iris discussed with the family her unhappiness and helplessness at Angeline's new situation.[90] Two days later, Rosaline and Iris reported Jubilee's bruises and their concerns to DOCS. Just before the New Year, Iris rang Angeline to ask about Jubilee's preschool arrangements. Angeline told Iris that Jubilee would not be attending preschool and would be homeschooled instead. Iris then heard Brody in the background saying, 'they do not have to tell you what to do'.[91] A few weeks later, Iris and Papadino received a call from Angeline asking for an amount of money she had previously placed with Iris for safekeeping. Iris became distressed because they had agreed to save the money for Jubilee. Angeline, unhappy with Iris' response, threatened to take legal action. She also threatened that if her parents visited she would call the police to remove them from the house. That week, Iris received back the gifts she had sent to Angeline and Jubilee; Iris then visited DOCS and showed an officer the things Angeline had returned in the post. In that same week, Iris received a threatening call from Brody telling her to give them the money.[92] Iris thought she heard Angeline being choked and told Angeline to run away, but her message was met by Angeline's incoherent response. Brody then threatened that Iris would never see Angeline and Jubilee again.[93] Iris wanted to ring the police immediately, but Papadino stopped her. The next morning, the police came and informed them that Jubilee was dead.

Rosaline's story[94]

Rosaline, Angeline's sister, knew that Brody had somehow charmed her sister. She warned Angeline about Brody. When Rosaline heard Angeline had tried to withdraw a large sum of money, she thought it was strange and irrational because Angeline was always careful with her finances. Rosaline felt something was amiss after hearing stories from her parents about Angeline. When the family drove up to visit Angeline, she noticed that Angeline did not greet them with the same warmth, happiness, talkativeness and loving manner as she normally would. Jubilee appeared not to recognise Rosaline. There was something different, cold and disturbing about Angeline's behaviour. Rosaline noticed Angeline was inconsistent about her intentions for the money she required, and Angeline was shocked when she heard Jubilee call Brody 'Daddy'. Rosaline asked Jubilee if Brody hit Angeline, and Jubilee replied 'sometimes'.[95] Angeline was not her

90 Report 'IS1', taken on 23 February 2000 from Iris Soprano in Wollongong at police station S, 9.
91 Ibid.
92 Ibid 11.
93 Ibid 12.
94 This account is written from Rosaline Soprano's perspective and is extracted from report 'RS1', taken on 25 February 2000 from Rosaline Soprano in Wollongong at police station S, and report 'RS2', taken on 26 January 2000 from Rosaline Soprano in Wollongong at residence P.
95 Report 'RS2', taken on 26 January 2000 from Rosalina Soprano in Wollongong at residence P, 4.

usual talkative self that day, and appeared to Rosaline as though she were in a trance. Her usual speech pattern, vocabulary and intonations had changed. That evening, Rosaline spoke with a police officer about her concerns. When she asked about Brody's criminal record, the officer replied that '[Brody] is well known with the police'.[96]

A friend of Angeline's called Mary, a bank teller at the bank where Rosaline went to withdraw the money, told Rosaline the following day that she saw bruises on Jubilee's arms and legs. Mary said when Angeline could not withdraw the money that Brody reacted violently and had to be restrained. Mary said Angeline behaved strangely, like 'looking right through [me]',[97] and was not listening. Angeline told Mary she was going to give the money to Jesus. Later, Rosaline also heard from other friends and acquaintances of Angeline, including Jubilee's kindergarten teacher, that they saw bruises on Jubilee and that Angeline's appearance had changed. Rosaline felt extremely worried and lodged a report with DOCS. A DOCS officer informed Rosaline that nothing could be done because there was insufficient information and it was still early days.

After the New Year, Angeline isolated herself from her family and friends. Rosaline heard from her parents, who had visited Angeline, that the house had changed. Iris felt that there was a strong presence of death in the house. Brody was chanting bible verses and lost his temper in her parents' presence. During this time, Rosaline found Ross Kitaro, Brody's brother, in the telephone directory. Ross informed Angeline that Brody was unwell and needed to be hospitalised. Through Ross, Rosaline came to know Atlas Weatherburn, who was part of the mental health team. By this time, Rosaline was convinced Brody had drugged and manipulated Angeline to make her believe he was Jesus Christ. Rosaline also heard that Jubilee's behaviour had changed for the worse.[98] Atlas Weatherburn told Rosaline that, when he and the mental health team visited Angeline, Angeline and Brody denied everything and were going to pursue legal action against her parents. Rosaline decided to arrange an AVO for Iris because of Brody's death threats, but before this could happen the police came with news that Jubilee was dead.

Ross' story[99]

Ross, Brody's brother, reported that their father was an aggressive man who was abusive towards his wife and children. Out of all the children, Brody bore the brunt of his father's beatings. When he was 6 years old, Brody was assaulted by

96 Ibid 6. Later, Rosaline heard from Angeline's real estate agent and Brody's colleague that Brody had a history of mental illness, thought himself to be a healer, and had a criminal record for vehicle theft.

97 Ibid 7.

98 Ibid 12. Jubilee started swearing at other children and at her babysitter.

99 Ross is Brody's brother. This condensed account is based on report 'RK1', taken on 30 February 2000 from Ross Kitaro in Wollongong at police station K.

a teacher. He later attempted suicide. At 19, he joined the army but went AWOL. A few years later, he injured his spine in two car accidents and this left him feeling depressed and worthless. He became unemployed, as the pain affected his mobility and once-active lifestyle. After their father died, Brody regretted not making peace and seeking paternal approval. The following year, Brody was immersed in spiritualism and came to believe that he was God. Worried, Ross contacted the acute care team at the Alumni clinic, who took Brody in. After his discharge, Brody embarked on two relationships, in both of which AVOs were taken out against him by his partners. Two years after leaving Alumni, Brody went back twice, but was quickly discharged the third time despite a court order to stay for three weeks. Brody then started using drugs. Ross did not hear from Brody again until Rosaline's call regarding Brody controlling and manipulating her sister. Ross informed Rosaline about Brody's mental illness and told her to contact DOCS, while he rang Alumni. Six days later, Ross heard that Brody had threatened their mother. The police were called, but they did nothing. Ross then rang Alumni and instructed them to see Brody immediately. However, the Alumni team said that the best they could do was to pressure the police to check on things. The next day, Ross heard that Jubilee was dead.

Angeline's story[100]

Angeline described her upbringing as strict and patriarchal in that her father ruled the household.[101] Growing up was about pleasing, and being subjected to, her parents' direction, especially her father's control.[102] Her need for this type of relationship continued in her adult life. Angeline described herself as naïve, shy and self-conscious as a teenager. She would become sick from stress at work. She was sexually taken advantage of twice, and had several casual relationships before meeting Hamish. They met through a mutual friend who had previously taken advantage of Angeline sexually; Angeline confided this to Hamish, who advised her to see a doctor. Angeline found that she had contracted a sexually transmitted disease, and felt betrayed when she later realised she had contracted the disease from Hamish and not from their friend. The disease made her feel that she was 'locked into Hamish'[103] and undesirable to others. As her parents were not supportive of the relationship, she became unhappy and overweight, and developed low self-esteem.

After Jubilee was born, Angeline described the marriage as 'smothering'.[104] Hamish constantly belittled her, drank and gambled. It was only when he was

100 This account is extracted and paraphrased from report 'AS1', taken during the period 4 February to 3 March 2000 from Angeline Soprano in Wyong at police stations W and K. Portions are written in first-person narrative to preserve Angeline's voice.
101 Ibid [11].
102 Ibid [16].
103 Ibid [30].
104 Ibid [33].

diagnosed with cancer that he started planning for their wedding. When Hamish died, Angeline was devastated. She had grown reliant on him for everything and suddenly felt vulnerable once more. When she first met Brody, she felt overwhelmed by his youth, vitality and magnetic personality.[105] Although she was still feeling 'empty'[106] from Hamish's death, she felt a connection with Brody.[107] But after Brody moved in, everything Angeline thought she knew about him changed. Brody's marijuana usage increased; he taught her to prepare the marijuana for him and encouraged her to smoke it. When Angeline asked Brody about the scratches and bruises on Jubilee's face, Brody told Jubilee, 'Your mummy is in charge of your discipline, not daddy'.[108] Angeline knew that this was wrong, but did not say or do anything to correct Brody. By then she had developed 'absolute fear' of Brody and had become 'totally subservient' to him.[109]

When the Alumni team arrived, Angeline did not know Jubilee's whereabouts because Brody told her that Jubilee had run away. Brody then warned Angeline to 'put on a good act . . . say very little'[110] and he will do the talking. He added, 'any time the police would come around, I can be anything I want to them, whatever they are looking for . . . if they want to see mentally and physically disabled, I will show them what they want to see'.[111] Angeline said:

> I was scared of the police because I did not know the whereabouts of my daughter. I knew I had to perform well for Brody if he was taking any medication. He told them that he did not need it. I remember the police mentioned Jubilee and I was starting to panic because I did not know where she was. Then very quickly and smoothly Brody changed the subject about how my mother would not give me money. Then the police started to give me some advice . . . Then . . . the [Alumni] team walked out. No one ever sighted Jubilee and I did not even know she was in the house until everyone left.[112]

Finally, Angeline confirmed that she changed completely after knowing Brody and could never forgive herself for not saving Jubilee.

Disempowerment[113]

Friends and relatives commented that Angeline had a vulnerable disposition. She was easily manipulated and led by other people's decisions. Angeline would

105 Ibid [105].
106 Ibid [54].
107 Ibid [61], [63], [95]–[98].
108 Ibid [289].
109 Ibid [199].
110 Ibid [299].
111 Ibid [299]–[302].
112 Ibid.
113 Here, disempowerment refers to a victim characteristic or predisposition that is particular to Angeline and that, it is argued, has a role in constructing the violence

follow instructions from Hamish (her husband) to the letter.[114] Hamish's friend described Hamish as controlling and Angeline as submissive, fearful and naïve, but a loving and overprotective mother.[115] After Hamish died, Angeline desperately wanted a father for Jubilee.

Dysfunctional intervention

When police officer Tindale received information from the bank that a woman was withdrawing a large sum of money, he thought at first she had been coerced into it. He visited Angeline and Brody. Angeline rationally informed Tindale that the money was hers and that she could do with it as she pleased. The money was to buy 'Jesus', referring to Brody, a car. Tindale noticed that Jubilee was also calling Brody 'Jesus', which appeared strange, but he thought nothing of it because Jubilee appeared happy and well cared for, with no signs of physical abuse. Brody told Tindale that Angeline's family did not trust him and were trying to split them up.[116] For some time, the police had been aware that there was an arrest warrant issued for Brody in relation to a previous police matter. They spoke with Angeline's family twice but there were no signs of anything suspicious. Angeline's family told Tindale that they had contacted DOCS.

The next intervention occurred three days before Jubilee died. The police were called to attend Angeline's residence at the request of Dr Critter from Alumni. Dr Critter's mental health team requested police attendance based on their knowledge of Brody, and the likelihood that he needed to be hospitalised. The police's role was to support the Alumni team in case Brody turned violent. However, this turned out to be unnecessary as Dr Critter concluded, following a psychiatric evaluation, that there were no signs of mental illness. Atlas Weatherburn was also present at the evaluation. He recounted what happened at the meeting:

> [Brody] voiced his indignation at our unannounced presence. He initially appeared pleasant and sociable offering us a seat and tea. It was [Brody] who initiated and kept the conversation flowing. [Angeline] appeared solemn and I recall she said very little but I remember at one point she had tears in her eyes. When she did speak it was only to back up or confirm [Brody's] words. It was at that point that I noticed the tears in her eyes. She gave no signs in

towards the child. This is not a criticism of Angeline, but her vulnerability in the context of events cannot be totally separated from the surrounding interactions, particularly in the physical and verbal communications between Angeline and the family.

114 Report 'MJG', taken on 27 February 2000 from Moses Peter Brown in New South Wales at police station M.

115 Report 'GW1', taken on 25 February 2000 from Grange Williams in New South Wales at police station R.

116 Report 'FIVO', made 29 February 2000 from Commissioner Burrell in New South Wales police station Q.

> what she said or her behaviour that she wanted to be apart from [Brody]. The whole scene was tense. [Dr Critter] later told me that he had not seen the child only that he thought that he had heard her. This was after we had left the house. I was concerned when I learnt this because I wanted to sight the child and now I was unable to go back to the house. [Brody's] answers to the doctor's questions were always appropriate; he did not display signs of mental illness. We tried to lengthen our stay but it was difficult as we were running out of things to say.[117]

The police later said that Brody was able to 'through various devices disguise his mental condition to the point where an experienced mental health team was not able to find signs of mental illness when they assessed him'.[118] Two days later, Brody's sister received a call from Brody that he wanted to go to the Alumni clinic before he killed someone. The police were told there were concerns for Jubilee's welfare. The police attended but could not enter the premises because the gate was padlocked. Because the house was quiet, they decided not to force entry. The next day, they received a call from Iris that Brody had threatened to harm her, Angeline and Jubilee. That night, they received an emergency call that screaming was coming from Angeline's residence. They attended and incapacitated the out-of-control Brody, and found Jubilee dead. Later, a DOCS worker explained that there were insufficient staff and resources to deal with the family's concerns, but the case should have received a level 2 (48 hours for semi-urgent) response.[119]

Media representation[120]

The newspaper reporting of the case centred on the nature of assaults by Brody on Jubilee and Angeline, and the family's desperate calls to DOCS for help. The media portrayed DOCS and the agencies involved as absent and lacking in their capability after the revelation that the families' concerns went unheard prior to the killing.[121] For example, one report quoted a family member saying, '[T]he woman at DOCS took notes but said there was not enough evidence and there was nothing they could do.'[122] The reports questioned the effectiveness of the

117 Report 'HW1', taken on 5 February 2000 from Atlas Weatherburn in Wollongong at police station H, 31–35.
118 Report 'FIVO', above n 116.
119 Report 'VLH1', taken on 7 February 2000 from Verona Hump in Campbelltown at police station J. There were at least five risk of harm reports lodged by the Soprano family to DOCS.
120 This section is based on secondary sources and media reports from the public domain.
121 Report 'BK2', *Sun Weekly*, New South Wales, 3 February 2000; report 'BK4', New South Wales, 3 February 2000; the headlines of reports 'BK5' and 'BK6', *Sun Herald*, New South Wales, 10 December 2000; and report 'BK7', New South Wales Parliament, 23 November 2000.
122 Report 'BK2', ibid.

mental health system, and blame was cast on the overall system, which became the scapegoat.[123]

Concluding remarks

The central analytical conclusions that can be drawn from this story highlight the following themes.

- *Dysfunctional intervention:* In Chapter 2, it is argued that in this story the failure of the intervention team enabled the violence perpetrated against Jubilee. The failure to unmask the risks of child endangerment added another layer of 'hiddenness' to the existing dysfunctional conditions in the home, and further exacerbated the threat of violence to the child. It is argued that the violence in this case is symbolic violence,[124] because it was expressed and was deeply embedded within the normal and symbolic channels of communication.
- *Representation:* In Chapter 4, Jubilee's case is used to illustrate models of degrees of representation, which are postulated as being able to chart representations about risk to the child. In this case, these representations include reports of harm made by the parents to DOCS; outward appearances, such as Angeline's changed behaviour; and descriptions of the perpetrator, such as those given by Rosaline, Ross and police officer Tindale. The models of representation developed are used to interpret the emerging data on risk and representation.
- *Masking:* In Chapter 5, Jubilee's case is employed to support an argument made about the nature of representation. It is argued that Brody was able to feign rationality, and present himself as rational to the intervention team, because he imitated the appearance of 'the reasonable man'.[125] It is suggested that Brody had to wear a reasonable man mask to enact that role to convince others of his rationality. Here, the story is used to support the theorising of representation.

Capello Steppenwolf[126]

Summary: *This story is about the killing of Capello Steppenwolf, aged 2 years and 7 months, by his mother, Elizabeth Kramer, and about the displacement of Elizabeth's*

123 Report 'BK3', *Sydney Morning Herald*, New South Wales, 18 June 2003.
124 Pierre Bourdieu, *Masculine Domination* (Stanford University Press, 2001) 2.
125 Baudrillard's theory on dissimulation is relied upon here to explain Brody's ability to do this: Jean Baudrillard, *Simulacra and Simulation* (University of Michigan Press, 1992) 2–4.
126 Capello Steppenwolf is an Indigenous child. This case was identified in the public domain in late 2007. It was not one of the cases in the coronial sample even though the coronial file was later accessed, but it revealed little information. This case study

anger at her ex-spouse, Peter Steppenwolf, onto the child victim. Capello reminded Elizabeth of Peter's violence towards her before he was incarcerated. Because of Elizabeth's projection of Peter's image onto Capello, she did not appear to see Capello as a separate, distinct individual. As with Capello, Elizabeth in fact used all her children as outlets for her anger towards her ex-spouses. There was an ongoing residence and contact battle for Capello between Elizabeth and Peter's mother, Gabrielle. At times, Elizabeth appeared torn between letting go of Capello and keeping him. Finally, Elizabeth took out her anger on Capello, but not before she rang the Family Court and a caseworker to ask for him to be removed from her care because she knew she was not in control of her anger. By the time the recovering order issued by the Family Court was executed, it was already too late to help Elizabeth or Capello.[127]

Background

Elizabeth had three children by different fathers. In 2004, Capello's parents, Peter and Elizabeth, were charged with assault. When Elizabeth was in prison custody, Peter's mother, Gabrielle, cared for the children and subsequently looked after the children a few days a week. When Elizabeth met Charles, her third partner, Capello's relatives forcibly removed Capello from Elizabeth's care. The following year, Elizabeth applied to the Family Court for an order for residence (custody) of Capello. The court granted interim child residence to Gabrielle and defined contact for Elizabeth. At Elizabeth's second exercise of the contact order in July 2005, she did not return Capello to Gabrielle. She threatened to kill Capello before he went back to Gabrielle.[128] Gabrielle filed an application for a recovery order, which would empower the police to remove Capello from Elizabeth. During this time, a family support caseworker, Yvonne,

---

is based on the following reports obtained from the court judgment and attendance of the sentencing hearing: *R v Kramer*, Supreme Court, New South Wales, 2009, Supreme Court No. EK1; report 'EK2', made by Mr Marlo Brandy on 18 August 2009 in Sydney in courtroom R; report 'EK3', made by Mr Marlo Brandy on 8 October 2009 in Sydney in courtroom R; report 'EK4', made in December 2009 by Agency T in Sydney, at the New South Wales Reporting Office J; report 'EK5', made on 19 October 2007 at the Department of Forensic Medicine in Sydney at hospital A; and report 'EK6', made on 20 October 2007 by police officer A in Sydney at police station L.

127 The reader may well arrive at the conclusion that the intervention came too late to stop Elizabeth from carrying out the killing. However, a conscious decision was made here to view the perpetrator as someone who the intervention would have helped rather than as someone who was to be stopped. This is because Elizabeth was known to DOCS seven years before the killing, and, in spite of DOCS' knowledge of Elizabeth's history of violence, its intervention was inadequate: Report 'EK4', made in December 2009 by Agency T in Sydney at the New South Wales Reporting Office J. This suggests that Elizabeth was as much a victim of violence as she was a perpetrator, and, had she been helped by intervention earlier, the need for her to be stopped might not have arisen later.

128 Report 'EK2', above n 126, 19.

visited Elizabeth. She noted that Capello appeared well and that Elizabeth was feeling emotionally attached to Capello.[129] However, before the recovery order hearing took place on 28 September, Elizabeth dismissed her lawyers and did not attend court. The matter was adjourned to 11 October. Between September and October, Elizabeth contacted the Federal Magistrates Court several times to ask that Capello be retrieved.[130] The recovery order was granted on 11 October but was not executed by the police until 18 October. When the police attended Elizabeth's residence, she told them that she had already dropped Capello at DOCS. A few days later Capello's body was found under a bridge. Elizabeth pleaded guilty to murder.

Family and perpetrator representations

Elizabeth's story[131]

Elizabeth became extremely fearful after Peter, her second partner and father of Capello, was released from jail in August 2004 and threatened to kill her.[132] Peter always told her that if she left him he would take Capello from her. After that, Elizabeth believed that Gabrielle, Peter's mother, was colluding with Peter. Elizabeth became irritable and did not want Capello to touch her arms because it brought back violent memories, such as when Peter kicked her stomach when she was pregnant and held a knife to her throat. Elizabeth and Charles, her partner, frequently argued over Capello's discipline. Elizabeth felt angry that Capello did not listen to her.[133] Charles and Elizabeth were marijuana users, but while Charles was decreasing his usage Elizabeth increased hers, though she stopped days before Capello died. The withdrawal left her frustrated and she felt overwhelmed, disorganised, depressed and unable to cope. Elizabeth felt she should have been given more help and support. On the morning of 11 October, Elizabeth rang the court to enquire, unsuccessfully, about the recovery order status. She requested Yvonne, her caseworker, to take her to DOCS, but Yvonne, who knew she was struggling, told her that DOCS would take the children away if she approached them,[134] and Elizabeth believed her.[135] Then the accumulated weeks of spiteful emotions towards Peter overcame Elizabeth and she reacted violently towards Capello. She later said:

129 *R v Kramer*, above n 126, [8]. Yvonne had been in regular contact with Elizabeth for the past year.
130 Report 'EK2', above n 126, 4, 17.
131 Elizabeth Kramer told her story to the Crown's psychiatrist on 11 and 26 June 2009. Her story is based on report 'EK2', above n 126, 18–21.
132 Ibid 19.
133 Ibid.
134 Ibid 17, 20. The sentencing judge did not accept the truth of this statement: *R v Kramer*, above n 126, [75].
135 *R v Kramer*, above n 126, [34].

> I shook him ... I just kept seeing his father and couldn't stop myself. I could see myself doing it, but I didn't think it was me. I tried to love him ... the media are portraying it as if it is real evil.[136]

From August 2005, Elizabeth had grown resentful and critical of Capello's behaviour. She believed 2-year-old Capello was rebellious and disobedient because he was spoiled by Gabrielle. She punished him severely and frequently, and described him to others as 'little bastard' and 'asshole'.[137] Whenever Capello sought Elizabeth's affection, she became angry and saw him as overly clingy.[138] Elizabeth told people that Capello reminded her of his father, who she loathed and feared, and that Capello was ruining their lives.[139] Capello turned to Charles for affection instead. Charles noticed that Capello was unusually terrified of Elizabeth.[140] From Elizabeth's punishments, Capello developed bruises that were visible to Elizabeth's mother and friends. Elizabeth explained that she disciplined him because she feared he would do the 'same things [Peter] did to [her]'.[141]

According to Yvonne's notes regarding Elizabeth's phone call to her, Elizabeth was stressed when the court officers informed her that the matter would return to court on 18 October.[142] Elizabeth did not want to attend court and wanted Capello to be picked up by the police as soon as possible. Elizabeth was tense whenever Capello came near her, as she could not stand him. She suggested leaving Capello at DOCS. Yvonne suggested Elizabeth ring Gabrielle's lawyer.[143] Yvonne also suggested meeting with Elizabeth, but Elizabeth wanted to wait for her mother and then decide on her course of action. Yvonne then asked Elizabeth if she felt she might harm Capello, and informed her that, if so, she would have to make a report to DOCS. Elizabeth replied 'no'.

Report 'EK4'[144] later concluded that Family Support Services provided irregular and inadequate support to Elizabeth because they lacked clear and adequate understanding of the family's history.[145] By October, Capello was at risk of harm and Yvonne 'did not take adequate steps to facilitate [Capello's] return to [Gabrielle]'.[146]

136 Report 'EK2', above n 129, [27].
137 *R v Kramer*, above n 126, [9]. See also report 'EK2', above n 126, [12].
138 Ibid.
139 Ibid [10]; and report 'EK2', above n 126, 4.
140 Report 'EK2', above n 126, 5. Charles considered notifying DOCS because Elizabeth was taking matters too far with Capello.
141 Ibid.
142 Ibid 7–8.
143 At the time, Gabrielle's lawyer was unavailable.
144 All the information derived from report 'EK4' is based on an independent review into Capello's death undertaken in December 2009 by Agency T in Sydney at the New South Wales Reporting Office J. As Elizabeth had a prior history with DOCS, the review assessed the information and evidence regarding the adequacy of intervention.
145 According to report 'EK4', there was also misleading and inaccurate written information provided by Yvonne to various agencies involved with the family.
146 Report 'EK4', above n 144, 11, 12. DOCS responded that the Community Services Grants Program, which funded all family support organisations, needed reform.

Media representation

Media reports covered the community's anger over Capello's death.[147] The media's focus on DOCS was specific. It portrayed DOCS as having failed the family because the intervention 'came too late'.[148] Many of the reports contained piecemeal and repetitive reporting on the facts and context of the killing. The media portrayed DOCS negatively, while Elizabeth was, in some reports, cast as a victim of the system's deficiency.[149] Suggestive of DOCS' failure was the media's focus on the number of Helpline calls regarding Capello made by family members,[150] but according to report 'EK4' these calls were also made by health professionals and police officers. This led DOCS to respond defensively about its capabilities.[151] In some reports the media appeared sympathetic towards Elizabeth,[152] but these reports juxtaposed the manner of killing against the community's condemnation of the killing,[153] which negated any sympathetic interpretation of it.

Legal and judicial narratives

The prosecution submitted that motive had aggravated Elizabeth's culpability and that a message of deterrence was necessary.[154] The prosecution argued that

147 For example, report 'Media-4', *Sunday Age*, Victoria, 21 October 2007; report 'Media-6', Australian Associated Press, New South Wales, 21 October 2007; report 'Media-7', *Herald-Sun*, Victoria, 19 October 2007; and report 'Media-11', *Sun Herald*, New South Wales, 21 October 2007.

148 Report 'Media-1', *Sydney Morning Herald*, New South Wales, 22 October 2007; and report 'Media-13', *ABC News*, New South Wales, 10 December 2009.

149 Report 'Media-6', above n 147.

150 Report 'Media-1', above n 148; and report 'EK4', above n 144, 3–8. I did not have access to DPP files, police investigation materials and DOCS records. I am not able to state knowledge of information in these files. However, this information is provided in report 'EK4', made in December 2009 by Agency T in Sydney at New South Wales Reporting Office J, which reviewed the relevant agency records pertaining to Capello Steppenwolf, agencies that Capello and Elizabeth were involved with. The contents of report 'EK4' are discussed following the legal representation section.

151 Mr Kevin Greene (New South Wales Minister for Community Services) said that there were 240,000 calls made to the DOCS Helpline annually and that, because the cases were extremely complex and some required urgent attention, particularly where various parents were involved, different relationships and surnames made it more difficult to identify the calls related to Capello: report 'Media-1', above n 148.

152 Report 'Media-12', *Sun Herald*, New South Wales, 21 October 2007.

153 Examples of the community's anger are seen in the following media reports: report 'Media-11', above n 147; report 'Media-1', above n 148; report 'Media-6', above n 147; and report 'Media-9', *Sunday Mail*, New South Wales, 21 October 2007.

154 The information in this section is extracted from report 'EK3', made by Mr Marlo Brandy on 8 October 2009 in Sydney in courtroom R. The prosecution cited *R v Horace Faulkner*, above n 2, in which Justice Grove, at [41] and [42] cited *R v Hull* [1997] SASC 6087 *per* Justice Lander.

Elizabeth's feelings towards Capello were based on her irrational perception that Capello was a reminder of Peter, and on a desire not to acknowledge that she was not a failed mother.[155] As such, her aim in keeping Capello was ultimately to prevent Peter from having him. Her motivation was steeped in 'her hatred, resentment and anger towards Capello as well as a desire to prevent others from having the benefit of the court order'.[156]

The judge accepted the prosecution's submissions that Elizabeth 'breached a position of trust and authority' and that 'Capello was entitled to love, protection and nurture',[157] and rejected Elizabeth's statement that Yvonne talked her out of taking Capello to DOCS.[158] The judge observed that there were inconsistencies in Elizabeth's story. Because Elizabeth chose not to give oral evidence, her voice was suppressed, and this calls into question the veracity of her statements.[159]

Dysfunctional intervention[160]

DOCS received 34 risk of harm reports concerning Elizabeth's children.[161] Since 1999, DOCS had been aware of the domestic violence history between Elizabeth and her partners, and of Elizabeth's drug and alcohol use.[162] Elizabeth was in custody for several offences at various periods of time, which resulted in her irregular care of the children, who DOCS placed with family members during these times. Because Elizabeth moved between various temporary refuges, different DOCS officers handled these harm reports. A number of them were closed because of 'competing priorities'.[163] In 2005, DOCS' early intervention services gauged the family ineligible because of its extensive child protection history.[164] Given this knowledge, report 'EK4' found that there were repeated failures to adequately respond to the harm reports regarding the children.[165]

155 Report 'EK3', ibid 3–4.
156 Ibid.
157 *R v Kramer*, above n 126, [87].
158 Ibid [75].
159 Ibid [46].
160 'Dysfunctional' here refers to the inadequacy and ineffectiveness of the intervention, which exacerbates the risks of violence to the child and/or allows the threats to the child's safety to continue. In the context of state intervention, it refers to the failure to intervene in situations where it is arguable that intervention would have made a difference. Information in this section is extracted from report 'EK4', an independent review made in December 2009 by Agency T in Sydney at the New South Wales Reporting Office J.
161 Report 'EK4', ibid 3. At least nine reports concerned Capello (Elizabeth's second child) and 12 reports concerned Elizabeth's first child. A total of 15 reports was assessed by Helpline as indicative of medium to high risk, but none received the completion of a comprehensive risk assessment.
162 Ibid 4.
163 Ibid.
164 Ibid 7.
165 Ibid 9.

In spite of at least three opportunities for intervention to address the violence,[166] there were none. Report 'EK4' listed the problems as follows:

> There were issues with quality of documentation by DOCS staff, including inconsistencies in record keeping and the transfer of information. A number of 'missed opportunities' for intervention where recommended responses given to reports warranted a more comprehensive or higher level response . . . the known information at the time should have combined to create a picture of a higher level of risk. At times, there was problematic use of language and emphasis placed on information in records, resulting in somewhat misleading information about risks to the children. There were also periods in the case where a level of analysis was lacking.[167]

The capacity of DOCS to respond effectively to children who are the subject of risk of harm reports was identified by report 'EK4' as a consistent issue of concern.[168] It concluded with the following advised reforms: requiring effective response to risk of harm reports; expanding service capacity and the role of non-government agencies; information exchange; and risk assessment.[169]

Concluding remarks

The central analytical conclusions that can be drawn from this story highlight the following themes.

- *Dysfunctional intervention:* The problematic recording of information, such as identified by report 'EK4', is discussed in Chapter 2 as being an obstruction to the interpretation of risk. The failure of proper recording practices and the problematic use of language in this process masked the existing violence from the authorities. From this perspective, the intervention was dysfunctional, thereby exacerbating, rather than assisting, the state of familial dysfunction and ultimately the risks of violence to Capello.
- *Sympathetic reinterpretation:* In the contest of perpetrator representations, it is argued in Chapter 4 that there is evidence that Elizabeth consistently referred to external events, such as the conversation with Yvonne, to explain her actions. It is argued in Chapter 7 that Elizabeth's conversation with

166 Ibid.
167 Ibid.
168 Ibid 13–14.
169 Ibid. These reforms were suggested in conjunction with those raised by the Wood Inquiry. See the Hon James Wood AO QC, *Report of the Special Commission of Inquiry into Child Protection Services in New South Wales: Executive Summary and Recommendations* (State of NSW through the Special Commission of Inquiry into Child Protection Services in NSW, November 2008).

Yvonne illustrates the perpetrator's distrust of DOCS, also identified as a recurrent theme in the case studies of Hannah Bromley and Juniper Berry.[170]

- *Symbolic violence:* Elizabeth's use of violent language towards Capello, it is argued in Chapter 2, is a form of symbolic violence that could have alerted others to the potential harm to the child. Elizabeth's projection of Capello's father onto Capello is, it is argued, violent to the child, because the projection allows Elizabeth to take out her anger and frustrations on the child rather than the father.

Hannah Bromley

Summary: *Hannah Bromley's story*[171] *is unique in that it is about the peculiar nature of violence behind closed doors, a form of cruel and unusual treatment amounting to torture. Hannah was imprisoned in a room and starved to death by her parents. Hannah's imprisonment is compared to, and contrasted with, a concentration camp.*[172] *The juxtaposition of the home and the camp gives birth to a horrifying symbology – that both can co-exist in the one space, the home that is traditionally represented as a safe, protective and nurturing space. Her parents' treatment of Hannah ties in with the theme of ownership of children. Both her parents believed they had the right to treat her this way, and their position is reinforced by their reluctance to allow DOCS*

170 See also the discussion in Chapter 7 on distrust as one of the conditions of risk.

171 This case study was one of the two cases identified in the public domain and not part of the original coronial sample. It is based on the official account of the story told in court and is derived from my observation of the trial proceedings in court, reported case law, the coronial file (which I requested and obtained), and secondary sources such as newspaper reports, magazines and independent government report 'HB4'. The coronial file contained the police report of death, charge sheet and autopsy report. I acknowledge that the official account represents the legitimated version on which subsequent media reports are based. Portions of this account might be contested, but there was no opportunity to obtain perpetrator police statements and first-hand stories.

172 Randall Jerrall, 'On Preparing to Read Kipling' in E Gilbert (ed), *Kipling and the Critics* (New York University Press, 1965) 133–149, 146. In his essay, Jerrall uses the term 'God's concentration camp' to describe his observation of abused children who grow up in dysfunctional families; they become like camp inmates who, he argues, identify with the persecutors and take on the guilt of their deeds. In Hannah's story, her deprivation and imprisonment are comparable to conditions in a concentration camp. In report 'MEDIA-HB3', *The Monthly*, New South Wales, February 2010, 38, the author likens Hannah's family to Jerrall's description of 'God's concentration camps'. I think this description is fitting in this particular case study because of the extreme state of deprivation into which Georgina and Quentin placed Hannah. I juxtapose the home with the concentration camp to accentuate to the reader the acute state of dysfunction in this particular family. This comparison is not new. See Leonard Shengold, *Soul Murder Revisited: Thoughts About Therapy, Hate, Love and Memory* (Yale University Press, 1999) ch 6 and also Eva Hoffman, 'Home as Concentration Camp', *New York Times* (online), 17 October 1999 www.nytimes.com/books/99/10/17/reviews/991017.17hoffmat.html.

officers to sight the children, because they did not want another child to be taken away. The inability of child protection officers to sight Hannah is a significant failing of the Department. This, as well as repeated failures to investigate nine risk of harm reports concerning the children, reflects the dysfunctional nature of State intervention, which directly contributed to the perpetuation of the hidden violence in Hannah's room.

Background

Hannah, in contrast to her two siblings, lived in a room with no toys or furniture. There was just one mattress and a Victorian painting. The window was boarded up entirely. The room smelt of stale urine.[173] Compared to the rest of the house, which was relatively clean and tidy, Hannah's room was the opposite.[174] Forensic pathologists had never encountered a death so horrible and extreme. Hannah weighed three times less than expected. Her socks had melded to her skin. There was no food or moisture in her wasted body. Her pink lungs suggested no contact with the outdoors for months.[175] The prosecutor and later the media described Hannah's body as comparable to 'a holocaust victim' and as 'mummified'.[176]

Hannah had autism. Her parents, Georgina and Quentin, did not follow up with medical or therapeutic services offered to them.[177] Seven years after birth, Hannah was growing minimally and her weight was below average.[178] The last time the doctors saw her prior to her death in November 2007, she looked well. In none of the previous consultations were any concerns raised about her health and well-being.[179] At 6 years old, Hannah did not attend school even though the school arranged her transport to and from home.[180] In 2006, a neighbour saw Hannah once but never again, and claimed that she could hear Hannah making noises and crying for her parents in her room for long periods of time.[181] That year, the window in Hannah's room broke and was boarded up. When the family moved out in mid-2007, the neighbour reported to DOCS and the Department of Education and Training ('DET') the squalid state of Hannah's room, which had faeces and urine in it.[182] The last person from the outside to see Hannah was the removalist, who saw Hannah in the new home in August

173 *R v Georgina and Quentin Bromley*, Supreme Court, New South Wales, 2009, Supreme Court No. GQHB, [60].
174 Ibid [66].
175 Report 'MEDIA-HB3', above n 172, 37. Also see the description of the death in *R v Georgina and Quentin Bromley*, above n 173, [39]–[44].
176 Report 'MEDIA-HB4', *Daily Telegraph*, 2 October 2009.
177 *R v Georgina and Quentin Bromley*, above n 173, [13].
178 Ibid [18].
179 Ibid [25].
180 Ibid [26].
181 Ibid [29]; and report 'MEDIA-HB3', above n 172, 38.
182 Ibid [31]. Also see report 'MEDIA-HB3', above n 172, 38.

2007. The removalist reported that Hannah was 'sitting down, just staring . . . unusually skinny'.[183] A television technician noticed that Hannah's room was closed and a rope tied between two door handles, preventing the opening of the door from inside the room.[184] During this time, there was an attempt by a DOCS caseworker to interview the parents and physically assess the three children, but the caseworker did not sight Hannah.[185] In November 2007 Georgina found Hannah dead in her room, but it was Quentin who rang for help.

Perpetrator legal representations

Georgina and Quentin pleaded not guilty. They portrayed themselves as devoted parents who made foolish mistakes.[186] They alleged Hannah was fed, was eating and was mobile prior to her death, but the trial judge found their story implausible.[187] Quentin remembered Hannah as bubbly and smiling. He saw Hannah only twice. He was in his 'own little world with Valium'.[188] He admitted that he did not pay appropriate attention to Hannah's health and well-being and obstructed social workers from monitoring the children.[189] On these representations the judge said, '[Hannah] did not receive the love of her parents. They were both so absorbed in their own lives that they did not care about her.'[190] The lack of parental love was indicated by the parents' locking Hannah up and excluding her from family celebrations.

Georgina alleged that she had had abusive parents.[191] She met Quentin at age 17 and married, and by 27 they had four children. Their relationship was one-sided, with Quentin controlling her. For example, he deterred her from having contact with her parents and was physically abusive towards her. She felt she lost the capacity to act for herself and had little say in the care of their children.[192] She also suffered health problems that caused her addiction to prescription medication.[193]

Quentin left school at an early age to work but stopped after his father went to prison. He came to rely on disability pensions and became addicted to Valium

183 Ibid [32].
184 Ibid [35].
185 Report 'HB4', made in October 2009 by Agency T in Sydney at the New South Wales Reporting Office J, 13.
186 Report 'MEDIA-HB3', above n 172, 37; and report 'MEDIA-HB33', *Australian*, 12 June 2009.
187 *R v Georgina and Quentin Bromley*, above n 173, [54], [55].
188 Ibid [71].
189 Ibid [72].
190 Ibid [81].
191 Ibid [85].
192 Ibid [88], [91]. She alleged Quentin controlled the finances, did not permit her to drive or leave the house without his permission, and forced her to engage in bondage: [94].
193 Ibid [92], [93].

from age 18 while suffering anxiety and panic attacks and neurosis.[194] His poor memory was alleged to be because of his addiction. Quentin did not at first admit responsibility towards Hannah but later changed his position, and explained, 'I was in my own world there'.[195] He admitted that he did not trust DOCS because DOCS had previously removed one of their children.[196]

Judicial narrative

The trial judge did not accept Georgina's story, in particular her contradictory and inconsistent accounts of the history of her marriage. The judge did not accept the following contested facts: the level of violence, control and domination by Quentin;[197] the amount of medication she consumed;[198] and the medical opinion that Georgina had developed learned helplessness because of her abusive relationships, which would have enabled her to raise the 'battered woman syndrome' defence.[199] The judge justified this rejection on the ground that the assessing doctor did not have the benefit of viewing the tape recording of the police search of the house, in which Georgina appeared to be the dominant and assertive one compared to Quentin, who was cooperative and compliant.[200]

The judge did not accept that Quentin was remorseful.[201] He rejected the parents' claim that abuse of drugs blinded them to Hannah's deteriorating condition. He described Quentin as a father who showed 'no less love to [Hannah]' and was completely oblivious to Hannah's existence, which was an abrogation of parental responsibility to the extent it amounted to 'abject cruelty'.[202] He described Georgina as 'cold, callous, cruel and heartless'.[203] The judge opined that the sentencing of both parents needed to reflect the 'objective gravity' of the offences, the importance society places on the value of children's lives, and the trust placed in parents.[204] A message of deterrence to society was

194 Ibid [134].
195 Ibid [144].
196 Report 'HB5' taken on 11 June 2009 by Janice Sim in New South Wales at courtroom M.
197 Ibid [119].
198 Ibid [120].
199 Ibid [102].
200 Ibid [106]. The doctor later conceded that her behavioural traits in the video were not indicative of someone suffering from battered woman syndrome: [108].
201 Ibid [145].
202 Ibid [162].
203 Ibid [188].
204 Ibid [178]. The judge cited the Greta Sheng case in support of the general deterrence element in sentencing in negligence cases: *R v Gerald Sheng*; *R v Caitlin Sheng*, Supreme Court, New South Wales, 2009, Supreme Court No. SHG13, [153]. The judge in the Greta Sheng case enunciated that a message of general deterrence was required to impress upon the community the serious consequences of parents breaching the trust reposed in them to care for their infant children, because the protection of children is of fundamental importance to society.

needed that Hannah's parents' conduct was unacceptable.[205] Quentin was sentenced to 16 years' imprisonment and Georgina to life imprisonment.

Dysfunctional intervention

Report 'HB4' was constructively critical of the various state departments involved with the family: DOCS, DET, the Department of Ageing, Disability and Home Care ('DADHC'), the Department of Housing ('DOH') and the New South Wales Police. There had been a prior history of dysfunction in relation to the other children. DOCS had removed the parents' fourth child when the child failed to thrive and after they failed to comply with DOCS requirements.[206] In 2002, the Children's Court ordered the three older children to remain in their parents' care provided Georgina and Quentin undertook to ensure the children's school attendance.

Between 2005 and 2006 DOCS received a total of nine risk of harm reports made by community members and state agencies (DET and DADHC) concerning the children regarding their absence from school; the parents' lack of capacity to manage Hannah's behaviour; concerns for Hannah being locked up and her window boarded; the poor state of the family's home; and domestic violence.[207] None of the five reports in 2005 were allocated for risk assessment. Report 'HB4' found DOCS' response to these reports unsatisfactory, inadequate and inconsistent. None of the reports at the initial assessment stage identified the child protection history in the family. Many of these harm concerns were 'minimised' over time, and repeated concerns such as the children's absence at school became an 'educational matter'.[208] None of the reports were allocated to a caseworker for the purpose of visiting the family and undertaking a risk assessment, despite one report rated as 'high' risk.[209] Most of the reports ended up closed due to 'competing priorities'.[210]

There was inadequate record-keeping of conversations between DET and DOCS regarding the children in 2006, and incomplete history checks.[211] In 2007, a DOCS caseworker was instructed to interview the parents and the children and, if necessary, take steps to see that a police search warrant would be obtained.[212] The caseworker contacted a housing worker, who reported

205 Ibid [179].

206 Report 'HB4', above n 185, 4. Report 'HB4' is an independent review that examines the critical systemic issues pertaining to state intervention. This is a summary of report 'HB4's findings. Only key issues and chronology relevant to the book will be highlighted.

207 Ibid 12.

208 Ibid. There were delays with processing the risk assessment. At times, the incomplete provision of information compromised Helpline's analysis of risk.

209 Ibid 4, 12.

210 Ibid.

211 Ibid 13.

212 Ibid.

that Quentin was evasive and would not allow them to sight the children. The housing worker expressed concerns that the children might be imprisoned in their bedrooms, and the family might be relocating. When the caseworker finally spoke to Quentin, he said he was arranging for the children to be home-schooled.[213] Arrangements were made for the children to attend medical assessments, but Quentin later refused to give consent, saying that their youngest child had previously been taken away as a result. When the caseworker again visited the family, the two older children were sighted. They appeared normal. However, Quentin did not permit Hannah to be seen.[214]

There was a transfer of files to a new caseworker.[215] The new caseworker visited the family and realised the family had moved. DET and DOH could not ascertain the family's whereabouts. DET informed the caseworker that the application for homeschooling was rejected. Report 'HB4' found that the first caseworker did not take sufficient steps to progress the risk assessment or follow up with the arranged medical appointments.[216] In particular, DOCS' assessment of the case was fundamentally flawed: DOCS assumed that, because the older children were reported healthy, Hannah was no different.[217] However, this was untenable because by then DOCS had information that Hannah had significant disabilities, had never attended school, had received no services, lived in squalid conditions with her room boarded up, and had not been seen by a professional in 2007. To compound matters, the two risk of harm reports received in September 2007 reporting that the filthy conditions of the family's previous residence and the boarded window were classified as 'information only' on the basis that the information was already known to DOCS.[218]

Report 'HB4' found the DET and DADHC responses were inadequate even though some appropriate steps were initially taken.[219] The inadequacy pertained to exchange of information and poor communication between departments,[220] failure to meet responsibilities such as the children's school absenteeism, and poor assessment and classification of information.[221] Report 'HB4' also questioned the adequacy of police actions to locate the family. The police justified their poor response on the basis of misunderstanding of the phrase 'well-being' – the police thought DET officers meant the children's non-attendance at school rather than imminent risk of harm.[222] Because of this misunderstanding, less emphasis

213 Ibid.
214 Ibid.
215 Ibid 14.
216 Ibid.
217 Ibid 16.
218 Ibid 17.
219 Ibid ch 5 and 6.
220 This observation was made with regards to DOH, whose responses towards the filthy property were found to be reasonable and consistent even though there were minor communication discrepancies.
221 Ibid 42, 47.
222 Ibid.

was placed on pursuing enquiries with the removalist, and this impacted on the efficiency of DOCS' subsequent intervention to track the family down.[223] Report 'HB4' concluded that there was little evidence of effective interagency collaboration, which should be an integral part of an effective child protection system.[224]

Media representation[225]

There were three distinct media foci of the reporting of Hannah's death: DOCS; the parents' representations; and representation of Hannah's death. Media reporting was largely confined to selective comments made by the lawyers to the jury on the parents' representations. Some of the comments were depicted in the headlines. I observed the reporting of the trial to be selective and repetitious of the court proceedings, with little contextual reporting on the social circumstances leading to the death. The general focus tended to be on the horrific manner of Hannah's death and the parents' 'excuses' regarding their treatment of Hannah and their dysfunctional lifestyle.

Concluding remarks

The central analytical conclusions that can be drawn from this story highlight the following themes.

- *Symbolic violence:* In Chapter 2, the symbolism of hidden violence in the representation of Hannah's death is unpacked. The discussion also centres on the violence of the parents' treatment as a symbol of their ownership and control over Hannah. Their treatment, it is argued, reveals marked indifference to Hannah's suffering, which suggests that violence can easily be masked by the perpetrators' interpretation of 'love'.
- *Dysfunctional intervention:* Hannah's case illustrates how dysfunctional intervention can jeopardise the safety of a child. The failure of state agents to investigate and sight the child is set amid the numerous risk of harm reports, including concerns regarding the non-attendance of the children at school. This brings into focus the nature of dysfunctional intervention. It is argued in Chapter 2 that it amounts to symbolic violence, which, in this context, suggests the complicity and negligence of state agents in Hannah's death.

223 After the address was retrieved from the removalist, DOCS transferred the family's child protection files to offices near the family in October 2007. Before the files could be allocated to a caseworker, DOCS was notified of Hannah's death (in early November): ibid 5.

224 Ibid 49.

225 Due to word constraint, this analysis of media reports is confined to key observations.

- *Perpetrator representation:* The reader may well have noticed Quentin's sympathetic reinterpretation of his actions to the judge. Chapter 4 discusses this technique of self-representation in the context of perpetrator representations of what they have done. It is argued that perpetrators such as Quentin appear to have to wear a mask to not just reinterpret the killing to themselves, but for their audiences. The mask also conceals from the authorities what should have been indicators of risks of violence to the child, such as the poor state of the family home, non-attendance at school, boarding up of windows and parental refusal to engage with support services.
- *Judicial narrative:* The reader may have noticed that in this case the perpetrators made representations in court that were discredited by the judge. In Chapter 5, the unmasking function of the court is discussed. It is argued that the court can be the unmasker of false representations. This is significant in the larger conceptualisation of representation, which is central to the symbolic processes of giving voices to certain representations.

Danny Burrow

Summary: *This story is about 5-year-old Danny Burrow, who was killed by his mother, Saskia. Her animosity towards Danny is apparent in her brutal choice of words when talking to him, which mirror the violent manner in which she treated and 'disciplined' him. Saskia felt she had the right to treat Danny violently. She saw Danny as a representation of the object of her anger, Danny's absent father, George Pigeon. Her abusive treatment of Danny reveals harsh discipline based on ownership of the child, in the social sense, masking the existence of severe physical and symbolic violence. The judicial and media narratives were highly critical of Saskia's 'otherness', which was positioned against the archetypal 'good mother' symbol. Two other emerging themes are social isolation and dysfunctional state intervention. Social isolation sits among a number of indicators of dysfunction, such as domestic violence and drug and alcohol intake. It is clear that, after Saskia moved away from her family and lost the frequent physical contact she had with them, the combination of her isolation and her inability to cope with two young children on her own was cataclysmic. Even though these indicators of dysfunction and risk were reported to DOCS on several occasions, DOCS did not appear to have any concerns for Danny.*

Background

At the time of Danny's birth, Saskia had been with George, who was recorded on the birth certificate as Danny's father, though paternity is not certain (see below). She eventually broke up with George and, after a few other relationships, began going out with Evans Runnings, with whom she had had an earlier relationship. After Danny's death, Saskia wrote from prison to Evans professing her love for him. She also wrote to her parents saying that George had been her only love, and of her grief when she lost him, which was the reason she turned to drugs. She saw herself as a bad person and hated herself for the drugs, but she maintained she did not kill Danny.[226] At first Saskia blamed everyone but herself. Finally she admitted hitting Danny with a wooden spoon until he could not walk. She was punishing him for hitting his sister Mary.[227] She could not stop herself.[228] Then she left him by the open fire unclothed, causing burns to his body. The next morning, Saskia found Danny lifeless in the bathroom. Danny was rushed to the hospital. He died hours later.

Perpetrator and family representations

George's story[229]

George was addicted to drugs when he got together with Saskia, and later said he remembered little of the past because of his poor health and poor memory. They broke up shortly after because Saskia was involved in other relationships. When Saskia informed George that she was pregnant, he moved back with her, not knowing whether he was the father. As no one came forward to claim paternity when Danny was born, George was recorded as the father on Danny's birth certificate. George's parents did not believe George to be Danny's father – because of his heavy drugs usage they did not believe he was capable of producing children. On the few occasions George lived with Saskia, he never saw Saskia mistreat Danny. A few years later, Saskia informed George that she was pregnant with Mary, and that George was the father. George never met Mary, because of an AVO Saskia took out against George and George's father, Mark.

Following George, Saskia had short-term relationships with two men, Christopher and Sonny; they claimed they never saw Saskia discipline Danny with excessive force.[230]

226 Copies of letters ('SB2') from Saskia Burrow dated 21 August 2000 from Grafton, New South Wales, at prison X. Saskia's claims here are not consistent. She had also given different accounts of the events leading to Danny's death to the police. See *R v Saskia Burrow*, Supreme Court, New South Wales, 2001, Supreme Court No. SB1, [5]–[11].

227 Report 'SB3', taken from Saskia Burrow on 5 July 2000 in Grafton, New South Wales, at police station Y.

228 Ibid.

229 This account is written from report 'GP1', taken from George Pigeon on 31 May 2000 in Grafton, New South Wales, at police station Y. The account has been paraphrased and identifiers have been changed to comply with the book's privacy undertakings.

230 These accounts are based on report 'CI1', taken from Christopher Injera on 29 May 2000 in Grafton, New South Wales, at police station Y, and report 'SG1', taken from Sonny Giles on 30 May 2000 in Grafton, New South Wales, at police station Y. The accounts are about Christopher's and Sonny's perceptions of Saskia during their brief relationships with her.

Evans' story[231]

Evans had known Saskia since their teenage years. He was with his mother, Susanna, when he met Saskia and her children. Susanna invited Saskia to live with them. Following this encounter, Saskia and Evans resumed their relationship. Evans noticed Saskia usually treated the children well, except when she disciplined Danny. She yelled mainly at Danny, 'You little bastard, you're just like your father, if you don't stop playing up, I'll send you back to him.'[232]

Evans did not believe Danny deserved such scolding. Whenever he spoke to Saskia about the severity of her punishments, she told him to mind his own business.[233] Evans recalled that Saskia said:

> [George] used to bash me and [Danny] all the time . . . [George] was on heroin . . . I have a domestic violence order . . . to keep [George] away . . . after [George] . . . kidnapped [Danny] one day. Ever since [Danny] came back, he's like his father and won't do anything I tell him to do.[234]

Saskia lost her temper whenever Danny did not listen to her. She would beat him hard with a spoon, and said at one time: 'Get in the fucking room, you are just like your fucking father, I'll fucking send you back to him, stay in there and don't come out until tea time. If you come back out, I'll give you more.'[235] The hits were full, hard swings. Once, Evans suggested to Saskia that she make Danny stand in the corner of the room instead of beating him, but Saskia would remind Evans not to interfere. The next day Saskia punished Danny according to Evans' suggestion, but was unhappy when Evans allowed Danny out of the corner earlier than she expected. Quite frequently, Saskia would scold Danny with comments such as:

> You're a naughty boy, you're like your father.[236] You're a naughty boy, you're just like your father.[237]
>
> Wait to you get home you little bastard, I'll give you a flogging, you won't do as your told.[238]

231 This account is written from report 'ER1', taken from Evans Runnings on 14 April 2001 in Grafton, New South Wales, at police station K. It is written from Evans' perspective regarding his knowledge of, and relationship with, Saskia. Portions have been written as a first-person narrative to accentuate Evans' point of view and to preserve his voice.

232 Ibid 3.

233 Ibid.

234 Ibid. Saskia's allegation that George kidnapped Danny was not corroborated by Saskia's family.

235 Ibid 4.

236 Ibid 7.

237 Ibid.

238 Ibid 10.

> I'm so sick of you little bastard, I'll be glad when I can get rid of you. I'll send you back to your fucken father, just like your fucken father.[239]

Most times after the beatings, Saskia would lock Danny in the bathroom without food, despite his pleas from afternoon until night, when Saskia and Evans would have their regular smoke before bedtime. Once when Danny stole the neighbour's dog bowl, Saskia screamed at him and beat Danny all afternoon. This time Evans tried to intervene. Saskia told Evans that she would raise Danny however she wanted,[240] and said, 'I told you before, mind your own fucking business. I don't fucking care, the little bastard kicked me.'[241]

On the day of Danny's death, Saskia beat him and threw him into the wall of the shower, which cracked under Danny's weight. She continued beating him for another 20 minutes on and off. By late afternoon, Danny became silent. In the evening, Saskia let Danny out of the bathroom at Evans' insistence, and left him in front of the open fire. Evans noticed Danny had blisters on his back; Danny then rolled towards the fire and burnt his knee. Evans suggested Saskia should treat the burn with cold water. Saskia then dragged Danny to the bathroom. Saskia insisted on smoking cannabis because she was too upset and needed to calm down. During the night, Danny crept into Evans' bed to sleep next to Evans. The next morning Saskia proceeded to retrieve Danny from his bath so that Evans could take him to the doctor, but instead she found him lying lifeless there. They rushed Danny to the hospital but it was too late to revive him.

Susanna's story[242]

Susanna, Evans' mother, recalled an exchange with Saskia after Danny broke an ornament at Susanna's house. Saskia said:

> I'm not bringing [Danny] here, he's too much of a naughty boy, I can't handle it and I'm not bringing him to your place anymore . . . He is always playing up, won't eat, won't do as I tell him, throws tantrums, runs away and he tells lies.[243]

Susanna suggested that Saskia should contact DOCS to see if they can help with Danny in case he needed special care. She also offered to accompany and support Saskia.

239 Ibid 13.
240 Ibid.
241 Ibid 16.
242 This account is based on report 'ERM2', taken from Evans Runnings' mother on 14 April 2001 in Grafton, New South Wales, at police station K. It is written from Mrs Runnings' perspective of her experience with Saskia.
243 Ibid.

Another time, Susanna noticed Danny's bloodshot eyes and questioned Danny. Danny replied that it was Mary who did that to him. Saskia then interjected, 'with . . . one of those mixing spoons'.[244] Susanna suggested that Saskia take Danny to the doctor. Saskia said, 'Yes I have, there is nothing wrong with him. He is always a naughty boy. He is naughty all the time, aren't you Danny?'[245] Danny replied 'sometimes'.[246] Susanna told Saskia not to say that to Danny, to which Saskia replied, '[Danny] always plays up and won't do anything I tell him'.[247] The next time Susanna saw Saskia was at the hospital. Susanna commented:

> [Evans] smokes yarndie sometimes but does not drink alcohol . . . I know [Saskia] smokes yarndie . . . From when I met [Saskia], she has constantly complained to me [Danny] was a naughty boy, he threw tantrums, would not eat his food unless it was McDonald's. She even told me he did not eat for three days. I have never seen [Evans] or [Saskia] hit the children. I never saw [Saskia] play with [Danny], she always told him to go and play. She would also say to him, *'you are just like your father'*. [Evans] and myself are of Aboriginal descendants. I was an Aboriginal foster parent.[248] (Emphasis added)[249]

Saskia's parents' story[250]

Saskia's parents, West and Janis, had ten children, of whom Saskia was the youngest. When Saskia was 18, she was beaten and raped by three men. After the incident, Saskia changed and became rebellious towards her parents.[251] When Saskia informed her parents she was moving into Evans' caravan, Janis was unhappy, but she spoke to Saskia regularly and maintained close contact. A month later, Janis ran into Saskia at the clinic and noticed Saskia's bruised face.[252] West confirmed he knew about the domestic violence, but it was never reported to the police because Saskia always returned to Evans.[253] A few months later, Saskia moved into a separate caravan and met George.

244 Ibid.
245 Ibid.
246 Ibid.
247 Ibid.
248 Ibid.
249 The emphasis here is a reference to Saskia's projection of the absent George Pigeon onto their son Danny.
250 This account is based on reports 'JBM1' and 'JBM2', taken from Janis and West Burrow respectively on 9 July 2000 in New South Wales at police station Z. This account is written from the parents' perspectives on the events in Saskia's life and their involvement and interaction with her and the children.
251 Ibid, report 'JBM1', 5.
252 Ibid 6.
253 Report 'JBM2', above n 250, 2.

When Saskia first introduced George to her parents, they were supportive of the relationship.[254] Janis and West helped the happy couple relocate nearer to them, but Saskia and George soon encountered problems because of George's drug habit. To compound matters, George's father, Mark, constantly interfered in the relationship and tried to get George to leave Saskia once he found out Saskia was pregnant. Eventually, George left Saskia three months into the pregnancy. Janis said:

> [Mark] on a number of occasions took [George] away for four or five days at a time. This put a lot of stress on [Saskia] and after about eight months, I contacted [Mark] and asked him to stop interfering in [Saskia] and [George's] relationship.[255]
>
> [Mark] was still interfering in their relationship and [George] again turned to drugs . . . I don't think [George] could handle his relationship with his father. [Mark] appeared to have a very strong influence over [George] which caused [George] a lot of stress.[256]
>
> [Mark] told [George] that his mother was very sick and that she needed [George]. [George] made his decision and left [Saskia].[257]

Saskia was devastated when George left. The couple reunited briefly with Janis' help. George stayed with Saskia for three months after Danny's birth before he left again. Janis noticed Saskia was lonely without George.[258] Soon after, Janis and West helped Saskia to move into a Housing Commission home and visited her regularly. West said:

> I could say that [Saskia] was coping with motherhood well. I think she was lonely but she was looking after [Danny] and made sure he was always clean and tidy . . . [Danny] was always running around . . . I heard [Saskia] yell at [Danny] a couple of times when he was doing something wrong and I saw her smack him on the leg with her hand a couple of times when he played up. On occasions, I saw [Saskia] strike [Danny] with a wooden spoon . . . on the legs . . . a couple of individual times during our visits . . . In all the times that I went to [Saskia's] house I never saw any bruises on [Danny] that were out of the ordinary for a young child.[259]

Whenever Saskia's parents visited, West took Saskia shopping and paid her rent while Janis cared for Danny. After Danny's first birthday, Saskia took out an

254 Report 'JBM1', above n 250, 8.
255 Ibid 8. Mark claimed that George was incapable of having children.
256 Ibid 9.
257 Ibid.
258 Ibid 11.
259 Report 'JBM2', above n 250, 5.

AVO against George and Mark for harassment. West noticed that Saskia became affected and was lonely.[260] Three months later, George reunited with Saskia briefly.[261] Danny was delighted to see his father. But when Saskia became pregnant with Mary, George left and Saskia was again devastated.

West and Janis again helped Saskia to relocate. West noticed Saskia, when left on her own, began showing signs that she was not coping.[262] She scolded Danny for no reason apart from taking out her frustrations on him. No amount of West's persuasion could dissuade Saskia from scolding Danny. West also noticed that the previously good relationship Saskia had with her sister Carrie became strained. This was because Carrie contacted DOCS about Danny. West said:

> I understand that welfare did nothing about the report, so I thought it must have been incorrect. During this time, [Carrie] used to bring [Saskia] and [Danny] back over to our place a lot and sometimes my wife and I would travel over to see them. On all the visits I never saw [Danny] show any signs of distress towards his mother or show any sign of injury.[263]

After Mary was born, Janis and West had to relocate. This made Saskia upset, but she continued to receive support from her siblings, who regularly visited to supervise Danny.[264] When Janis and West relocated again, they lost physical contact with Saskia and this was compounded when Saskia relocated to live near Evans. West and Janis could not visit Saskia like before because West was unwell, but they maintained telephone contact.[265] After news of Saskia's relocation, the next piece of news was Danny's death.[266]

Saskia's sisters' stories[267]

After Danny was born, everything appeared well. Danny was happy as he was surrounded by many caring, supportive family members. The first signs that Saskia was not coping showed when she was pregnant with Mary. Saskia often rang one of her sisters, Leanne, for help. Leanne sometimes cared for Danny overnight. Leanne never saw any abnormal bruising on Danny. After Mary was born, Saskia rang Leanne frequently because she could not cope with the children. Danny was always running away because Saskia was constantly yelling at him.[268]

260 Ibid.
261 Report 'JBM1', above n 250, 14.
262 Report 'JBM2', above n 250, 7.
263 Ibid, 8.
264 Ibid 9.
265 Ibid 10.
266 Ibid 11–12.
267 This account is based on report 'JS1', taken from Leanne Burrow on 10 July 2000 in New South Wales at police station Y. It is written from Leanne's point of view, as the second-youngest child in the family, on her youngest sister, Saskia.
268 Ibid.

Leanne noticed that Saskia gambled heavily, but she could still pay rent and buy food because their parents supported her whenever she was short of money. Leanne lost contact with Saskia after Leanne relocated interstate.[269]

Saskia's sister Carrie recalled that Saskia was traumatised by the rape and the subsequent court experience, where the perpetrators threatened Saskia in court. Saskia had terrible nightmares and was never the same person again. She used to be happy, but after the incident she became depressed and started drinking and smoking. Things did not improve after Saskia met Evans. Saskia told Carrie about the violence in her relationship and that Evans 'raped and bashed' her.[270] After separating from George, Saskia turned to drugs and alcohol. Carrie said:

> I was fighting with [Saskia] because she was drinking, taking drugs and gambling all the time. Her errant habits became worse . . . During this time, [George's] parents forced [George] to take out a restraining order against [Saskia] . . . [George] told me that his father had made him do it and threatened him. When [Danny] was 1 year old, [Saskia] gave him a lot of attention, the house was clean and [Danny] was well fed. [Danny] started being naughty when he started pre-school . . . He would throw things at people and rip books up. Around this time, [George] also started to re-enter [Saskia's] life and [Danny] was asking questions about his father. He was also having nightmares and this was when he started misbehaving in school. After [George] left again, [Saskia] began having visitors who would sometimes stay over.[271]

Around this time, Carrie realised Danny was behaving strangely in her presence, which was unusual. On one visit Carrie observed that Danny did not enjoy his baths like he always did before. Carrie asked Saskia what was wrong with Danny. Saskia said she did not know but that Danny was naughtier than before. He frequently ran away from home. The police would be called to look for him. One time, Carrie saw Saskia beating Danny with a cooking spoon. Carrie was incensed and warned Saskia not to hit Danny again. Saskia then told Carrie she was pregnant again. Carrie said:

> In my opinion, [Saskia] went too far that night with how hard she belted [Danny] . . . I have never seen [Saskia] like that before, she was wild when she was hitting him . . . I went to see my doctor about my concerns regarding [Saskia] and brought her to see him. I would often hear [Danny] screaming and would run up to [Saskia's] place to check his body for bruises . . . A month later, [Saskia] was staying at a friend's place. When I visited, I found

269 When Leanne visited Saskia in prison, Leanne noticed Saskia was telling her a number of lies, such as the extent of her drug addiction.

270 Ibid 3.

271 Ibid.

the place to be . . . terribly filthy . . . I fought with [Saskia] over this. I remember thinking that this was out of character for [Saskia] because she was fastidious about cleanliness in her own house. When [Danny] came to bid me goodbye, he flinched when I hugged him saying 'I'm sore'. I took off his clothes and saw bruises all over his body. I asked him what happened to him. He said, 'people hit me and mummy did too because I was naughty'. I asked him again, 'what other people hit you' and he just said 'over there, over there'. I do not know what he meant. When I looked for [Saskia] to confront her about the bruises, she had already gone. I then rang DOCS and reported what happened. [Saskia] was away for a few days before DOCS spoke with her. DOCS told me that [Saskia] told them that [Danny] often gets into such accidents . . . DOCS did nothing so I rang the police. [Saskia] was booked in, she was supposed to take [Danny] to the doctors for a physical examination. She immediately left and no one knows where she went to . . . She . . . would not speak to me because I told her that it was I that reported her . . . I had very little contact with the family after . . . No one would speak to me because I had dobbed on [Saskia].[272]

Dysfunctional intervention

After DOCS received its first report from Carrie regarding Danny's bruises,[273] DOCS officers spoke with Saskia, who reassured them. Without supporting documents to validate the original notification, the file was closed. DOCS then received another report from Carrie a year later that the children were being neglected. DOCS found that Danny had not been attending preschool, but that he presented as well dressed and cared for.[274] Due to 'competing workload pressures',[275] the case went unallocated. A month later, Carrie rang DOCS with concerns regarding Saskia's drinking and smoking habits, her neglect of the children and Danny's behavioural problems.

In one of the three recorded calls regarding Danny's welfare and safety, DOCS was told by the caller that 'Danny is scared of his mother. Danny said he was scared to go home.'[276] DOCS recorded that they were unable to assess risk based on the information.[277] In another call, the caller reported that Danny said 'Mummy hit me with a stick'.[278] The caller also reported evidence of bruising on

272 Ibid 7.
273 Report 'DF5', dated 5 July 2000 in New South Wales at DOCS Office W.
274 Ibid.
275 Ibid.
276 Report 'CR3', dated 13 September 1999 in New South Wales at DOCS Office W and report 'DF5', dated 5 July 2000 in New South Wales at DOCS Office W.
277 Ibid.
278 Report 'CR4', dated 27 November 1998 in New South Wales at DOCS Office W. Additional calls related to Saskia's drug and alcohol lifestyle, her inability to afford rent and the neglect of the children.

Danny, and Saskia's verbal threats towards Danny. In spite of this information, whenever DOCS checked on Saskia, Danny presented as clean, well dressed, happy and interactive.[279] The allegations of drug abuse were denied by Saskia and the alleged injuries were explained as accidents. Even when Saskia failed to attend the medical check-up ordered by DOCS, there were no concerns of possible risks of harm to Danny.

Judicial narrative

The court was critical of Saskia's aggressive discipline, which was held to be was unlawful and dangerous. The fact-finding exercise by the court rejected Saskia's version of events,[280] and constructed her as dishonest. Reference was made to Saskia's neglect of her duties as a mother, which was seen as accentuating the gravity of the offence. The court said:

> The injuries inflicted on this poor unfortunate child were brutal and extensive . . . what aggravates the criminality involved is that these injuries came from *his own mother, the person from whom above all he was entitled to expect care, nurture, love and protection*. (Emphasis added)[281]
>
> Whilst the offence of manslaughter is always serious as it involves the unlawful killing of another human being, the Court regards the killing of children as *particularly serious, especially when such killings are at the hands of a parent or family member*.[282] (Emphasis added)[283]

Saskia pleaded guilty to manslaughter and was sentenced to eight and a half years' imprisonment.

Media representation[284]

News reporting of the case was confined to the basic facts of the killing and the judicial pronouncements on the representation of Danny's death (ethnicity was not reported), the seriousness of the offence and Saskia's criminality. The judicial

279 Report 'FCR', dated 1 December 1998 in New South Wales, recorded at residence Z1.

280 *R v Saskia Burrow*, above n 226, [5], [6], [8]. The court did not discuss Dr Tijuana's assessment of Saskia, which suggested she had a Medea complex: report 'SB5', taken on 23 November 2001 from Dr Tijuana in New South Wales, prison X.

281 Ibid [22].

282 Ibid [39].

283 The purpose of the emphasis in both of these quotes is to illustrate the legal symbolism and representation of the mother archetype.

284 This section is based on report 'SB6', Australian Associated Press, New South Wales, 18 December 2001 (source: Factiva); and report 'SB7', *Daily Telegraph*, New South Wales, 18 December 2001 (source: Factiva).

comments published by the media (see above) highlighted the horrific nature of Danny's death, and the gravity of the offence committed by Saskia as Danny's mother. The media representation stressed the horrendous nature of Danny's punishment, which was represented as a tortuous ordeal, while portraying Saskia as a cruel, aggressive and unflinching disciplinarian.

Concluding remarks

The central analytical conclusions that can be drawn from this story highlight the following themes.

- *Symbolic violence:* In Chapter 2 it will be argued that Saskia's violent language towards Danny amounts to symbolic violence on two levels. First, language as violence, when uttered by the perpetrator and when used symbolically and directly to the child, exposes the child physically and psychologically to violence. Second, the use of violent language is capable of transforming to physical violence, such as exemplified by the punishments Danny received from Saskia; also, however, it is reflective of Saskia's negative labelling of Danny, in particular her frequent characterisation of him as resembling his absent father, George. For Danny, the violence is normalised, which is evidenced by his acceptance of his mother's labelling. In Chapter 5 it is argued that Saskia and Danny imitate a shared desire for George. For Saskia, the desire relates to George's absence as a partner in the family, and for Danny it relates to a desire for his absent father. This is analysed in the context of Girard's theory on mimesis, which argues that the struggle for shared desires leads to eventual conflict.
- *Receivership of meaning:* In Chapter 5 it is argued that the audience has an important role, because they are the receivers of meaning and they give meaning to certain actions or inactions. As such, meaning-making is important with regard to the interpretation of reports of harm such as the report made by Carrie to DOCS. It is argued in Chapter 2 that DOCS' failure to properly investigate Carrie's risk of harm report represents symbolic violence. This is of special significance to meaning-making, as the DOCS response can be seen as pivotal to the confirmation or rejection of Carrie's report of harm. DOCS' action, it is argued, has an impact on the audience – in this case, Saskia's parents, who subsequently interpreted Carrie's report as baseless and untrue.
- *Judicial selectivity:* The other angle given to this theme discussed in Chapter 5 is the examination of the selective representations in the judicial narrative. Connected with this is an argument that the court is central in the meaning-making process, particularly as the ultimate arbiter that selects and gives 'voice', legitimacy and authority to certain representations, such as the 'bad' or 'good' mother. In Danny's case, the legitimated representation emerging from the narratives is predominantly of Saskia as a 'bad' mother. This representation is discussed in Chapter 3, which examines the relevance of

mythologised representations of the good and bad male and female parent in the law.

Jack Drummond

Summary: *This story is about a family's crusade for disability assistance and support for their autistic son Jack, and his mother's eventual killing of him. This is a unique case because Melanie Drummond, the parent perpetrator, was sentenced to a five-year good-behaviour bond, contrary to the conventional sentence for filicide, although such a sentence is not unconventional for filicide cases*[285] *in which the perpetrator kills as a result of severe mental illness. This sentence was later criticised by the appellate court as manifestly inadequate. More significantly, there was a significant amount of sympathetic reinterpretation of Melanie's actions in the judicial and media narratives in spite of the severity of the crime. The media portrayed an overwhelmingly sympathetic audience to Melanie's representation as the good mother. At the trial, the good mother symbolism appeared to have triumphed over the voice of the victim. In the judicial narrative, Jack was constructed as the reason for the parents' breakdown and separation, and their loss of community ties. In other words, he was constructed as the provocateur and as the 'Other', rather than as the victim.*

Background[286]

Melanie and David Drummond married young. They had two children, Athena and Jack, the latter of whom was diagnosed with autism at the age of 1. Jack's autism caused his parents immense stress. While Athena was the perfect child, Jack was the complete opposite.[287] At 18 months, Jack was rejected by an early intervention school because there was no available position. From then, Melanie went on a crusade to locate a position for Jack.[288] When David finally threatened

285 The judges in *R v Cooper* [2001] NSWSC 769 and *R v Pope* [2002] NSWSC 397 imposed bonds on these perpetrators, who pleaded guilty to the offence of infanticide under section 22A of the *Crimes Act 1900* (NSW). In *R v Li* [2000] NSWSC 1088, a bond was imposed on the perpetrator, who pleaded guilty to manslaughter of her child on the basis of substantial impairment. In *R v Sette* [2000] NSWSC 648, a two-year sentence imposed on the perpetrator was fully suspended; the perpetrator was convicted for manslaughter of her 15-month-old child by reason of substantial impairment. In *R v Richards* [2002] NSWSC 415, the perpetrator pleaded guilty to the manslaughter of one child and the attempted murder of her other two children. She availed herself of the defence of mental illness and was sentenced to 15 months, the time that she spent in prison. See *R v Rg* [2006] NSWSC 21, [45]–[49].

286 This background is written from various statements from family members, including David and Melanie Drummond. The account details the different stages of parenting Jack and the lack of support services the parents had to overcome.

287 Report 'DD1', taken from David Drummond in Sydney on 9 September 2003 at police station A.

288 Ibid.

legal action against the school two years later, it gave Jack a place. Then Melanie and David had to run their food business and take care of the children without family support, which they had left behind in Sydney when they moved to Penrith Bay.

When Jack was assessed at 2½ years old by a Dr Tutu, the doctor informed Jack's parents that Jack was not progressing because of the lack of substantive early intervention. Dr Tutu predicted Jack would end up as a ward of the state.[289] The next day, David suffered a nervous breakdown, which cost him his employment for the next two years. Melanie and David sold their business and experimented with alternative therapies for Jack. Melanie saw that being the sole primary caregiver for the children and an advocate for Jack was '[her] job', which she did to the best of her ability.[290] She worked and supported the family the whole time while David sought treatment.[291]

Because of Jack's behavioural problems, finding a school with the capabilities to handle Jack was a difficult process. The task fell to Melanie. She faced problems with DET because Jack was attending school three days a week. But there were no other schools that could take Jack, and David had to threaten the school with legal action in order for them accept Jack. By this time, both Melanie and David were frustrated and distraught as the responsibilities of looking after him grew harder. According to Melanie, Jack placed an immense strain on everything, including their friendships, their relationship with Athena and their marriage.[292] To Melanie's cousin Louise they appeared stressed and the marriage appeared dysfunctional due to the physical and mental abuse by David on Melanie, David's alcohol abuse and the delicate balance between work and the children.[293] David was suffering depression and did not help Melanie much. Melanie too became depressed as a result. There was no family support, and Jack was not getting the services he required even though Melanie fought very hard for him.[294]

When Jack was 7, Melanie confided in her mother, Christina, that she had thoughts of submerging Jack in the swimming pool across the road from her house.[295] Christina was shocked and worried, and spoke with David, who reassured her things were under control. Christina would visit Melanie twice a year, and after Melanie became depressed Christina helped Melanie whenever she visited Sydney so that Melanie and David could have some time to themselves.

289 Ibid.
290 Report from Dr Iceberg ('MD3') dated 5 December 2003, New South Wales, residence D, 3.
291 Ibid [29]. Also extracted from report 'CHR1', dated 24 May 2004, Director of Public Prosecutions Office, New South Wales.
292 Report 'MD4', taken from Melanie Drummond in New South Wales on 8 January 2004 at police station A.
293 Report 'LTA1', taken from Louisa Tina Abarvini in Sydney on 6 September 2003 at police station A.
294 Ibid.
295 Report 'PSCR1', taken from Christina Rhubarb in Sydney on 10 September 2003 at police station A, 9.

Melanie also told her cousin Louise she had thoughts of hurting Jack and herself. Louise became extremely worried because she could see that Melanie was spiraling downhill. When Louise asked Melanie if she would carry out her thoughts, Melanie replied, 'No, it's just going around my head all the time.'[296]

The Drummonds decided to move back to Sydney so they could have family support. However, things did not improve and Christina warned Melanie that the visits were proving too much. Melanie did not cease her crusade for Jack's school placements. Whenever a school rejected Jack, the Drummonds would threaten legal action. Every few months, they met with DET to review the funding available to Jack. David resumed full-time employment while Melanie worked part-time. The stress did not go away.

Things became worse for the family when it was discovered that Jack's sister, Athena, aged 13, had been suffering abuse. One day, Christina informed Melanie that Melanie's stepfather, Levi, had been sexually assaulting Athena. Melanie was devastated and furious. It dawned on Melanie that while she and David had been encouraging Athena to spend more time with Levi, because Levi complained to Christina and Melanie that he did not see Athena enough, Athena had been trying to distance herself from Levi. What tore Melanie apart was Levi's betrayal of her trust. Levi was Melanie's 'safe haven'.[297] He was the father who she loved and respected. She was angry with Christina for supporting Levi after that. Melanie felt that the abuse caused Athena's behaviour to change for the worse. Melanie and David met with the Joint Investigation Response Team ('JIRT') at the DOCS office after weeks of waiting for an appointment. When they finally attended, there were two police officers and no community worker because DOCS was insufficiently staffed. The officers knew about Jack's autism, the assault and the domestic violence. JIRT applied for an AVO for Athena, but no referral was made to the sexual assault unit. Melanie said, 'due to someone's negligence in the Department, none of us received the support that would have assisted us through that difficult time'.[298]

A month later, Melanie's biological father died. The death plunged Melanie into deep depression, from which she did not recover.[299] In the following weeks, Melanie and David agreed that they would never relinquish Jack to state care despite Dr Tutu's prediction. However, they were worried about Jack's social behaviour in public, and were frightened by the thought that Jack would enter adolescence soon.[300] On the morning of Jack's death, David and Melanie discussed obtaining support for the family and their fears about Jack's socialisation

296 Report 'LTA1', above n 293, [13]; and report 'CHR1', above n 291.

297 Ibid.

298 Ibid.

299 Report 'DD1', above n 287. According to David, the series of unfortunate events – Athena's abuse; Levi's betrayal; Melanie's biological father's death; the loss of their previous home; the loss of family support with Levi's betrayal; and existing depression – contributed to Melanie's depression, grief and stress.

300 Ibid.

as he was growing older. When David later visited Melanie at the hospital after her attempted suicide after killing Jack, she told him that she did not want to live anymore.[301] Later, Melanie described her thoughts and feelings at the time of the killing:

> At that time, my feelings of inability to trust were overwhelming me. We thought [Jack] should not stay in bed for too long but it is difficult to get him up. After he got up, he would not let me dress him and ran downstairs . . . That was when it became overwhelming. I felt 'I cannot keep doing this anymore'. I held his nose and covered his mouth . . . [Jack] was struggling, trying to remove my hands . . . There were a lot of thoughts going through my mind like how difficult it is to have [Jack] and then how I can be doing this, *I just want to be a good mum*. I just cannot do this anymore. It was like it was not me . . . I knew how wrong it was but I do not know I knew . . . I guess I knew what the consequences were . . . that [Jack] would stop being so demanding. My intention was not to have [Jack] around anymore and that intent was driven by the fact that I wanted to have a normal family. After he stopped struggling . . . *I realised I was not this perfect mum anymore and I could not live with that* . . . I felt guilty for the things that had been going wrong. I was feeling bad the night before – depressed, dark, doomed . . . I was not thinking of ending [Jack's] life at the time. I had intentions of going to work that morning.[302] (Emphasis added)[303]

Ongoing domestic violence: Melanie's perspective

After they got married, Melanie and David experienced problems as a result of David's gambling and drinking habits.[304] There were at least ten incidents of domestic violence, physical and verbal, from David towards Melanie. David attended anger management classes, but whenever he drank his behaviour would change. Weeks before Jack died there was an incident of violence in the car, which nearly caused Melanie to have an accident.[305] Melanie said her world then consisted only of the children: 'my children were and will always be my world to me'.[306] A social worker, Shirley, said Melanie feared leaving David and they had

301 Ibid.
302 This account is extracted from report 'MD4', taken from Melanie Drummond in New South Wales on 8 January 2004 at police station A. After killing Jack, Melanie attempted suicide. See *R v Melanie Drummond*, New South Wales District Court, 2004, District Court No. MD1, [37], [38].
303 The emphasis here is a reference to the theme of Melanie's self-labelling and is discussed in Chapter 5.
304 *R v Melanie Drummond*, Court of Criminal Appeal, New South Wales, 2004, Court of Criminal Appeal No. MD2, [14].
305 Report 'MDM1' taken from Melanie Drummond in New South Wales on 8 January 2004 at prison A.
306 Ibid.

worked together on strategies to enable Melanie to cope with her feelings of powerlessness and isolation in the relationship.[307] DOCS was aware of the domestic violence in the family.[308] A social worker and domestic violence coordinator, Katherine, described Melanie as 'very fearful of David because of his behaviour and threats towards her'.[309] Katherine said:

> [Melanie] always presented as a caring mum who went out of her way to look after both children, especially [Jack] . . . she never missed appointments and followed up on latest interventions for children with autism and how she could assess them. I never anticipated she would harm [Jack].[310]

Later, Melanie wrote:

> My children have always been the most important things in my life. The reason for my existence . . . It is painful to think how I felt so empty . . . This time, I can clearly see the reasons for my emptiness. *For the 18 years of my marriage, my husband slowly eroded my self-esteem. The physical but worst of all the verbal abuse and intimidation destroyed my person* . . . I supported [David] during that time, even though I told him to leave. During our separation, I encouraged him to visit the children . . . But during his daily visits, he rarely spent time with the kids. Instead he would be with me telling me how much he loved and missed me . . . When [David's] family needed me, I was there for them. *They all know how hard I strived to be the best mother I could to both of my children.* I feel very hurt that none of them will even look at me now, especially when . . . his family was aware of . . . the physical and verbal abuses.[311] (Emphasis added)[312]

Judicial narrative

The court, in the first instance, found Melanie guilty of manslaughter and sentenced her to a five-year good behaviour bond subject to supervision.

307 Report 'SH1', taken from Shirley Hanson in Byron on 12 September 2003 at police station C.
308 DOCS had at least six reports relating to Jack, all of which related to domestic violence, mental health issues and Jack's autism. The family was identified as a family in crisis in the reports. One record stated that the children were never removed from the home due to concerns for their safety. Another record stated that the children had been removed once, but the circumstances were unknown. This information is extracted from report 'MDCI-1', Coroner Court, Westmead, New South Wales, 4 April 2005, Coroner Report File No. MD.
309 Report 'KC1', taken from Katherine Cow in New South Wales on 12 September 2003 at police station D.
310 Ibid.
311 Report 'MDM1', above n 305.
312 The emphasis here is a reference to Melanie's self-labelling and self-perception.

The court opined that Melanie's circumstances were so exceptional that they justified the imposition of a non-custodial sentence. Prior to sentencing, the court had painstakingly reconstructed the events leading to the killing, including Jack's autistic characteristics and their impact on Melanie and on the marriage. Each representation of Melanie from the family pertained to her role as a mother and primary caregiver and supporter of the family,[313] and her responsibilities towards Jack were highlighted as a 'never-ending task that very few people' can understand.[314]

The judge concluded, based on the expert evidence, that Melanie's 'moral culpability was significantly diminished' because of her depression.[315] There were numerous representations of Melanie's depression and her dedication as mother,[316] but little mention of the impact of domestic violence on her and her depression. Rather, the judge opined that Melanie's 'crusading behaviour also contributed to conflict within the marriage'.[317] The appellate court, on the other hand, held that the trial judge had erred by taking into account David's victim impact statement, which attested to Melanie's good mother image.[318] Against this image was the judicial representation and interrogation of Jack's autistic characteristics, which portrayed him as the 'problem'.[319]

The appeal

Following the trial there was a public outcry regarding the leniency of Melanie's sentence.[320] On appeal, the prosecution changed its original position and appealed for a custodial sentence on the grounds that the non-custodial sentence failed to reflect the objective seriousness of the crime.[321] However, the appellate court held that, even though the sentencing judge had erred, the prosecution's initial failure to press for a custodial sentence and Melanie's changed circumstances at the time of the appeal did not warrant the court reversing the original sentence.[322]

313 *R v Melanie Drummond*, New South Wales District Court, above n 302, [10], [30].
314 Ibid [28].
315 Ibid [55].
316 Ibid [76], [77].
317 Ibid [70].
318 Ibid [78].
319 *R v Melanie Drummond*, Court of Criminal Appeal, above n 304, [8], [9], [51]–[53]; *R v Melanie Drummond*, New South Wales District Court, above n 302, [30], [34].
320 Luke Clements and Jane Read (eds), *Disabled People and the Right to Life: The Protection and Violation of Disabled People's Most Basic Human Rights* (Routledge, 2008) 63.
321 Report 'MED2', *Sydney Morning Herald*, New South Wales, 30 September 2004.
322 Melanie's circumstances had changed. She obtained a child residence order for Athena and had an AVO against David. She was maintaining contact with her domestic violence counsellor and psychiatrist while making progress in her rehabilitation and depression. As such, imposing a custodial sentence would be 'disruptive': *R v Melanie Drummond*, Court of Criminal Appeal, above n 304, [46].

Two out of the three presiding judges concurred that the initial sentence was 'manifestly inadequate'.[323] By then David had also altered his initial position in his victim impact statement and now called for Melanie to be jailed.[324]

The appellate judgment stressed the value of human life – including lives of the disabled, handicapped, criminal, derelict and friendless – and the right to be protected.[325] The judges emphasised that abnormality of mind, while diminishing an offender's responsibility for the killing, does not negate that responsibility.[326]

Coronial narrative

The coronial narrative, unlike the judicial narrative, dealt with the issue of public support agencies and whether better assistance could have been provided. The coroner stated that the agencies involved with the family had 'failed to identify the special needs of [Jack]'.[327] It stressed the need for DADHC to provide support to a child with disabilities, to assess the degree of support needed and to recognise that the level of support would vary among families.[328] The same warning extended to DOCS. The coroner said agencies should be able to identify a family in crisis when faced with circumstances such as domestic violence, abuse of another child in the family, notifications of risk of harm and death in the family.[329]

Media representation

Following Jack's death, the *Daily Telegraph* ran sympathetic headlines that emphasised the tragedy of the family.[330] These stories generated reader support and empathy, especially from parents who were at the time in a similar dilemma with a disabled child. The issues in the media revolved around the pressures of caring for autistic children,[331] the lack of external intervention and resources,[332] the pressure on family relationships[333] and the isolation[334] parents such as Melanie faced. Letters[335] from sympathetic readers were published calling for the system

323 Ibid [40].
324 Ibid [30]; and report 'MED1', *Inclusion Daily Express*, New South Wales, 30 September 2004.
325 Ibid [31].
326 Ibid [34].
327 Report 'MDCI-2', Coroner Court, Westmead, New South Wales, 13 October 2006, Coroner Report File No. MDD.
328 Ibid.
329 Ibid.
330 Report 'MED12', *Daily Telegraph*, New South Wales, 13 August; and report 'MED10', *Daily Telegraph*, New South Wales, 20 August 2003.
331 Report 'MED9', *Daily Telegraph*, New South Wales, 13 August 2003.
332 Report 'MED6', *Daily Telegraph*, New South Wales, 15 August 2003.
333 Report 'MED10', *Daily Telegraph*, New South Wales, 20 August 2003.
334 Report 'MED11', *Daily Telegraph*, New South Wales, 9 August 2003.
335 Report 'MED7', *Daily Telegraph*, New South Wales, 14 August 2003; and report 'MED8', *Daily Telegraph*, New South Wales, 15 August 2003.

to shoulder the blame. The media's focus was on a particular audience supportive of Melanie and her fight against a system that was represented as letting families down.

The reports represented Melanie as grief-stricken and isolated from her family while in prison. The stories constantly returned to issues related to the plight of parents with disabled children and community support for Melanie's pain. The *Daily Telegraph* stories portrayed the system as not doing enough to meet 'a desperate community need for government assistance'.[336] The stories highlighted characteristics of autistic children, particularly those with communication difficulties and lacking in public acceptance, which were portrayed as social issues that needed to be publicly addressed. Other news sources, however, presented a different debate. In an online publication, activists argued that if Jack did not have a disability the support in favour of Melanie would have been different.

Around the same time, an article was published about a New Zealand mother who killed her autistic daughter and whose sentence was reduced, allegedly, because of public empathy. She was quoted as saying, 'I only served one year because the public did not want me to be in prison'.[337] This story and Melanie's story in the *Daily Telegraph* were, arguably, designed to impact on audiences. Such a representation is observed in Chapter 5 to be one-sided: while appearing to present the facts it also presents a distorted picture that is value ridden, using emotions to manipulate its audience.

Concluding remarks

The central analytical conclusions that can be drawn from this story highlight the following theme.

- *Representation:* This story revolves around Melanie's representation as the good mother, juxtaposed against the court's construction of Jack as the Other. In Chapter 3, it is argued that the good mother symbol originates from myth. In Chapter 5, it is argued that this symbol had a profound symbolic effect on the audience. The perpetrator stereotype created for Melanie by the media and the judicial narratives was the image of the good mother. This is a perennial and universal symbol that is associated with all-encompassing qualities represented as inherent to motherhood, such as loving, devotion, dedication, nurturance and sacrifice. In Chapter 3, it is argued that this symbol is reinvented against the majority of the other perpetrators in the case studies in this chapter. The purpose of this, as argued in Chapter 5, is social governance of the wider society.

336 Report 'MED6', above n 332.
337 *R v Albury-Thompson* (1998) 16 CRNZ 79. Also see report 'MED4', *Daily Telegraph*, New South Wales, 19 August 2003; and report 'MED3', *Daily Telegraph*, New South Wales, 16 August 2003.

Conclusion

These six stories reveal the main analytical themes of masking; symbolic violence (to be discussed in Chapter 2); representation and the receivership of meaning (Chapters 4 and 5); victim and perpetrator disempowerment (Chapter 6) associated with parental ownership and control of the family in the social sense (Chapter 2); and risk (Chapter 7). Representation is the main umbrella theme that ties together all the smaller themes. Regarding representation, the analysis to follow examines the representation of violence in the case studies (Chapter 2); perpetrator representation in relation to their style of representing the event and themselves (Chapter 4); legal representation and media representation (Chapter 5); and representation by family members of the perpetrator and risk (Chapters 4 and 5).

From the broad theme of disempowerment, the sub-theme of victim and perpetrator disempowerment emerges out of two observations: first, the male perpetrator sense of disempowerment implies the male's belief in his right to power and control over his wife and children; and second, female perpetrator disempowerment implies their belief that the children will be defenceless without them. In the Jubilee Soprano story, the disempowerment pertains to Angeline Soprano, whose vulnerable disposition did not enable her to break away from the violent situation in the home, and this impacted negatively on the best interest of the child, Jubilee. In the discussion to follow, perpetrator disempowerment is seen in Chapter 6 as threatening for certain fathers who, when faced with the potential 'loss' of the children, reassert their power and control in a disproportionate manner by resorting to violence. Angeline's disempowerment is discussed in Chapter 2 in the context of modelling representation. There it is argued that her predisposition, arising from her inaction, makes her complicit in the killing and can be understood as constituting symbolic violence.

Parental ownership and control of the family is discussed in Chapters 2, 3 and 6. In these chapters, it is suggested that, in spite of the rise of feminism and human rights, the male's belief in the right of power and control over the family is still embedded in many sectors of society and can be seen particularly in the case studies involving male perpetrators: Horace Faulkner, Mark and Libby, and Paul and Isabel (short stories in Chapter 2). In Chapter 7, the patriarchal meltdown and reassertion illustrated by these case studies is questioned in light of socio-legal developments in children's and women's rights in international law and in the national context, in particular regarding domestic violence. It is argued in Chapters 3 and 7 that, even though the selected cases studies appear to suggest that something positive might have been lost in making the argument that there is a collapse of male assumed right to ownership in these families, it should be pointed out that these cases are not representative of the wider population of male-perpetrated filicide cases and certainly not representative of families in which filicide does not occur. This said, it is still a genuine concern, particularly in light of recent debates over a handful of male-perpetrated filicide cases in Victoria and New South Wales. Patriarchal dysfunction in this particular context is one of the conditions of risk discussed in Chapter 7, in which it is suggested that there need to be more options to address this problem.

The belief in parental ownership, in the social sense, is not confined to male perpetrators: some female perpetrators appear to believe that they are entitled to use violence on their children. In other words, mothers can be as embedded in the ideology of patriarchy as fathers.[338] In Chapters 2 and 3, it is argued that this assumed right to treat children violently is sometimes masked as discipline or love, and that the masking by such symbols conceals the risks of child endangerment. Masking is introduced in Chapter 2 as an analytical tool and dramaturgical device to explain the nature of perpetrator representations and the reason for the authorities not detecting risks of harm when confronted with them. Relevant to this theme is the prevalence of mother and father symbols in mythology and in the law, an issue that is teased out in Chapter 3. This issue is again taken up in Chapter 5, which examines the purpose of these symbols in the law.

Finally, a discussion on risk is featured in Chapter 7, which brings together observations about conditions of risk as opposed to factors of risk. Risk in this book is seen as emerging from the state of dysfunction in the family as well as the lack of support in the community.[339] Chapter 7 concludes with some suggestions on bringing to prominence the visibility of the child in light of international developments and Australia's national framework on child protection.

338 Gerda Lerner, *The Creation of Patriarchy* (Oxford University Press, 1986) 217.
339 The state of dysfunction is a theoretical conceptualisation that is discussed and defined in Chapter 6 as a state in which the conditions of basic child safety are not met.

2 Symbolic representation

Forms of filicidal violence

Introduction

Central to this book are the six cases of filicide presented in Chapter 1. The pivotal event in each of these is the killing of a child. This act of violence is the root from which future actions and recriminations flow and become justified by the perpetrator. The character of this violence is mainly expressed as emotive (including anger, frustration and oblivion) and threatening (including abuse and assault). These expressions of violence, the book will show, appear unmediated within everyday normal and symbolic[1] channels of communication, and they appear in recognisable forms such as action (e.g. physical violence) or threat (e.g. psychological, physical and emotional violence), and sometimes in unrecognisable forms such as non-action (e.g. omission, spoken and unspoken language) and symbols *representative* of violence, including symbolic violence.[2] Even though the violent act in each of the cases is usually the ultimate act of killing, violence can occur over a period of time, as abuse, or during a sudden, momentary lapse of control, such as an expression of anger.

This chapter focuses on the expressions of violence seen in the cases, and the representation and symbolism of these expressions in, and after, death. In its widely recognised form, violence is visible and physical. Notwithstanding this, this chapter demonstrates that violence towards children often takes other *different* forms, and sometimes appears in unrecognisable forms that depart from commonly held beliefs about violence.

The analysis begins with a broad examination of the symbolism of children and the impact of filicidal violence in Western society. Following this, four main forms and expressions of violence that arise from the cases (violence as *symbol*, violence as *language*, violence as *action*, and violence as *threat*) are discussed. Within each of these four expressions of violence, the analysis focuses on how

1 Pierre Bourdieu, *Masculine Domination* (Polity Press, 2001) 2.

2 Bourdieu defines symbolic violence as 'a gentle violence, imperceptible and invisible even to its victims, exerted for the most part through the purely symbolic channels of communication and cognition (more precisely, misrecognition), recognition, or even feeling': ibid 2. For the purposes of this book, Bourdieu's definition is adopted.

the violence is not recognised for what it really is. To demonstrate this, I take the reader through the contextual layering of the cases to show that the violence had been masked by social appearance and dysfunctional intervention, which represent 'symbolic' violence. For example, in the case of Greta Sheng, the reader meets the final expression of violence symbolised as 'punishment'. Three short cases presented in this chapter illustrate the themes of 'hidden' violence and masking specific to this argument on symbolic violence. These cases are: Mark and Libby, Paul and Isabel and Greta Sheng. These short case analyses are intended to give the reader a broad social interactionist perspective on the different forms of violence and the interpretations of such violence.

Violence in child killing: meaning and context

What is it about the killing of a child that in most cases causes people to react more strongly than in the case of the killing of an adult? The expression of public condemnation is itself a violent reaction.[3] During my field research, I came across evidence of strong public condemnation and violent reaction, as represented in letters to the prosecutor from members of the public demanding that a child killer be brought to justice and severely punished.[4] Why is the death of a child so abhorrent to Australian society? In general, people do not like to discuss or hear about death, particularly the death of a child. Paul Wilson,[5] for example, elucidates the social effects of child killing and the question of responsibility during a detailed exploration of child killers. Wilson argues that the death of a

3 In the Hannah Bromley case, the court referred to the community condemnation of violence against young children: *R v Georgina and Quentin Bromley*, Supreme Court, New South Wales, 2009, Supreme Court No. GQHB, [181]. In its judgment, the court also cited *R v Hoeler* [2004] NSWCCA 184; 147 A Crim R 520, [42], where Chief Justice Spigelman referred to the 'sense of outrage in the community' concerning the manslaughter of a young child by an unlawful and dangerous act of violence being 'so strong that the element of retribution must play a prominent part in the exercise of the sentencing discretion'. This element of retribution, derived from the common understanding of the maxim 'an eye for an eye, a tooth for a tooth', has its foundation in both Eastern and Western penal philosophy. It is communicated in two ways: societal reaction and legal response that is seen as a justifiable response, and arguably a violent one, to an act of unlawful violence. The judicial legitimation of the retributive element supports my argument that the criminal justice system meets violence with violence. The difference is that one form of violence is lawful and the other is not.

4 Examples of public condemnation are seen in the following media reports in the Steppenwolf case: report 'Media-11', *Sun Herald*, New South Wales, 21 October 2007; report 'Media-1', *Sydney Morning Herald*, New South Wales, 22 October 2007; report 'Media-6', Australian Associated Press, New South Wales, 21 October 2007; and report 'Media-9', *Sunday Mail*, New South Wales, 21 October 2007. Also see Ch 1: Capello Steppenwolf.

5 Paul Wilson, *Murder of the Innocents: Child-Killers and Their Victims* (Rigby, 1985) 21–36.

child is symbolically powerful and emotive. This is because, he suggests, in Western societies, the fear of death is prevalent, along with an inability to incorporate death into the social fabric.[6] More so is the temporality, or finite nature, of life that makes death a taboo subject. He argues that, when a child dies, adult vulnerability is made sharply manifest, and on a symbolic level the killing of a child subverts the fundamental principle of human survival – that it is children who carry on the culture and beliefs of the community.[7] The symbolism of child killing casts doubt on the image of Western society as civilised;[8] the killing of children weakens this image, as well as being an outrage against humanity, and the reason for this outrage is that society sees children as powerless and defenceless, and hence believes them to be innocent. From this perspective, their killing represents unacceptable violence against the essence and the innocence of humanity. So, children's deaths carry this deeply symbolic meaning.

In addition, the death and abuse of children affects society on other profoundly symbolic levels. Wilson argues that the killing of a child symbolises the invasion of the sanctity of the family and threatens the belief that parents play a protective and constructive role in raising the young. The threat to this parental role reaffirms the position in Western societies that the state should play a more significant role in the upbringing of children.[9] Wilson suggests that it is easy and convenient for society to view child killers as aberrations, monsters or madmen rather than 'as outgrowths of our cherished beliefs concerning the nuclear family, the cult of individualism, the emphasis on material goods, or other such values we hold as being essential parts of the capitalistic ethos'.[10] Thus, the central argument regarding responsibility for child killing is about complicity that makes it 'in a very real way, more convenient for us to blame individuals for murderous acts than for us to blame those communities and values we ourselves have helped to construct'.[11] Wilson's interpretation of child killing and its broad symbolism and effect on Western society sits well in this book and supports the position that the state and the community share the responsibility for the death of a child, particularly in situations where the death results from their failure to protect.

'Complicity'[12] regarding violence is a recurring theme for Wilson, and it is one of the central themes in this book. The theme of complicity, in the social sense, refers to the idea that there are various competing contributory factors that

6 Ibid 114.
7 Ibid 32.
8 Ibid.
9 Ibid.
10 Ibid.
11 Ibid 33.
12 The term 'complicity' here is not the same as complicity in the law, which deals with the liability of individuals who encourage or assist the perpetrator(s) to commit a crime. Such a crime is found in Part 9 sections 345–351B of the *Crimes Act 1900* (NSW). In this book, complicity has a non-legal meaning, which is that of having knowledge, awareness or involvement.

'participate' in causing, or bringing about, the violence. This idea is important because, as argued in symbolic interactionist theory,[13] violence is situated within the structural network (including the social audience) surrounding the family, as opposed to being located solely within the individual. While Wilson looks to the environment and societal factors that drive parents towards committing violence to a child, this book looks towards understanding the surrounding precipitating and contributory social and familial factors and influences that precede the violence in child killing and the contextual representations of such violence before and after the killing. The way the book sets about examining these precipitating factors is, first, to unpack the nature of violence and the form(s) taken by such violence and, second, to critically assess the adequacy of external intervention measures to neutralise[14] this violence.

The literature on filicide is replete with discussions of the presenting risk factors in the family in crisis and the families in which child killing occurs. Factors such as social isolation and lack of social support networks, drugs and alcohol abuse and addiction, prior criminal conviction, prior history of violence, low socioeconomic background, unemployment, low education, social instability, social and economic hardship, and mental disorder or incapability[15] characterise the typical profile of a child killer and of families in which child killings are likely to occur. These factors, perceived as contributing to the violence, find their way into risk assessments that social and medical professionals apply to the general population. Such families have at one time or another some contact with social and medical professionals and support networks.[16] Social and medical professionals might consider families that present with these factors as 'risky', and their cases may well become reportable to child protection authorities. Arguably, these factors are general identifiers that, if present, suggest such families have the propensity to kill children. One might argue that the likelihood of child killing occurring in these conditions is higher than in families where these circumstances are not present. Criminal profiling is based entirely on the assessment of risk based on accumulated factors in the past that have been shown to be associated with child killing. Risk assessment in the field of child protection is about identifying families that have the likelihood or the propensity to harm children. This is encapsulated in section 23 of the NSW *Children and Young Persons (Care*

13 David Downes and Paul Rock, *Understanding Deviance* (Oxford University Press, 2003) 180–195, 181.

14 In this book, I use the term 'neutralise' to mean counteract or negate the violence. This is employed in the context of police intervention in response to existing violence.

15 Ania Wilczynski, *Child Homicide* (Oxford University Press, 1997) 70–85. Also see Wilson, above n 5, 71 and 73. These risk factors are discussed more fully in Chapter 7. See also Peter Reder, Sylvia Duncan and Moira Grey, *Beyond Blame: Child Abuse Tragedies Revisited* (Routledge, 1993); and Peter Reder and Sylvia Duncan, 'Conflictual Relationships and Risks of Child Abuse' (1999) 6 *Journal of Child Centred Practice* 127–145.

16 Ibid 97–100.

and Protection) Act 1998 ('CYP Act').[17] The effect of this legislation is to place the responsibility to protect on child protection authorities – to ascertain and make decisions on the families that appear to satisfy the risk criteria, and to neutralise child endangerment in such families. In many of the cases in this book, child protection authorities *did* identify a child at risk, but action to secure and incapacitate the risks of child endangerment was often not taken, or was poorly implemented.[18]

While risk assessments show deviance and violence to be situated in demographic and individual factors, such assessments as a means to detect potential filicide risks are not always successful. This is because, while society attaches blame to individual deviance, it does not address the larger problems that add to and perpetuate individual deviance, such as social inequality,[19] and because, where deaths can be attributed to the failures of the system, society does not attach similar sanctions to those failures. It is arguable that one contributory and precipitating factor in the complicity of violence is the relationship and interaction between child protection authorities and the family unit. This is precisely Wilson's argument: that society expects the state to play a more direct and intervening role in the family unit, but paradoxically its contributory role in the violence in subsequent criminal or civil investigations is seldom questioned. This is evident at the criminal trial, where the focus of the trial is on the degree of blame accorded to, and punishment of, the offender instead of also enquiring into the failure(s) of child protection services and other agencies to protect the child. Although such agency actions do not escape public and judicial scrutiny, the recommended systemic reforms and corrections often arrive well after the fact. This is seen in the cases of Hannah Bromley, Capello Steppenwolf and Jack Drummond.[20] In these cases, several systemic problems were identified, and these same problems were again identified later in a different inquiry into a different child death by an independent review body. This suggests that the systemic reforms recommended and implemented have not necessarily been the appropriate ones and that they are either insufficient or ineffective in addressing the problem.

17 Section 23 of the CYP Act is more fully discussed in Chapters 6 and 7.

18 For example, see Ch 1: Jubilee Soprano; Ch 1: Danny Burrow. The issue of DOCS' capacity has also been addressed by report 'EK4', made in December 2009 by Agency T in Sydney at the New South Wales Reporting Office J, 13–14 in the Capello Steppenwolf case.

19 Wilson, above n 5.

20 For example, in the Hannah Bromley case, report 'HB4' identified systematic problems such as lack of interagency collaboration and sharing of information: Ch 1: Hannah Bromley. Similarly, in the Capello Steppenwolf case, report 'EK4' identified problems related to information exchange and sharing: Ch 1: Capello Steppenwolf. These issues have been identified by The Hon James Wood AO QC, *Report of the Special Commission of Inquiry into Child Protection Services in New South Wales: Executive Summary and Recommendations* (State of NSW through the Special Commission of Inquiry into Child Protection Services in NSW, November 2008) i–iv. Also see Ch 1: Jack Drummond.

In the majority of the cases in this book, the protection authorities (including some members of the public) had prior information and notice that a child was at some risk of being harmed,[21] but this fact only emerged after the death of the child. An example is the Hannah Bromley case. After Hannah's death, the media portrayed the state as failing in its authority to ensure the welfare and protection of children's lives.[22] The media's messages are ways to publicly re-emphasise and reinforce the value that society places on children. What is this 'value', and how is it a reflection of the symbolic status of children? Wilson explains that this 'value' is tied to the child's place in Western society and their (non-existent) legal and social status.[23] Wilson is pointing to the paradox that is inherent in the phenomenon of child killing: on the one hand, the gross violation of innocence that receives immediate outrage and condemnation in a dramatic fashion and, on the other, the absence of security for children in the law. This paradox is also revealed in some of the cases, suggesting that the value of children's lives and the role of the state are inextricably bound with the meaning and symbolism of the violence in child killing. In this sense they are part of the violence. As the intersections between the state child protection services and the family in the cases will show, the violence committed against a child takes on a specific form, but is also revealed to have a deeper social and symbolic meaning.

In the following discussion, the focus will be on representations of violence that violate Western society's fundamental duty towards the protection of children. The cases reveal that dysfunctional state intervention is complicit in engendering the risks of violence to the child. The following analysis centres on revealing certain forms of violence as *symbolic* because they are masked by dominant symbols such as parental ownership (in the social sense), love and discipline. Because of the appearances of these symbols, the violence is not recognised for what it really is, and it eludes early detection. Before delving into this analysis, it is useful to briefly introduce the concept of masking, which is an analytical and dramaturgical theme used throughout the book to illuminate the nature of representation.

21 Since giving effect to the recommendations in the *Report of the Special Commission of Inquiry into Child Protection Services in NSW*, section 23 of the CYP Act was amended on 2 December 2010. The previous 'risk of harm' provision under section 23 has been changed to 'at risk of *significant* harm'. The change also included a new subsection (bi) and subsection (2). The insertion of 'significant' adds a layer of seriousness to the original meaning of 'risk of harm', and therefore the new amendment suggests that there are at least two levels of child endangerment harms.

22 For example, the media published a dramatic headline pointing blame at the agencies involved with the family: see report 'MEDIA-HB5', *Sydney Morning Herald*, 6 October 2009. This news report quoted a sentence from the independent review body looking into the actions of child protection services; this sentence was reinterpreted by the media as casting blame on the agencies that had the knowledge of the family's dysfunction but took no effective action to intervene.

23 Wilson, above n 5, 26.

Masking: an introduction

In this book, masking is discussed as a symbolic interactional technique, in the context of dramaturgy, for analysing the nature of perpetrator violence and uncovering the reason(s) behind dysfunctional state intervention. Dramaturgy is a perspective that emphasises the use of symbols to convey impressions to an audience.[24] Relevant to this perspective in the context of filicide is the employment of the mask as a dramaturgical device. The theme of masking is significant in a number of cases discussed, such as those of Horace Faulkner, Jubilee Soprano, Juniper Berry, Greta Sheng and Mark and Libby. In these cases, the representation of the loving parent is seen as masking, or concealing, the appearance of risks of violence. The conceptual discussion of masking takes place in Chapter 4. It is argued there that the loving parent representation enables masking because it embodies a social utility and social status, which allows for adherence to social conventions and thus bypasses detection. The purpose of this, as argued in Chapter 5, is social governance and, by implication, social control.[25] Masking is discussed in Chapters 3 and 4 in relation to perpetrator representation. In this chapter, however, masking is discussed in the context of symbolic and physical acts of violence to the child. It is appropriate to discuss masking here because it is so evident in the cases and is pertinent to the discussion on violence, particularly on the masking of violence towards the child. In this context it will be argued that certain social symbols, such as parental ownership, control and discipline, have the power to mask certain forms of violence, along with other dysfunctionalities that are not normally recognised as violence. As such, masking is perceived as enabling the perpetuation of violence towards the child.

The act or series of acts of violence on their own, without a context, have little meaning. The following section uses the cases to illustrate and examine the contexts in which situational social variables interact with the violence in child killing. Here it can be seen that the violence in child killing takes meaning from the contextual and situational surroundings, and sometimes the evolving meaning of such violence involves recognising the presence of social and intervention influences that shape the violence in the domestic space.

24 Peter Manning, 'Theorizing Policing: The Drama and Myth of Crime Control in the NYPD' (2001) 5(3) *Theoretical Criminology* 315–344, 316; and see Erving Goffman, 'The Interaction Order' (1983) 48 *American Sociological Review* 1–17, 1. Young and Massey argue that, by its separation of the social from the natural world, dramaturgy makes visible the flaws of law and is a 'powerful instrument and a valuable adjunct to the construction of a social reality imbued with vitality and wisdom': T R Young and Garth Massey, 'The Dramaturgical Society: A Macro-Analytic Approach to Dramaturgical Analysis' (1978) 1(2) *Qualitative Sociology* 78–98, 81.

25 This is further elaborated and discussed in Chapter 5.

Forms of violence

The home has traditionally been, and still is, a private space,[26] which means that much of the violence that takes place is hidden. As such, it is imperative to uncover the contextual layers and forms of hidden, and symbolic, violence. This will also reveal the nature of such violence and its capacity for destruction. Four particular forms of violence are seen in the cases: violence as symbol, violence as language, violence as action and violence as threat. I have chosen these four categories because they indicate the ways in which representations and meanings are communicated between audiences, such as between the parent and the child, between family members (e.g. the parents or the immediate and extended family) and the community, and between families, observers and the authorities, including social and medical professionals and law enforcement officers. Categorising violence this way allows for an interrogation of the appearances of violence. In particular, the categorisation explains the reason(s) for the authorities not recognising the danger and risks to the child when some of the forms of violence had been present. The misrecognition of risk by the authorities in some of the cases suggests that some forms of violence have the propensity to elude early detection by authorities.

Violence as symbol

Here, I unpack the violence contained in two of the six cases, Horace Faulkner[27] and Hannah Bromley.[28] In both cases the nature of the violence was deeply symbolic. The violence took place behind closed doors in the safety and sanctuary of the domestic private space, the home. This sort of violence is a gross violation of the symbol[29] of the home, because the home is traditionally associated with emotions and understandings relating to relationships of love, intimacy, trust and safety for children.

In Hannah's case,[30] analysis of the violence reveals another layer of 'hiddenness', or invisibility, in that it was confined to a room in which Hannah was kept over an extended period of time. The only window in that room – the only link to the outside world – was boarded up, thus cutting her off from the outside,

26 Katherine O'Donovan, *Sexual Divisions in Law* (Weidenfeld & Nicolson, 1985) 36.

27 The reader will recall that this case is about a vengeful father who drugged and drowned his three children in order to send a message to his ex-wife.

28 The reader will recall that this case is about child neglect. Hannah's parents kept Hannah confined in her room and starved her to death.

29 In this chapter, symbols refer to instruments of social integration. They are also instruments of knowledge and communication, because there is a shared consensus on the meaning of the social world. This meaning, Bourdieu argues, is a fundamental contribution to reproducing social order. See Pierre Bourdieu, *Language and Symbolic Power* (Harvard University Press, 1991) 166.

30 See Ch 1: Hannah Bromley. Also see report 'MEDIA-HB3', *The Monthly*, New South Wales, February 2010, 38.

adding another layer of invisibility. This symbolises the violation of the home, with her bedroom becoming a prison. The fact that Hannah was a prisoner in her own home in her own room, coupled with the fact that Hannah's family had been known to child protection officers from the time the first of four children in the family was born, accentuated the potency of this symbolism and the invisibility of the violence. The symbolism is deepened by the knowledge possessed by the different state agencies involved with the family, including the child protection officers,[31] who did not, and were not able to, rescue Hannah.

Structural and spatial layers of violence

The symbolism in Hannah's death lies not only in the dysfunctional condition of her home but also in the state of her body in death, the actions of the perpetrators (her parents, Georgina and Quentin), and the dysfunctionality of the responses of agencies monitoring the family at the time. The violence is seen as symbolically structural – in the walls of the home and her room, and within the familial and agency relationships around her. These representations of Hannah's death, when drawn together, allow the reader to grasp the full measure of the various contextual layers of dysfunction[32] surrounding her death. As will be argued, such dysfunction is a representation of symbolic and physical violence.

The space in which Hannah was confined as prisoner, and in which she was subjected to chronic starvation and imprisonment, has been described as 'one of God's concentration camps'.[33] This connection was also made by the prosecutor at the trial when he compared Hannah's emaciated body to 'that of a holocaust victim'.[34] This theme was subsequently developed by the media.[35] The post-death construction of Hannah's death was made through the legal narrative, and the media legitimated this symbolism by aligning her death with the deaths of Holocaust victims. At the heart of this symbolism is the juxtaposition of the symbols of the home and of the concentration camp in Hannah's case, where the particular symbol of the camp has been socially constructed for the audience to

31 Ibid. Findings in report 'HB4', conducted by an independent review body, indicated that much of the intervention by the different state agencies was inadequate in spite of the knowledge they possessed about the state of dysfunction. This knowledge pertains to the state of the filthy house, Hannah's autism and the children's absence from school.

32 This dysfunction is characterised by a number of factors: the parents' prescription drug abuse; neglect; starvation; the dysfunctionality of the family home, which is filthy and unkempt; Hannah's imprisonment; the children's absenteeism from school; and the repeated failure of child protection workers to sight Hannah.

33 Bromley, above n 3; and report 'MEDIA-HB3', above n 30.

34 Ibid. Also see report 'MEDIA-HB4', *Daily Telegraph*, New South Wales, 2 October 2009.

35 Ibid. For examples of the media reporting, see report 'MEDIA-HB6', *Sydney Morning Herald*, 6 November 2007, and report 'MEDIA-HB8', *Sydney Morning Herald*, 22 November 2007.

fully represent the dysfunction leading to her death. In order to understand this juxtaposition, it is important to contextualise the meanings behind these symbols.

The suggestion that the room, in Hannah's case, symbolises the concentration camp is a disturbing thought. Shengold, in *Soul Murder Revisited*, argues that there is a paradigmatic parallel between the wilful abuse and neglect of children by adults that is of sufficient intensity and frequency to be traumatic (which he terms 'soul murder') and the abuse and destruction of the individual in the concentration camp.[36] Looking at this juxtaposition, it is not difficult to connect the violence in Hannah's room to the concentration camp as a specific, representative symbol.

The concentration camp is a socially constructed symbol that, over the course of history, has taken on a special significance. The expression of the 'camp', according to Giorgio Agamben, is historical in that the camp has been, and still is, associated with 'the extension to an entire civilian population of a state of exception linked to a colonial war'.[37] In other words, according to Agamben, the camp is born out of the state of exception, a situation or 'a temporal suspension'[38] that is exceptional to, or outside, the normal state of law, and martial law.[39] The political theology that Agamben uses to define the camp, however, presents a comparable but different analysis to, and therefore can be distinguished from, the meaning of the 'camp' in the context of Hannah's case. In both contexts the camp sits – structurally, spatially and symbolically – outside and beyond the normal. In reality and symbolically, the violence against Hannah was made invisible to the outside world, and the outside world was unable to see through the layers of symbolic and real imprisonment by the parents.

Hannah's room can be understood as a space that was outside the Bromley's normal family life. This is because, unlike her sisters, Hannah did not get to move around the house or go out; she could not look out of the window, which had been boarded up, and she did not watch television or participate in family activities. Instead, she was kept confined in a room (a camp) within a larger space in the house. No one knows the reason for Hannah's imprisonment or for her concealment in this manner. Was it because of her autism, or the tediousness of appointments that her parents could not keep? Because the two other children were not similarly imprisoned, it seems that Quentin and Georgina locked Hannah up to shut her out from their consciousness, in an attempt to erase from their minds their additional parental responsibilities towards her, such as attending to her disability. Their act of confining Hannah, by keeping her imprisoned in a room, is symbolic in that they did not want Hannah to remind them of reality because they were too absorbed in their own 'normal' lives;[40] Quentin and

36 Leonard Shengold, *Soul Murder Revisited* (Yale University Press, 1999) 97.
37 Giorgio Agamben, *Means Without End: Notes on Politics* (Vincenzo Binetti and Cesare Casarino trans, University of Minnesota Press, 2000) 38.8.
38 Ibid 38.9.
39 Ibid.
40 Bromley, above n 3.

Georgina were caught up in their world of prescription drugs and Hannah represented a reality that was not their own.

Similarly, during the Second World War Hitler kept the Jews in a camp that was outside the normal juridical order of German society.[41] The distinguishing factor between Hannah's camp and the Jewish concentration camps is the element of the political function of the camp. In spite of this difference, there is a shared effect conveyed by the symbol of the camp in both the political and juridical context and the psychosocial context. This shared effect is that of the violent abuse on its victims. Shengold and Jarrell compare the psychological and behavioural ramifications of child abuse and violence among children to the effects of violence and abuse in concentration camp prisoners. From these perspectives, the violence located in the symbology of the concentration camp has three layers: spatially, where the violence sits outside the normal space; psychologically, where the violence is evident in the inmates; and physically, where the violence is represented by the physical boarding up or fencing of the camp. The combination of these three arrangements creates a territorial stronghold of power and ownership of the captives by the captors, or dominators, and a debilitating, powerless and helpless situation for the victims, the dominated. This structural relationship of violence – dominator/dominated – is precisely the kind of violence that Bourdieu describes in his version of symbolic violence.[42]

Violence as symbol is also represented by the intervention in Hannah's case. The intervention was dysfunctional[43] because it was complicit in engendering the invisibility of the violence to Hannah. First, this is a form of symbolic violence because of the structural perpetuation of the violence, predicated on the unequal relationship between the law and the state as dominators and the family as dominated.[44] The law (via the CYP Act) and the state (represented by its agencies) could be characterised as dominators because of their objective social structures, which have the power to shape the relations, and actions, within the family. As such, the dysfunctionality of this relationship is accentuated here because the symbol of the state as protector of young children from violence is undermined.[45]

41 Agamben, above n 37, 39.

42 Bourdieu, above, n 1, 38–42.

43 This is confirmed by the findings in report 'HB4', which reviewed the actions of the five different state agencies (DOH, DET, DOCS, DADHC and the NSW Police Force) in contact with the family prior to the killing and found the agency responses to be inadequate, unsatisfactory and inconsistent: Bromley, above n 3. The inadequacy of the five agency responses is characterised by this book as dysfunctional because, when read as a whole, the responses exacerbated the endangerment to Hannah when steps could have been taken to neutralise that danger.

44 Bourdieu, above n 1, 37. Bourdieu uses the example of post-independence Nigeria, in which he argues that symbolic violence is associated with linguistic domination of the British accent over the native language.

45 CYP Act section 8 sets out the primary responsibility of the state to protect young children from violence.

Second, the intervention was complicit in engendering the invisibility of the violence because of the failed attempts by child protection workers to sight Hannah in spite of their concerns for her safety and welfare.[46] To compound this failure, the responses by the agencies, such as DET, DOH and DAHDC, were found to be inadequate and hence dysfunctional.[47] It appears that these failures and the failure of child protection services exacerbated the invisibility associated with the nature of hidden violence in Hannah's room. Such intervention, it could be argued, is symbolic violence because of this misrecognition.[48] That is to say that the exacerbation of harm by the lack of action by the agencies is generally not recognised or regarded as violence.

Marked indifference to suffering

The final representation of violence as a symbol, and as symbolic violence, in Hannah's case is that of her parents' maltreatment and abuse of their daughter. In most of the selected cases, there does not appear to have been a lack of parental 'love' for the child, acknowledging that 'love' in these circumstances is too ambiguous to define. But in circumstances such as Hannah's, Eekelaar argues that there can be a marked indifference by parents to their children.[49] This indifference stems from the sense of parental ownership and parental entitlement over children. Seeing parental ownership from this narrow perspective allows for the conceptualisation of such violence – as a symbol of indifference in which the indifference is in regard to the suffering of the child. This indifference can be masked or revealed as love, or ownership and control over the child. A handful of cases highlight this profound symbolism.

The negligent treatment of Hannah by her parents can be described as symbolising gross indifference to her suffering. Examples of their maltreatment include Hannah's lack of schooling, her parents' reluctance to engage with available support and therapy services for her, and the squalid state of her room.[50] Hannah's parents' acts of withholding these basic childhood rights from Hannah reveal that they believed they had the right to treat her that way; the violence of their treatment is a symbol of their ownership and control of Hannah.

The second example of marked indifference to suffering as a form of symbolic violence is seen in the Horace Faulkner case. The reader will recall that Horace arranged the scene of death in a horrific manner in order to send a message to his ex-wife, Melissa. Upon entering the home, she would have encountered the sight of a disfigured stuffed monkey, one of the children's toys, hanging from a noose fashioned from an electrical cord; further inside there were messages for

46 Bromley, above n 3.
47 Ibid.
48 Bourdieu, above n 1.
49 J. Eekelaar, 'The Emergence of Children's Rights' in H D Krause (ed), *Child Law* (Dartmouth Publishing, 1992) 38.
50 Bromley, above n 3.

Melissa on the walls, the computer screen and the children.[51] The court recognised the manner in which the scene of death was arranged and said that the state of the home and the ritualistic way Horace placed the children after he killed them reflected his disturbed state of mind.[52] It further stated that '[t]here is no doubt at all that he genuinely attempted suicide after killing the children. There was something symbolic in the fact that he attempted to drown himself as he had drowned the children.'[53] This was not the first time Horace had attempted suicide; it was his fourth attempt. Horace's anger was not only directed at his ex-wife but also at himself, and this was reflected in the way he chose to kill his children and attempted to kill himself at the same time. The violent way in which he drugged and then drowned his children is a symbol of his indifference to their suffering, as well as a symbol of ownership of and control over them. The court said:

> Paradoxically the killings were in part a testament to his deep feelings for [the children]. There is nothing to suggest that the offender had ever harmed his children before this weekend. He only seriously thought of injuring them when he became so mentally disturbed that he was suicidal. Under the effects of his mental disorder, he became obsessed with their safety and their welfare, fearing that they would be sexually molested or mentally abused if they were permanently separated from him. And yet he believed that the only way they could be saved was to kill them.[54]

At first sight, one might be swayed by the court's argument that because Horace had never harmed his children it logically follows that he loved them. What did the court mean by 'deep feelings'? This question begs a more perspectival frame of analysis: what do welfare agencies, the media, the law and the public think indicates love? And what did Horace think indicates love? These questions allude to the possibility that love can be represented as violence, or as something more insidious, such as indifference to suffering. In other words, 'love' can mask violence. Horace's case parallels the case of Edward Williams in 1924, who killed his three daughters out of 'love'.[55] Williams said:

> I decided to murder all three daughters. I say murder because it is murder. When I did it I pictured them happy in Heaven . . . When I killed my children . . . was the moment I loved them most intensely. Far from being a callous act, it was to me an act of great love.[56]

51 Ch 1: Horace Faulkner.
52 Ibid. Also see *R v Horace Faulkner*, Supreme Court, New South Wales, 2004, Supreme Court No. HF1, [50], [51].
53 Ibid.
54 Faulkner, above n 52.
55 Wilson, above n 5, 63–66.
56 Ibid 65.

Like Horace, Williams saw that his life was locked in a cycle of poverty, misery and hopelessness, and he could see no future for the children.[57] Wilson comes close to an explanation of the killing, arguing that the parent could no longer distinguish himself from the children.[58] There are clear indications here that the overriding representation of 'love' that manifested itself as violence in the Faulkner and Williams cases is the symbol of ownership.

Parental ownership

The symbol of parental ownership over children does not, in this book, refer to proprietorship of children as chattels in legal theory. Instead, the book explores the concept of ownership in the social sense. Parental ownership or parental entitlement over children here refers to the sense of control and entitlement, social and physical, over children. This is best illustrated by Horace Faulkner's case. Many of Horace's verbal expressions regarding the children illustrate this expression of ownership. He stressed constantly that the children belong to him, and that he had a role as owner and protector of them. Reading his words, one gets the sense that, by stressing that the children belong to him, he is trying to assert his authority and dominion over them. Here are some examples (emphasis added):

> *My* kids were going to be *taken away* by my wife and I told her that *my kids* would always *be with me*.[59]
>
> My children were my world. I killed my kids because I had to protect them.[60]
>
> I love the children more than you. You do not deserve to *have them*. Don't tell me I haven't warned you. I told you, *you would never take the children away from me*.[61]

Horace lamented: '*[M]y* poor kids . . . I didn't say I didn't love *my kids*. I love *my kids* more than anything.'[62] Horace's constant references to *his* children and his right to have them show the overwhelming possession, control and ownership he felt he was entitled to have over the children. Horace did not deny that his main desire to punish Melissa stemmed from his fear that *his* children might be sexually abused by Melissa's new boyfriend, who, Horace believed, would own his children and replace him as father to *his* children.[63] Arguably Horace used *his*

57 Ibid 66.
58 Ibid.
59 Faulkner, above n 52.
60 Ibid.
61 Ibid. The emphasis in italics references the theme of possession, control and ownership Horace feels he is entitled to have over the children.
62 Ibid.
63 Ibid.

children as pawns to wrest control from his ex-wife, who he saw as the initiator of the separation and the residence proceedings. The following statement indicates Horace's belief that he had the right to kill the children. This belief can arise when a person believes that he or she has ownership of the object of their concern (emphasis added):

> There is one thing that I am glad that I killed my kids, they won't have to suffer. I have put them out of their misery, I have saved them from pain. *For once, my wife was not in control.*[64]

Horace's references to the children's pain in his statements 'I have put them out of their misery, I have saved them from pain' and '[i]t was so that they did not have to go through what I had to'[65] appear to be a reflection of or reference to his own pain. One might read the symbology in the children's deaths as an act of selfish expiation through the act of killing the children (the displacement of his anger towards his wife onto the children).[66] Horace believed he was saving the children from the future consequences of the broken marriage, which was the greater evil in his view. The reason he gave for killing the children was altruistic, and his altruism justified the killing for him,[67] but the actual reason was revealed to the audience when he said, '[f]or once, my wife was not in control'. So, the actual reason for killing the children was to punish his wife by using the children as pawns. By using his children in this manner, he began the process of expiating his own suffering. Three observations arise from this: during the killing, he was impervious to the children's intense struggle to live; his reasoning revealed the extent to which he was divorced from reality, but he did not completely lose his sanity in that he knew exactly what he was doing; and he had to wear a mask[68] to relieve his own anguish in order to kill the children.

Horace's case is an example of the instances where violence can be masked as discipline or as 'love'.[69] Masking also appears in the story of Danny Burrow. In the Burrow case, violence masqueraded as discipline. In that case, Danny's mother, Saskia, 'disciplined' Danny by beating him with a wooden or plastic

64 Ibid. Again, this emphasis is on Horace's proprietary attitude and belief in his entitlement to control and possession over the family.

65 Ibid.

66 Ibid. Horace said that the monkey he stabbed represented his wife. He also said that what he did was a message to his wife because his anger was about her.

67 Ibid. Horace said, 'I did not look at it like I'm going to kill my kids. I looked at it like I don't want my kids to go through the pain and suffering and insecurity I had to go through.'

68 See Ch 1: Horace Faulkner, for evidence of Horace's various masks (victim, social misfit and failure, sacrificial father, loving father, violent husband, child). Horace admitted taking drugs and self-medicating with alcohol in order to kill the children. At one point, he distanced himself from the act of killing by justifying the killing with altruistic motives.

69 Ibid.

spoon and then locking him in the bathroom. Her discipline was often carried out in a violent manner. This violent manner of punishment was masked as discipline, and is a symbolic reflection of Saskia's anger and frustration towards her son. She also admitted to Evans[70] that Danny resembled and reminded her of his father, George, and presumably their broken relationship. Again there is the presence of masking: masking the true nature of the violence. When violence is masked as love and/or discipline it is not easily identifiable, because love and discipline are not immediately associated with violence as commonly understood.

Masking as an analytical device can be seen as relevant to understanding perpetrator violence expressed as language, action and threat. But because these expressions are built into the structures and experiences of everyday life,[71] they are not at first recognised as representing violence as commonly understood. The following section discusses examples of language *representing* violence. The academic discourse on language is a massive field ranging from aesthetics to semiotics.[72] Here, language is presented within the symbolic interactionist framework as central to the construction of meanings around representation and risk. In this context, language consists of both verbal communication and non-verbal communication, such as body language. Language is analysed as the interpretive mechanism by which meanings are interpreted by the audience as observers to perpetrator representations and their perceived risks of child endangerment. From this standpoint, it is important to recognise in these cases the power of language as a dominant structure in symbolic violence because of its power to define and shape meanings.[73]

Violence as language

Language is a form of violence when language expresses emotional and verbal abuse. In this context, language can be seen as being important to *representing* violence and as a response to violence, and its importance as a representative mechanism is discussed in this framework. Two arguments are canvassed: first, language can represent violence when it takes the form of verbal abuse; and, second, language is pivotal to the construction of meanings, particularly in child endangerment. This means that language can add a layer of invisibility to the violence, thereby masking existing violence, or it can interpret and construct risk meaningfully with a view to unmasking the violence. The first argument is

70 Ch 1: Danny Burrow. Also see these excerpts discussed below.

71 Bourdieu, above n 1, 33–42, 34–35, 37, 43. For Bourdieu, symbolic violence has to be understood in the context of structures of domination, which he argues makes relations of domination appear natural. Some of these structures would include families, the church, the education system and the state, all of which reflect a more pervasive system of domination – patriarchy.

72 Norman Denzin, *Symbolic Interactionism and Cultural Studies: The Politics of Interpretation* (Blackwell, 1992) 2–3.

73 Bourdieu, above n 29, 165.

demonstrated by the stories of Mark and Libby and Danny Burrow, where the violence expressed as verbal abuse was transformed into physical violence. This sort of abuse can set the scene for future opportunities for parents to act violently to each other and towards their children.

Analysis of these stories, for example those of Mark and Libby, Paul and Isabel and Horace Faulkner, reveals that, even though domestic violence is present between the parents, the parties (the parent receiver and surrounding family members) seldom perceive a risk of harm to the children. This perception existed because there had been no overt evidence of physical threat in the form of physical violence from the parent towards the child, and it was clear to the parent receiver that the parent perpetrator was a loving parent.[74] On the other hand, the authorities often do not take verbal abuse and verbal threats seriously. The appearance of verbal abuse as non-violent or harmless is misleading. Such an appearance misled the authorities in the Mark and Libby story, which is set out below.[75] The stories of Paul and Isabel and Greta Sheng are set out as short stories in later sections of this chapter.

Short study: Mark and Libby[76]

Libby and Mark had two children over their 11 years together. In the eighth year, there were allegations of emotional, verbal and physical abuse made by each of them against each other. In the tenth year, they separated, and Libby filed for a child residence order. When Libby found her couch slashed during the period of separation, she lodged a police report and requested an AVO to support her child residence application, but as she stated that she had no fears for the children's safety she was told that she did not qualify for one. In her child residence affidavit, she alleged Mark did not return the children to her at their agreed time. During this time, Mark was unable to obtain legal representation in time for the hearing. The court granted interim residence orders to Libby. Mark started exercising his regular contact rights with the children pursuant to these orders.

74 For example, in the Mark and Libby case, discussed at length in Chapter 6, Libby did not qualify for the AVO application on behalf of the children because she stated that she did not have concerns for their safety. This observation will not be dealt with here as the purpose of this section is to illustrate the symbolism of violence contained in language. The same occurred in the Faulkner and Paul and Libby cases.

75 This case will be used in this chapter and in Chapter 6, but it will only be set out in full in this chapter. This and two other short cases, Paul and Libby and Greta Sheng, are set out in the body of this chapter to allow the reader ease of reference to the cases without having to refer to Chapter 1 and the Appendix. These three cases form part of the nine cases selected for case writing to illustrate the specific themes relevant to the book.

76 This case is based on the following reports: reports 'ML1', 'ML2', 'ML3', 'ML4', 'ML5', taken from NSW Coroner Office P on 12 November 2008, 13 November 2008, 16 November 2008 and 11 January 2009.

Three months later, Libby agreed to Mark's request to have the children during his three weeks' leave from work. When the children were delivered to him, he told Libby, 'I've got a proposal for you. I want to keep [Mary].[77] *I want you to think about it and give me an answer on Sunday. If your answer is no, you'll never see the children again.' The police and DOCS were contacted. DOCS requested the police assess the children and circumstances under which they were being cared for. The police attended the premises on Sunday and noted that the children were happy to be with their father. Mark denied making such comments to Libby and said she was trying to cause trouble for him over their child residence dispute. The police left satisfied that the children did not appear to be in immediate risk of harm. Following this, DOCS was to attend the premises on Monday to perform a welfare check but did not. The following week Mark became uncooperative towards Libby on the phone because she did not give him the answer he wanted, and he again threatened her. An urgent application was filed to discharge the earlier contact orders and replace them with supervised contact between father and children, and an order was sought for a warrant authorising police to take possession of the children.*

At the hearing, the court issued a court order that Mark present himself and the children at a police station, and directed Mark to facilitate telephone contact between Libby and the children. Mark complied with the court order the next day. As the children appeared well cared for to the police officers, they had no immediate concerns for their safety. On the same day, Mark also purchased videocassette tapes. However, when Libby was not able to speak to or contact her children, DOCS was contacted. They attended the premises two days later but failed to locate Mark and the children. Two days after this, Libby expressed her concerns before the court. Based on those concerns, the court granted a recovery order. Two days later, police located a vehicle with three deceased bodies, Mark and the children, along with the videocassette tapes containing his last words.

Mark's body language and possibly the conversation he had with the police officers on the day he complied with the court order gave the police officers the impression that everything was fine when it was not. By presenting the children as clean and well cared for, Mark managed to convey to, and convince, the police that he meant no harm to them. This presentation – using verbal and non-verbal communication – projected the image of the loving parent. This is to say that, even though Mark's earlier language towards Libby was violent, on the day he presented himself to the police his language towards them was not. This indicates that language acts as the facilitator, carrier and conveyor of meanings.[78] As the police interpreted the loving parent representation as harmless or not risky, the representation masked Mark's intention to use violence on the children. It is crucial to recognise this particular way in which language masks violence, because of its pivotal role in constructing meanings around perpetrator representation and risk such as occurred in this case.

77 According to Mark, Mary had previously expressed a desire to live with her father.
78 Denzin, above n 72, 95–96.

Language as symbolic violence

The case of Danny Burrow[79] is illustrative of the way language can become physically violent and coercive in a different way from the Mark and Libby case. In the Burrow case, language is central to the construction of violence committed against the child. The reader will recall that the story of Danny is about a boy who became the victim of his mother's frequent abuse. Danny was the receiver victim of the angry advances and abuses of his mother, Saskia. (I use the phrase 'receiver victim' because in all of the cases the child is on the receiving end of the violence and a victim as well.) Saskia would use brutal and violent language towards Danny whenever he did not behave the way she expected or wanted him to. However, she had not always had this violent attitude towards him. Her attitude progressively worsened after Danny's father, George, left the family. As such, the violence towards Danny has to be understood in the context of Saskia's relationship problems.

At first when Danny's father George left the family, Saskia was devastated.[80] However, after some encouragement and help from her family to get them back together, George and Saskia were briefly reunited.[81] During this time, Saskia found out she was pregnant again. George informed his unhappy parents, who rejected Saskia's pregnancy as they were against the relationship. George eventually left Saskia again.[82] Her parents noticed that, soon after the relationship breakdown, Saskia became 'regularly upset', she 'started to show signs that she was finding it difficult to cope again' and there was 'an increase in [her] yelling at Danny'.[83] This was the point when the language Saskia started employing towards her son took on a violent character.

Saskia's father said that he observed that 'Saskia would yell at Danny for no other reason than she was upset in relation to her present position'.[84] Some of the language Evans heard Saskia use supports the contention that language expresses violence. The following examples show the violence contained in Saskia's choice of words (emphasis added):

> Ever since [Danny] came back, he's like his father and won't do anything I tell him to do.[85]

79 Ch 1: Danny Burrow.
80 Ibid.
81 Ibid
82 Ibid. According to Saskia's father, the reason George left Saskia was that he could not bear the responsibility of the child and that he resumed his drug habit or was smoking drugs at the time when the pregnancy was revealed.
83 Ibid; and report 'JBM2', taken from West Burrow on 9 July 2000 in New South Wales at police station Z, 7.
84 Ibid.
85 Ibid.

> You little *bastard*, you're just like your father, if you don't stop playing up, I'll send you back to him.[86]
>
> Get in the *fucking* room, *you are just like your fucking father*, I'll *fucking send you back to him*, stay in there and don't come out until tea time. If you come back out, I'll give you more.[87]
>
> You're a naughty boy, you're like your father. You're a naughty boy, you're just like your father.[88]
>
> Wait till you get home *you little bastard*, I'll give you a flogging, you won't do as you're told.[89]
>
> I'm so sick of you little bastard, I'll be glad when I can get rid of you. I'll send you back to your fucken father, just like your fucken father.[90]
>
> I told you before, mind your own fucking business. I don't fucking care, the *little bastard* kicked me.[91]

The type of language employed by Saskia is crucial in understanding it as violence. This function of language in this case is symbolic. For example, Saskia's violent language reveals the image that she projects on to Danny and reflects the violence she inflicts on him as a result of this projection. Her violent language also reflects the anger she has towards Danny's father. This image is important because Saskia constantly labelled Danny as his father, George. Implicit in this labelling are George's negative traits, such as his drug addiction and his reneging on his responsibilities as a parent. Adding to this negative image that Saskia projects onto Danny was the poor relationship between George and his father, and the dominating influence of George's father, which, according to Saskia's parents, had a part in the relationship breakdown.[92] In addition to this, Saskia characterised Danny as 'naughty' and a 'little bastard', and even described Danny as 'the little bastard' to Evans on numerous occasions.[93] According to Evans, she punished him for being naughty and for being like his father. Even when it became apparent to Evans' mother that Saskia was being too harsh with Danny, she could do nothing more than reason with Saskia about scolding Danny and tell her it was normal for Danny to behave this way. Saskia's labelling as violence is evident in her projection of Danny as his father ('you are just like your father').[94]

86 Ibid.
87 Ibid.
88 Ibid.
89 Ibid.
90 Ibid.
91 Ibid 7.
92 Ibid. The evidence for this statement is Saskia's mother account, in which she described some of Saskia's and George's problems maintaining their relationship.
93 Ibid.
94 Ibid.

So, the language that Saskia employed when scolding Danny can be seen as violent. This is significant because in Saskia's mind she is directly associating Danny with his absent father and the 'violence' that George had inflicted on the family by abandoning them. Saskia's projection, created through her use of imagery – the juxtaposition of Danny and George – is a violent representation because it describes the violence that is being inflicted on Danny. The violence in this representation is not apparent at first and is in a 'nearly invisible form',[95] much like Bourdieu's description of symbolic violence,[96] which suggests that this type of violent language has been normalised for Danny.[97]

Saskia's projection can be analysed on two levels. First, the imagery of Saskia's language creates a representation for her that Danny is violating her. Implicit in her labelling are her feelings of anger and resentment towards Danny for being like George, and Saskia sees this projection as violating her memory of the relationship with George.[98] Second, the representation of Danny as his father violates Danny's identity as separate from his parents. This goes back to the argument demonstrated by this case that language is the key that connects representation with violence.

Interpreting risk out of language

The second argument in this section concerns the connection between language, meaning and the interpretation of risk. In this book, risk refers to the high

95 Nancy Armstrong and Leonard Tennenhouse (eds), *The Violence of Representation: Literature and the History of Violence* (Routledge, 1989) 9–10. Armstrong and Tennenhouse explain that the representation of violence becomes the violence of representation through a holistic interpretation of language. They stress the importance of the structure of the words used to convey meanings of violence. Even though their argument is constructed around the representations and analogies contained in *Jane Eyre*, the discussion is not limited to fiction but locates itself between the discourses of cultural, political, historical and gender studies. The novel serves as a reflection for the broader ideas related to hegemony, patriarchy, identity and social power. In this context, there is a parallel between Bourdieu's version of symbolic violence and representations manifesting violence.

96 Bourdieu, above n 2.

97 The use of normalisation in this context refers to Danny accepting and internalising this pattern of verbal abuse: Ch 1: Danny Burrow.

98 Examples of Saskia and George's relationship can be found at Ch 1: Danny Burrow. These representations characterise the relationship as loving at first. Later, the relationship turned sour because of George's father (Mark's) interference. In spite of this, it is highly possible that Saskia did not reject the early memories of her relationship with George. This is evidenced by her language towards Danny and her parents' observations of Saskia's mood and overall disposition when Saskia and George reconciled. Even though there was the allegation by the sister that Saskia did not always tell the truth, it is arguable and believable based on the collaborated accounts that she believed her relationship with George was genuine. Her declaration of affection for Evans must be read in the context that she had lost all contact with George and Evans was, at the time, one of the few persons she had meaningful contact with.

likelihood or high possibility of foreseeable danger to the child.[99] Discussed first is the case of Capello Steppenwolf,[100] in which language can be seen as adding another layer of invisibility to the existing violence, thereby masking violence. The reader will recall that Capello's story is about his mother, Elizabeth, harbouring ill feelings towards her ex-partner, Peter, Capello's father. Elizabeth could not cope with caring for Capello and killed him. She later claimed that he reminded her of Peter. The Family Court and DOCS were involved in the family to the extent that they intervened whenever Elizabeth could not physically care for the children. At the time of Capello's death, there were two applications before the Family Court: an outstanding residence application for Capello between Elizabeth and Capello's maternal grandmother, Gabrielle; and a recovery order to retrieve Capello from Elizabeth's care, which was applied for on the day Capello died but was not executed by the police until eight days later.

Following Capello's death, an internal DOCS review, 'EK4', reported that the problematic use of language in the records led to misleading information being given about risk to the children.[101] DOCS' records should have indicated a high level of risk, which should have been addressed but was not.[102] Attention is drawn to the report's concerns that DOCS misunderstood Helpline's reports of risk of harm to Capello because of the inconsistencies in record-keeping and transfer of information. The concern appears to be that the strength of the language used to report risk was not properly conveyed in DOCS' records, thereby causing the level of risk to be wrongly assessed. This indicates that the risks were not appreciated by child protection officers[103] because of poor information-gathering and record-keeping. Language in this context is revealed to be crucial to DOCS' interpretation of representations of risk based on recorded language. If the recorded narrative is inconsistent, the possibility that it might lead to a misinterpretation of risk should be recognised. For example, in a transfer of information between the person transmitting the representation of risk and

99 'Risk' is a complex phenomenon in criminal justice discourse even though it is often presented as a value-neutral term. The common dictionary definition of risk associates it with danger and peril, but this later grew to include taking chances and calculating the odds. See Hazel Kemshall, *Understanding Risk in Criminal Justice* (Open University Press, 2003) 3–8, 4. In this book, 'risk' refers to its meaning in the law of torts, where risk is a 'high likelihood' of foreseeable harm. See *State of New South Wales (Department of Education and Training) v Maurice O'Sullivan* [2005] NSWIRComm 198, [123]. This case also distinguishes the principle of 'relevant risk' from 'general' and 'specific', and 'actual' and 'potential' risk. See also above n 18, 86 at [4.13], where a 'risk factor' is defined as a factor that increases the likelihood of a future negative outcome for a child. Also see Pat O'Malley, *Crime and Risk* (Sage, 2010) 57. Risk is again discussed in Chapter 7.

100 Ch 1: Capello Steppenwolf.

101 Ibid.

102 Ibid.

103 The reader may well question this given that there were 34 risk of harm reports regarding Elizabeth Kramer's children in the seven years before Capello's death: ibid.

the Helpline receiver recording the concerns, if the narrative is misunderstood or not recorded accurately, there is a higher likelihood that the meaning of the violence will be lost at the receiving end. As implied by the report's observations, because the language of note-taking as well as verbal and non-verbal communications provides the critical framework from which risk is analysed, the accuracy of record-keeping and information transfer must not be misleading. Such an analysis includes the construction and interpretation of representations about risk. This suggests that language functions as the bridge between the meaning of representation and the meaning of violence. It is one of the foundations upon which risk assessments are conducted. From this perspective, language can mask or unmask existing violence. Language can *sustain* violence when it is not understood by the receiver to be a means by which actual violence can be masked, resulting in a lack of intervention, such as in the Steppenwolf case. This could be seen as a violent response to the child because the lack of intervention enables the violence to continue and to be sustained.

Language is seen here as having the power – through written communication such as recorded language, and verbal communication such as speech and body language – to deny, reject, give meaning to, represent and/or unmask violence. In this discussion, it is conceived within the broader framework of representation and as a dominant tool of construction in both action and threat. In this broad sense, language underpins these forms of violence. Language is able to do all this because it is a symbolic instrument that has the power and capacity to ***know*** and *construct* the world of objects,[104] including the power to give meaning to representations of risk and violence. This is to say, one can perceive language as having two significant purposes when it comes to constructing and interpreting violence – verbal utterances of violence, and recording and interpreting violence.

Verbal utterances of violence

Language represents violence against a child when it is uttered and used symbolically by the perpetrator against a child, for example Saskia's language towards Danny. A similar example in which there were suggestions of overt utterances of violence is the case of Capello. In this case his mother frequently described him as a 'little bastard' and an 'asshole' to others, and she punished him severely because he reminded her of his father.[105] The ramifications of children's exposure to domestic violence have been documented as harmful to their development and well-being, and against their best interests.[106] These types of cases in which the parent is verbally violent towards the child are illustrations of symbolic violence, in particular, the symbolic and physical effects of uttered violence.

104 Bourdieu, above n 29, 164.
105 Ch 1: Capello Steppenwolf.
106 Nancy Ver Steegh and Clare Dalton, 'Report from the Wingspread Conference on Domestic Violence and Family Courts' (2008) 46(3) *Family Court Review* 454–475, 456.

Recording and interpreting violence

It is suggested also that language 'does' violence to the child when the reporting of violence is recorded inaccurately, or when the reported risk of harm to the child is misunderstood and not given the appropriate meaning by the authorities. The importance of recognising the role of language in reporting indications of physical violence is emphasised here. For example, in the Hannah Bromley case, DOCS did not actively investigate the risk of harm reports regarding the poor condition of the family's home and instead minimised their significance by classifying the information as nothing new.[107] The centrality of language in constructing and communicating urgency of risk is also evident in Hannah's case. The police officers misunderstood the language used by DET and as such they did not react promptly in their efforts to trace the family.[108] The significance of language as, first, a mechanism for meaningful interpretations of risk and violence reporting and, second, as physical and symbolic, such as verbal utterances of violence when used on a child, should not be downplayed.

In the following two sections, violence as action and violence as threat are explored. Here, the reader might at first consider that violence as threat and action are easily categorised as violence. However, upon reading the cases further the reader might realise that this is not the case when it boils down to certain types of threats and actions that are not at first sight identifiable as dangerous or violent. This book argues that some forms of violence as threat and action are not easily identifiable because they are made invisible, or are hidden behind a particular representation that allows for the risks of child endangerment to be concealed, namely the representation of the loving parent. In both cases, the perpetrators had appeared as loving fathers towards their children. Another important aspect focused on in these sections is the relevance of the role of the state[109] in the reinterpretation of the meaning and expressions of violence. The state in these cases is seen as the dominant instrument that constructs and gives meaning to the violence for the wider social audience. This role is symbolic because the subjective expression of the perpetrator violence is given an objective meaning. This symbolic function of the state is achieved through the symbolic role of the court in the criminal justice system, and here the reader can begin to see the violence of punishment meeting perpetrator violence in the broader context of symbolic violence.

Violence as action

Very often when there is violent action or inaction that is immediately identifiable as violence, there is a clear law enforcement response to it. However, there are

107 Bromley, above n 3.
108 Ibid.
109 Chapter 6 picks up from here with a discussion on the implications of dysfunctional state intervention.

certain situations in which an action or inaction that is violent does not appear as violence, or is not classifiable as violence, initially. 'Action' for the current purposes is deemed to be an act or an omission to do something. Two categories of action will be discussed here: the first is perpetrator action and inaction that may not appear violent, and the second includes law enforcement action and inaction that do not, at first, appear violent. The latter is seen as one of the social interactive forces[110] that are complicit in the violence against children in the studies in this book. In the foregoing section on violence as threat, threat was conceptualised as involving action, language, or both, such as occurred in the Paul and Isabel and Mark and Libby cases. In regard to these cases, the visibility of threats not taken seriously was discussed.

The case of Greta Sheng exemplifies the first category. The case, described below, illustrates that a parent can believe that he or she is acting for the benefit of the child but that that belief can be misplaced. Greta's parents acted with the belief that the homeopathic medicine they applied to her was improving her condition when it was not. The parents were charged and convicted for manslaughter by criminal negligence. Their crime was their negligence towards Greta in not providing the appropriate medical treatment, which, the court said, should have been conventional medicine. The violence in Greta's case is both perpetrator action in treating Greta with homeopathic medication and inaction or omission for not seeking appropriate conventional medical treatment. It is also, in the broader context of symbolic violence, the symbolism of punishment.

Short study: Greta Sheng[111]

Greta Sheng died at 9 months. At 3 months, she was diagnosed with eczema. One month later, Greta's eczema worsened. A nurse recommended Greta see a skin specialist. Instead her parents, Caitlin and Gerald, consulted Gerald's uncle, a practising homeopath (as was Gerald), who recommended homeopathic treatment for Greta. Two months later, a general practitioner recommended Greta see a specialist dermatologist. But the parents did not heed this advice. Greta's weight dropped and her skin became

110 In this book, the majority of the cases were known to the state prior to the killing. As such, the state and its agents are seen as influential in shaping some of the outcomes in filicide cases. Again, this conceptualisation of the state within the symbolic interactionist framework is not new; see Howard Becker, *Outsiders: Studies in the Sociology of Deviance* (Free Press of Glencoe, 1963) 9. Other social interactive forces that may play a role in shaping the family in crisis include the extended family and social and support services and networks such as schools and children's playgroups.

111 This case is a summary of *R v Gerald Sheng*; *R v Caitlin Sheng*, Supreme Court, New South Wales, 2009, Supreme Court No. SHG13. It does not appear in Chapter 1 and the Appendix. This case was identified in the public domain and was not part of the original coronial sample. This case is based entirely on reported case law, newspaper reports and my observations of the trial proceedings in court. All identifiers have been changed. The case has been diluted and pared down to focus on the themes relevant to the book.

itchy, reactive and elevated. A nurse observed Greta's suffering and urged the parents to see a skin specialist. Arrangements were made for Greta to see a paediatrician, Dr Matombo, the next day. During this consultation in February, Greta's parents informed Dr Matombo that they were treating her with both conventional and homeopathic medicines. Dr Matombo advised against homeopathic treatment but said they should continue with the conventional ointment. Two weeks later, Greta's condition improved. Still, Dr Matombo advised the parents to consult a paediatric dermatologist. An appointment was made for April.

A few days later, the parents rang Dr Matombo to inform him that they were travelling to country X, and could not attend the April appointment. Dr Matombo expressed his unhappiness at the travel, saying it would be 'cruel' to Greta. Not being able to change the parents' minds, he advised them to consult a specialist there. Prior to this, no homeopath had physically examined Greta, but Gerald admitted later that he had treated Greta with homeopathic medicine prior to the travel.

In country X, Greta saw a paediatrician and skin specialist, who prescribed conventional medication. Greta's condition improved and she did not attend the follow-up appointment. When Gerald joined his family, Gerald observed that Greta's condition had improved minimally and sought homeopathic treatment for her.

At the end of April, the family returned to Australia. Greta's skin was inflamed and bleeding. Greta's pain was noticed by passengers on the flight, who commented that she was inconsolable. Once home, Gerald went back to work. A week later, Greta's eye developed a rash. Because the parents were tired that day they did not take Greta to the hospital immediately. The next day, Saturday, Gerald went to work. Greta's condition worsened. On Sunday morning, Gerald attended church. When Greta was finally admitted to the hospital that afternoon, her condition shocked the doctors. The eczema had completely eroded away the epidermis on Greta's body. She presented with severe malnutrition, evidence of grey hairs, delayed developmental milestones, and a melting cornea, which could not be saved. Days later, Greta died. Gerald and Caitlin pleaded not guilty at the trial. The jury found them guilty. They were convicted of manslaughter by criminal negligence and sentenced to imprisonment.

The form of violence to Greta in this case is twofold: perpetrator action and perpetrator inaction, which constituted omission in law, which means the parents breached a legal duty to act.[112] The parents' act of consulting doctors, homeopathic or conventional, on its own is not normally seen as violent. Their act appeared non-violent because they believed they were treating Greta's condition by consulting with homeopaths and applying homeopathic medication, sometimes together with conventional medication. In this regard, the violence committed by Greta's parents to Greta did not appear as violence. However, when placed in the broader context of the medical advice given to the parents, a pattern in the parents' behaviour emerges, namely their recurrent failure to seek appropriate

112 Simon Bronitt and Bernadette McSherry (eds), *Principles of Criminal Law* (Lawbook, 2nd ed, 2005) 487–488.

treatment for Greta. It is this inaction that the court held was breaching the law, and as violent and deserving punishment and condemnation. The court said:

> The sentences to be imposed must also denounce the conduct of the Offenders in failing grossly to take necessary and readily available action to treat Greta's curable condition and must recognize the harm done to the victim, Greta, and the community.[113]

The judicial narrative in this instance is significant regarding the broader context of symbolic violence. The symbol of the court is its representation of the ideology of justice, and its representation as an institution that is instrumental in seeing that justice is done. This is to say that the court is instrumental in seeing that individuals who break the law are punished. In this way, the court participates in symbolic violence that is both legitimate and justified.[114] Punishment is symbolic because it lies directly at the root of social order.[115] As an instrument for articulating society's moral sentiments,[116] the judicial pronouncement in this case was particularly illustrative of this symbolic function. The moral issue for the court was whether the standards expected of a reasonable parent and reasonable homeopath were breached. As Gerald admitted in his evidence he had, at times, treated his daughter in his capacity as a practising homeopath, and that added a layer of responsibility to his duty as a parent. In the process of setting straight these standards for the wider social audience, the court role can be seen as both educative, which is a symbolic function, and punitive in instituting punishment; it is instrumental in educating the wider social audience and punishing, or correcting,[117] offending behaviour. To illustrate these functions, I cite this principle from the court's judgment in Greta's case:

> It is the responsibility of the courts to protect and preserve human life and to punish those who unlawfully take it: *R v [Melanie Drummond]*.[118]

113 *R v Gerald Sheng; R v Caitlin Sheng*, above n 111, [160].

114 A kind of punishment that is conceivable as symbolic violence incorporating both symbolic and violent punishment is the death penalty. In the twenty-first century, most Western countries have abolished the death penalty but some jurisdictions, such as Singapore and Texas in the United States, continue to justify the active use of the death penalty.

115 David Garland, 'Frameworks of Inquiry in the Sociology of Punishment' (1990) 41(1) *British Journal of Sociology* 1–15, 11.

116 David Garland, 'Perspectives on Punishment' (1991) 14 *Crime and Justice* 115–165, 122.

117 Michel Foucault, *Discipline and Punish: The Birth of the Prison* (Alan Sheridan trans, Penguin Books, 1977) 179 [trans of: *Surveiller et punir: Naissance de la prison* (first published 1975)].

118 *R v Melanie Drummond*, Court of Criminal Appeal, New South Wales, 2004, Court of Criminal Appeal No. MD2, [31]; *R v Gerald Sheng; R v Caitlin Sheng*, above n 113, [155]. Both case names cannot be revealed here as they are both cases in this book.

> Without leading to a position of double punishment, the sentence to be imposed upon [Gerald Sheng] must also reflect an element of general deterrence directed to alternative health providers who may fail to ensure a patient receives conventional medical treatment where the patient is not responding appropriately to alternative treatment.[119]

The trial observation component of the fieldwork allowed me to observe the perpetrators' behaviour at the trial. I observed that Gerald's status as a practising homeopath was held to be of importance by the observers, such as the media and the legal actors. This interest can be attributed to Gerald's professional position, which was seen as accentuating the gravity of Greta's death. The gravity of his position was also an important consideration in the court's judgment at sentencing.[120] In particular, the court was unequivocal that the sentence for Gerald should reflect an element of general deterrence.[121] This warning has a symbolic function: a warning to the audience, as well as potential future victims, to be careful of the mask of the loving parent and mask of the practising homeopath, which were the two masks that Gerald wore.

Before going on to discuss Gerald's masks, I should point out that Greta's case is different from all the other cases in the fieldwork in that Greta's parents do not fit into the conventional profile of a family in which child killing is likely to occur. In spite of this, this case is similar to Hannah's case in that they are both cases of child neglect. Both cases involve the symbolic rejection of the child.[122] However, the situation in this case is unlike Hannah's case in the sense that Hannah's parents shrank from external contact with doctors and social professionals. Greta's parents, by contrast, took Greta to consult with various doctors. More importantly, unlike in Hannah's case, there was the presence of masking in Greta's case where the father perpetrator wore two masks. These masks must be seen in conjunction with the fact that both Greta's parents had a tertiary education, were in employment at the time, had no prior criminal convictions,

119 Ibid [154].

120 Ibid [143].

121 Ibid [154]. To be sure, homeopathy is a popular alternative to conventional medical treatment, but this does not detract from the legal position that was confirmed by the court in this case that conventional medicine takes precedence and must be sought when alternative treatments fail. See Dana Ullman, 'Homeopathic Medicine: Europe's #1 Alternative for Doctors' *Huffington Post* (online), 3 March 2010 www.huffingtonpost.com/dana-ullman/homeopathic-medicine-euro_b_402490.html. At the trial, the court accepted the universal view of homeopathy as complementing conventional medicine, but it was not intended to substitute for the treatment of conditions requiring conventional medical assessment and treatment: above n 113, [141].

122 Capello Steppenwolf is another case that involved the symbolic rejection of the child: see *R v Kramer*, Supreme Court, New South Wales, 2009, Supreme Court No. EK1, [83]. The judge held that Elizabeth's method of disposing Capello's body was a further sign that she loathed him.

and, importantly, had the benefit of a supportive family and a supportive and stable upbringing.[123] They were also well regarded in their community.[124]

The presence of masking here is different from some of the other cases in Chapter 1, such as Hannah Bromley and Horace Faulkner, where the fathers covertly manipulated others in order to present themselves as loving fathers, or not mentally ill, as in the Soprano case. Here, Gerald's masks appeared not to have implied some deliberate covering up of malign intent at first sight. However, this is not to say that his masks did not, in fact, conceal the violence (including the negligent treatment of Greta) from the doctors who attended to her. In such a context, the mask can be perceived as a functional, malleable and representative device that is worn by social actors to achieve different purposes and outcomes.

One might ask what was the mask worn by the mother, Caitlin. My argument is that Caitlin was subsumed into, and concealed behind, Gerald's masks, because Caitlin played the role of the submissive wife who relied on her husband to make decisions on behalf of the family.[125] For example, the court noted that Gerald was the dominant one and that Caitlin was the 'compliant and non-assertive woman who was deferential to authority'.[126] This was evident in the fact that Caitlin was mostly silent on Greta's needs, particularly in the final days of Greta's life when Gerald was afforded the time to work and attend church while Greta's condition worsened. As such, the court concluded that Gerald's 'offence is objectively greater than [Caitlin's] offence, given his dominant role and her reliance upon his homeopathic knowledge'.[127] The court highlighted the gross failing of Caitlin as a mother, observing: '[Caitlin Sheng] was [Greta's] mother, the person from whom, above all others, the child was entitled to expect nurture, care, sustenance and protection, and she failed the child in her most important duty, with fatal results'.[128] This judicial statement entrenches the universal symbol of the Mother (which is further discussed in Chapter 3) as a symbolic force,[129] conceived as pivotal to the construction of meanings associated with representations of parenthood. It is interesting to note that it is the court that articulates this representation and that itself lends credence to the court's symbolic role in articulating punishment.

The revealing of Gerald's masks was also critical to the court's symbolic role. His masks concealed the violence from the nurses and from Dr Matombo, who

123 *R v Gerald Sheng; R v Caitlin Sheng*, above n 111, [15], [16], [112], [113].
124 Ibid [114]–[116].
125 Ibid [117], [143]. The immersion of the mother into the perpetrator's mask also occurred in the Jubilee Soprano case.
126 Ibid.
127 Ibid.
128 Ibid [144].
129 Bourdieu, above n 1, 38. For Bourdieu, symbolic force refers to a form of power that is exerted on bodies directly, and without physical constraint, to affect the deepest level of the body. He cites the symbolic efficacy of religious messages and religious socialisation, such as catechism and church-going activities, as examples.

were attending to Greta at the time. Although Dr Matombo recognised Greta's parents' overseas trip as 'cruel',[130] he did not report his concerns to DOCS. Dr Matombo's usage of the word 'cruel' alluded to the inappropriateness of the parents' care of the child. However, this non-reporting was not an issue raised by the defence at the trial. Could the reason for this be that both Gerald and Caitlin did not fit the profile of parents who would put their child at risk of harm? Perhaps this demonstrates that the social and professional status of the perpetrators functioned to mask the underlying dysfunction in their duty towards Greta. The court's role in unmasking this façade and its reinterpretation of the parents' treatment as violence is the key to understanding the broader context of symbolic violence and the symbolic expressions of violence in the phenomenon of child killing.

A different expression of violence that could be seen as symbolic violence is the absence of intervention, which can be generally conceived as inaction by the state and its agents. Some examples are seen in the following cases. In the Jubilee Soprano case,[131] DOCS did not respond to Iris' and Papadino's concerns, and in the Danny Burrow case (discussed below), DOCS did not constructively determine the nature of the risk. DOCS' reactions in these cases can be seen as pivotal to giving meaning to the representation of risk. The reader will recall in the Burrow case that DOCS chose to believe Saskia over her sister Carrie. In so doing, DOCS rejected Carrie's concerns regarding the physical bruises on Danny, and gave new meaning to the violence. To illustrate the gravity of this particular point, the context of Carrie's report merits some discussion. In the Burrow case, the reader will recall, Carrie saw bruises on Danny's body and rang DOCS to report her concerns for his welfare.[132] When DOCS did nothing about her report, Carrie rang the police and Saskia was questioned by the police.[133] Carrie said that Saskia was supposed to take Danny to the doctor for a physical examination, but did not. Later, Saskia's father, West, noticed that DOCS did nothing after Carrie's report to DOCS. He therefore assumed that Carrie's concerns were incorrect and untrue.[134]

West's assumption here is significant because it reveals that DOCS rejected Carrie's interpretation of child endangerment. DOCS said that they were 'unable to ascertain assessed risk based on [the] given information',[135] and that whenever they saw Danny he presented to them as clean and appropriately dressed.[136] Contained in these responses is the representation of DOCS as the medium

130 *R v Gerald Sheng*; *R v Caitlin Sheng*, above n 111.
131 Ch 1: Jubilee Soprano. This case is further discussed in Chapters 4 and 5.
132 Ch 1: Danny Burrow.
133 Ibid.
134 Ibid.
135 Ibid; and report 'CR3', dated 13 September 1999 in New South Wales at DOCS Office W. The reader will recall that DOCS gave a similar response in the case of: Ch 1: Jubilee Soprano.
136 Ibid.

through which meanings of risk and violence are constructed and determined. Because DOCS has the authority to determine the legitimacy of the violence, its absence of intervention[137] gave the reported violence a different meaning and altered the significance of the original violence. The new meaning given to the original violence by DOCS was that the violence did not exist, and this interpretation impacted on West's belief. He came to believe that Carrie's concerns were incorrect and he accepted *as fact* that the violence did not take place. This means that DOCS' interpretation and West's acceptance both counteracted and negated the meaning of the original violence on Danny.

This is an important observation because it reveals child protection action/inaction to be critical in determining the meaning and significance of violence for the audience. DOCS' language, evidenced in their record-keeping, their lack of verbal and written responses to the family and their inaction, sent one or more of these messages to the family as the audience: the actions were not interpreted as violence; the actions were acceptable; they were unimportant. This is to say that it added another layer of invisibility to the violence. DOCS' lack of intervention appears all the more grave when considered in the light of its obligation under the CYP Act as substitute parent when the child is at risk of harm.[138] This was also the case in the case of Hannah Bromley.

The short study of Paul and Isabel (below), in addition to that of Greta Sheng (above), illustrates the visibility of certain types of threat, such as those posed by Paul and Gerald as loving fathers. In the Sheng case, the visibility of the threat might not have been easily identifiable at first. These examples are set as a contrast to the short study of Mark and Libby (above) where the threat to the children appeared invisible and was masked by Mark's representation as a loving parent. All these short studies build on the concept of masking as a technique for concealing risk; and both the Mark and Libby and Paul and Isabel cases investigate the symbolism of parental ownership in the context of marital separation or relationship breakdown. In these cases the analysis focuses on the symbol of parental ownership as shaping the primary motivation behind the wearer of the loving parent mask to use violence on the children; in the Sheng case, the focus is on how parental ownership shaped the parents' belief that they were entitled to treat Greta however they thought fit and in a way that suited their schedules. The child's safety and well-being was not a priority for the Shengs or the Bromleys, because they felt they were entitled to treat their children as non-persons.[139]

137 Here, the violence as inaction should be read in the larger context of language, particularly the meaning that DOCS' response gave to the violence. In the final section of this chapter, violence as action and inaction is discussed in the context of physical law enforcement responses or the lack thereof.

138 As determined by sections 23 and 49 of the CYP Act.

139 The concept of the child as non-person is further discussed in Chapter 5, where it is argued that in some mercy killing cases, such as the Drummond case, involving a child with disabilities, the value of the child's life is devalued by the judgment of the

Violence as threat

Violence can be seen as taking the form of a threat or threats. A threat can be an action or it can be verbal (language), or both. The cases of Isabel and Paul (below) and Mark and Libby (above) illustrate the dangerous potential of open and veiled threats made in the context of an acrimonious divorce and residence disputes over children, and against the backdrop of bitter separation. To be sure, when a person makes a threat it does not necessarily follow that the person will act on it, and it is difficult to establish when a threat is about to be realised. In fact, delineating between the stages of constructing, realising and actualising a threat is almost impossible. The lines at which the threat made in anger crosses over to become the threat realised, and the threat realised crosses over to become the threat actualised, are almost indistinguishable, if not invisible. Does the moment of visibility in which threats can be neutralised come before they are actualised? Before expanding on the relevance of visibility, the following case is introduced in order to provide an understanding of the context from which threat arises.

Short study: Isabel and Paul[140]

In April in the fifth year of Isabel and Paul's relationship, relations had deteriorated to the extent that ***Paul had told Isabel that if she ever left him he would track her down and kill her****. By the end of the month, both parties had effectively separated, and Paul had lost his job. However, Paul continued to see their children whenever he wanted to. Three months later, he tried to reconcile with Isabel but she rejected him.* ***He then started to realise his threats of violence towards Isabel and threatened often to kill himself.*** *In one incident, he threatened her with a knife in the presence of the children. The police were called but no further action was taken. The police spoke with Paul and told him to seek counselling. Two days later, he sought counselling but was told that the normal waiting time was ten weeks. On the same day, an AVO was taken out against*

---

court. It is also argued there that children with disabilities have been, historically and culturally, treated as non-persons. In the Sheng and Bromley cases, it could be argued that the parents believed they were entitled to treat their children as non-persons. In these cases, the reader will recall that Hannah suffered autism and Greta suffered eczema. These were children in need of appropriate medical treatment and services that were not provided to them.

140 This case does not appear in Chapter 1 and is set out in full here. This case is again discussed in Chapter 6, which examines the theme of masculine disempowerment, and in Chapter 7, where the disempowerment is seen as a condition of dysfunction predisposing risk of child endangerment. This case is a summary of the following sources: report 'P4', Coroner Court, Westmead, New South Wales, 11–15 July 2005, Coroner Report File No. PPP; report 'P3', Coroner Court, Westmead, New South Wales, 15 July 2005, Coroner Report File No. PPP; report 'P2', made by police detective LH on 13 December 2003 at police HQ3; and report 'P1', taken from police officer R on 15 September 2003 in New South Wales at residence G. The emphases in bold are intended to highlight the visibility of Paul's threats.

him, and DOCS was notified. The AVO conditions were for Paul not to approach or contact Isabel except to arrange for contact with the children, and not to enter Isabel's home. Despite the AVO, ***Paul repeatedly breached its conditions*** *by calling and visiting Isabel. The police were contacted about the breaches. However, Isabel did not want to press charges, though she agreed for the police to speak with him regarding his responsibilities under the AVO.*[141] *In the next two weeks, there were three failed attempts to negotiate contact with the children. After the last failed attempt, Paul broke into Isabel's home with a knife and sexually assaulted her. After she calmed him down, he informed her of his suicide intentions, which he promised to retract. Paul then left for work. Isabel left the children with her father, contacted the police and went to the hospital. When the police took her home, she was met with the deaths of the two children, whom Paul had killed. (Emphasis added)*

It is observed that the police at the time did not respond appropriately because they did not take seriously Paul's threats of physical violence. Part of the reason for this was that Isabel did not want to press charges at the time. This is especially symbolic because the very institution that is entrusted with law enforcement and protection failed to neutralise Paul's violence. This theme also arises in the Mark and Libby case, where the police and the Family Court were involved. Both interventions failed to neutralise the father's violence towards their children.

The moments of visibility of threats arise on a number of occasions prior to the killing. In the Paul and Isabel case, the visibility of the threat arose during Paul's repeated breaches of the AVO. The threat was not neutralised, as the police intervened but took no action.[142] In the Mark and Libby case, it could be argued that the visibility of the threat, although present, was not as clear. For example, when the police intervened on the request of DOCS to check on the children and when Mark presented himself and the children at the police station, one might think that the police could have intervened to apprehend Mark. However, there was nothing suspicious in Mark's behaviour or demeanour that would have alerted the police to the threat of harm to the children, unless they knew they were looking for a particular type of representation that posed a risk to the children.

In the Mark and Libby case it can be seen that the police chose to believe Mark because the children appeared well cared for, in that they 'were happy to be with their father' and 'did not appear to be in immediate risk of harm'. There was a mask that the police did not pierce to reveal the hidden risk behind Mark's threats. This risk was hidden behind Mark's presentation to the police as

141 The coronial inquest later found that the police should have arrested Paul on the morning of the murders and that there were shortcomings in their handling of the domestic violence incidents: Media 'PK1', *Hawkesbury Gazette*, 27 July 2005.

142 Under the recent NSW law in relation to breaches of AVOs, the police are mandated to arrest perpetrators for breaches of AVOs. This is further discussed in Chapter 6, which has been accepted for publication as, 'Loving Fathers? Implications of State Intervention' (2009) 28(2) *University of Tasmania Law Review*, 242–264.

a loving father. Similarly, in the case of Paul the risk was contained in Paul's threats of violence but hidden behind his appearance as a devoted father. In this regard, the violence here fulfils Bourdieu's description of symbolic violence as 'invisible' and exercised for the 'most part through purely symbolic channels of communication'.[143] There is no other symbol that has the propensity to mask risk of harm and violence to children more than the symbol of a loving parent, which is discussed throughout the book.

Having established that certain hidden threats can be actualised as real violence, it is imperative to discuss the relevance of the theme of parental ownership of children that arises in these cases and recurs throughout the book. This theme allows the reader to uncover the motivations behind this form of violence. In both the Paul and Isabel and Mark and Libby cases, the violence was directed towards the children as a response to the perception of failed negotiations for contact and residence of the children. In both cases, the children were at the centre of the separation and in this sense their situation is similar to that of the Horace Faulkner case, in which the ownership of the children framed the context for the violence. For example, when attempts at negotiating contact (for Paul) and residence (for Mark) of the children failed, both perpetrators resorted to violence as a solution to the conflict in the marital separation. Both used the children as pawns to negotiate with their spouses. Like Horace, they believed they had a right to do this because they believed they had ownership of their objects of concern, their spouse and children.[144] The fact that the violence directed at the children was not intended *for* the children indicates that the perpetrators used what they saw as their ownership over the children as weapons, because they felt they were entitled to have and use them. This context is important because it alludes to the question of support available to conflicted families. It is noteworthy to consider that, even though various state interventions were available at the time, these were ineffective in assisting the perpetrator in dealing with the family conflict.

In these cases, the police had a key role to play in shaping the subsequent course of the violence by the perpetrators towards the children. The role of the state as intervener was also significant in the Jubilee Soprano case. The reader will recall that in this case a medical team and the police interviewed the perpetrator three days before the killing, but they all failed to pick up the progressive worsening of the perpetrator's mental illness and the unusual behaviour of Angeline.[145] The intervention team also did not sight Jubilee.[146] The dysfunctionality of state intervention in these cases is one of the expressions of violence identified. That is to say that, because the failure to neutralise a threat to child

143 Bourdieu, above n 1.

144 However, unlike the Faulkner case, in these cases there is a strong presence of police intervention prior to the killing in which the police failed to neutralise the violence.

145 Ch 1: Jubilee Soprano.

146 Ibid.

endangerment perpetuates the existing violence, the failure to neutralise is argued to be *part* of the violence. This echoes Wilson's argument about the state's passive, complicit role as protector and as *in loco parentis*,[147] or substitute 'parent', which is one of the interactive forces central in shaping the outcomes of the violence in these cases.

Conclusion

In sum, this chapter has argued that certain forms and expressions of violence towards children are hidden behind masks and are symbolic. Although in the cases discussed the violence was not perceived or understood as an indicator of potential filicide, it can be seen as risking child endangerment when the mask of the loving parent and/or the dysfunctional layers are peeled away. In these cases, the violence was masked such that it was not perceived as an indicator of lethal violence to the children. This lack of recognition needs to be addressed. Crucial to establishing this misrecognition is an understanding that the mask of the loving parent and the different expressions of violence, physical and symbolic, must be better understood in order to define the nature and context of filicidal violence to children.

The symbol of the parent as owner, disciplinarian and loving/devoted parent in the child neglect cases, such as those of Hannah Bromley and Greta Sheng, exemplifies the way this particular type of representation of the parent is used against the child, and masks the symbolic rejection of the child by the parents. In these and the cases of Mark and Libby, Paul and Isabel, Danny Burrow and Horace Faulkner, a closer examination of the perpetrators' language reveals their deep sense of parental ownership, control and entitlement. Drawing on the perverted symbol of parental ownership in these cases, it is argued that ownership can be used as a form of violence against the child.

The reader might consider the symbol of the rejected child in contrast to the good and whole child. In a symbolic sense, it is argued that the state can also be seen as rejecting the child in a similar way by responding inappropriately to recorded concerns of violence. The symbol of the child rejected by the family runs in parallel to the neglect by the state *in loco parentis*, as seen in the Mark and Libby, Paul and Isabel and Danny Burrow cases, where the failure or absence of intervention had a role in the construction and perpetuation of the subsequent violence. The risks of child endangerment in every family are risks for both the parents and the state.[148] In the Sheng case, the court stated unequivocally that

147 The state steps in as *in loco parentis* (or substitute 'parent') or guardian when the functionality of the parents fails. In these cases, there is an assumption of guardianship responsibilities by the state that include the power to make decisions on behalf of the child with secondary regard to the familial unit: sections 8, 9, 36(c), 43, 48, 233, 49 CYP Act.

148 The role and significance of the state, as *in loco parentis*, in enabling the state of dysfunction in the family, and/or the crisis, by not neutralising the existing risks of child

'the protection of children is of fundamental importance to society'.[149] The symbolism of the vulnerable and innocent child permeates every level of society, and hence violence towards children violates the fundamental duty on both individuals and state agents to protect them.

---

endangerment are further discussed in Chapters 6 and 7. This position is also in line with the national framework on protecting children, which outlines a responsibility shared by both the state and the community: Council of Australian Governments, *Protecting Children is Everyone's Business: National Framework for Protecting Australia's Children 2009–2020* (Australian Government, Canberra, 2009) 8.

149 *R v Gerald Sheng*; *R v Caitlin Sheng*, above n 111.

3 Mythical representations

From myth to law

Introduction

Until the recent development of the 'best interest of the child' principle, the symbol of the child was seldom seen as distinct from that of the parent. Parent representations have been the central symbols in filicide mythology and in the law. This chapter examines the presence of mythologised representation in filicide perpetrator representations in the law. It discusses the representations of two Greek myths – Medea and Heracles – in Western culture, both of which involve parents killing their children. The purpose of this chapter is to demonstrate the symbolism of certain time-honoured representations of the parent and the child. Straddling myth and reality, this chapter charts the developing presence of these representations and posits one of the book's key themes – parental ownership,[1] or proprietorship, towards children – as relevant, universal and inextricably tied to the notion of duty in the social and legal sense. Parent representations in these two myths are discussed at some length in order to draw out the subtext of parental ownership of children. The reader may come to realise, as will be pointed out, that myth and law are mainly constructions of patriarchy. The chapter also introduces the theme of patriarchal dysfunction (which is picked up in Chapter 6), taking the reader through the developing representation of female perpetrators in the law on infanticide. In this book, patriarchal dysfunction refers to a situation in which the male's assumed right to authority and ownership is challenged but is reaffirmed in extreme cases by a parental claim to the right to kill their children. In the cases, the tenacity of the male's reassertion of authority leading to the collapse creates a state of dysfunctionality which impacts on the safety and well-being of the children.

1 Throughout this book there are reminders that ownership refers to ownership in the social and not legal sense. Parental ownership in this book refers to the sense of control and entitlement, social and physical, over children. This chapter postulates that such a sense of ownership might arise from existing legal obligations towards the child, such as financial payments for maintenance, or it might arise from the patriarchal belief in male proprietary attitude towards one's wife and children.

Before delving into the myths, it is noted that myth and law share one characteristic: they are unifying and transcendental traditions that bind society together.[2] Fitzpatrick contends that it is possible to trace remnants of myth in the law since modern law has its basis in Judaeo-Christian mythology, which is characterised by the dominance of the Father.[3] This is supported by Lerner's contention that the father's ownership of their wives and children is a condition of patriarchy.[4] Fitzpatrick argues that law negates the mythical realm, which it initially relies upon, and its denial allows law to mythologise itself.[5] His insightful observation of the law is the basis upon which this chapter is built. The chapter begins with an introduction to the Greek myths of Medea and Heracles. Here, the theme of parental ownership of children is discussed in relation to the children's subordinate statuses as inseparable from their parents. Following this, the chapter relies on Fitzpatrick's argument to make the link between myth and law by arguing that the law develops legal archetypes (of the filicide perpetrator) that are based on mythologised representations. It is argued that these archetypes are sustained through the law's autonomous, self-legitimating nature in its judicial narratives.[6] The second part of the chapter looks at the development of the law on infanticide, which, the book argues, constructed the filicidal female perpetrator archetype. The law is critiqued as representing and stereotyping female perpetrators as weak – as the 'Other' – and susceptible to their biological reproductive systems.

The chapter then proceeds to present archetypal representations of parent perpetrators from the cases in order to supplement the overarching argument – filicidal representations, while of a socio-legal nature, are myth-like because of their inherent contradictions. Representations of filicidal perpetrators have been sustained and legitimated in the law, media and social narratives. For instance, as a mask can reveal and conceal at the same time,[7] the perpetrators can sometimes be concealed behind the mask by a dominant representation such as by their repositioning as 'aberrations'[8] in society, or they can be revealed as false representors by the court. The chapter concludes with the observation that the prominence of children in the cases and in the myths has been mystified. This observation is further developed in the final chapter, which will draw together some insights on the representation of the child in the family and in the law.

2 Peter Fitzpatrick, *The Mythology of Modern Law* (Routledge, 1992) xii, 9–10.
3 Ibid chs 1, 11, 25, 55.
4 Gerda Lerner, *The Creation of Patriarchy* (Oxford University Press, 1986) 217.
5 Fitzpatrick, above n 3.
6 Ibid 3–9. See also Gunther Teubner, *Law as an Autopoietic System* (Blackwell, 1993) 35.
7 The masking function of representation is further discussed in Chapter 5.
8 Ania Wilczynski, *Child Homicide* (Oxford University Press, 1997) 144. See also Paul Wilson, *Murder of the Innocents: Child-Killers and their Victims* (Rigby, 1985) 32.

Mythology

Myths represent many things – natural phenomena, absolute truth, mental patterns, and so on. Myths can be conceptualised as allegories and/or personifications of animate and inanimate forces, which transcend everyday notions of time and space.[9] Myths are sometimes told and enacted to entertain and to illustrate a particular morality. Their conclusions are left open-ended to allow the audience to formulate their own opinions. The characters in myths are supernatural beings;[10] when they are enacted, the actors wear costumes and sometimes masks to conceal their faces. In this way, myths are gentle in that they tell stories and may even go so far as to reflect an aspect of reality, but do not fully represent reality.[11] Myths can be conceptualised as symbolic, primordial,[12] allegorical representations because their messages and meanings create a filter between the realms of the symbolic and the real and/or between 'inner' (the subject) and 'outer' (the object) life.[13] Myths can traverse realms because they are 'provinces of meaning detached from everyday life and endowed with a peculiar reality of their own'.[14] Their symbolism lies in their meaning and representation, and in the power of storytelling. As such, they have been defined as oral or written testaments that directly or indirectly present a description of a cultural and social crisis or phenomenon; their narrative often involves supernatural or imaginary elements and characters.[15] Looking at the Medea and Heracles myths, it becomes apparent that mythologised violence appears as acceptable because they remain in the realm of the symbolic, the supernatural and the divine. In reality, however, the violence is unacceptable socially, morally and legally speaking. While the reception of violence in myth does not parallel reality, the archetype parent in myth, as will be shown, contains some parallels to the parent stereotype in reality. This parallelling is important because mythologised representations, as will be argued, are relevant to the judicial narrative in explaining the nature and execution of filicidal violence in the cases.

9 Legend is a type of myth. Unlike myths, legends have some historical basis steeped in the human past about great deeds of human heroes and heroines; myths are stories handed down orally and represent the universal in that their meanings have collective importance for society as a whole and not merely for the individual: Barry B Powell, *Classical Myths* (Pearson Education, 5th ed, 2001) 2–10.

10 Mircea Eliade, *Myth and Reality* (William R Trask trans, Harper & Row, 1963) 5–6.

11 Ibid 8–10.

12 Ibid 11, 18.

13 Ibid 75–91. Also see Mircea Eliade, *Myths, Dreams and Mysteries* (Philip Mairet trans, Harper & Row, 1975) 23–38 [trans of: *Mythes, Rêves et Mystères* (first published 1960)].

14 Peter Berger and Thomas Luckmann, *The Social Construction of Reality: A Treatise in the Sociology of Knowledge* (Doubleday, 1966) 89.

15 René Girard, *The Scapegoat* (Johns Hopkins University Press, 1986) 24.

Myth-making

Myth-making is a form of symbolic action that is an important tenet of society, used to create meaning and centralised on the enforceability of morals. In the contexts of mythology and law, myth-making can be seen as a means by which complex phenomena are explained, as well as a way to action rights and protections for minorities.[16] In mythology, myth-making is about the search to understand the complexity of relationships at the level of human and divine, and one way to do this is to weave a story for the audience in order for them to make sense of the morals, so that they can be edified by them. The process of myth-making involves not just the creation but also the interaction of representation and symbols that give meaningful insights and convey messages to the audience. On a symbolic level, when the myth is enacted, myth-making utilises dramaturgical devices such as masks to convey meanings of representations and symbols; masks both reveal and conceal meaning.

Myth-making is relevant because it provides a means by which to uncover the meanings of symbols and representation. The utility of the Medea and Heracles myths, for example, is that they contextualise the discussions of the loving father representation to follow. Myth-making is deeply symbolic not only because of the way the process legitimises certain representations and key symbols, but also because its interaction with these representations creates a particular meaning around morality, which then becomes a way to give meaning to the inexplicable. The storytelling process of imparting morality to an audience through fictional characters reveals an underlying need for uniting different groups in society with dominant stories, symbols and representations. Particular to this purpose of myth-making is the morality around parental relations. Greek myths, in particular the ones discussed here, are created out of patriarchal ideology, which locates the father at the centre of the family and society, specifically the symbol of the state that is predicated on the archetypal Father symbol as revealed by Greek and Judaeo-Christian mythologies. Myth-making creates an enriched understanding of the symbolic importance of symbols, such as the Father archetype, and legitimises a particular meaning for it by universalising the symbol through storytelling. The analysis and discussions of the loving father representation and symbol in Chapters 2 and 6 reveal the complexity of parental love. The symbol of love can be celebrated, yet equally it can endanger the child by a distortion and perversion of its meaning. This distortion can only be understood through an appreciation of the myth-making behind the symbol.

In other representations found in mythology, such as the vengeful spouse or the silent child, it is important to note the centrality of representation as promoting particular meanings and revealing differential power relations and tensions between parents, and between parent and child. Myth-making reveals this process to be layered and complex because social roles are situated behind

16 Judith Bessant and Rob Watts, 'History, Myth Making and Young People in a Time of Change' (1998) 49 *Family Matters* 5–10, 7.

dominant symbols, which are deeply embedded in society. For the social analyst, filicide reveals the power of symbols and the possibility of endangerment for the child when these symbols are reversed and perverted. More importantly, such an interactionist understanding provides a framework within which to explain the failure of state intervention (as discussed more fully in Chapter 6) and reasons why risks to the child in the cases were not adequately identified, addressed or understood.

In the myths of Medea and Heracles, the audience is presented with dramatic and tragic events exemplifying representation of good and evil. The characters are complex, and while they reflect human characteristics they also embody elements of divine powers. Medea, for example, is represented as a witch and mother, while Heracles is represented as a superhuman hero with divine origins. The symbols of witch and divinity reconnect the audience with the primordial, and the characters' humanness bridges the realms of the symbolic and the real so that the audience can relate to them. Myth-making in the sense discussed below creates meanings around universal symbols and representations, and some of these are unwrapped in the analysis to follow, in order to reveal myths' relevance to the law.

The myths: Medea and Heracles

There are two very powerful and well-known myths in Greek mythology[17] which contain mythologised filicide perpetrators:

- The myth of Medea in the story of Jason and the Golden Fleece, which has over centuries represented the tragic and murderous element in a jilted union, and the depth of emotions in a woman scorned.
- The myth of Heracles, which has over centuries represented the powerful union between the divine and the mortal. More significantly, the myth represents an aspect of Roman law, historically the Roman *paterfamilias* – a father's legal right of life and death over his children.

The first of these myths is told in one of Euripides' plays, *Medea*.[18] Medea represents many things to many people.[19] In the play, Medea is portrayed as a foreigner[20] and as a disillusioned woman with genuine emotions of despair,

17 Greek myths were chosen for this chapter because they, more than others, are rich in their stories about dysfunctional families and parenting. Additionally, Greek myths are popular and resonate in Western popular culture. More importantly, they demonstrate key themes in the cases, particularly patriarchal ideology and endangerment to children.
18 Euripides, *Medea and Other Plays* (Philip Vellacott trans, Penguin Books, 1963) 17–61.
19 Powell, above n 9, 519.
20 Donald Mastronarde (ed), *Euripides Medea* (Cambridge University Press, 2002) 22–28.

sorrow, rage, jealousy and doubt following Jason's betrayal.[21] In Seneca's version of the same myth, Medea is represented as a cold, bloodthirsty sorceress.[22] The tragedy begins with the flourish of love, passion and hope between Medea and Jason but ends in Medea's bitter revenge on Jason and the murder of their children. This is a story about a woman's jealousy and revenge following her husband's betrayal of their marriage. The story unfolds as follows: Medea, daughter of the King of Colchis, sorceress and heroine, leaves home (and her father) to help Jason acquire the Golden Fleece. After Medea and Jason acquire the fleece, they flee Colchis with Medea's brother in pursuit. Medea then lures her brother into a trap and Jason kills him. Following their escape, Medea marries Jason and from their union two children are born. Soon after, Jason meets Glauce, daughter of Creon, the ruler of Corinth. Jason then plans to forsake Medea and becomes betrothed to Glauce. When Medea hears this, she is furious. Creon notices Medea's rage and banishes her, but she pleads for one extra day. Medea is reproached by Jason, who chastises her for not submitting to the sovereign power, and for having provoked her sentence by her own violent temper. In reply, Medea reminds Jason of what she has done for him – helped him acquire the Golden Fleece, assisted him to win his battles, betrayed her own father and people, murdered Pelias (the King) – all these, she has done for his sake. Unknown to Jason, Medea has already secured her escape plan with Aegeus, ruler of Athens, who has promised her refuge. Medea then turns her thoughts to vengeance. Medea first begs Jason's forgiveness. She despatches poison robes disguised as wedding gifts for Glauce. Glauce wears them and dies, and Creon too is poisoned when he tries to save her. In a dramatic finale, Medea leads her sons to the house and murders them. Jason arrives too late to save the children. In their final confrontation, Jason curses Medea while he mourns for the dead children.

In both variations of the myth, Medea is constructed as a woman who feels she has ownership and entitlement over the children. Like Horace, Medea sees the children as 'property'[23] belonging to her and as pawns she could use against Jason 'to break [his] heart'.[24] She does not deny that her ultimate purpose is to 'work revenge on Jason'[25] for his betrayal. For example she says:

21 Harry Hine, *Seneca Medea* (Aris & Phillips, 2000) 10–11.
22 Ibid.
23 Here, the notion of children as 'property' refers to ownership in the social sense, not the legal sense. This perception was also noted by Adams, who argues, using the context of Medea to illuminate the nature of child residence (custody) disputes, 'children are necessary to men, generally as property or as an affirmation of their masculinity. Thus, the vengeful woman wreaks vengeance, ultimately, by destroying a man's masculinity': Michele A Adams, 'Framing Contests in Child Custody Disputes: Parental Alienation Syndrome, Child Abuse, Gender, and Fathers' Rights' (2006–2007) 40 *Family Law Quarterly* 315–338, 327.
24 Euripides, above n 18, 59–60.
25 Ibid 25.

I will kill my sons.
No one shall take my children from me. When I have made
Jason's whole house a shambles, I will leave Corinth
A murderess, flying from my darling children's blood.
Yes, I can endure guilt; however horrible;
The laughter of my enemies I will not endure.[26]

Medea justifies her killing by using her enemies as a reference point: 'I'll never leave sons of mine to be the victims of my enemies' rage'.[27] Medea appears more concerned about her enemies and their mocking her than the children's security and well-being. Undoubtedly, Medea is worried that the children will be ill-treated by Creon and Glauce if she leaves them behind. Medea's acceptance of guilt reveals the children's status was not as important to her as her enemies' perception and mockery, while simultaneously acknowledging the horror of her intended killings.[28] By appearing to be worried about her enemies' treatment of the children and her reputation, she appears to use her enemies to justify the killing of the children.[29] The justification enables her to cast a sympathetic reinterpretation on herself,[30] and the murder to follow, for the audience. This means that she is able to justify the killing of the children by reinterpreting the killing in a sympathetic fashion, such as arguing that the killing is necessary or the better of two evils, in order to make the killing appear acceptable to herself and the audience. Medea next reveals the true motive for the children's murder, which is to use the children as tools of revenge against Jason:

Now let things take their course. What use is life to me?
I have no land, no home, no refuge from despair . . . when I
Was ready to desert my father's house, won over
By eloquence from a Greek, whom with God's help I now
Will punish, he shall never see alive again
The sons he had from me.[31]

Here Medea explains that this is the only way to 'deal Jason the deepest wound',[32] that is, to punish Jason by inflicting on him the maximum amount

26 Ibid 41.
27 Ibid 50. For a different rendition, see Euripides, *Medea* (online) (E P Coleridge trans, ebooks@Adelaide, last updated 28 August 2010) at Ebooks@Adelaide http://ebooks.adelaide.edu.au/e/euripides/medea/: 'never will I hand my children over to their foes to mock and flout'.
28 Ibid.
29 Ibid 49.
30 Ibid 55. Medea hardens herself to prepare for the killing and simultaneously pleads for the audience's sympathy, saying 'Life has been cruel to me'. Sympathetic reinterpretation is discussed in this chapter as a technique of explaining and justifying a horrific crime or deed to make it appear acceptable to the perpetrator.
31 Ibid 41–42.
32 Ibid.

of pain through the death of the children. There is a polarisation of Medea's representation in the play: as a devoted mother and as a manipulative, powerful witch. Medea appears to be socially and symbolically transformed once the knowledge of betrayal dawns on her. Her symbolic transformation is reflected in the emotions she oscillates between – rage, anger, pity, betrayal and grief – which are suggestive of the momentous and morally challenging task she has chosen to undertake. Her social transformation is from her social role as devoted mother to murderess. How did she accomplish that? The chorus gives the audience an insight into Medea's tumultuous state of mind and the dramatic transformation she is undergoing:

> Where will you find hardness of purpose?
> How will you build resolution in hand or heart
> To face horror without flinching?
> When the moment comes, and you look at them –
> The moment for you to assume the role of murderess –
> How will you do it?
> When your sons kneel to you for pity,
> Will you stain your fingers with their blood?
> Your heart will melt; you will know you cannot.

The chorus reveals that Medea would have to wear ('assume') the mask ('role') of the hard-hearted murderess in order to be able to commit the murder. Following this, Medea does indeed don several masks to change appearances: from rational (towards Jason by asking for forgiveness),[33] to loving (towards the children to lure them to her),[34] and to cold and heartless (during the killing of Glauce and the children).[35] Like Lady Macbeth, Medea invokes the supernatural/divine deities of Themis and Artemis, daughter of Zeus, to enable her plea for revenge, that is, to 'see Jason and his bride ground to pieces in their shattered palace',[36] and to help her overcome her gender frailties. In between these different role transformations, Medea plays the part of grieving spouse, constantly referring to her pain even while she despatches the poisonous gifts to Glauce. The fact that she uses the children and the appearance of their innocence to send the deadly gifts to Glauce reveals her deceptiveness and her ability to use the children as tools for achieving her ultimate revenge. After Medea kills the children, she confirms the ascription of her 'otherness', as Colchian sorceress.[37] On a symbolic level, the killing of the children represents a rejection of her maternal instincts and of her betrayed marriage. Fundamental to all this is that Medea has no doubt that her children are hers to do with as she pleases.

33 Ibid 43–44.
34 Ibid 46, 48–50.
35 Ibid 41, 52, 55–56.
36 Ibid 22.
37 Mastronarde, above n 20, 15.

Medea's 'otherness', representing the elements of deviousness and deviance, has since developed in medical literature as the 'Medea complex',[38] which refers to parental entitlement to use violence on the children as a form of revenge directed towards the opposite spouse. From this, the Medea complex has been termed 'spousal revenge'[39] or 'retaliated killings' in the criminological literature.[40] The Medea complex does not only refer to women; it can also apply to men who do the same. For example, in the Faulkner case, as discussed later in this chapter, Horace killed the children to exact revenge on Melissa, who he saw as the culprit who was taking the children away from him.[41]

On an academic, cultural and social level, early representations and stories of Medea have pervaded, on some conscious or unconscious level, our collective consciousness and knowledge about filicide in Western culture. For example, the Medea myth has, over time, given voice to certain dominant values and gender stereotypes in Western society, such as the practice of monogamy in marriage; the taboo of adultery, which is a ground for divorce in most common-law countries; and the characteristics of spousal betrayal.[42] This is to say that mythology has a deep symbolic and constitutive role in organising society. It could be argued that the construction of Medea has had a role in falsely shaping the stereotype of women as vindictive and angry in acrimonious divorce proceedings.

And yet Medea appeals to the timeless imagery of the deviant mother archetype in mythology and judicial narratives to some extent. Deviant women, especially women who kill their children, are often represented as non-maternal and either

38 Edward Stern, 'The Medea Complex: The Mother's Homicidal Wishes to Her Child' (1948) 94(395) *Journal of Mental Science* 321–331, 321. For example, in the Burrow case study, Saskia was medically assessed as possibly showing signs of the Medea complex: report 'SB5' taken on 23 November 2001 from Dr Tijuana in New South Wales, prison X. Her killing of Danny was contextualised by the psychiatrist as retaliation against the men in her life who had harmed her.

39 Phillip Resnick, 'Child Murder by Parents: A Psychiatric Review of Filicide' (1969) 126(3) *American Journal of Psychiatry* 325–334, 330.

40 Above n 8, 45.

41 For a recent unreported case, see Amelia Bentley, 'Mother Gets Life Sentence for Killing Children', *Sydney Morning Herald* (online), 24 November 2010 www.smh.com.au/queensland/mother-gets-life-sentence-for-killing-children-20100224-p2yo.html.

42 For instance, the phrase 'Hell hath no fury like a woman scorned' is a well-known idiom in popular culture that generally stereotypes vengeful women in Medea-like situations: Adams, above n 23, 327, 328. The phrase originated from playwright William Congreve, see William Congreve, *The Mourning Bride: A Tragedy* (Dodo Press, 2008). The phrase was then applied to the Medean context of the pathology of a vengeful mother's attempt to sever the father–child bond by using the child to revenge the injury inflicted on her by the father or ex-spouse: J W Jacobs, 'Euripides' Medea: A Psychodynamic Model of Severe Divorce Pathology' (1988) 42(2) *American Journal of Psychotherapy* 308–319.

mad and/or bad,[43] in direct contradistinction to the Universal Mother. The social and conceptual dichotomised representation of deviant women into 'either/or' roles, for example 'Madonna' and 'whore', has been pervasive in ancient and modern cultures.[44] While it is possible to juxtapose qualities of good and bad, and/or mad, in the mythological deviant mother, it is very rare to do the same in reality.[45] An example of this juxtaposition in mythology is the painting by Delacroix of the half-naked Medea holding a dagger in one hand and her two wriggling children in the other hand. This layered representation symbolises the duality of the forces of creation and destruction in the Mother symbol. It represents the complexity in the violence of emotion and the brutality in destruction, which is juxtaposed against nurturance, protection and devotion, qualities associated with motherhood and representative of creation and birth. The juxtaposition of these polarising forces in this painting reveals the dichotomy in the Mother archetype and in the representation of filicidal women, where the dichotomy is particularly apparent.[46] The stereotype is 'holy motherhood', in which mothers are expected to act always in a loving, warm, selfless and protective manner towards their children.[47] Reneging on this 'holy mother' stereotype results in the imposition of the deviant label, which categorises the deviant as the 'Other',[48] such as happened in the case of Susan Smith[49] in the United States.

The 'holy mother' is a patriarchal stereotype which can be traced back to the symbol of the iconic Madonna, whose representation across cultures stands for,

43 Ania Wilczynski, 'Images of Women Who Kill Their Infants: The Mad and the Bad' (1991) 2(2) *Women & Criminal Justice* 71–88, 72. Also see F Heidensohn, *Women and Crime* (Macmillan, 1985) 90–96; P Pattullo, *Judging Women* (National Council for Civil Liberties, 1983) 8–9; and Wilczynski, above n 8, 118.

44 Sarah Pomeroy, *Goddesses, Whores, Wives and Slaves: Women in Classical Antiquity* (Schocken Books, 1975) 8; and Anne Summers, *Damned Whores and God's Police* (Penguin Books, 1994) 313. Also see Heidensohn, ibid 90; and Susan S M Edwards, 'Neither Bad Nor Mad: The Female Violent Offender Reassessed' (1986) 9(1) *Women's Studies International Forum* 79–87, 82–84.

45 An example of such a rare instance, as argued, is the case of Melanie Drummond, which is discussed in the following section and in Chapter 5.

46 Wilczynski, above n 8, 73. Also see Edwards, above n 44.

47 M D Pagelow, *Family Violence* (Praeger, 1984) 184–185.

48 Simone de Beauvoir, *The Second Sex* (Vintage, 1997) 16–29.

49 Susan Smith confessed to killing her two children and was convicted of murder, and sentenced to life imprisonment. The community argued that the death penalty should be imposed. Media representation of Smith was negative and there was a 'lynch-mob' atmosphere in which angry crowds screamed at Smith at her first court appearance. It was later pointed out that Smith was reviled because she violated sacrosanct views about families and mothering such that her crime represented 'the mother of all crimes', and her so doing made the community feel vulnerable: R Grant, 'Mother of All Crimes', *Sydney Morning Herald* (New South Wales), 11 March 1995, Section V, 1, 6A; and A Gordon, 'Murder Most Foul', *Daily Telegraph Mirror* (Australia), 24 July 1995, 11. A factor that compounded Smith's crime was that before the crime she had appeared to be a 'good mother': Wilczynski, above n 8, 133–134.

provides and supplements culturally acceptable images and stereotypes of the good mother. The symbol of the Madonna nursing the child Christ at her breast connotes an image of humility, chastity and nurturance, all qualities associated with good motherhood.[50] Given the significance and meaning of the Virgin Mary in the theological context, it suffices to say that the representation of Madonna and child embodies a profound and visual symbol in Western cultural and social milieu, which is the sublime message that a mother's place is with her child. According to Gold, the representation of Madonna as Mary has developed over time to encompass images of tenderness, graciousness, humaneness, intimacy and solemness.[51] The humility of the Madonna's representation alongside the adult Christ – whose posture is erect while Mary is bent further over – symbolises the man's authority over his wife.[52] Although the opposite of the Medea figure, this Madonna symbolisation is also one based on patriarchy; it is suggestive of a state, structure or system, of hierarchical organisation that requires domination and submission and is pervasive and elemental.

Both mythological representations, then, arose out of patriarchal construction. It is noteworthy that the story of Medea is far more engaging and dramatic than that of Heracles when the focus is on the killing of the children. This observation sheds light on the male construction of the deviant woman stereotype and her characteristics, such as irrationality and pathology.[53] In the next section it will be argued that this male construct and symbol took on a special relevance to women in general when it became enshrined in one of the earliest laws on infanticide. The categories, such as 'villain' and 'hero',[54] used here must be recognised as social constructs for the purposes of making the argument. Such dichotomised categories, even though portrayed in popular culture as being distinct and separate, are really not different from each other. Just like great heroes in Greek mythology, such as Zeus, the Father symbol in Western Christian mythology possesses both 'villain' (negative) and 'hero' (positive) qualities. The 'negative' qualities are generally played down or are portrayed as part of a strong male character, such as 'righteous anger', in popular representations of this symbol.

The normative male archetype in mythology is far more ambiguous than the female.[55] To a child, the father archetype encompasses a hero/divine and daemon-

50 Penny Schine Gold, *The Lady and the Virgin: Image, Attitude and Experience in Twelfth-Century France* (University of Chicago Press, 1985) 64. Later in the Middle Ages, her humility is increasingly emphasised. This is evidenced in the art of that period showing her on her knees before Christ. Also see Beth Williamson, *The Madonna of Humility: Development, Dissemination and Reception, c.1349–1400* (Boydell Press, 2009) 132–148.

51 Ibid 66.

52 Ibid 65.

53 Wilczynski, above n 43.

54 For Jung, these two symbols structure a person's libido or unconscious structure of the psyche: Carl Jung, *Aspects of the Masculine* (R F C Hull trans, Routledge, 2003) ch 1, 1 [first published 1989].

55 R W Connell, *Masculinities* (University of California Press, 2nd ed, 2005) 12–15.

type figure.[56] The positive father archetype in Western mythologies usually has two main characteristics: paternal qualities, such as a loving, sacrificial and protective nature; and heroic qualities, such as authority, power and strength, as demonstrated in both the Zeus figure and the Judaeo-Christian God.[57] Yet ambiguity emerges, as both are also vengeful and punitive. They are portrayed at times as demanding the wholesale slaughter of people and the deaths of innocents as a sign of loyalty. And the heroic qualities are characteristics also found in a stereotypical male hero archetype such as Heracles. It is notable that that power lies at the centre of both positive and negative father archetypes. An example of patriarchal power in the positive father archetype is the importance of the Roman paterfamilias to Judaeo-Christian mythology.[58] In the negative father archetype, such as the male villain, representations of power revolve around the desire for control and dominance, although these qualities are often held up also as positive male traits.[59] In popular culture, the deviant counterpart to the hero, such as the Devil, developed quite late in religious history. He is usually portrayed as having characteristics that the positive father archetype of the early Christian centuries does not normally possess, such as an aggressive and violent disposition,[60] the ability to be manipulative and a capacity for great evil.[61] Over time, the male deviant, delinquent or villain became increasingly romanticised in popular culture.[62]

In filicide mythology there is one main fallen but divine and mortal hero, Heracles, who, in terms of this book, straddles the image of the filicidal perpetrator and the redeemed hero. Heracles is technically not a villain, and nor is he known as one, because legend has it that he performed many good deeds for humanity, including ridding the human world of monstrous beasts through the performance of his 12 labours. These labours were undertaken after he murdered his wife and children in a fit of madness inflicted on him by the goddess Hera, Heracles' stepmother. The labours represent a form of punishment and expiation for this

56 Jung, above n 54, 74–77.

57 Ibid 73. Also see James George Frazer, *The Golden Bough: A New Abridgement* (Oxford University Press, first published 1994, 2009 ed) 673–674; and Joseph Campbell, *Myths To Live By* (Penguin, first published 1972, 1993 ed) ch VIII, 149, 154, 156–158.

58 Ibid.

59 Carl Schmitt, *The Leviathan in the State Theory of Thomas Hobbes: Meaning and Failure of a Political Symbol* (George Schwab and Erna Hilfstein trans, University of Chicago Press, 2008) 22–23 [trans of: *Leviathan in der Staatslehre des Thomas Hobbes* (first published 1938)].

60 In the context of familial and non-familial homicide, Alder and Polk argue that most male perpetrators who commit filicide usually resort to aggression and violence as solutions to existing problems: Christine M Alder and Kenneth Polk, 'Masculinity and Child Homicide' (1996) 36(3) *British Journal of Criminology* 396–411, 399–400.

61 Carl Schmitt, above n 59.

62 Ibid. See also Judith Allen, 'The "Masculinity" of Criminality and Criminology: Interrogating Some Impasses' in Mark Findlay and Russell Hogg (eds), *Understanding Crime and Criminal Justice* (Law Book Company, 1988) ch 1, 1–24, 10.

atrocity. Even though Heracles is generally regarded as a hero, he is flawed. In his life, he committed terrible crimes followed by humiliating expiation. He sought atonement for violating two sacred human codes – the first for the murder of his family and the second for killing his guest Iphitus. Additionally, Heracles died a horrible death. After he died, he was apotheosised by the gods for the completion of his labours.

Such is the standard version of the story, but Euripides, in his play *Heracles*, tells the story in a different order. Heracles' 12 labours come before his madness and the murder of his family.[63] He then finishes his labours and returns home to find his family taking refuge from the tyrant Lycus. Heracles rescues his family but then the madness, sent by Hera and her agents, strikes and causes him to murder his wife and children. The remainder of the play shows Heracles regaining consciousness and sanity, and confronting the full horror of his actions. In this version, it seems Heracles is first portrayed as a great hero at the peak of his success and good fortune before his catastrophic downfall. Euripides' technique, in reversing the order of the labours, is to emphasise the effect of madness on Heracles' mind and life, and to show how little the effect of the expectation of divine justice is justified.[64] Euripides' play appears to focus more on human suffering and compassion than on Heracles' heroic prowess.[65] It is as if Euripides wants to show the humanness in Heracles in contrast to his divine aspect, and against divinity itself. Arguably, Euripides intended to expose the antagonism between human nature and divine intervention.

There are two important representations to take from the Heracles myth. The first is the representation of physical violence, which emerges from Heracles' madness. Throughout the story of Heracles, there is an ever present sense that the theme of physical violence is deeply interwoven in Heracles' life. The theme of physical violence is portrayed as an extension of masculinity and strength in Heracles, such that, even when the gods choose to destroy him by inducing madness, they do so through patterns of behaviour that are already characteristic of Heracles' disposition.[66] It is noteworthy that the representation of male physical violence, such as illustrated by the killings of Heracles as a means of achieving masculinity, or as an unpremeditated act, has been associated with male filicidal perpetrators.[67] But such representations often do not adequately reflect the diversity of violent filicidal scenarios.[68] The second important representation is the portrayal of madness as incapacitating reason. For instance, the character Madness in Euripides' play says, '[T]he slayer will not know that

63 Powell, above n 9, 378, 380. Also see Euripides, *Heracles and Other Plays* (John Davie trans, Penguin Books, 1963) 3–6.
64 Ibid 4.
65 Ibid 5.
66 Shirley Barlow, *Euripides' Heracles* (Aris & Phillips, 1981) 1.
67 Above n 60, 396.
68 Ibid 409.

he has killed his own until he is free of my frenzy'.[69] The effect of the extended description of Heracles' madness, including his composure as 'a different man',[70] develops the conception of madness as a malignant and dominating influence that dispossesses a person's normal capacity for reason, awareness and consciousness. Two schools of thought emerged in early Western representations of madness. Following Hippocrates and Plato, madness has been seen as having organic and social origins.[71] In the Middles Ages and the Renaissance, when the church was the most influential force in society, madness was believed to be an affliction from supernatural forces such as demonic possession.[72] In summary, then, Heracles is portrayed sympathetically as a hero who has been taken over by madness sent by Hera, whereas Medea is portrayed as a manipulative and wicked woman (the opposite of the good mother) who is in her right mind when she kills her children.

In the context of filicide, both representations that emerge from the myths will be shown to have some bearing on the cases and the law. The focus of the next section is broadly on the representation of madness and its relevance in the law, especially in early infanticide legislation, which is discussed in the subsequent section. Additionally, the discussion uncovers the relevance of the archetypal Mother and Father symbols when applied to understandings on filicide in the law and the judicial narratives of the perpetrators and the killings.

Developing socio-legal archetypes

Myths take on universal characteristics because they elevate the everyday to the level of universality.[73] Quite often, a social institution in a dominant position, such as the law, creates a myth in the image of the present to lend sanctity, rightness and legitimacy to its actions undertaken in the present.[74] One way for the law to achieve this moral, social and legal legitimacy is to attribute the existence of a myth or image to the divine or to give it supernatural symbolic status or both, and then to mythologise its own legal text.[75] The juxtaposition of the parent perpetrator representation against a fixed symbol such as the Universal Mother, or the good and holy mother, allows the law to categorise and

69 Euripides, above n 63, 29.

70 Ibid 31.

71 For example, see Hippocrates, *On the Sacred Disease* (Francis Adams trans, The Internet Classics Archive) http://classics.mit.edu//Hippocrates/sacred.html.

72 Craig B Little, *Deviance and Control: Theory, Research and Social Policy* (Peacock, 3rd ed, 1995) ch 4, 103–104.

73 Peter Halder, 'Myth-Understood' (Spring 1994) 5(1) *Law and Critique* 113–123, 114.

74 Nandini Rao, 'Interpreting Silences: Symbol and History in the Case of Ram Janmabhoomi/Babri Masjid' in George Clement Bond and Angela Gilliam (eds), *Social Construction of the Past: Representations as Power* (Routledge, 1994) 160.

75 Halder, above n 73; and Fitzpatrick, above n 2, ch 2, 41, ch 6, 210.

explain inexplicable behaviour as 'otherness', and to partake in its own myth-making.[76] From this, the legal archetype of the good versus the bad parent is conceived. That is, legal archetypes of the good and bad parent can be remotely located in the archetypal mother and father symbols. By measuring the parent perpetrator against the legal archetype, direct references can be made with regard to the mythology of the legal archetype. So, mythologised socio-legal symbols act as a means of interpreting the perpetrator's unacceptable and inexplicable killing of their child.

It could be argued that the law takes from the myths of Heracles and Medea the characteristics of the deviant perpetrator, which are conceived and shaped accordingly. These pre-Christian mythological characteristics are evident in most early societies along with patriarchal values and have been appropriated by more recent religious and cultural traditions such as Christianity. From the Judaeo-Christian mythology, the law adopts and develops for its purposes the characteristics of the good Father and Mother symbols, which have been applied universally.[77] In the following section, the discussion will centre on the development of parent archetypes in the law, with a particular focus on the characteristics of the deviant parent as demonstrated by the cases. This section also examines the role of madness (or in legal terminology 'insanity', and its successors, better known now as mental disorders) in shaping the deviant parent archetype in the law.[78] It begins with a discussion of early social developments that led to laws in England designed to curb child killing, and later the codification of the concept of madness in the development and evolution of infanticide legislation. As this is not a historical account, the section only summarises the social and cultural representation and context of child killings at the time. The next section also discusses the law in relation to women's status, which is tied to, and emerges from, patriarchal ideology and volatile social conditions. The crucial observation coming out of this discussion is the emergence of broad stereotypical labels that construct the female filicidal perpetrator (but not the male).

Following this, the discussion turns to the uncovering of the representation of these labels in the cases and it is argued that these labels have roots in mythology and that historically they have been used against women. As such, they shed little light on the nature and circumstances of the perpetrators or on the act of killing. Although there are fathers who kill children, historically the focus has been on the mother, and the discussion highlights some views on this focus over the past couple of centuries. It is then argued that the legal archetype of the filicidal parent was constructed against the backdrop of Judaeo-Christian mythology and genuine concerns for the diminishing status of a child's personhood.

76 Ibid; Fitzpatrick, ibid 10.

77 Fitzpatrick, ibid 9–11, ch 3; *Bowman v Secular Society Ltd* [1917] AC 406, 425, 464. Also see *Milirrpum v Nabalco Pty Ltd* (1971) 17 FLR 141, 200 (Blackburn J) ('*Gove Land Rights Case*').

78 Little, above n 72, 106.

The role of law: evolution of infanticide law

The first legislation in England outlawing child killing was enacted by Puritan legislators in 1623 in Stuart England ('the 1623 Act').[79] Prior to this, the utility verses polemic dichotomy in child killing had always reflected the harsh reality of survival pitted against the social and cultural developments regarding the role, place and symbol of the child. The first offence was sex-specific in that it targeted unmarried women for concealment of the death of a newborn child, rather than murder, although both murder and concealment were separate offences included within the literal reading of the 1623 Act. This law defined the women perpetrators as 'lewd' and 'shameful', clearly reflecting these women's subordinate status due to having a child out of wedlock. Additionally, the accusation of witchcraft against women in this period had infanticide woven into it as evidence of a specific female form of criminality. Without a doubt, the 1623 Act represented one of the means by which this patriarchal society attempted to control women. Its emergence from the dire social conditions leading to widespread child abandonment[80] was further strengthened by the failure of the church to curb the problem of illegitimate children. On the religious front, the church had attempted to stigmatise unmarried single women as 'descendents of Eve' and 'naked Bathshebas',[81] but its failure to achieve any meaningful change meant that more urgent measures were needed.[82] The advent of the 1623 Act, which was essentially enforced against unmarried women, revealed them as reasoned, immoral and premeditated, as opposed to married women, who would have no reason to conceal a birth. The use of this law against unmarried women as such embraced Judaeo-Christian conceptions of the fallen woman as temptress, witch, Eve and whore, and maintained male superiority. There was no equivalent legislation or punishment for fathers.

In 1803, Lord Ellenborough's Act repealed the 1623 Act. This enacted that trials under the 1623 Act should proceed as trials for murder and included an

79 21 Jac. I, c. 23, 1623. Also see Davis D Seaborne, 'Child Killing in English Law' (1937) 1 *Modern Law Review* 203–217, 213; and Mark Jackson 'Infanticide: Historical Perspectives' (1996) 145 (6736) *New Law Journal* 416–420, 417.

80 William L Langer, 'Infanticide: A Historical Survey' (1974) 1(3) *History of Childhood Quarterly* 353–366, 359.

81 Peter C Hoffer and N E H Hull, *Murdering Mothers: Infanticide in England and New England 1558–1803* (New York University Press, 1981) 11.

82 The church represented one of the several social attempts to raise social awareness of the disregarded lives of children. Unmarried women were powerless and vulnerable to seduction and rape, so pregnancy was a 'double-edged sword' for them because their good character and financial status and future marriage prospects were diminished. See Johanna Greyer-Kordesch, 'Infanticide and the Erotic Plot: A Feminist Reading of Eighteenth-Century Crime' in Mark Jackson (ed), *Infanticide: Historical Perspectives on Child Murder and Concealment 1550–2000* (Ashgate, 2002) 99, 127; and Katherine O'Donovan, 'The Medicalisation of Infanticide' (1984) *Criminal Law Review* 259–264, 260.

alternative verdict allowing the jury to acquit if there was concealment of birth, which was a crime with a maximum sentence of two years' imprisonment.[83] In spite of the severity of these laws, there was a decline in conviction rates as in a majority of the cases the sentence of death was altered.[84] Judges at the time, such as Shee, B Bramwell and Lord Cranworth, were of the view that infanticide was never practically treated as murder because most juries acquitted defendants on the ground that there was lack of proof that the infant was born alive, or substituted a verdict of concealment in the alternative.[85] Seaborne suggests that the law broke down because the public disliked capital punishment.[86] So it appears that attempts at social change began with piecemeal efforts to use the law as a tool of social governance aimed specifically at emerging forms of female criminality viewed by men as threatening the social fabric. But the unpopularity of this law over time meant that it was ripe for change.

The next attempt at socio-legal reform was to introduce insanity into the law, around the end of the eighteenth century. There were in England already a handful of recorded cases where a mother had killed her child in a fit of madness, or 'phrenzy'[87] as it was called then. Physicians such as William Hunter argued that mental distress associated with childbirth could explain why some women irrationally concealed their child's dead body, and sometimes even drove them to commit suicide.[88] Even though Hunter's argument stemmed from his observation of the socio-economic plight of women at the time, his bio-social[89] explanation constructed women as passive victims of their biological pathology, which invariably meant that their criminal and moral responsibilities under the law were diminished. The *Infanticide Act 1922* was thus inaugurated to countenance the gap between the law and social awareness on the motives and plight of women who killed their child at birth.

83 Catherine Damme, 'Infanticide: The Worth of an Infant Under the Law' (1978) 22 *Medical History* 1–24, 13.

84 O'Donovan, above n 82, 261. According to Langer, infanticide was committed almost with impunity, and, even if the offender was brought to trial, juries refused to convict, holding that capital punishment was too harsh: Langer, above n 80, 360.

85 J R Dickinson and J A Sharpe, 'Infanticide in Early Modern England: The Court of Great Sessions at Chester, 1650–1800' in Mark Jackson (ed), *Infanticide: Historical Perspectives on Child Murder and Concealment, 1550–2000*, above n 79, 43–44.

86 Seaborne, above n 79, 217. In addition, throughout the nineteenth century in England there were scandals over burial clubs and baby farming, and numerous acquittals for lack of proof that the child had been born alive: O'Donovan, above n 82; and Langer, above n 80, 360–361.

87 William Hunter, 'On the Uncertainty of the Signs of Murder, in the Case of Bastard Children' in *Medical Observations and Inquiries by a Society of Physicians in London*, vol 6 (T. Cadell, 1784) 266–290, 271.

88 Kirsten Johnson Kramer and William D Watson, 'The Insanities of Reproduction: Medico-Legal Knowledge and the Development of Infanticide Law' (2006) 15(2) *Social & Legal Studies* 237–255, 240–241.

89 Ibid 241.

This new law reduced the offence of murder to manslaughter where a woman had not fully recovered from the effects of childbirth, resulting in disturbance or imbalance of the mind.[90] The disturbance of the mind observation was further medicalised by John Stanley Hopwood, who later identified two forms of insanity arising in pregnancy: puerperal and lactational.[91] This provided a new dimension to understandings of childbirth and its impact on women. Following this, another wave of change swept the pre-eminent legislation on infanticide by introducing new definitions such as 'newly born' and 'effect of lactation'.[92] This change was embodied in England in the *Infanticide Act 1938*, which was subsequently introduced to the legislatures of New South Wales, Victoria, Tasmania and Western Australia, as well as to New Zealand and Canada.[93] In New South Wales, the present law on infanticide is found in section 22A of the *Crimes Act 1900*.

No doubt the infanticide legislation is considered a partial defence to murder for women, but historically the law singled out unmarried women and constructed them as 'fallen' and passive victims of men.[94] Smart argues that, even so, the law reflected a degree of understanding of women's economic situation, particularly the predicament of working-class women.[95] However, the predominant social view was that women were 'frail' and at the mercy of their reproductive systems.[96]

90 *Infanticide Act 1922* section 1(1). See also O'Donovan, above n 82, 261.

91 Kramer and Watson, above n 88, 247–248. See also John S Hopwood, 'Child Murder and Insanity' (1927) 73 *Journal of Mental Science* 95–108, 96–97, 101–102. See also *O'Donoghue* (1927) 20 Cr.App.R. 132, 133 for the judgment of 'guilty but insane' against a defendant who killed her 35-day-old child. The medical evidence was that the mother had symptoms bordering on puerperal insanity at the birth of her first child.

92 O'Donovan, above n 82, 261.

93 New South Wales Law Reform Commission, *Partial Defences to Murder: Provocation and Infanticide*, Report 83 (New South Wales Law Reform Commission, 1997) [3.2]. In the United States, there have been calls to recognise post-partum depression and psychosis in the law as a partial defence for infanticide, see: Christine Anne Gardner, 'Postpartum Depression Defense: Are Mothers Getting Away with Murder?' (1990) 24 *New England Law Review* 953–989; Jessica Butterfield, 'Blue Mourning: Postpartum Psychosis and the Criminal Insanity Defense. Waking to the Reality of Women Who Kill Their Children' (2006) 39 *John Marshall Law Review* 515–537; Susan Ayres, 'Newfound Religion: Mothers, God and Infanticide' (2006) 33 *Fordham Urban Law Journal* 335–356; and Jacob M Appel, 'When Infanticide Isn't Murder' *Huffington Post* (online) 8 September 2009 www.huffingtonpost.com/jacob-m-appel/when-infanticide-isnt-mur_b_279703.html.

94 Tony Ward, 'The Sad Subject of Infanticide: Law, Medicine and Child Murder, 1860–1938' (1999) 8(2) *Social & Legal Studies* 163–180, 164–165.

95 Carol Smart, 'Disruptive Bodies and Unruly Sex: The Regulation of Reproduction and Sexuality in the Nineteenth Century' in Carol Smart (ed), *Regulating Womanhood: Historical Essays on Marriage, Motherhood and Sexuality* (Routledge, 1992) 7–32.

96 Anne Digby, 'Women's Biological Straightjacket' in Susan Mendus and Jane Rendall (eds), *Sexuality and Subordination: Interdisciplinary Studies in Gender in the Nineteenth Century* (Routledge, 1989) 192–200.

This view is a far cry from the portrayal of Medea, who forsook her maternal instincts and embraced masculine traits to enable her to wreak revenge on Jason. Equally dominant in the infanticide legislation was the perception that women were dangerous and, if not controlled, they could be witches and could wilfully murder their children. It is also noteworthy to mention the split in the offences of murder of children and infanticide; the latter offence developed out of the medical sphere's attempts to medicalise the crime, even though there might have been no medical basis for it.[97] On a symbolic level, it could be argued that the madness incorporated into the law on infanticide was intended to be exculpatory, much like the temporary madness that caused Heracles to kill his children.

Infanticide law from the late nineteenth to twentieth century has persisted. However, its enforcement has since declined. Since 2000 there have been few infanticide cases[98] in New South Wales. There have been calls by the New South Wales Law Reform Commission to abolish the offence of infanticide since the defence of diminished responsibility is sufficient and achieves the same result of reducing culpability from murder to manslaughter or not guilty on the ground of insanity.[99] The Commission has also pointed out that this archaic law simply reflects an anachronistic and paternalistic view of women, and reinforces the myth of women as weak and pitiable.[100] The Commission's argument should be taken seriously. The persistent refusal to abolish the crime of infanticide reinforces the law as patriarchal, which perpetuates a subordinate view of women, in particular, the polarisation of female criminality in filicide into the 'mad', 'bad' and 'sad' categories.[101] Images of women are divided in popular culture: the weak/incapable woman, and the bad woman/mother. Both of these images, as noted already, arose from patriarchal ideology. The Commission's position seeks to address this by viewing women as human beings. This approach takes into account all the appropriate mitigations that can apply equally to men and women charged for the crime of murder.

97 O'Donovan, above n 82, 263. O'Donovan points out that the Butler Committee in 1975 was of the view that the medical principles informing the *Infanticide Act 1938* were no longer relevant as puerperal psychosis was now regarded as no different from other psychoses, and childbirth was simply a precipitating factor: Butler Committee (UK), *Report of the Committee on Mentally Abnormal Offenders, Cmnd. 6244* (London: HMSO, 1975) 245. This position was accepted by the Criminal Law Revision Committee (UK), *Offences Against the Person, Cmnd. 7844* (Fourteenth Report: Criminal Law Revision Committee, 1980) [103].

98 For example, *R v Cooper* [2001] NSWSC 769; *R v Pope* [2002] NSWSC 397; and *R v Keli Lane* [No. 17] [2010] NSWSC 1544.

99 New South Wales Law Reform Commission, above n 93, [3.18]–[3.26].

100 Ibid [3.31].

101 Ania Wilczynski, 'Mad or Bad? Child-Killers, Gender and the Courts' (1997) 37(3) *British Journal of Criminology* 419–436, 421–424. See also Lisa Appignanesi, *Mad, Bad and Sad: A History of Women and Mind Doctors from 1800 to the Present* (Virago, 2008) ch 1, ch 3.

This said, outside of the infanticide legislation, the position of the law reinforces and confirms some remnants of Judaeo-Christian mythology by representing filicidal women in contradistinction to the good mother symbol, as will be demonstrated below by reference to the cases.

Filicidal men

Regarding filicidal men, the cases suggest that the law appears to apply similar labels of 'mad', 'bad' and 'sad'. However, according to Wilczynski, filicidal men are sometimes viewed as 'sad' but are usually viewed as 'bad' – that is, morally blameworthy and reprehensible – while relatively few filicidal women are viewed as 'bad'.[102] It is Wilczynski's view,[103] and also this book's position (as will be discussed further in Chapter 5), that these labels by which the perpetrators are socially represented usually affect the length and type of their imposed sentence. Even though this might be an ancillary effect of label application, the labels do not merely stereotype perpetrators into very broad categories, but they are also made with reference to the Universal Mother and Father symbols.

The good and bad mother and father symbols in the law (particularly in relation to the law's expressive function as discussed above),[104] when read together, represent the mythical, but existential duality of creative and destructive forces that Medea and Heracles embody. However, these symbols are also active in the law's facilitative function as it relates to the prevention of harm and management of risk, such as embodied in the CYP Act. The discussions in the following chapters concern symbols and representations with respect to the latter role of the law. It is argued that myths and symbolisms mask the potential of harm and risk to the child. Yet, irrespective of these functions, the relevance of myth and symbols in relation to perpetrator construction in the law in its facilitative and expressive roles cannot be understated. This seemingly irreconcilable position of dualistic representations underlies the irrational conundrum that makes filicide such a complex phenomenon.

Socio-legal filicidal parent representation: the cases

The judicial narratives in the cases reveal some remnants of mythological representations with regard to descriptions of the perpetrators. The focus and position of the law with respect to filicide emphasises the importance of parental duty

102 Ibid 424.
103 Ibid 424–434.
104 The law's expressive role concerns the institutionalisation of values and morality through punishment, which is different from its facilitative role as an instrument for shaping social behaviour by threatening sanctions, see: Bronwen Morgan and Karen Yeung, *An Introduction to Law and Regulation* (Cambridge University Press, 2009) 5–6.

towards children. Additionally, the law, such as the *Family Law Act 1975* (Cth) and the CYP Act (NSW) have developed to reflect the best interest of the child principle in order to bring to prominence the position of the child's needs in the family and society. In these cases, however, the child's position in the family is less than visible to both the authorities and the parents. It is only after the child dies that the legal and media narratives refocus on the dead child. Prior to the child's death, as shown in the cases, the focus of child protection workers and court interventions is on the parent. The attention on the parent also emerges from the stereotypes constructed around their representations. For example, various labels and classifications about the filicidal perpetrators have emerged in the literature to describe their characteristics and motivation for killing.[105] While such labels might aid filicide offender taxonomy, I would suggest they are no more than attempts to pathologise the perpetrator – 'good', 'mad', 'bad' – and do not adequately reflect the complex circumstances and interactional forces faced by most parent perpetrators. Because these types of labels tend to stereotype perpetrators, they do not really assist understanding of the social conditions of these families, and by focusing only on the parent they further reinforce the position of non-existence of the child in the family.

The judicial narratives on the representations of the parent perpetrators in several of the cases are discussed below in light of the preceding discussion on mythological and socio-legal constructions of parents who kill their children. The purpose of the discussion is to demonstrate that these representations are partly myth-derived, partly socio-cultural and partly legal archetypes, constructed out of a fundamental ideology of parental proprietorship, or ownership in the social sense, of children. This theme gives rise to two sub-themes that are discussed throughout the book: the tenacity of the male's reassertion of his belief in proprietary ownership of women and children, also termed patriarchal dysfunction, which is discussed in Chapters 2, 6 and 7; and the rights and representation of children, which is discussed in Chapter 7.

Judicial narratives, as opposed to media narratives, are chosen as the focal point here because they give certain representations authority and have the force of law and sanction. Additionally, judicial narrative is seen as pivotal to the construction of the perpetrator and the killing, and, as will be discussed in Chapter 5, gives authority to the voice of certain representations. Like myth, the law transcends society but at the same time is part of it.[106] As Fitzpatrick points out, both myth and law take existence and validity from their self-referential sources and in this sense they are self-serving.[107] Therefore, unquestioning legal authority that emerges from the judicial narrative, which reflects the law's expressive function, gives meaning to perpetrator representations which sustain their existence as myths.

105 Above n 8, ch 3.
106 Above n 2, 9.
107 Ibid 204.

Socio-legal constructions of the filicidal perpetrator

Filicide classification by motive, such as Wilczynski's classification, usually showcases the various socio-legal constructions of filicide perpetrators. Such a classification could be as follows: retaliatory killings due to spousal revenge (Medea complex);[108] killings due to jealousy of, or rejection by, the victim;[109] killings due to there being an unwanted child;[110] killings as a result of discipline; altruistic or mercy killings committed out of the belief that it would be in the best interest of the child;[111] killings due to the parent being psychotic;[112] killings due to Münchausen syndrome by proxy ('MSBP');[113] killings secondary to sexual or ritual abuses of the victim; killings in which there was no intention to kill or injure the child, for example, deaths by accidental killing or where there are no known motives to kill.[114, 115] Cases might straddle one or more of these motives, such as occurred with Horace Faulkner, whose killings were characterised by both retaliatory and altruistic motives. Within these classifications, the perpetrator characteristics in the myths of Medea and Heracles are evident in the retaliatory killings and parental psychosis classifications respectively, as discussed below.

Male perpetrator representations

The discussion in this section is drawn from the judicial narratives in the four cases involving male perpetrators, namely the cases of Horace Faulkner, Jubilee Soprano, Hannah Bromley and Greta Sheng (bearing in mind that the Bromley and Sheng cases involved both female and male perpetrators). Two cases – those of Paul and Isabel, and Mark and Libby – involving male perpetrators were excluded because the male protagonists committed suicide after killing the children, so there were no judicial narratives available. The first case in which a

108 Examples in the cases in this book include Capello Steppenwolf, Danny Burrow, Mark and Libby, Paul and Isabel and Horace Faulkner.

109 According to Wilczynski, this is an exclusively male category where the male perpetrators resented the children they killed for various reasons, such as knowing they were not the child's biological parent or the attention received by the child from the mother: Wilczynski, above n 8, 47.

110 The Bromley case study falls under this category, primarily because the parents were so disengaged from Hannah and rejected her physically and symbolically, as argued in Chapter 2.

111 Examples in the cases include Jack Drummond and Horace Faulkner.

112 An example of this is the Jubilee Soprano case.

113 Above n 8, 58–60. Münchausen syndrome by proxy (MSBP) involves the faking and/or inducement of illnesses in a child by an adult caretaker who presents the child for medical assessments and care, often repeatedly. Wilczynski points out that MSBP is a hidden form of abuse because the perpetrator usually induces symptoms by smothering, poisoning and provoking seizures.

114 An example of this category is the Sheng case study.

115 Above n 8, 43–62.

link may be made between the law and myth is that of Jubilee Soprano, and the link is the representation of madness. In the Soprano case, the reader will recall that the perpetrator, Brody Kitaro, was suffering mental illness at the time of the killing. Brody, according to the court, 'was delusional and his behaviour was severely disturbed'.[116] The court found that Brody was unable to reason about the wrongness of his actions.[117] It is possible to compare the representation of Brody's mental illness to that of Heracles' madness.

The second example of the link between myth and law is the case of Horace Faulkner. The reader will recall that Horace killed the children to punish his ex-wife, Melissa, but he tried to convince others and himself that he was doing it for the children's sake. The court recognised the Medea element in the case: 'I am satisfied beyond reasonable doubt that his motivation in killing the children was at least in part to punish his wife for her conduct towards him.'[118] The judicial narrative cast Horace as 'selfish', 'vindictive', 'disturbed' and 'loving'.[119] The court also stressed the position of trust and duty of a father to care for their children, particularly when they are away from the mother. Again, this harks back to proprietorship of children, in the social sense, that is functional. As with Medea, parental duty breaks down when an existing marital union disintegrates. The collapse of his relationship revealed Horace's belief in his proprietary ownership of the children and his ex-wife,[120] who he feared was going to take the children from him. The act of using the children as punishment and revenge is symbolic of this proprietary perception of social ownership and control over the children, founded in patriarchal ideology and mythology.

In the three cases that involved male perpetrators who were charged together with female perpetrators, two of the male perpetrators, Quentin Bromley and Gerald Sheng, were charged jointly with their female counterparts and one, Toby Mansfield in the Ford case, pleaded guilty to a lesser charge, the malicious infliction of grievous bodily harm. Quentin was charged with murder but found guilty of manslaughter, while Gerald was charged with manslaughter by gross negligence and found guilty. In the Bromley case, the sentencing judge focused on the neglectful attitude of the parents and their failure to adequately care

116 *R v Brody Kitaro*, Supreme Court, New South Wales, 2000, Supreme Court No. BK1, [21].

117 Ibid.

118 *R v Horace Faulkner*, Supreme Court, New South Wales, 2004, Supreme Court No. HF1, [38].

119 Ibid [39], [50].

120 Carolyn-Harris Johnson, *Come with Daddy: Child Murder-Suicide after Family Breakdown* (University of Western Australia Press, 2005) 129–130. According to Johnson, masculine possession is a factor in familicides, that is, murder-suicide by a parent, which are characterised by suicidal masculine depression, in that the man's perception of ownership apparently gives him the belief that he has the right to kill his spouse and/or children. The other cases in this study that showcase this sort of patriarchal dysfunction are Paul and Isabel and Mark and Libby, which are further discussed in Chapter 6.

for Hannah.[121] In particular, the judicial narrative portrayed Quentin's overall disposition and parental attitude as oblivious, uncaring and unloving.[122] In the Sheng case, the sentencing judge came to the conclusion that Gerald was unrepentant and 'arrogant',[123] because he 'continues to see the blame for his daughter's death lying with others'.[124] Gerald was also openly represented as a patriarch according to the judicial narrative: he 'operated upon the attitude of [Caitlin], who was inclined to defer to her husband'.[125] Here, the court recognises the operative system of male ownership and control over his family.

The judicial representations of both Horace and Brody appear to conform to the view that male perpetrators are 'bad' and 'sad' while female perpetrators are 'sad' or 'mad'.[126] These categories have been constructed to leave little space for other types of representation. For example, in many of these cases studies, such as Mark and Libby, Paul and Isabel, Horace Faulkner and Greta Sheng, the fathers appeared 'loving' prior to the killing but were revealed as 'bad' by the court after the killing. Yet in none of these narratives is the appearance of 'loving' represented by the courts as significant to the interpretation of violence and endangerment.

Female perpetrator representations

The discussion in this section is drawn from the judicial narratives in the five cases involving female perpetrators, namely the cases of Danny Burrow, Capello Steppenwolf, Hannah Bromley, Greta Sheng and Jack Drummond (bearing in mind that the Bromley and Sheng cases involved both female and male perpetrators). Three prominent types of filicide emerge from this cohort: the Medea-type or spousal revenge killings typified by the Steppenwolf and Burrow cases; killings motivated by altruism, typified by the Drummond case; and killings due to mental illness, illustrated by the Drummond case. In these cases, which are similar to the male perpetrator cases, the judicial narratives stressed the importance of parental duty to children and emphasised the mother–child symbolism. For example, in the Burrow case the sentencing judge held that: 'these injuries came from his own mother, the person from whom above all [Danny] was entitled to expect care, nurture, love and protection'.[127]

121 *R v Georgina and Quentin Bromley*, Supreme Court, New South Wales, 2009, Supreme Court No. GQHB, [81].
122 Ibid, [71], [72].
123 *R v Gerald Sheng*; *R v Caitlin Sheng*, Supreme Court, New South Wales, 2009, Supreme Court No. SHG13, [134]
124 Ibid [159].
125 Ibid [134].
126 Wilczynski, above n 101.
127 *R v Saskia Burrow*, Supreme Court, New South Wales, 2001, Supreme Court No. SB1, [22].

In the Steppenwolf case, the sentencing judge said, '[Elizabeth] acted in breach of a position of trust and authority in respect of a victim who was her own son. [Capello] was entitled to love, protection and nurture.'[128] The mother symbol especially was reiterated when the judge commented that Elizabeth held her own interests above concerns for Capello.[129] This symbolism emerged with the juxtaposition by the judge of Elizabeth as self-centred rather than sacrificial. Even though the court found Elizabeth was suffering from a severe personality disorder, it was not sufficient for her to qualify as a psychotic parent.[130] The Medea element was evidenced in this case, in which the judge recognised and was satisfied that Elizabeth prioritised her interests over her son Capello's welfare and 'used' Capello for vengeful purposes, even though she was unlike Medea, who did not loathe her children in the same way as Elizabeth did. The judge said Elizabeth, 'came to loathe [Capello] because he reminded her of his father towards whom she held ambivalent feelings . . . prior to the murder she was in fear of [Paul] and, in that period, she more hated than loved him'.[131] The Soprano case was also a portrayal of the psychotic parent suffering from mental illness. In the Sheng case, the gender slur on the mother Caitlin as submissive was evident in the way she was portrayed as deferential to her husband.[132] Additionally, the judicial voice enunciated that Caitlin failed in her duty as parent towards the child, who was 'entitled to expect nurture, care, sustenance and protection'.[133] In the Bromley case, the perpetrator, Georgina, was predominantly labelled by the judicial narrative as 'bad', given that most of the judicial narrative, where it commented on her representation, was devoted to demolishing her credibility due to the conflicting stories she told.[134] In these cases it is clear that the overriding judicial emphasis is on the failure of motherly duty to the child. In conjunction with the upholding of this duty, also present in the judicial narratives are symbolisms related to the mother, with labels such as 'bad' sometimes being applied to the perpetrators. These usually arose from the judicial iteration of the perpetrators' motives and conduct, and were indicative of the level of the perpetrators' moral culpabilities.

In the Drummond case, the tone of the judicial narrative is different to that in the cases described above. This case could be classified as a mercy killing, but it could equally be classified under the unwanted child classification. The reader may recall that Melanie had been suffering a prolonged depressive disorder. At the time of the killing she felt that she could no longer cope or measure up to

128 *R v Kramer*, Supreme Court, New South Wales, 2009, Supreme Court No. EK1, [87].
129 Ibid [92]. Here the judge recognised that Elizabeth displayed antisocial tendencies with her callous disregard for Capello after his death.
130 Ibid [90].
131 Ibid [78].
132 Above n 125, [134].
133 Ibid [144].
134 Above n 121, [119], [127].

the standard of her expectations of being a good mother.[135] Concurrently, she revealed that she harboured feelings that she longed for the family to be 'normal' again, and therefore would be better off without Jack.[136] Both of these symptoms are characteristic of both classifications, according to Wilczynski's categorical descriptions. In terms of symbolism, it is noteworthy that Melanie was predominantly stereotyped by the media, and to some extent by the court, as the good mother.[137] The implications of this representation are more fully discussed in Chapter 5. Suffice to say here that the representation of Melanie as the good mother is an example of a mythical representation in the law. As argued, the symbol of the good mother is a reference to the universal symbol of the Mother. The references in Melanie's case can be contrasted to references to the 'bad' or 'wicked' mother such as occurred in the Ford, Steppenwolf and Burrow cases, where the perpetrators were juxtaposed against the qualities inherent in the good mother symbol, such as love, nurture and protection.

Mythological constructions

Within the subtext of the judicial narratives shown above, the labels and symbols were generally used to represent the perpetrators. These labels appear to represent very broad generalisations and constructions against which the offenders' actions are judged generally, but they do not sufficiently describe the context of the cases, which, as seen in Chapter 1, are varied. For example, in the Sheng case the label 'sad' is unfairly applied to Caitlin on the basis of her judicial representation as subservient and passive to her husband's influence and control; such a label might not have taken into account factors such as her cultural background. In the Drummond case the same label, 'sad', can be applied to Melanie's situation but for very different reasons. The label appears to describe the circumstances of the killing and the way Melanie was portrayed by the media and the courts. The label 'bad' can also equally be applied to Melanie but the overwhelming representation of her was as the good mother in both the judicial and media narratives. An argument could be made that Melanie could have been labelled as 'bad' given that she had abused the position of trust in relation to the special and vulnerable circumstances of Jack, who was disabled.[138] As such, it would appear that labels such as the good mother tend to stereotype perpetrators in broad categories that arise out of their representation in the narratives in court through the force of judicial authority, and which in turn reinforce them.[139]

135 Ch 1: Jack Drummond.

136 Ibid.

137 Ibid.

138 For example, the appellate court in their judgment recognised the seriousness of the offence and the inadequacy of the sentence at first instance: *R v Melanie Drummond*, Court of Criminal Appeal, New South Wales, 2004, Court of Criminal Appeal No. MD2, [40].

139 Patricia Allatt, 'Stereotyping: Familism in the Law' in Bob Fryer and Alan Hunt (eds), *Law, State and Society* (Routledge, 1981) ch 8, 177–199, 180.

The purpose here is to show that these labels can be arbitrary and can reflect mythical constructions. The labels can be likened to masks, whose function to conceal from, or reveal to, the audience either illustrate or hide the individual circumstances and background of the actors.[140] The revealing function of the mask shows the authority of the judicial narrative to give voice to certain representations over others. Even though the labels might reveal characteristics of the case and perpetrator representations very broadly, it is argued here that they do not assist in understanding some of the underlying complexities that motivate perpetrators to kill, as will be discussed in the following chapters. The labels are at best superficial and mythical, because they tend to stereotype filicide perpetrators according to categories that do not accurately reflect the reality or context in which the killing occurred.

For Wilczynski, the pathologising function of labels fulfils an important ideological function, which is to stereotype the perpetrators as 'other' or as 'bizarre aberrations', in order that they can be set apart from 'us' who are the rest of society.[141] The social governance implication arising from the application of labels is more fully discussed in Chapter 5. The starkest evidence of myth in the law is the construction of the child, whose place has been constructed as firmly with the mother. This symbolism of mother and child is prevalent in narratives involving female perpetrators. In myth and in the law, there are elements of masking and unmasking of the perpetrators. For example, unmasking is crucial in revealing Medea's motives and Heracles' unintentional killing as a result of his temporarily inflicted madness. In the judicial narratives, the unmasking function of the court also reveals the perpetrators' motives, though it has been argued that the labels can be affixed to the perpetrators by judicial authority through its selective rearticulation of the perpetrators' representation, such as in the Drummond case. This can sometimes mask the nature of the killing and present it as something other than it is.

Conclusion

This chapter has posited that Western mythology has a relevant place in the present-day law, particularly within judicial narratives and socio-legal articulations of the representation of filicidal perpetrators. It has been argued that the symbolic representations of the Father, Mother and mother–child archetypes are founded in mythology, and that they continue to influence, and be sustained in, the law through the force of judicial authority.

The chapter has focused on the process of myth-making regarding parent perpetrator representations in the myths of Medea and Heracles and in the

140 Masking as a dramaturgical device and analysis tool was introduced in the previous chapter and will be used to analyse the context of perpetrator representations in the next chapter.

141 Wilczynski, above n 8, 144.

judicial narratives of the cases. In the narrative of Medea it is notable that the children are mostly silent throughout the play. Additionally, the transformation of Medea from loving spouse to jealous and revengeful woman, and then to sorceress, embracing 'the Other', is a mythical, cultural and historical narrative that has been retold countless times in the representation of women. From the narrative of Heracles it can be observed that the representation of madness is a prevalent theme in mythology and in the law. In addition, the representation of Heracles as hero, god and fallen but redeemed hero has had an influence in mythology and popular culture, through such things as the Father archetype and the romanticisation of the male villain. So, although most people in Western societies do not know these myths by name or the detailed stories, their views have been infused with the symbolism arising from these myths that have permeated Western culture for millennia. The socio-legal representations of filicidal perpetrators as susceptible to the labels of 'mad', 'bad', 'sad' and 'loving' come, it has been argued, from myths. These labels can be seen as descriptions of Medea and Heracles as much as of the perpetrators in the cases in a general way that does not accurately reflect their reality. And yet the dualistic and conflicting forces of good and evil seen in these mythical characters are the same dominating complexes that make filicide a complex phenomenon.

The overarching mythology in Western societies appears to be dominated by the symbol of the Father, whose ideological and mythological presence has been constructed and maintained by patriarchy. This patriarchal sense of ownership between the state and the family and between the father and his wife and children has, ironically, helped shape the legal conceptions and development of parental duty and rights of women and children. However, in the cases where the system of male ownership and authority was challenged in society but was reasserted by the perpetrator, the position of the child in the family was hidden and risks of endangerment to the child developed easily. In such a context, the rights of the child appear threatened.

In these narratives, it can be observed that the status and place of children are largely invisible, because the focus is on the parent. The child is also concealed because the child is represented in symbolic terms as inextricably part of, and tied to, the mother and as subject to the control of the father. In the discussion about the laws on infanticide, it was seen that the status of children has been an issue of increasing social concern, particularly in relation to a child's rights as an independent person. Within this socio-historical context it could be argued that legal conceptions such as parental duty and the best interest of the child have emerged as prominent in the debate on the rights and safety of children.

Myths take on power when they become a mechanism for broadcasting a particular morality. The cases on their own have no such power, but in the broader context of mythology the child is concealed behind parental symbols. Perhaps a starting point for repositioning the child in a visible space is the recognition that mythological symbols and ideological representations have pervaded Western social consciousness, that these have influenced the law, and that they cannot be discounted if inroads into understanding the pathways to filicide and the influence of these symbols and representations on risk are to be made. Certainly, understanding the power of myths and the symbol of the child in mythology could be a useful policy tool, if only to provide insight into some of the representations that mask the visibility of the child and the child's safety and place in the family and society. The exploration of mythology in this chapter indicates that not only is representation part of symbolic interactionist theory as a deeply embedded social and symbolic force, but it also interacts with social processes such as human decision-making to produce certain acceptable or unacceptable meanings.

4 Modelling representation

Introduction

Social representation is theorised to be at the centre of the filicide perpetrator construction. It will be suggested here that perpetrator representations are constructed based on several sources situated around the perpetrator, such as the perpetrator, witnesses, family and friends, the media and the law. In this chapter I unpack perpetrator representation as a theoretical social construct and explore the various human sources that participate in constructing the perpetrator's multifaceted representation following the event of killing. The ideas for this theoretical construct of representation are drawn from the case studies of Jubilee Soprano, Jack Drummond and Horace Faulkner, in which Brody Kitaro, Melanie Drummond and Horace Faulkner are the perpetrators, respectively.[1] I build into the initial perpetrator construct the social representations made by other parties and the subsequent representations by the media and the law. The final representation of the perpetrator and the killing are thus based on social, media and legal, including judicial, representations. This is designed to show that the perpetrator and the killing representations are multilayered and multifaceted, although in the legal narrative these reconstructions are diluted in order to create for the audience[2] a particular, if not specific and limiting, representation of the perpetrator and of the killing in retrospect.

In terms of the structure of this chapter, first the parameters of the chapter are defined. This is achieved by explaining the concepts used. Second, a discussion on the theoretical conceptualisation of representation through modelling is presented and the utility of the model is illustrated through the Soprano and Drummond cases. The function of this modelling is twofold: it charts the way the perpetrator is represented as a person by parties directly or indirectly involved

1 This theoretical construction is not limited to the Soprano, Drummond and Faulkner stories. These three stories were chosen for the richness of their narrative. The stories that are not modelled will be referred to as illustrations of aspects of the theory wherever relevant.

2 There is a further discussion on the constitution of the audience and the relevance of its significance to representation in Chapter 5.

in the conflict, and it charts representations of the event of killing. The purpose of these conceptualisations is to illustrate the contextual nature of representation and the importance of its role in decisions taken about intervention. In addition, the models illustrate how I have used the contextual richness of the data sources to build this theoretical conceptualisation of representation. This chapter should be read together with Chapter 5, which discusses the theoretical underpinnings of representation.

Definitions

What is *representation*? Consistent with orthodox understandings and usages in sociological and social construction theories,[3] this book refers to representation as a depiction of an idea or message in the form of a text – a written or auditory or visual object – that can be analysed and read for meaning that is in itself a product of representation.[4] To frame the definition in another way, Griselda Pollack argues that the word *representation* 'stresses that images and texts are no mirrors of the world, merely reflecting their source. Representation stresses something refashioned, coded in rhetorical, textual or pictorial terms, quite distinct from its social existence.'[5] In other words, representation possesses the power to redefine, refashion and restructure a way of thinking, acting and even ordering in society. In addition, it can be said that representation embodies language, image, conduct, sign and behaviour; as such, representation demonstrates by its appearance, its text or subtext, the nature of a relationship that is readily associated with another ideological object, meaning or dimension; that is, representation is about the repositioning and redefinition of an object or text or visual for the audience. However, representation is not synonymous with *symbolism*. Within the discourse of symbolic interactionism, a symbol is a social object that is socially created or purposely established for the purpose of representation; it is an object that can be used intentionally in many different situations in many different ways, and it has a shared meaning among the users and its audience.[6] Symbols have wide applicability in the sense that most of them are universal within a particular culture; this unique quality is particular to the symbol because it enables the understanding of abstract reality from different perspectives.[7] A symbol can be used to represent and to communicate meaning and intention;[8] it is not simply a sign.[9] It can be differentiated from a

3 Peter Berger and Thomas Luckmann, *The Social Construction of Reality* (Doubleday, 1966) 33–43, 67–74, 172.
4 Susan Goodwin and Joanne Finkelstein, *The Sociological Bent: Inside Metro Culture* (Thomson, 2005) 163, 165.
5 Griselda Pollock, *Vision and Difference* (Routledge, 1988) 6.
6 Joel M Charon, *Symbolic Interactionism: An Introduction, an Interpretation, an Integration* (Pearson Education, 9th ed, 2007) 49.
7 Ibid 67.
8 Ibid 50.
9 Ibid 56.

representation because its power is not to redefine, restructure or to refashion, but to communicate meaning. As such, a symbol can be described as being one step further removed from a representation.

In this chapter, an overarching view of representation is taken that includes social, symbolic, media and legal, including judicial, representation. This book presents representation as a theoretical and analytical tool that is used within symbolic interactionism to describe both the legal (e.g. legal representation) and social (e.g. self-representation) processes. Representation is also used to describe the social world in which there might be overlapping understandings of presentation and symbol. For example, much of the news in the media is represented; that is, what constitutes news reporting is arguably a repositioning of facts by the media and the occasional use of symbols such as icons or celebrities to portray a particular image, brand or ideology.[10] Representation within interactive theories is utilised as a device for understanding the processes by which the image of the parent perpetrator is reconstructed and represented by the court in Western society. The argument explaining the purpose of this phenomenon is that perpetrator representation is constructed and reconstructed more than once in order to create a specific meaning and particular symbol. It was argued in Chapter 3 that this symbol was grounded in mythology. A non-deviant or deviant parent representation in this context is a symbol in itself. For example, non-deviant parent symbols are typically represented by: the Virgin Mary, the symbol of the perennial good mother; the Mother-Goddess, the symbol of the Universal Mother;[11] or the One Male God, the symbol of the Father. By contrast, the deviant parent representation is epitomised in the symbol of the mythological sorceress, Medea for example. The evil father symbol is typically represented by a villain that is the opposite of the good father but is much less defined.

10 For instance, Alexander argues that celebrity icons are objects of worship: Jeffrey C Alexander, 'The Celebrity-Icon' (2010) 4(3) *Cultural Sociology* 323–336, 325. The iconic status of The Beatles, for example, extended beyond the mere representation of the British rock/pop genre in popular culture. It is undeniable that the group did, and still does, symbolise an era of popular subculture whose ideologies were sometimes seen as associated with the Left: Mark Sullivan, '"More Popular than Jesus": The Beatles and the Religious Far Right' (1987) 6(3) *Popular Music* 313–326, 318. The band was also a symbol for teenagers worldwide: John Muncie, 'The Beatles and the Spectacle of Youth' in Ian Inglis (ed), *The Beatles, Popular Music and Society: A Thousand Voices* (Palgrave Macmillan, 2000) ch 3, 35–52, 41. Muncie argues that on a cultural level the symbol of the Beatles questioned the culture of elitism, work, freedom and sexuality. Also see John Street, 'Celebrity Politicians: Popular Culture and Political Representation' (2004) 6 *British Journal of Politics and International Relations* 435–452 and Irving Lewis Allen, 'Talking about Media Experiences: Everyday Life as Popular Culture' (1982) 16(3) *Journal of Popular Culture* 106–115.

11 Gerda Lerner, *The Creation of Patriarchy* (Oxford University Press, 1986), 148, and James Preston, *Mother Worship: Theme and Variations* (University of North Carolina Press, 1982) 341.

The interest in representation is not limited to its current understandings in labelling theory, dramaturgy, masking or the legal literatures. As a theoretical socio-legal concept, representation has an important place outside the pre-existing understandings in these discourses. As an analytical device, representation is a form of interaction between the various social forces and social ideas. From this interactive perspective, it is argued that representation can be used as a form of power to construct a social and political reality that can be described as being the dominant reality in Western society.[12]

Applying these definitive parameters here, the reader may well arrive at the conclusion that the refashioning of perpetrator representation takes place as a result of a number of socio-legal interactions drawn from various outside social forces at various stages of the perpetrators' lives. This is not an unusual conclusion. The real difficulty the models reveal is the influence of disingenuous representations that mislead and conceal the existing risks of child endangerment.

Degrees of representation

When Goffman theorised about the presentation of the individual in daily activities, he was essentially writing about a multilayered representation of the individual in various social contexts.[13] Relying on dramaturgical theory, Goffman argues that the individual can be likened to an actor who plays various roles on various stages before an audience, depending each time on what each stage demands.[14] Drawing from Goffman's sociological perspective on this, I have reconstituted this theory into a generic representative model that is not only indicative of the layered contexts in the individual that Goffman theorises about, but also of the layered context of the event of filicide.

Symbolically, layers can be uncovered to reveal what is beneath. This meaning of layering can also connote contextualisation. By this I mean the circumstances in which an event occurs or, bluntly, the circumstances within which a killing

12 'Dominant reality' in this book refers to the normative context of women's status in Western society that is predicated on deeply held structures of the patriarchal state: R W Connell, 'The State, Gender, and Sexual Politics' (1990) 19 *Theory and Society* 522–523, 527–528. Particularly in relation to family and state relations, the dominant reality is constructed around the state's capacity to regulate this relationship, including the cultural boundary between public and privates spheres. An example of such regulation is the NSW *Crimes (Domestic and Personal Violence) Act 2007* on the issue of domestic violence.

13 Erving Goffman, *The Presentation of Self in Everyday Life* (Penguin, first published 1959, 1990 ed) 15–27, 17. Goffman argues that the individual will behave in such a way as to convey his or her interests to the audience or the other party. He argues that the actions of the individual will influence the definition of the situation, and, depending on the kind of impression the individual wants to create, he or she will behave in such a way as to evoke that specific response he or she wants to obtain.

14 Ibid 9, 15–17; and Norman Denzin, *Symbolic Interactionism and Cultural Studies: The Politics of Interpretation* (Blackwell, 1992) 97.

occurs. Each layer connotes a particular situational context, and in both models the contexts are important. A layer can be added on top of another layer in space, and, over time, each layer becomes contextual in that the reader cannot understand one layer without comprehending the layers beneath that layer. For example, the reader would have lost some insight into the Jack Drummond conflict had the domestic violence element of the conflict been suppressed. If the layer of domestic violence were absent, it is arguable that the court and audience would not be able to give meaning to Melanie's depression, which subsequently led to the killing.

The term 'layers' adds a novel interpretation to Goffman's interpretation of social roles. Each layer can be comparable to a social role or even social label, and as such the individual wears various layers as various social roles for each part he or she plays for the audience. A subtle distinction is that layers, unlike social roles, can be grafted on top of each other. For example, they can be merged to create a combination of social roles. This is not to say that roles cannot perform the same – a working mother is a combination of two social roles, for example. But a social role leans towards *action*, that is, the act of enacting or doing, whereas a layer can exist outside of role-playing. In other words a layer can still exist even though the actor is no longer in his or her role. To give a hypothetical example, Annie retains her work persona even though she is not at the workplace, but she will have discarded this social role in favour of her mother persona when she is with her family. In the narrow context of masking used in this book,[15] an actor can wear a mask to exhibit a layer or to play a role. The mask is the dramaturgical and interactive device used by the actor to create a specific representation. From this perspective, this model combines criminology theory and dramaturgical analysis, and when these are merged in this context a multilayered understanding of the nature of filicidal representations emerges. It is my argument that this contextualisation of the killing allows for a greater understanding of the motivations of the perpetrator, in particular the social interactive forces that prompt the killing, such as external intervention and support (or the lack thereof).

Before we delve into modelling of the data, the reader needs to understand the reason for using models to explain representation theory and why the models come before the theorising. There is utility in using models to better understand conceptual schemes and theories in the social sciences.[16] In this book, the models are graphical representations[17] of the social and interactive processes of representation theory and are believed to be useful in explaining the conceptual

15 In Chapter 2, masking was used to analyse hidden violence. Here, it is used in the context of perpetrator violence to analyse and describe perpetrator representations.

16 R Hanneman and S Patrick, 'On the Uses of Computer-Assisted Simulation Modeling in the Social Sciences' (1997) 2(2) *Sociological Research Online* www.socresonline.org.uk/2/2/5.html. Also see N Giere Ronald, 'How Models Are Used to Represent Reality' (2004) 71(5) *Philosophy of Science* 742–752, 747 www.jstor.org/stable/10.1086/425063.

17 Hanneman and Patrick, ibid [2.1].

nature of representation.[18] The models arise from the case studies, and it is believed that the models should be presented as an extension of the data. The reason for this is that the models are employed here to bridge the gap between reality, practice and theory,[19] and to assist the interpretation of the stories in a meaningful way.

The models introduced

Both models sit in the context of the surrounding representations of the individual and of the event. The purpose is to give the reader an insight into the hypothesis that representation can exist as a theoretical concept, and that the conceptual and layered nature of representation explains the ability of representation to conceal, reveal, deceive, mystify and change. Although both models appear similar, they are not. The dissimilarity is the subject matter of the models. Model 1 is about perpetrator representation and Model 2 is about the representation of the killing, that is, event representation. In both models the representation is associated with the origin point at the centre of the model.

Model 1 (see section 'Model 1 explained' below) is about the degrees of the various understandings of the perpetrator. The centrepiece of this model is the perpetrator. The model sits in the context of the perpetrator and his or her self-representations, where they are made known. The model is about the way in which the perpetrator is represented, and about the closeness or intimacy of the representor in relation to the perpetrator, making the representation at various points in time.

Model 2 (see section 'Model 2 explained' below) describes representations of the killing, which stem from events pre-death and post-death in relation to the original event, the death of the child. The model represents the chronology, or the 'building up' or contextualising, of the story, in which the events are seen as central influences in relation to the death of the child. Events are significant; these include the developmental and social milestones in a child's life, such as familial celebrations, inoculation visits, birthdays and parents' anniversaries. Arguably, these events are definitive of the structure of family life and, hence, their representations are crucial to identifying risks of child endangerment.[20]

18 Ibid [5.4].

19 Ibid [6.2]. For example, models can be used to represent aspects of social reality or social practice that theory is not able to conceptualise visually or graphically: Ronald, above n 16. As such, modelling bridges understandings of social practice and theory, or social reality and theory, in a way that allows for in-depth analysis and conceptualisation. In this sense, modelling and theory can inform each other simultaneously.

20 For example, in the case of Greta Sheng, Greta had not been achieving her developmental milestones due to her eczema. This should have alerted the nurses and doctors who saw her that something was amiss. Arguably, the doctors did not see the need to report the family to DOCS because the parents appeared as loving, educated and caring towards Greta when in fact they had been negligent in seeking the appropriate treatment for her.

In both models the space inside the circles represents contexts, which can be conceptualised as layers. The more layers there are, the further away the representation is from the centre. This implies that the representation is less believable. This is also to say that, if the centre represents the truth, then the further the distance from the site of representation the less believable is the context of 'truth'.[21] However, there is an exception to this observation: the court. In both models, the court is a constant feature in the circle entitled 'third-degree representation'. This is an important observation. The court, being the legitimating authority in criminal cases, has the final say on whether a representation is discredited or affirmed. This symbolic function of the judicial narrative gives voice to certain representations, which then become legitimated by the court through the pronouncement of the legal judgment. The selected representations, which have been legitimated, are then disseminated by the media to the rest of society. The court's legitimating function has a twofold significance – giving voice to the dead, and giving authority to the voice of representation. That is, judicial authority not only gives legitimacy and authority but also believability to representations and facts that have been legitimated as *truth*. Without the court, the representations of the perpetrator and the killing would be nothing more than ghosts and the voices of the dead children unrepresented and disbelieved. Judicial legitimation in the context of third-degree representation in this sense is exceptional, because it counteracts the influence of distance and gives authority to the voices of certain representations. This process of legitimation, which is discussed in Chapter 5, is important because it has the power to unmask and unravel the layers of first-degree and second-degree representations, and provides the foundation for the judicial narrative.

In the models, the circles also represent layers in that the bigger circles encapsulate, surround and cover the smaller circles, causing the layers to surround and hide the centre. Each model can be likened to an onion, which when cut reveals the bulb at the centre. The word 'layer' is appropriate because its meaning is 'to cover', that is, to hide what is underneath. Layers can also be uncovered to reveal what is beneath. The word 'degrees', on the other hand, is used broadly to signify representation as perspectival,[22] in that there are various ways to represent a person or event. While each perspective is connected, it is not the same, and there are varying degrees of difference. This is further elaborated in the next section.

21 For 'truth' as a legal, objectively indefinable concept, see Ch 1, 'Recounting the voice'; and 'truth' as distinct from 'fact', see below n 80.

22 Perspectivism as a method introduces a critical attitude towards conceptualising experience, and therefore it has a theoretical utility: Nikolas Rose, *Powers of Freedom: Reframing Political Thought* (Cambridge University Press, 1999) 20. Applied in this context, representation as a perspectival method provides a critical analysis of the subject matter – in this case, the event of killing and the perpetrator.

Degrees

As noted above, degrees are not the same as layers. The reader might sometimes get the sense that they are used interchangeably because the models illustrate both degrees and layers. Yet degrees are about perspectives while layers, as already explained, are about situational contextualisation with the ability to reveal or cover up. Perspectives depend on a particular discourse.[23] In the law, for example, the offence that is similar to complicity[24] defined in this book is the crime of being an abettor and/or an accessory. This offence sets out the criminal liability for individuals who assist perpetrator(s) to commit a crime.[25] This offence is dependent on three different perspectives: principal, second-party and third-party representation.[26] The discourse on representation presented here is not dissimilar. Implicit also in the meaning of perspectival or perspective are temporal and spatial progressions of time and space, which impact on the degree of representation.

To illustrate this, here is another hypothetical example. Annie tells Duncan, her doctor, that she is not herself and she might do something 'silly'. The next day, Annie tells Edwin, her husband, that she is losing her mind and has considered killing herself and their baby. Duncan and Edwin reach the same conclusion about Annie's representations to them – that she is unwell – but Duncan's and Edwin's representations of Annie are not the same even though Annie has essentially made similar representations to them. The degree in which their representations differ is found in the temporal (e.g. the timing) and the spatial (e.g. the locality and the level of intimacy). When these temporal and spatial variables are read together, they impact on the interpretations Duncan and Edwin give to the meaning of Annie's representations. What is the degree of representation? The degree of representation is that made by an actor at varying intersections of temporal and spatial variables in the context of social interaction.

The representation of the event or perpetrator differs in each account from different individuals involved in the event. For example, Rosaline Soprano at first sees Brody Kitaro as manipulative, while Ross Kitaro sees Brody as a sick brother needing medical assistance. Prior to the killing event, Ross and Rosaline are related through Brody, the perpetrator, and following the killing through the death of Jubilee. These representations of Brody are different, but they are also the same. The representations are different because they arise from different points in time, yet they are essentially the same because what Ross and Rosaline see in Brody are the manifest characteristics of his mental illness. What they both see in Brody, whether they know it or not at the time, is his mental illness,

23 To illustrate with a simple example, the perspectives on what constitutes risk in the child protection discourse will be different from the perspective of risk in the discourse on terrorism.

24 The meaning of 'complicity' for the purposes of this book has been discussed in Chapter 2.

25 *Crimes Act 1900* (NSW) Part 9, sections 345–351B.

26 Ibid.

which brings out the manipulative streak in him. This is not to say that Brody may not be manipulative by nature, even if he were not unwell. This is not known. What is known from the start is that Brody was unwell and that he could sometimes behave in a manipulative manner.[27] When looking at the degrees of representation of Brody as a whole, it is noteworthy to observe that one representation, Brody as manipulative, comes across more strongly than the other representation of him. The reasons for this are that the representations are generated at different points in time and emanate from different perspectives. This supports the proposition that social actors wear different masks in different social situations.

Degrees also take into account distance, which includes both time and space.[28] Distance cannot be viewed separately from the models. This is because the constructions of the perpetrator and event to the receiver, who is the person the representation is made to, are dependent on the distance the representor is from the perpetrator, as well as on the distance the representor is from the event. Therefore, degrees not only connote differences in perspectives, but also represent distance. This means that the representation informing one perspective is built on participation in or observation of the event or perpetrator, or both. However, the perspective coming from person A is not the same as that coming from person B, and the degree to which perspective A differs from perspective B can be explained by their distance from each other and their distance in relation to the event or the perpetrator. Applying this to the Jubilee Soprano story, the reader may well observe that Ross' perspective and Rosaline's perspective of what was happening to Angeline are informed by different circumstances. The degree of representation by which both perspectives differ can be explained by the proximity of each party to Brody. This is an important observation because it reveals, as will be illustrated in Model 1A (see Figure 4.2), that third-degree representation – in this case the representation by the intervention team members – of the perpetrator prior to the killing event did not take into account their distance from the perpetrator, and hence they were not able to make a successful assessment of the perpetrator's state of mind and the risks associated with the domestic arrangement of Angeline and Brody at the time.

27 For example, he instructed Angeline to leave the talking to him prior to the interview with the intervention team, and he tried to manipulate Angeline into believing that she disciplined Jubilee: Ch 1: Jubilee Soprano.

28 Time and space together connote the presence of distance. In the West, time has been conceptualised by the Judaeo-Christian school of thought, in the Bible, as a linear process, but it has also been conceptualised by Eastern schools of thought, in the Vedas for example, and other non-Western cultures (the Mayans and Hindus are some examples) as cyclical: see Michelle Bastian 'Inventing Nature: Re-writing Time and Agency in a More-than-Human World' (2009) 47 *Australian Humanities Review* 99–116, 101. Also see Mircea Eliade, *Myth and Reality* (William R. Trask trans, Harper & Row, 1963) 75–76. In both models, time is represented by a line showing linear progression, while space is represented by the lines of concentric circles.

Nature of representation in the case studies

The stories of Jubilee Soprano, Jack Drummond and Horace Faulkner show representations of the perpetrator and the conflict event to be layered. This means that an observer would find it difficult to understand the conflict without first understanding the context and background of the family dynamics. For example, in the Jubilee Soprano story, the vulnerable predisposition of Angeline must be understood in order to grasp the effect of Brody Kitaro's mental illness on her when she met him. In the Jack Drummond story, it is difficult to understand Melanie's depression without an appreciation of the domestic violence context, the parenting upheavals regarding the children and the lack of external assistance in terms of respite and support services. In the Horace Faulkner case, there were a number of layers to the conflict: Horace's disturbed childhood; his ex-wife Melissa's complex personality, as portrayed by Horace;[29] Horace's feelings of guilt, revenge and jealousy stemming from his disturbed past; Horace's mental instability; the third-party relationship; domestic violence; and, finally, the role of the children. In all three case studies, the perpetrators had represented the event of killing differently and the actors had represented the perpetrator's personality as contrary to that of a cold-blooded killer.

Styles of representation in relation to the actors

For our purposes, 'style', as defined by Findlay and Zvekic,[30] is a material representation of impressions and intended meaning. The creation of a style is dependent on the negotiation of meanings within a particular context. In this context, the style of representing an individual or an event, the represented, is dependent on the physical and emotional distance between, and the nature of the relationship between, the representor and the represented. The meanings within this specific relationship are negotiated by degrees of social relatedness, such as social status (e.g. between friends, relatives, colleagues and neighbours), relationship status (e.g. between parent and child and between spouses) and intervention status (e.g. between the social worker and the individual, the lawyer and their client). Relevant to this are also degrees of temporal and spatial relatedness, such as locality and time, which are variables that cannot be discounted. Underlying such a relationship is the presence of the voice. An influential and leading voice, such as the protagonist's narration, can give authority by neutralising distance and thus enhance believability.

In the Jubilee Soprano story, the perpetrator, Brody, is represented as a sick patient (by Ross), a manipulative person (by Rosaline), and a magnetic and

29 Ch 1: Horace Faulkner.

30 Findlay and Zvekic write that style is a way of doing as well as a manner of representation: Mark Findlay, Uglješa Zvekic and United Nations Interregional Crime and Justice Research Institute, *Alternative Policing Styles: Cross-Cultural Perspectives* (Kluwer Law and Taxation, 1993) 7.

charming person (by Angeline). In the Jack Drummond story, the perpetrator, Melanie, is represented as a loving mother by David and Athena. In the Horace Faulkner story, the perpetrator, Horace, is represented by Melissa, his ex-wife, as a loving father but also as an absent and uncommunicative husband with a disturbed past. This reveals that an actor represents a different social role to different people and his or her social role changes in different social contexts. Arguably, this means that an actor displays different styles of representation depending on the context and on the person to whom the representation is made. Equally, though, the person observing the representation may interpret the representation differently to another depending on the observer's relationship with the actor, their understanding of the actor's context and their own self-interest in the situation.

Styles of representation in relation to the event

When examining representation in relation to the event, it has to be stated at the outset that in very rare instances the event, that is the killing, is known to be a potential event to the actors beforehand. Most representations of the event are post-killing. This is not to say that representations of the event in retrospect are not important. The actors' perceptions of the event after the killing has occurred are important because they shed light on the contextual nature of the killing. For example, they can reveal the intention of the perpetrator – whether he or she acted deliberately and planned the killing, or whether the killing was spontaneous. On the other hand, there may be some instances where the actors are able to, prior to the event, glimpse or foreshadow what might occur. For example, Iris Soprano had a premonition that something bad was about to happen in Angeline's house.[31] It is usually the case that such premonitions come from persons, especially family members, within the second-degree representation. The perpetrator, though, often plans the killing event and provides representations of it to those for whom the killing is meant to mean something. For example, telling the mother that she will never see the children again is a representation of punishment and 'just deserts' for the separation.

When looking at representational styles in relation to events, it is important to recognise that style is heavily dependent on the representor and his or her proximity to what is being represented.[32] For example, a representor from a third-degree representation, such as the court or the perpetrator's lawyer, would have a different style of representation to that of a representor from second-degree representation, such as the parent of the victim, who would have a subjective style of representing that is characterised by his or her relationship to the victim and the event. When it comes to perpetrator representations of events, the style in which the perpetrator represents the event of killing can be dependent

31 Ch 1: Jubilee Soprano.
32 Above, n 30.

on the proximity of the killing to a different event, such as an ongoing court matter or a previous DOCS intervention. In some of the case studies,[33] it can be observed that the perpetrators represent their motivations for killing or neglecting the children with reference to an ongoing child residence battle in court or to a previous DOCS intervention in which a child was removed from the family.

This style of representing the killing was usually characterised by the perpetrator's response to the other event, which the perpetrator saw as justifying his or her motivations for killing. For example, when referencing previous DOCS interventions, the perpetrators in some of the case studies claim they did not approach DOCS because they were fearful DOCS would remove the child from their care. For example, in the Mark and Libby story, Mark made this statement *at* the time of the killing:

> This is just a quick little message for you, just to let you know how unfair and biased the system seems to be . . . I've been put through nothing but punishment and abuse and treated like a common criminal. And for what? I was a good husband, a good father and a good worker. I did all the right things that a father's supposed to do . . . My children mean everything to me. They were my life and my life is non-existent anymore. I'm expected just to sit back and watch it all take place around me, I'm sorry but I just could not do that . . . I've put up with nothing but torture, abuse and punishment . . . yet I did everything to the best of my ability . . . I was the best father I could be. I was the best worker and husband I could be and yet for some people it just isn't enough.[34]

In the Capello Steppenwolf story, the reader will recall that there was an ongoing care application by Elizabeth's ex-partner's mother, Gabrielle, for Capello. The DOCS reference in Elizabeth's statement (see below) references a previous incident when DOCS removed Elizabeth's children from her care and placed them with family members because of her incarceration.[35] Elizabeth later resumed care of the children, but relinquished care again when the children went to live with family members.[36] As a response to the history of child removals by DOCS

33 For example, Elizabeth Kramer in Ch 1: Capello Steppenwolf; Georgina and Quentin Bromley in Ch 1: Hannah Bromley; and Mark in Ch 2: Mark and Libby. The cases of Capello Steppenwolf and Mark and Libby will be discussed here. This is because they contain examples of the two types of interventions referred to here: DOCS and judicial (involving child residence application). These cases demonstrate the link between the perpetrators' representations of the killing in relation to a previous or ongoing intervention.

34 This excerpt is extracted from the transcription of the tape recordings left behind by the deceased father: report 'ML5' taken from New South Wales Coroner Office P on 11 January 2009.

35 Ch 1: Capello Steppenwolf.

36 Ibid.

and family members, Elizabeth's reluctance to surrender Capello is evident in her statement. When Elizabeth was asked about the timing of the killing, she said:

> [Yvonne] turned me off about DOCS, because I told her I said I want to take him to DOCS now . . . and she turned me right off against DOCS. She said if you take him, you are concentrating on one child but it probably backfire in your face and . . . other kids taken . . . She kept telling me that. And that's why I did not go to DOCS. That is why I was scared of going to DOCS.[37]

It appears from both the above cases that the perpetrators' style of representing the killing was to cast blame away from themselves by referring to a previous DOCS event. Arguably, this is done to explain the situation in which the perpetrators find themselves, particularly where the perpetrators see no alternative solution to end the conflict. This is an important observation because it supports the earlier contention in Chapter 2 that state actors are complicit in filicide. This suggests and supports the symbolic interactionist framework used in this book, namely that there are social and interactive forces that influence and shape a perpetrator's decision to kill.

Perpetrator representation of what they did

The perpetrators in the case studies almost always provide a representation of what they did after the killing even though they might have planned the killing and their explanations beforehand. In the Mark and Libby story, however, the perpetrator made representations on an audiotape before he committed suicide. In this exceptional case, the self-representation was contemporaneous. This means that the representing was done prior to, if not at the same time as, the killing. Arguably, this gives the audience a rare insight into the motivations of the perpetrator. Retrospective self-representations are sometimes put together in a police statement, usually as a result of the police investigation, which depends on second-degree representations or hearsay, that is, statements obtained from people expressing what the perpetrator had said about himself or herself and his or her actions. Perpetrator self-representations may be conveyed through the perpetrator's lawyers, but this is not to say the 'Self' (the person) and the representation made are necessarily the same. However, a full and honest representation is rarely found in police statements.[38] There are in fact two questions in relation

37 Ibid. Elizabeth also told her mother she had decided against surrendering Capello to DOCS because that might result in her other children being taken away: *R v Kramer*, Supreme Court, New South Wales, 2009, Supreme Court No. EK1, [34].

38 In most of the cases reviewed, the perpetrator would not tell the full story of the killing or events leading to the killing in the first police interview. The bits and pieces only emerged after further police investigations through phone intercepts or

to how perpetrators represent what they have done to themselves and to others: what sorts of techniques do they use to represent the nature of their actions, and how are such techniques employed?

There are two techniques[39] observable in the case studies that allow perpetrators to represent what they did: masking and sympathetic reinterpretation. In the discussion of these, the reader will find that sometimes the perpetrator utilises both techniques to make sense of the killing. This is not uncommon. Masking and sympathetic reinterpretation complement each other because their purposes are the same, that is, to give meaning to an otherwise unacceptable act of violence. The reader will recall that in Chapter 2 masking was discussed as a symbolic interactionist technique and as a dramaturgical device for analysing the nature of perpetrator violence. Here, masking is analysed in relation to the perpetrator as the wearer of the mask. It will be argued that perpetrators wear a mask in order to take on a different paternal or maternal representation in order to make themselves look different, to themselves and to others. Sympathetic reinterpretation, on the other hand, entails perpetrators self-justifying or self-rationalising their actions by casting themselves in a sympathetic light to the extent of masking their true motives. The purpose of this appears to be the need to give acceptable meaning to an otherwise unacceptable act of violence. The perpetrators Horace Faulkner, Elizabeth Kramer, Saskia Burrow, Mark (in the Mark and Libby story) and Georgina and Quentin Bromley illustrate these techniques of self-representation.

In the Horace Faulkner story, the evidence of both masking and sympathetic reinterpretation lies in Horace's explanation of his increasingly unstable state of mind. Horace sees himself in a number of roles: as a victim of childhood[40] and later as a victim of his marriage;[41] as a loving father but also a failure at being the ideal father to the children;[42] and as a 'social misfit'.[43] The clearest example of the use of masking and sympathetic reinterpretation is when Horace represents his killing of the children:

> [D]o you know how hard it was for me to kill my children. I took drugs to do it, otherwise I couldn't have done it. There is one thing that I am glad

subsequent interviews in which the perpetrator recounted his or her earlier statements. In some cases where the perpetrator was reluctant to cooperate with the police and provided different versions or explanations of the events leading to the killing, the court found the perpetrator's account of the events inconsistent, and this would be an adverse inference drawn against the perpetrator. Some examples of these observations flow from the cases of Danny Burrow and Hannah Bromley.

39 This book recognises that there can be other techniques, such as self-denial and self-rationalisation. However, the focus in the book will be on masking and sympathetic reinterpretation.

40 Ch 1: Horace Faulkner.

41 Ibid.

42 Ibid.

43 Ibid.

> that I killed my kids, they won't have to suffer. I have put them out of their misery, I have saved them from pain.[44]

Horace took drugs to give him Dutch courage to kill the children. This meant that he had to step into another role or wear a different cloak[45] in order to perform the killing. Arguably, Horace wore the mask of the loving, protective and sacrificial father in order to convince himself that he was saving his children from the emotional and physical pain that he was experiencing. By doing this, he represented himself differently. He reinterpreted the negative image of himself by injecting the image with a positive affirmation of the exemplary Father symbol. He rationalised the horror of his killing as follows: 'I think I knew it was against the law but I thought it was best for them. I did not think it was wrong'[46] and 'I was not thinking in terms of killing them. I was going to save them from a broken marriage.'[47] In regard to Horace's explanation it could be said that he had to rationalise his actions to himself and others in a way that would give acceptable meaning (saving the children from the broken marriage) to an otherwise unacceptable act of violent killing. He also saw himself as a victim of the marriage[48] and of his past,[49] and his victimhood status added to this sympathetic reinterpretation of his actions. It is as though he wanted the audience to feel sorry[50] for him, particularly when he was recreating the scene of death as a message for his ex-wife. In addition, this story provides an insight into Horace's image of 'father' and the meaning of 'father' and its symbolism. This is the image he believed he was representing to the children and to himself. He said that he had a desperate wish to be a better father and a better parent than his own parents had been to him.[51] This statement reveals that Horace had an image of the ideal father and how such a father should behave. He clearly saw such an image as opposite to that of his own father. As such, he came to believe that he was saving the children. This he saw was opposite to what his father had done, which was to walk away from him and the family. In spite of the fact that the image Horace had of his father was flawed,[52] Horace chose to enact the symbol of the Father by wearing the mask of the loving parent in order to rationalise the killing of the children to himself and his audience. When the court unmasked

44 Ibid.

45 The term 'cloak' is employed in Chapter 6, where it is seen as a representation or device such as a mask, which is worn in order to conceal underlying dysfunction.

46 Ch 1: Horace Faulkner; report 'HF3' taken on 31 January 2001 from Dr Costello in Sydney at prison F.

47 Ibid.

48 Ibid.

49 Ibid.

50 For example, Horace's father, Alan, described Horace as someone who used others to make them feel sorry for him when he did not get his own way: ibid.

51 Ibid.

52 Ibid.

the true nature of Horace's representation, it revealed that the only motivation for the killing was revenge.[53]

In the Capello Steppenwolf and Jack Burrow case studies, both Elizabeth Kramer and Saskia Burrow were overpowered by their hatred of their ex-spouse, suggesting in both cases that they might have had a Medea complex.[54]Arguably, the mask of Medea allowed the perpetrators the luxury to feel anger towards their ex-partners for the violence they had suffered at the hands of these partners. The mask allows the wearer to do what he or she would otherwise not do; it provides for this capacity because it mixes both man and beast.[55] For example, in the Burrow story, the reader will recall that Saskia's violence was masked as discipline. To both Elizabeth and Saskia,[56] the victim represented and reminded them of their previous partners, from whom they had suffered abuse, violence and/or abandonment. Elizabeth said, for example, that she did not want Capello to touch her arms because it reminded her of the time when Peter kicked her stomach and threatened her with a knife.[57] She also expressed her loathing for Capello, which is evident in her belief that he would grow up and become his father: 'What about when he grows up . . . what if he does the same things his father did to me . . . I don't even look at him like he is my son.'[58] Elizabeth's self-representation, which emerged after the killing, reveals that she viewed herself as a victim of Peter's violence and the child protection system, which she felt did not give her sufficient support.[59] It could be argued that the victimhood status she and Saskia[60] felt somehow gave them the entitlement to wear the mask and to use violence on the children.

This theme of victim empowerment arose also in the story of Mark and Libby. The reader will recall that story was different from the rest because Mark killed the children and committed suicide; he therefore made his statement about doing 'all the right things that a father's supposed to do' (see quote earlier in this chapter) *at the time of* the killing.[61] Mark's statement reveals that he perceived

53 Ibid.
54 The Medea complex is explained in Chapter 3, in which the relevance of the myths of Medea and Heracles is discussed.
55 René Girard, *Violence and the Sacred* (Johns Hopkins University Press, 1977) 167. The theorising behind masking, especially Girard's usage of 'mask', is discussed in the next section on the purpose of representation.
56 Saskia's situation was discussed in Chapter 2 under 'Violence as language'. It was argued there that Saskia saw in Danny the representation of the absent father, George: e.g. Ch 1: Danny Burrow. Her anger towards George was reflected throughout the story in her labelling of Danny and the violent punishment she inflicted on him.
57 Ch 1: Capello Steppenwolf.
58 Ibid.
59 Ibid.
60 Saskia Burrow was a victim of an assault when she was young. She did not shake off this victim status: see Ch 1: Danny Burrow.
61 Mark and Libby, above n 33. This statement was not made retrospectively; that is, it was made before he committed suicide.

himself as a good father to the children. He believed that in spite of this goodness he was treated unfairly. He also perceived himself as a victim of the system. By casting himself in this victim role, he was able to justify killing the children to himself and the audience, his family.[62] He was at the same time reinterpreting the killing for his audience, because he wanted the audience to feel sorry for him. Implicit in the meaning of this message, and quite explicitly in the message[63] addressed to his ex-partner, was a message of revenge. In these messages, Mark reveals four different personas: the masks of the victim, the loving parent, the son and the vengeful spouse. Evident here is the interplay between the techniques of masking and sympathetic reinterpretation, which are used to cast a different meaning for the motivations for killing the children and committing suicide.

Similarly, in the Hannah Bromley story, the techniques of masking and sympathetic reinterpretation were evident in Georgina's and Quentin's representations in court.[64] They portrayed themselves as, and arguably were, victims of their drug addiction. They used their addiction, and the victim status associated with it, to mask and evade their responsibilities to Hannah. Quentin said that in the days leading to Hannah's death she was bubbly and smiling,[65] but he admitted he only saw her twice because he was in his 'own world'.[66] Quentin's representation of what he had done, or rather not done, for Hannah reveals the depth of his prolonged self-denial. This was the mask he wore for himself on a daily basis to evade the knowledge that Hannah was deteriorating. When unmasking Georgina and Quentin, the court revealed their dysfunctional lifestyle as cruel to Hannah and as an abrogation of their parental responsibility.[67]

Another observation worth mentioning is Quentin's representation to the DOCS caseworker in 2007. He told the caseworker that he was making arrangements for the children to be homeschooled and that the children were on medication.[68] He also allowed the two older children, but not Hannah, to be seen by the caseworker. It could be argued that he wore the mask of the loving parent to be able to represent to the caseworker that he was cooperating with DOCS, and so to mislead the caseworker into believing that he was concerned about the children's welfare. Quentin's mask and his subsequent explanation of his distrust of DOCS were revealed by the court to be misleading. This is evident in the sentencing judge's description of Quentin as 'cruel', uncaring and oblivious to Hannah.[69]

It is not clear whether these techniques of self-representation suggest that the available recourses to familial disputes such as separation and child residence

62 Two of his messages were addressed to his ex-partner Libby and his father. The remaining message was a general one.
63 Above n 33.
64 Ch 1: Hannah Bromley.
65 Ibid.
66 Ibid.
67 Ibid.
68 Ibid.
69 Ch 1: Hannah Bromley.

battles are inadequate. The voices of these perpetrators appear to suggest that there are no simple resolutions to disputes of such a complex nature. The very fact that the perpetrators felt that they had to wear a mask suggests that they were concerned about the representation of the killing and of themselves to the audiences. This kind of representation, particularly the loving parent, such as in Mark's story, did not present itself as a risk to the child. These are the kinds of representation that short circuit functional state interventions.

Model 1 explained

At the heart of Model 1 (see Figure 4.1) is the self-representation of the individual. The first circle (the smallest one), or first-degree representation, represents the perspectives of the persons around the individual perpetrator, such as those who have been in contact with the perpetrator at the time of the killing. These persons could be family members, community workers, police officers or even the victims. This is an 'inner circle' of witnesses who have intimate knowledge of the perpetrator's motives and background, and may even be a part of the conflict.

Although not shown in Model 1, there could be tiny circles[70] drawn inside the first-degree circle, which represents the perpetrator's self-representation (or first-person account) that may or may not be known. For example, in the Jubilee Soprano story, the first-degree representation comprises Angeline and Jubilee; there were no self-representations made by Brody. On the other hand, in the Horace Faulkner story there are a number of self-representations made by Horace concerning how he sees himself as a father and husband. In Horace's case, a tiny circle inside the first-degree circle would represent each of his self-representations.

The second-degree circle (the medium-sized one), or second-degree representation, represents persons at a step removed from the first-degree representation. In the Jubilee Soprano story, for example, they would consist of the mental health intervention team, the police officers, the health professionals and Brody's brother, Ross. These people have less intimate knowledge of the perpetrator's actions and are further away from the conflict; they do not live with the perpetrator such that they can form a daily 'database' of knowledge of the perpetrator's behaviour and motives.

70 If it were possible to provide a three-dimensional model, the perpetrator's self-representation or actual 'first-person' account would be clear. However, in this two-dimensional model, representing the first-person account could confuse the general purpose of the model, which is to illustrate degrees or stages of representation as a theoretical conceptualisation. Having said this, an actual 'first person' should be differentiated (on a three-dimensional model if possible) from the first-degree representation that includes the perpetrator's self-representation and representations made by close family members. Evidently the degree of intimacy between first person and representations made in the first degree is not parallel and should stand as a category on its own.

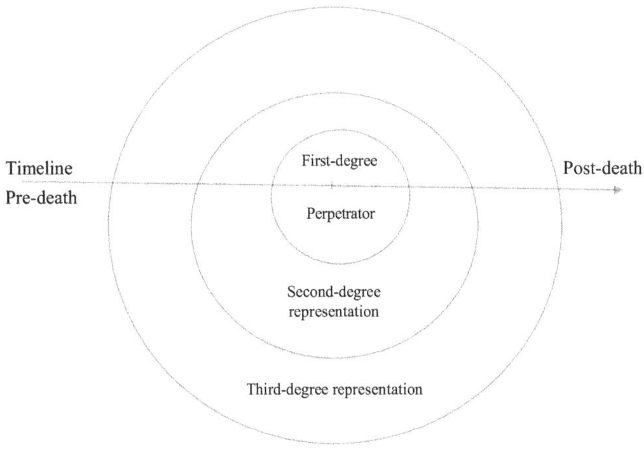

Figure 4.1 Model 1: degrees of perpetrator representation

For example, they might know of the perpetrator's background but lack the intimate connection with the perpetrator on a daily basis. There might be some difficulties placing persons into this category. One such person is Ross, who might at first appear to fall under the categorisation of first-degree representation; upon closer examination, however, it would be noted that he had lost touch with Brody some months before Brody met Angeline. Hence, this would preclude Ross from the first-degree circle. These persons, depending on their occupation and status, may have a measure of influence and control over the course of events.

The third-degree circle (the largest one), or third-degree representation, comprises persons who are furthest removed from the event. This group would include the media and the judge, who invariably play a role in defining the conflict for the audience. The representation from these people can be said to be equivalent to hearsay evidence, because they do not know the perpetrator and victim, or even their families, but have heard of earlier representations emanating from the perpetrator or victim through second-degree and third-degree representations. In legal narrative, hearsay refers to the oral testimony of one person as to the statement of another.[71] The judge in the courtroom is part of this circle but does not receive hearsay evidence if persons giving first-degree representations testify in person in court. However, the judge would still fit into this circle as third-degree representation because of his or her distance from the event.

71 Leslie Rutherford and Sheila Bone (eds), *Osborn's Concise Law Dictionary* (Sweet & Maxwell, 8th ed, 1993) 163. The general rule is that hearsay evidence (oral statements of a person other than one testifying or statements contained in documents offered to prove the truth of the contents) is not admissible. However, there are many exceptions to the rule. For example, see *Evidence Act 1995* (NSW) Part 3.2, sections 59 to 75.

As argued above, the layers represent the different perspectives of persons around the perpetrator. Understanding these perspectives is crucial to understanding which mask the perpetrator might wear in which situation. This understanding also supports the view that the perpetrator wears a different mask for each different social situation. In other words, studying these perspectives allows for the contextualisation of perpetrator representation for each different social situation or in each different situation in which there might be a risk of child endangerment. To illustrate this, the story of Jubilee Soprano is used to demonstrate how the different layers connect to the different perspectives of the parties to generate the representations of Brody. These different representations served to 'hijack' the efforts of the intervention team.

Model 1A (see Figure 4.2) charts a linear representation in which time is depicted as moving forward and backward from the point of origin and using different perspectives of Brody Kitaro, the perpetrator. This is different conceptually to Models 1 and 2, in which the centre event is the killing. In Model 1A, the point on the timeline to the extreme left represents pre-death, and the point on the timeline to the extreme right represents post-death. That is, representations to the left of the centre are representations of Brody before his mental illness manifested, and those to the right of the centre are representations of Brody after he met Angeline and when conflict first began to develop. The centre can then be conceived as the original point of conflict; in this book it is referred to as the relationship or marital rupture.[72] In Model 1A, this point of conflict resides in, and is represented by, the perpetrator. This is not to situate the breakdown of the marital relationship with the perpetrator alone. The perpetrator represents conflict and marital rupture because the rupture of the family begins with the conflict within the perpetrator and it is the perpetrator who manifests the conflict. This extreme manifestation is the killing of the children, but the focus of the representation of the conflict in Models 1 and 1A is on the perpetrator.

Model 1A is an expanded representation of Model 1 and can be superimposed on top of Model 1. The reason for having a separate model is that there is too much detail in Model 1A to fit into Model 1. Instead of having the circles seen in Model 1, the dotted lines in Model 1A show the points of intersection between the timeline and the circles. At the centre of Model 1A is the perpetrator, who is conflicted. The dotted lines to the left and right of the perpetrator mark the boundary of first-degree representation. This is followed by the boundary of second-degree representation; Iris and Papadino Soprano, for example, fall within the second-degree representation. The next set of dotted lines to the left and right of the boundary of the second-degree representation is the boundary for third-degree representation, into which the intervention team and Ross fall. As such, Model 1A is representative of the different perspectives of the perpetrator held by the parties.

72 This is discussed in Chapter 6.

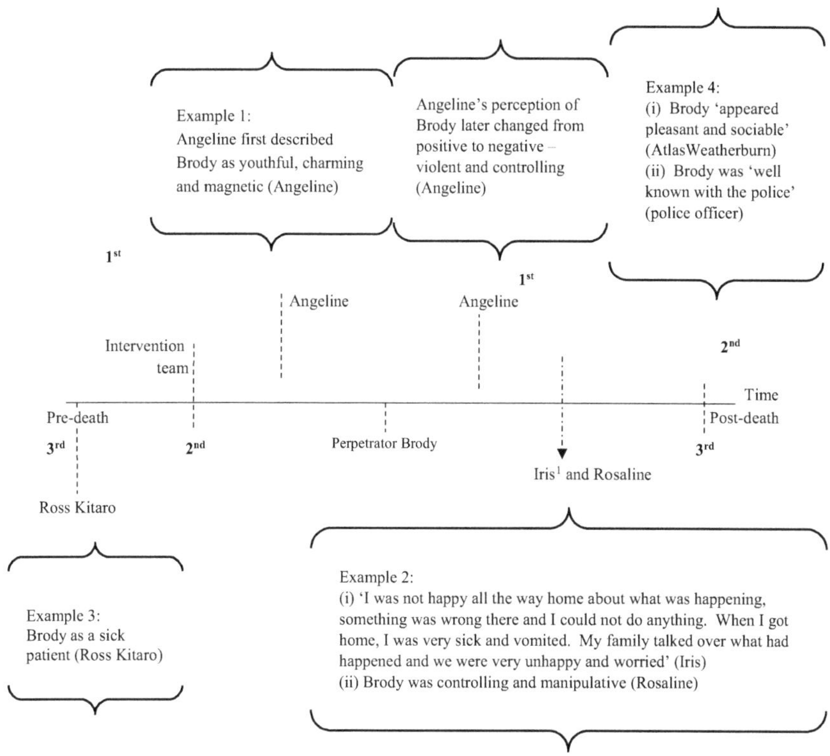

Figure 4.2 Model 1A: application to the Jubilee Soprano story[73]

73 Model 1A refers to the Jubilee Soprano story in Chapter 1. As this is a cross-section representation of Model 1, first-person account is not represented. If it could be, it would be contained within Perpetrator Brody. The purpose of Model 1A though is to illustrate the importance of understanding the significance of representations made by others about the perpetrator.

In Example 1, Angeline Soprano made two representations referred to in this model: the first a police statement after the killing with regards to the time when she first met Brody Kitaro, and the second in a police statement after the killing with regards to Brody's demeanour before the intervention team arrived.

In Example 4, Atlas Weatherburn, mental health worker, made this representation in a police statement after the killing with regards to the time when the intervention team interviewed Brody Kitaro at Angeline Soprano's residence. A police officer made this representation to Rosaline Soprano, Angeline Soprano's sister. Rosaline Soprano then repeated the police officer's statement in a police statement with regards to the time when she was researching on Brody Kitaro prior to the killing.

Iris Soprano, Angeline Soprano's mother, made the representation in 'Example 2' in a police statement after the killing with regards to one of her visits to Angeline Soprano's residence and her observation about what was happening to her daughter. Rosaline Soprano made the representation in 'Example 2' to Ross Kitaro, Brody Kitaro's brother, in a phone call to Ross. Ross then made this representation in a

Looking at Model 1A, it can be observed that the representations closest to Brody, such as those of Rosaline, Iris and Papadino, provide a more in-depth and detailed perception of his nature at the time than the representation of Ross. In other words, the second-degree representations provide a closer observation of Brody around the time of the killing than do the third-degree representation. The intervention team sits between the second- and third-degree representations across both models, but I classify them in Model 1A as third-degree representation. In Model 2A (see Figure 4.4), which also concerns the Jubilee Soprano story but from a different perspective, the team hovers between second- and third-degree representation but falls closer to second degree because of proximity to the killing. The intervention team had the opportunity to assess Brody just three days before the killing. This means that it should have been able to make a diagnosis of the perpetrator's state of mind prior to the killing, except for one obstacle: distance from the perpetrator. Because Model 1A is about *perpetrator* representation, the intervention team does not have the same level of relationship with the perpetrator as the persons in second-degree representation. However, Model 2A is about *event* representation, and in this model the intervention team is close to the event despite lacking an intimate connection. This suggests the team should have been able to recognise Brody's mental stability and the conflict situation prior to the killing.

This distinction between perpetrator and event representation is important because they are not the same. In the former, a relationship of intimacy and connection is crucial to the construction of the perpetrator representation, whereas in the latter such a relationship is not as significant; it can exist but only in so far as the relationship is one of the determinants in how the event is perceived. It could be argued that different people will perceive an event of killing the same way but will perceive the perpetrator in different ways depending on their level of relationship with the perpetrator. With perpetrator representation, the relationship is important because it signifies the relevance of having depth of knowledge about the perpetrator, which is crucial to the way he or she is represented by others. The distinction is a fine one.

The media and the sentencing judge fall under third-degree representation. This is because of their proximity to the perpetrator and their reliance on second-degree representations. As such, it is the reliance on what other people have said about the perpetrator that forms the basis of the media's and the judge's opinion about the perpetrator, in addition to oral testimony in court. As suggested before, the judicial narrative is a powerful voice because it gives authority, legitimacy and believability to selected representations and to the 'story'. Following from this, the media selects legitimated portions of the 'story'

---

police statement with regards to the time when Rosaline had rang him about Brody.

In Example 3, Ross Kitaro made this representation in a police statement with regards to the time when he spoke to Rosaline Soprano on the phone and to whom he made this representation.

and, as will be discussed in Chapter 5, it selectively endorses and adds to certain representations arising out of the judicial narrative rather than others. This process suggests that the nature of the relationship between these two agents is symbiotic. This symbiosis can sometimes result in the creation of a limited representation of the 'story' for the audience. Because this takes place at the third-degree representation, the emergent representations are physically removed from the centre and lacking any relationship of intimacy; yet, paradoxically, as third-degree representations they carry the most weight relative to the voices in the first- and second-degree representations.

Looking at the voices in the first- and second-degree representations in the Jubilee Soprano story, it must be noted that, at the time of the intervention prior to the killing, Angeline was not forthcoming with the intervention team regarding any concerning perception of Brody. Angeline did at an earlier point in time mention to her sister Rosaline in a telephone conversation that she had met this prospective partner, and Rosaline had warned Angeline to be careful.[74] Apart from this, there was no evidence of Angeline expressing her concerns to anyone about what was happening in the home. Angeline had been too frightened of Brody to voice her fears and concerns, and her vulnerable disposition made such expression even harder.[75] Angeline's representations evident in Model 1A were made after the killing. By charting this retrospective representation, it can be seen that Angeline could have been an important source of information for the intervention team or for any agency closely examining the dynamics of this conflict at the time. However, her voice could not be heard by anyone. Even though Angeline made these representations concerning Brody after the killing, it could be argued that her perception of Brody was more representative of his state of mind and his overall behaviour at the time (although she did not voice these prior to the killing) than the second-degree representations made, with the exception of Rosaline's view.

Examining the varying perspectives of Brody in Model 1A allows the reader to capture the changing nature of Brody's masks. The reader will recall that in Chapter 2 masking was discussed as a dramaturgical device for understanding filicidal violence. Masking was employed as an analytical lens through which the different forms of violence arising from the case studies can be understood. Here, masking is employed to understand perpetrator representations. Examining Model 1A, it can be observed that the perspective on Brody by Angeline in the first-degree representation is fairly accurate. This appears to indicate that the mask is manifested from afar. The representations made by the parties in the third-degree representation appear to capture the masks that Brody wore at that time. For example, the intervention team believed Brody to be rational because he put on the mask and represented himself as rational. His voice of reason, articulated through his mask, thus concealed his manipulation and mental illness.

74 Ch 1: Jubilee Soprano.
75 Ibid.

Once the intervention team left, the mask was torn down. This suggests that it is hard for the perpetrator to maintain the mask in the long term. It appears to be easier to wear the mask for a short period of time in order to convince a specific audience. There is a slight caveat to this argument: even though the mask is manifest from a distance (e.g. by third-degree representation), it is torn down when it is presented in the courtroom, which also belongs in third-degree representation, where unmasking usually occurs. At the trial, there are various witnesses from the first and second degree who make representations about the perpetrator. This offers the audience multiple perspectives of the perpetrator. It could be argued that the different masks are exhibited in the courtroom as a result of the unmasking function of the court. The court unmasks the perpetrator and reveals any hidden violence to be what it really is.

When examining Model 1A it is important to note that none of the representations can be discounted, because they can be pieced together to form a more complete understanding, though never a representational unity,[76] of what was really happening. Yet while these representations can never fully represent the conflict, they can be conceptualised as tools to allow the analyser to get a better grasp of the key players in the conflict and where they stand in relation to the perpetrator. The familial framework in which these players are structured is also important because it allows the analyser to build into the analysis the nuanced or sometimes layered contextualisation of the conflict; this will be further discussed in relation to Model 2A below.

Model 2 explained

At the centre of Model 2 (see Figure 4.3) is the event of killing. Like in Model 1, the first-degree circle encompasses representations about the events that are closest to, including immediately before and immediately after, the event of killing. Events found within this circle are considered according to the distance and the intimacy the event has in relation to the killing. In the context of the Jubilee Soprano story, the model is able to chart Angeline's retrospective representation of the killing.

Unlike in Model 1A, Angeline's event representation in Model 2A may be questionable and is not helpful because it is retrospective due to her silence prior to the killing. Her representation is questionable because of her relationship with the perpetrator, as this may cause her to provide a biased view. In theory, therefore, first-degree representations about an event should be approached with caution. However, Model 2 can also be used to represent various events.

76 Sarah Webster Goodwin and Elisabeth Bronfen (eds), *Death and Representation* (Johns Hopkins University Press, 1993) 324–330, 335. They argue that repetitive images, including duplicates of the original subject, are risky resemblances that attempt to represent the original identity that is non-replicable. Also see Walter Benjamin, *Illuminations* (Harry Zohn trans, Schocken Books, 1st ed, 1968) 217–252.

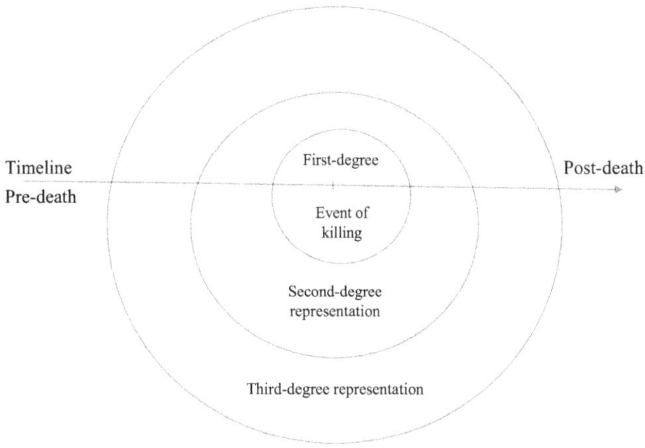

Figure 4.3 Model 2: degrees of event representation

Depending on the event's level of importance, its placement on the model can reveal its significance in the larger scheme of representations, particularly when considered in relation to the event of killing.

Again referring to the Soprano story, events that are theorised to be of significance can be charted on the model. In chronological order they are: Angeline's first meeting with Brody; the parents' visits; the mental health intervention; and the killing. When examining these as a complete chain of events, it is possible to pinpoint changes in significant events. The following explanation of Model 2 is based on Iris' and Papadino's representation of the chain of events leading to the killing.

Because Model 2, like Model 1, is about representation, the persons involved cannot be divorced from the event; they are intricately interwoven as participants who help to construct a particular perspective about what has happened. In this regard, Model 2 is similar to Model 1 in that the persons representing the events within the first-, second- and third-degree representations are the same. What is different is the subject matter of the representation. The separation of the event from the perpetrator in this manner allows for separate contextualisation of the different perspectives of the persons in the conflict. The analysis of these perspectives forms the basis of any objective and clinical assessment of risk and provides a method by which contextualisation[77] of the domestic conflict can be achieved in a methodical way.

77 In this book, 'contextualise' means putting into perspective the circumstances in which an event occurs. This means situating the event, such as the killing, within the broader social and familial framework, such as within relationships in the family, relationships and structures of violence and/or conditions for intervention.

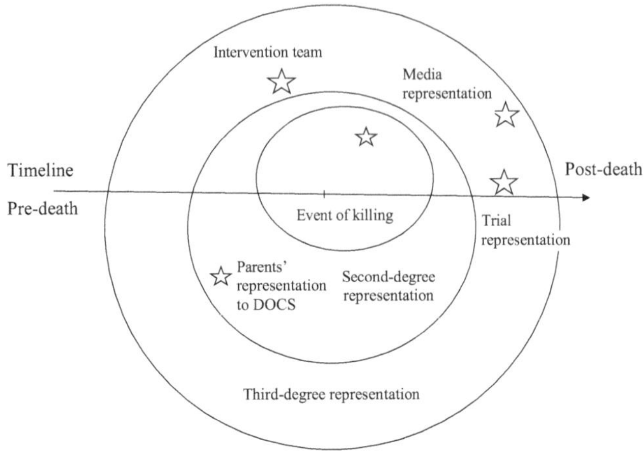

Figure 4.4 Model 2A: application to the Jubilee Soprano story

Before we proceed to an analysis of Model 2A (see Figure 4.4), this model has to be explained to the reader. The stars in Model 2A represent an event representation. This is to say that they are representations made by a party about their perception about an event they had witnessed. The timeline does not divide the top from the bottom; it is there to show a linear progression. The circles in Model 2A can be likened to a globe. The reason for this is that the events can be represented at various layers at the same time and/or within the degree or layer. In addition, the reader will notice that there are only three layers in the models. This is not to say that additional layers cannot be added. For the purposes of this book, the three layers are sufficiently representative of the structural framework that constitutes representation. Now the analysis of Model 2A and of the different degrees within it can begin.

The second-degree representation of events provided by Iris and Papadino Soprano, to use Angeline's parents as an illustration, is important because they are the next closest interaction Angeline had at the time (after that with Brody himself). The parents' developing perspective about the chain of events can be seen as crucial to understanding the context in which they understood their daughter. Their representation changed from being curious about the new arrival, Brody, to coming to a disturbing conclusion about the chain of events in Angeline's home. This shows the development of the risk of child endangerment to Jubilee. First, Iris and Papadino represented the event of their daughter's change of behaviour from her usual warmth to a cold and distant attitude. The events they represented in this manner included a number of phone interactions and social visits they had with her. Next, they noticed the change in Jubilee's normal routine. The events here included observing Angeline's and Jubilee's behaviour, listening to their stories and noticing the material changes in both Angeline's and Jubilee's lives. Their representations of the events were informed by their observations at the time and then were shaped, denied or confirmed by the conveyance of their perspective to an audience – a third party or each other. The parents, for example, conveyed their increasingly negative representation of Brody to DOCS. After this, they heard about Jubilee's change in routine, Angeline's attempt to withdraw money and the verbal threat from Brody. There were a number of significant points where it would have been obvious to DOCS that the event representations were indicative of an environment of risk. However, these risks were not immediately recognised, and inadequate action was taken to protect Jubilee.

When gauging the level of importance to attach to an event representation, it is important to recognise that first-degree representation, although it may provide accurate first-hand knowledge of the killing, may only provide a partial view with regard to other events. Caution must be exercised when a representation is made about an event which has previously impacted on the representor. Again I refer to Angeline's representation of the killing, which can be contrasted to her representation of her first meeting with Brody. It could be argued that Angeline consistently saw herself as a victim – when it came to her relationship with Brody, she reacted in the same way she had with her ex-husband. It is thus possible that through her disempowerment she was complicit in Jubilee's death. The fact that she had been silent all the way up to the killing is evidence of her complicity. Again, this harks back to the pervasiveness of symbolic violence and reveals that the phenomenon of child killing is not always only about the perpetrator.

Unlike in Model 1A, where the intervention team falls under third-degree representation, the intervention team in Model 2A is classified as second-degree representation, even though technically it sits at the border between second- and third-degree representation. This is because of its proximity, in terms of physical distance, to the event. The intervention team did not sight Jubilee Soprano or speak to Angeline and, as such, the team members could not make any assessments regarding the child endangerment concerns reported by Iris and Papadino. This could be because in their role as medical assessors they were sent primarily to ascertain Brody's state of mind and not the situation of the family as a whole, a role that would fall under the purview of DOCS. For this reason, the intervention team did not make any concrete assessment of the situation in Angeline's home at the time, except they noted that the atmosphere was tense.[78]

Using various perspectives of the event, I theorise that it is possible to contextualise the conflict using Model 2A. Because each version of the conflict cannot be discounted, the analyser has to read into the layered nature of each context. An interpretation of the layering of the conflict could be as follows. Angeline's sister, Rosaline, knew that Angeline was at a vulnerable stage of her life. She warned Angeline when Angeline first told her about Brody. Layered on top of this is the conflict between Angeline and her parents, in which she gave the impression that she did not want her parents' interference. Angeline's

78 Ch 1: Jubilee Soprano.

behaviour clearly did not make sense to her parents, and they rightly conveyed their concerns to DOCS. One could reason that Brody engineered Angeline's rebellion towards her parents and manipulated her to withdraw the money in defiance of her parents' wishes. Beneath this was Angeline's own representation of how she saw her parents. She described her father as 'authoritarian' and saw herself as a submissive actor under her ex-husband's influence.[79] For Angeline, meeting Brody was something extraordinary because initially he appeared to represent everything her ex-husband was not.

While Model 2A can be read in this way, the interpretation is not prescriptive. This means, practically speaking, that it would be difficult to predict when filicide will occur in families in which conflict is highly textured and where there are a number of different and changing perspectives. However, it might have been possible, in the Soprano case, to have made a number of reasonable diagnoses about possible turns of events and on that basis to have monitored events closely. This would require the analyser to be kept updated and to record each person's changing perception of a particular event, suggesting there is scope for better handling of potential filicides in future.

From a theoretical angle, another way of conceiving of the models is to view them as offering multiple perspectives on certain representations put forward by the judicial voice as preferred facts. The layering of representations gives the impression that perspectives revolve around the original event and depend on the distance they are from the centre. The claim that one story representing 'truth'[80] is only found at the centre is undisputable for the perpetrators and victims, but this version is often not readily available, and another claim, that there may be competing representations for other parties, is also valid.[81] In the context of judicial reasoning, truth has to be distinguished from fact. The adversarial nature of the trial process is designed to represent preferred facts as objective *truth* based on a discoverable objective reality and rational fact-finding.[82] Notions about objective truth are problematic in the legal context because, outside of this context, truth is seen as a social construct such as language, and as socially contingent,[83] rather than a consequence of legal

79 Ibid.

80 The notion of objective truth is highly contestable, particularly in law, where objective truth is a core assumption in the rationalist tradition: William Twining, *Rethinking Evidence: Exploratory Essays* (Blackwell, 1990) 76, ch 3; see also Donald Nicolson, 'Truth, Reason and Justice: Epistemology and Politics in Evidence Discourse' (1994) 57(5) *Modern Law Review* 726–744, 729. Here, 'truth' is representative in the context of storytelling and it serves to enforce the perspectives and beliefs of the different parties involved in the conflict.

81 M Davies, *Asking the Law Question* (Law Book, 1994) 304–305; A Hunt, 'Postmodernism and Critical Criminology' in B D McLean and D. Milovanovic (eds), *New Directions in Critical Criminology* (Collective Press, 1991) 71–94, 82; and see Berger and Luckmann, above n 3.

82 Twining, above n 80.

83 Richard Rorty, *Contingency, Irony and Solidarity* (Cambridge University Press, 1989) ch 1, 7; Ernesto Laclau and Chantal Mouffe, 'Post-Marxism Without Apologies'

reasoning.[84] In the socio-legal context of this book, truth and fact are presented as distinct. In Chapter 5, the process by which facts *become* a representation of 'truth' is further discussed. However, in the context of perpetrator representation, 'truth' must be confined to a limited context – from the perspective of the person making the statement or belief. In situations where the perpetrator does not testify in court, it is difficult for persons in third-degree representation to make any claim to knowledge. This implies that the court, when facing this lack of representation, will reject, or will not pass judgment on, the unrepresented voice. As a result, the voice will be denied legitimacy and credibility. As an example of this process of legal reasoning on the issue of fact-finding, the court's elucidation on this point in the Capello Steppenwolf case lends credence to this argument:

> [I]t is somewhat difficult to get a clear picture of the offender's life as there are inconsistencies in the history she gave to each of the report writers. I largely attribute this to the fact that third parties are relating a long story with varying degrees of detail and it is impossible to determine how accurately the story was told to them and how accurately they have recorded it. This is just one of the problems when the offender does not give evidence in sentencing proceedings but relies upon what has been reportedly said to others.[85]

This suggests that only one version of 'fact' can emerge, which entails a limitation on, and rejection of, the unrepresented voice. This was also seen in the Hannah Bromley story, in which the court also rejected the perpetrators' voices not as a result of a lack of representation but because their stories lacked consistency. The sentencing judge said:

> I accept there may have been some level of domestic violence in the relationship. If there was, it is more likely that it was relatively minor and occurred in years past rather than in more recent times. I cannot accept, however, that the level of violence, control and domination by [Quentin] was anywhere near that which [Georgina] had claimed. [Georgina] has a history of blaming others – doctors and government officials – for negative aspects in her life. There is some merit in the proposition put to [Georgina] by the Crown Prosecutor, although denied, that she was reduced now to blaming [Quentin] in an endeavour to minimise her responsibility for what occurred to her daughter.[86]

(1987) 166 *New Left Review* 79–106, 7, 85–86; and Michel Foucault, in Collin Gordon (ed), *Power/Knowledge: Selected Interviews and Other Writings, 1972–1977* (Harvester Wheatsheaf, Gordon *et al* trans, 1980 ed) 131.

84 Above n 82.

85 Ch 1: Capello Steppenwolf; *R v Kramer*, above n 37, [46].

86 *R v Georgina and Quentin Bromley*, Supreme Court, New South Wales, 2009, Supreme Court No. GQHB, [119]; and see Ch 1: Hannah Bromley.

The court's point is important because it suggests that the technique of sympathetic reinterpretation used by Georgina was not successful. Again, the court's role as legitimator of the official version is seen here.[87] The court's function to unmask the perpetrator also comes across clearly. Georgina's masks are manifested more clearly in the courtroom, and as such they are also more transparent to the court. The physical distance enables the court, in third-degree representation, to reject the perpetrators' inconsistent stories and to peel away the masks and layers to reveal the true nature of the violence to Hannah.

Developing from earlier analyses of third-degree representation and the judicial voice, the reader is presented with two competing voices here: the perpetrators' voices and the judicial voice represented by the sentencing judge. In this case, the latter prevailed over, and negated, the former. This is indicative of the court's symbolic power to legitimate certain representations, such as the representation of Quentin as an oblivious parent, and negate others, such as the representation of Georgina as submissive in the relationship.[88] More often than not, and as shown above, these selected representations end up as limited and diluted summaries, and, as will be argued in Chapter 5, they are presented by the media to its audience as preferred facts. The negation of the perpetrators' interpretation of Hannah's death also revealed the perpetrators' lifestyle and masks to be dysfunctional. This representation contradicted earlier representations of the parents as loving, which were revealed by the court to be misleading.[89] What was not revealed by the court was the risk of child endangerment embedded in and hidden behind the perpetrators' loving parent representations.

Conclusion

This chapter started with a working hypothesis that representations can be graphically conceptualised. In this regard, four models were employed to represent the data. Here, the modelling comes before the theorising in Chapter 5. This is because the positioning of the data is pivotal to the book. The models have been used to explain and to interpret the way the data is being analysed. In this way, they inform and add to the theorising, which references the models in order to explain and interpret the data in a meaningful way. The models function as a bridge between theory and reality. This unique positioning allows the reader to appreciate the richness of using modelling as an analytical lens through which to approach and interpret case study data across the disciplines of law, social sciences and criminology.

87 It was also evident in Horace Faulkner's story, where the court legitimised and hence confirmed Melissa's view on Horace and her version of events, including the history of the relationship and domestic violence: Ch 1: Horace Faulkner. This is significant because Horace and Melissa held opposite points of view on the relationship problems and domestic violence.

88 Ch 1: Hannah Bromley.

89 Ibid.

The conclusion that emerges from this marrying of the data with modelling is significant in that it reveals the nature of representation to be perspectival and layered. Representation is affected by the same kinds of cultural and social framing that people use to represent themselves and others. Types of cultural and social framing include proximity, which is indicative of relationship and familial status; emotional and physical distance, which is indicative of objectivity; and degree, which is indicative of perspectives taking into account variables such as time, space and distance. These kinds of framing are responsible for creating the response of the audience to a particular representation. They are also responsible for determining an actor's social role, which is dependent on the context of presentation. The models also illustrate the changing nature of perpetrator representation among his or her different social roles. This can be seen as revealing the points of change in perpetrator and event representations, illuminating the staged development of risk of child endangerment.

The layered nature of perpetrator representation is revealed through the different styles of representation in relation to the perpetrator, the event and the self-representation. The different styles of representation are seen as reliant on the same kinds of social and cultural framings. Applying these framings to an analysis of the case studies reveals that the act of killing is not a random decision, and for some it is dependent on the meaning of other events, such as the previous removal of a child or an unhappy court experience, which influence and shape the perpetrator's decision to kill.

The graphical breakdown of representation into first, second and third degrees also illustrates the importance of these social and cultural framings. For example, the judicial narrative is highlighted as significant because it perverts the distance/believability causality; furthermore, because of its symbolic function, the judicial voice is argued to endorse and legitimate certain representations over others. This becomes relevant in Chapter 5, where this process is discussed at length and is seen to be an important social interactive force of construction that gives meaning and purpose to representation in Western society.

In the context of self-representation, this chapter has highlighted two techniques used by perpetrators to rationalise the violence to themselves and others: masking and sympathetic reinterpretation. These techniques suggest that filicide perpetrators are social actors who, like actors in a play, believe that their masks reflect their true selves and at the same time, depending on the situation, they distance themselves from the mask on some occasions and accept the mask without reservation on other occasions.[90] These case studies show how the masking and sympathetic reinterpretation techniques are employed to give

90 Giorgio Agamben, David Kishik and Stefan Pedatella, *Nudities* (Stanford University Press, 2010) 47–48. Agamben makes a number of profound arguments here, but the primary argument which relates to this book is that the distance between the actor and his or her mask or persona is often blurred, and the actor's gaze on the mask reveals a special significance of the mask for the actor.

acceptable meaning to unacceptable violence. These techniques are employed by these perpetrators specifically for their audiences and themselves, and they are not unlike the techniques utilised by Medea and Heracles in classical Greek tragedies, as discussed in Chapter 3.

The mask enables the voice of the perpetrator to be heard. Yet the mask is a double-edged sword – it both reveals and conceals the nature of the violence, and enlightens and obfuscates the meaning of the actor's message. The point made here is that masking reveals representation to be the cornerstone of every decision and action taken by the state. Representation is an essential element in the creation of meaning and it is inseparable from risk. The voices of these perpetrators demonstrate that the processes of representation are not dissimilar to those in Greek mythology, and this representational parallel exists because these parent images have been and still are deeply embedded in the structures of patriarchy.

5 Theorising representation

Introduction[1]

The reader will recall the argument in Chapter 4 that representation can be conceptualised as layers that symbolise social roles, identities or labels that are constantly evolving depending on the context in which the role is being enacted and which mask is worn. It has been argued that the mask dictates, shapes and refashions the way the actor acts and is perceived by his or her audience. Now it is imperative to question the purpose of this mask and its representation in Western society. This chapter sets out to examine the socio-legal purpose of representation, which, the book argues, is social governance.[2] This broad purpose is contrasted with self-representation, whose purposes can be a good many things, such as personal reputation, image and first impressions. In the public domain, parental representations have been constructed in the law to preserve the existing

1 This chapter follows on from the Chapter 4 'Modelling representation' and builds on the modelling presented there.

2 Governance has a number of meanings: R A W Rhodes, 'The New Governance: Governing without Government' (1996) XLIV *Political Studies* 652–667, 653, 657. In the socio-political sphere, governance refers to a pattern of interactions by various social actors and organisations intersecting with the traditional arms of government: Nikolas Rose, *Powers of Freedom: Reframing Political Thought* (Cambridge University Press, 1999) 15. When applied to the context of this book, the term 'social governance' refers to the legal and non-legal interactions between formal and informal systems of regulation by traditional arms of government and social actors. An example of this would be the interaction between the legal system and parents as social actors or the interaction between a government organisation such as DOCS and parents. See also David McCallum, 'Coercive Normalization and Family Policing: The Limits of the "Psy-Complex" in Australian Penal Systems' (2007) 16(1) *Social and Legal Studies* 113–129, 114. The meaning of social governance is the condition of producing regulation and control of social actors, and in particular the regulation of the family: Jacques Donzelot, *The Policing of Families* (Pantheon Books, 1st American ed, 1979) 169–234.

social and cultural order in Western society.[3] Their ability to maintain a ubiquitous presence in Western society has been predicated on the governing forms of parenting behaviour deemed as deviant.[4] This form of governance creates homogenous control over the standards of parenting behaviour in the dominant society.[5] While this may not be the only purpose of parental representations,[6] the book suggests that their main purpose in the law and in the public social domain allows for a simplistic division of parents into categories of good and bad in order to preserve the hegemonic order between the state and the family.[7] This hierarchy allows Western society, through the use of the law, to regulate

3 Contrary to popular belief that the family is outside of public visibility, the family, especially regarding childhood, is intensely regulated through legislative obligations: Nikolas Rose, *Governing the Soul: The Shaping of the Private Self* (Routledge, 1990) xi, 121–122. The *Children and Young Persons (Care and Protection) Act 1998* (NSW) is an example of such regulation. Some examples of this are as follows. Section 38A on parent responsibility contracts at sub-section 5 provides a number of situations in which a parent responsibility contract is entered into between the parent as primary caregiver and the state through the Director-General of DOCS. Even though such a contract is not legally enforceable, it can be used as evidence to resolve a child's need for care and protection without bringing a care application under the *Children's Court Act 1987* (NSW).

4 Representations of motherhood, fatherhood, family life and parental conduct generated by expertise can infuse and shape individuals to regulate and evaluate their lives, actions and goals: Rose, ibid 129. Also see Donzelot, above n 2, 213, 225–231.

5 Edwin Schur, *Labeling Women Deviant: Gender, Stigma and Social Control* (McGraw-Hill, 1983) 8; and Vickie Jensen and Dudeck-Biondo, 'Mothers in Jail: Gender, Social Control and the Construction of Parenthood Behind Bars' in Stacy Lee Burns (ed), *Ethnographies of Law and Social Control* (Emerald Group, 2005) 121–142, 126.

6 Moscovici argues that the purpose of all representations is to make something unfamiliar, and unfamiliarity itself familiar; other purposes include: as a response to desirability, to imbalance; and as domination through control, and to control individual behaviour: Serge Moscovici, *Social Representations: Explorations in Social Psychology* (New York University Press, 2001) 36–37.

7 Hegemony harks back to Antonio Gramsci's usage in the political and historical sense, which is 'the consensual basis of an existing political system within civil society' and that is not the same as the concept of domination: Walter L Adamson, *Hegemony and Revolution: A Study of Antonio Gramsci's Political and Cultural Theory* (University of California Press, 1980) 170. In the socio-political sense, Gramsci sees the family as an institution of the state and civil society. The relationship between the family and the state can be conceptualised as hegemonic given that the state apparatus, including its institutions, can support and coerce the family through the 'microstructures of the practices of everyday life'. See Renate Holub, *Antonio Gramsci: Beyond Marxism and Postmodernism* (Routledge, 1992) 6. For the purposes of this book, hegemony refers to the state's existence as a structure of power, and related to this is the family as a domain of power in which its power is manifest. Closely connected to this domain are parent representations, which are intricately connected to the structures of power and authority in relation to the family. The sphere of domestic violence is one example of this intimate connection. See R W Connell, 'The State, Gender, and Sexual Politics' (1990) 19 *Theory and Society* 507–544, 520–522.

the family as a subordinate entity within its larger patriarchal structure.[8] Understanding the main purpose of representation, in general, is crucial within broader understandings of the contexts in which parent perpetrators are represented. This is important because, as the stories have and will further demonstrate, such contexts in which perpetrator representations are constructed are not usually painted in black and white.

The reader will recall in the Jack Drummond case study, for example, the media and subsequent trial representation of Melanie as the good mother was juxtaposed against the representation of Jack as the Other. This polarisation was evident in the trial court's reconstruction of Melanie's perpetrator representation, on the one hand, as '[i]t may well be that the offender's crusader behaviour also contributed to conflict within the marriage'[9] and, on the other:

> This offender was required to educate, feed, toilet, bathe, entertain and love Jason. She loved and cared for [her daughter] and did not neglect her despite the constant demands of raising an autistic child. She constantly lived with the fact that her son had lost his best chance of acquiring later life skills because of the failure of authorities to provide appropriate intervention during his early formative years. She carried the burden for her husband and supported him through his mental breakdown and general inability to cope with his life and [Jack] in particular. She did all this in an environment of physical and emotional abuse from her husband. She worked outside the family home to help support the family. She assisted others with handicapped children.[10]

This interpretation of Melanie was seemingly an overwhelmingly positive one in spite of her killing her son. Melanie was represented as the strong and loving woman, that is, the good mother, who sacrificed everything for her son and eventually succumbed to depression. This representation has been seen as one-sided. French and Kayess, for example, contend that both the trial and appellate courts appeared to have constructed Jack as the 'demonic Other'.[11] In so doing,

8 Gerda Lerner, *The Creation of Patriarchy* (Oxford University Press, 1986) 217; and Sarah Webster Goodwin and Elisabeth Bronfen, *Death and Representation* (Johns Hopkins University Press, 1993) 17.

9 Ch 1: Jack Drummond case study.

10 *R v Melanie Drummond*, New South Wales District Court, 2004, District Court No. MD1, [82].

11 Phillip French and Rosemary Kayess, 'Deadly Currents Beneath Calm Waters: Persons with Disability and the Right to Life in Australia' in Luke Clements and Janet Read (eds), *Disabled People and the Right to Life: The Protection and Violation of Disabled People's Most Basic Human Rights* (Routledge, 2008) 57–84, 64. For examples of this construction, see: Ch 1: Jack Drummond; *R v Melanie Drummond*, New South Wales District Court, above n 10, [30], [34]; and *R v Melanie Drummond*, Court of Criminal Appeal, New South Wales, 2004, Court of Criminal Appeal No. MD2, [8], [9], [51] to [53].

the courts devalued Jack's humanness and dignity and by implication offered a degree of excuse for the killing.[12] The court's reconstruction of Melanie also changed from Melanie as the good mother to Melanie as the sick patient. This explanation for the killing appeared to have been preferred over Melanie's moral culpability, which the sentencing judge said was 'very low'.[13] As such, the court, which has the final authority on the illegality of human conduct, including standards of parenting behaviour,[14] had enunciated that Melanie's behaviour and actions were understandable on the basis of her good parent image. The context Melanie's good mother image represented could be seen as misleading in light of the gravity of the offence, particularly when compared to the rest of the deviant parent representations in the other cases, all of which involve the death of a child.

Melanie's representation, whether as perpetrator villain or sacrificial heroine, was unclear because she appears to have been represented as both. Furthermore, the case itself was morally controversial and complex, especially on the question of responsibility. But, had the trial judge unravelled the various degrees of representations, he would have revealed the nuanced contextualisation in the case and might have arrived at a different judgment considering the gravity of the offence at first instance. A nuanced contextualisation might well revolve around the way the Drummond parents perceived their autistic son and whether that representation impinged on their responsibility towards him. On the issue of social governance, the appellate court's judgment was even less helpful because it reaffirmed Melanie's good parent representation at first instance. Having said that, Justice Dunford in the appellate court reinstated the deviant parent image in child killing by denouncing her conduct and holding the imposition of the good behaviour bond as 'manifestly inadequate'.[15]

Theorising representation

Representation is seen to be layered, and as having the ability to blur distinctions between the real and the unreal or the simulated, causing the audience to be captured by the mask of the unreal. This leads to a discussion on the ways in which meanings are received by the audience. The audience is posited as important because it is at the receiving end of representation, and it is the audience that gives meaning to the mask:

> Social groups create deviance by making the rules whose infraction constitutes deviance and by applying those rules to particular people and labelling them as outsiders. From this point of view, deviance is *not* a quality of the act the

12 French and Kayess, ibid.
13 *R v Melanie Drummond*, New South Wales District Court, above n 10, [65].
14 Ch 1: Hannah Bromley.
15 *R v Melanie Drummond*, Court of Criminal Appeal, above n 11, [40].

> person commits, but rather a consequence of the application by others of rules and sanctions to an 'offender'. The deviant is one to whom that label has successfully been applied; deviant behaviour is behaviour that people so label.[16]

The theorising in this chapter is informed by symbolic interactionism and key themes from the interactionist framework, such as intersections of interaction, biography, social structure, inter-subjectivity, interactional experience (including ethnographic and audiovisual representation) and enforced social identities, such as labelling.[17] In particular, the book uses a perspectival method for analysing perpetrator and event representation. This symbolic interactionist analytical lens reveals two things: first, there are various social and cultural framings that structure the representations of the perpetrator and event; and, second, the meanings embodied in these representations are shaped by audience reinterpretation, much like Becker's articulation on labelling, which makes the point that deviance – filicidal violence in this context – cannot be understood without a study of the social and interactive forces that play a role in shaping the options that enable or disable the killing.

The first of these (social and cultural framings) was discussed in Chapter 4. This chapter focuses on the second – the shaping, and receivership, of meaning. But first it is imperative to examine the formation of perpetrator self-representation in order to shed light on the purpose of the social actor in representing and his or her intention in shaping the meaning to be given to such a representation. The following discussion will make some reference to Model 1 from Chapter 4 (Figure 4.1); this model will be used as a reference tool for theorising on the nature of representation.

When looking closely at self-representations by the perpetrator it is, as noted earlier, possible to draw additional tiny circles within the first circle (first-degree representation) in Model 1. These additional circles represent perpetrators' representations of themselves; they are made to either persons around them, or to the perpetrators themselves. These representations give an indication of how perpetrators construct themselves and how they think of themselves in different contexts. These representations are argued to be important because they show how the perpetrator perceives the conflict, and the perpetrator's feelings about obstructions to conflict resolution. Using a legal analogy, the utility of having the perpetrator's self-statements is that they give insight into the state of his or her mind, and this can form the basis of criminal intention or *mens rea*. As discussed in Chapter 4, the cases of Mark and Libby and Horace Faulkner can serve as illustrations of this hypothesis.

16 Howard Becker, *Outsiders: Studies in the Sociology of Deviance* (Free Press of Glencoe, 1963) 9.

17 Norman Denzin, *Symbolic Interactionism and Cultural Studies: The Politics of Interpretation* (Blackwell, 1992) 20.

Pursuant to this, the question regarding the purpose and use of various self-representations will be explored: how and why does the Self perpetuate his or her own representations? The book's hypothesis is that, when attempting to hide dysfunction from prying external intervention, the Self often replicates the representation of a loving parent. This is enacted to the extent that the outsiders believe this representation. Baudrillard explains this in *Simulacra and Simulation*:

> It is no longer a question of imitation, nor duplication, nor even parody. It is a question of substituting the signs of the real for the real, that is to say of an operation of deterring every real process via its operational double, a programmatic, metastable, perfectly descriptive machine that offers all the signs of the real and short-circuits all its vicissitudes.[18]

Baudrillard is specific about the natures of representation and simulation. He argues that representation is imagery[19] and 'stems from the principle of the equivalence of the sign and of the real'.[20] However, he also argues that representation is not very different from simulation, though the distinction is a fine one; that is, while there are differences, there are also similarities. Simulation 'stems from the utopia of the principle of equivalence, from the radical negation of the sign as value, from the sign as the reversion and death sentence of every reference'.[21] Baudrillard compares the two and argues that 'whereas representation attempts to absorb simulation by interpreting it as a false representation, simulation envelops the whole edifice of representation itself as a simulacrum'.[22] In other words, according to Baudrillard, simulation creates a hyperreality, which can be thought of as being above and beyond the current reality; and he cites Disneyland as an example of this. However, because representation revolves around a reinterpretation, refashioning or redefinition of the real, it is suggested here that representation is one step below simulation, the difference being that simulation destroys any references to, and signs of, the real, while representation does not. For our purposes, Baudrillard is useful in so far as he sheds light on the processes of adopting the real and the transformation processes that follow.

Social actors, or 'simulators' in Baudrillard's phraseology, either dissimulate or simulate.[23] When an actor dissimulates, he or she is masking reality with his or her representation, but reality remains intact.[24] However, when an actor simulates, he or she is feigning to have something he or she does not have, and that,

18 Jean Baudrillard, *Simulacra and Simulation* (University of Michigan Press, 1994) 2.
19 Ibid.
20 Ibid, 6.
21 Ibid.
22 Ibid.
23 Ibid 3: '[T]o dissimulate is to pretend not to have what one has. To simulate is to feign to have what one does not have. One implies a presence and the other an absence.'
24 Ibid.

Baudrillard argues, threatens the difference between truth and falsity and between real and imaginary.[25]

Even though Baudrillard uses historical and psychiatric examples to illustrate his argument, his specificity on the nature of dissimulation can be applied to this book. His description of simulation can be interpreted, in the context of the child-killing cases in this study, to mean that any opportune moment for intervention prior to the death can be short-circuited by such an extreme form of representation – it is something that can be believed to be real – and with these cases it is that of the loving parent or the reasonable parent. Ancillary to this idea is the notion that such a simulation is a duplicated substitute for the real – the 'truth' – and that the substitute is thus an *unreal* representation. The image itself, and the character of the individual in that simulation or wearing the mask, is 'metastable', unstable and transient; when the situation no longer calls for the necessity of the mask, it is removed, when the individual thinks it safe.

To illustrate how Baudrillard's understandings of simulation and representation can apply to the perpetrator representations in the cases, I refer to the stories of Jubilee Soprano, Mark and Libby and Horace Faulkner. I will first illustrate the difference between simulation and representation using the Jubilee Soprano story. Next, I will use the stories of Mark and Libby and Horace Faulkner to draw out the nature of perpetrator representations and what these representations reveal.

The crucial observation in the Soprano story was that Brody was able to represent himself[26] as normal, reasonable and not insane, meaning that he did not appear as though he was suffering from mental illness. Even though Brody was highly likely to have been unwell at the time of the assessment, he warned Angeline to leave the talking to him. His belief in himself as someone who has the right to maintain control gave him the ability to put on a normal presentation, as opposed to a delusionary or irrational one, to the intervention team, doing this by engaging with them in conversation.

It is contestable whether the intervention team conducted a thorough professional assessment, but this is not the concern of this exercise.[27] What is pertinent is the presentation of Brody's sane and rational self despite his psychotic self being present, and the ability to deceive and mislead the intervention team. This deceptive representation could have occurred because Brody was able to imitate or dissimulate the conditions of the reasonable man. In other words, Brody was pretending not to have what he had – a mental illness. He could not be feigning, that is, simulating, rationality because it is questionable whether rationality can be simulated or feigned when it is absent; to feign is not the same

25 Ibid.

26 Ch 1: Jubilee Soprano. Report 'AS1' taken during the period 4 February to 3 March 2000 from Angeline Soprano in Wyong at police stations W and K, 19–20, [299]–[302].

27 Ibid [8]–[10].

as to pretend. Baudrillard elaborates on the layered nature of such a simulation using a different analogy:

> What can the army do about simulators? Traditionally it ***unmasks*** them and punishes them, according to a clear principle of identification. Today it can discharge a very good simulator as exactly equivalent to a 'real' homosexual, a heart patient, or a madman. Even military psychology draws back from Cartesian certainties and hesitates to make the distinction between true and false, between the 'produced' and the authentic symptom. 'If he is this good at acting crazy, it's because he is.' Nor is military psychology mistaken in this regard: in this sense, all crazy people simulate, and this lack of distinction is the worst kind of subversion . . . submerging the principle of truth.[28]

What Baudrillard appears to be saying here is that when 'simulators' have caught up with society such that they are able to replicate the real, society can no longer tell the difference between what is true and what is false. The distinction between the real and the unreal is blurred and even more difficult to unmask,[29] because all signs of the real have been destroyed. This quote is relevant to our scenario because Brody was able to replicate an aspect of the unreal in place of the real by dissimulating, that is, by representing himself differently. Essentially, Brody and 'the simulator' are closely related but not the same. They are both using representation to substitute the real and submerge the principle of truth. As argued, simulation and representation are different and yet similar. They both involve substituting the real, but in simulation what is being simulated does not exist in the simulator's person whereas representation via dissimulation can conceal, or even reveal, the truth. In this case, Brody was not simulating but representing, or dissimulating, and the distinction is a fine one. This does not detract from the overall argument that he used a mask to present as someone other than himself. Baudrillard's theory suggests that a perfect simulation cannot be unmasked, whereas a representation can be.

Mark and Libby's story illuminates the nature of the loving father representation and how Mark's representation concealed from the authorities the truth of his intentions. The reader will recall that Mark was ordered by the court to produce the children at a police station after he had threatened Libby on the phone and become uncooperative towards Libby regarding telephone contact with the children. Mark turned up at the police station with the children and, as the children appeared to the police to be well cared for, the police assumed Mark was a loving parent and allowed him to carry on with his unsupervised contact with the children. In retrospect, was there a particular representation that the police should have been looking for? If the children appeared at the police station

28 Baudrillard, above n 18, 4.

29 Baudrillard's application of masking here harks back to the masking discussions in Chapters 2 and 4.

unkempt and dirty, and if Mark had presented as drunk or unshaven, would such a representation have alerted the police that he was about to commit murder? It is likely Mark represented himself in the form he knew the police wanted to see and believe – a dissimulation of the real, which was that of the loving parent who was undergoing acrimonious divorce proceedings. Because this dissimulation occurred as a first-degree perpetrator representation, which emanated from Mark, the truth of the dysfunction was masked.

It is unclear whether the mask, or the invisible cloak,[30] was worn with the intention to conceal. The story of Horace Faulkner sheds light on this perplexing question. In Chapter 4, Horace was shown donning a number of masks for the various social roles he had created for himself. Quite naturally, tension between the masks and the Self would arise. Horace was very much aware of this tension between his masks and his Self. For example, he made the following statement:

> I did not look at it like I'm going to kill my kids. I looked at it like I don't want my kids to go through the pain and suffering and insecurity I had to go through and now I have to watch it all again.[31]

Again, the reader will recall the discussion on sympathetic reinterpretation in Chapter 4. Horace took drugs to give him courage to kill, and the drugs also allowed him to become the persona of the mask when killing the children. The tension is revealed in Horace's acknowledgement that 'I did not look at it like I'm going to kill my kids', which appears to be saying that he would rather not believe the truth that he was going to kill the children. Instead, he reinterpreted his intention to kill by giving it a sympathetic meaning. He did this by persuading himself that he had a good motive, that is, he was going to save the children from pain. This pain, however, was not the children's future pain, but self-referential in that it referred to Horace's own feelings of pain and insecurity. This statement is suggestive of dissimulation. In other words, Horace pretended that he did not have intention to kill when he did. As such, this was a false representation and the tension was resolved with Horace's ingestion of the drugs.

The riskiness of the loving parent representation becomes evident when examining Horace Faulkner's story using Model 2A from Chapter 4 (Figure 4.4), the events representation model. It is reasonable to argue that the existing legal safeguards in place at the time were inadequate to protect the children from harm. This is not to say that the safeguards were ineffective; there was, for example, an AVO in place against Horace primarily for Melissa's protection. But at no time did Melissa fear for the children's safety, because it was obvious to her that Horace loved the children.[32] The Family Court was involved to the

30 This metaphor was used in Chapter 6 to illuminate on the invisibility of the loving father representation.
31 Ch 1: Horace Faulkner.
32 Ibid.

extent that it was instructive on the issue of the children's day-to-day care, particularly regarding the agreement on the parents' contact times with the children and the application to take the children overseas. The police were also involved in some of the domestic violence incidents. In spite of these interventions, Horace was able to mask his intention to kill from persons in the first degree, including his mother and Melissa. And yet an analysis of Horace's statements reveals a disturbing and consistent presence of verbal threats, over the course of the volatile marriage, which were not taken seriously. To all observers Horace appeared as a loving and caring father, but ironically this loving father representation masked the threats of violence to the children. If the authorities had been aware such a representation could become a risk factor in child endangerment, their intervention efforts may well have been tailored to address this risk.

What do these perpetrator representations reveal about the nature of the conflict? Peeling away the layers of dysfunction will reveal not only the perpetrator's motives for the killing but also the hidden nature of the violence.

The following gives an example of how modelling may be applied to the nature of the conflict in Horace's story. This was not done in Chapter 4, in which Model 1 (Figure 4.1) pertained to perpetrator representation and Model 2 (Figure 4.3) to event representation. Here, the subject matter is the nature of the conflict. By analysing the nature of the conflict, revealing the perpetrator's motive for killing is made possible. The application of the general model to this context demonstrates the flexibility of the model in interacting with other variables of representation that are closely associated with the perpetrator and the killing, such as, in this case, perpetrator motive.[33] Even though motive is irrelevant to criminal responsibility in law, it could be relevant to understandings of the nature of child killing, the nature of violence and, in the broader academic framework, the discourse on punishment.

Applying the generic layout of both Models 1 and 2 to the conflict, it becomes apparent that the conflict within Horace was *layered*. The layers of this dysfunctional conflict were evident on at least three levels, corresponding to the three layers in Model 1. At the outermost layer (or circle), third-degree representation, the conflict was about the children and Horace's belief that they were vulnerable to exploitation by Melissa's lover. This conflict also centred on Horace, who feared his place as the children's father would be taken from him. This conflict is situated as third degree because this was the 'obvious' scenario presented to the outside world. The second layer of the conflict, second-degree representation, was about Horace's anger and frustration towards his ex-wife, Melissa, and the failure to communicate meaningfully with her. This second layer might not at first be obvious. This is because Horace made an effort to conceal from

33 Simon Bronitt and Bernadette McSherry, *Principles of Criminal Law* (Thomson Lawbook, 2nd ed, 2005) 175, 655. Also see mention of Horace's motive in: *R v Horace Faulkner*, Court of Criminal Appeal, New South Wales, 2005, Court of Criminal Appeal No. HFCA, [41]–[42] *per* Grove J.

others, and from himself, the message of revenge for Melissa. He did this by representing himself as a loving father. He used this representation to explain the killing by presenting the children and himself as victims to his audience. By giving himself and the children victimhood status, he was sympathetically reinterpreting the killing for his audience. In fact, Horace used the children as a shield or cloak to conceal the real message of revenge. At an even deeper level, first-degree representation, it becomes apparent that the conflict directly related to Horace's desire for, and therefore lack of, power over his family.

The layering of the conflict in this way reveals the nature of the killing to be multidimensional. Child killing is a complex phenomenon in which, as the modelling reveals, representation and perceptions of power in terms of perpetrator empowerment or disempowerment[34] have significant influence in determining the path of conflict and its outcomes. For Horace, disempowerment meant that he believed he had to resort to violence to resolve the conflict, and to re-establish in his mind the state of paterfamilias, that is, his belief that he held the power of life and death over the children and that this was, in part, what 'love' meant. This reveals the killing to be deeply embedded in patriarchal dysfunction.[35]

The flexibility of the modelling also demonstrates the multidimensional nature of modelling, which can be applied to the criminal justice paradigm.[36] For example, a positive utility of second-degree representation is that it can be used as a method for collecting data and for building context into a particular event or individual being studied, that is, framing the methodological analysis. An example of this is the process by which the police officers, through their investigations, constructed the case for trial based heavily on second-degree representation. Second-degree representation as a method for constructing cases is useful in that it also enables, to some extent, self-reflexivity,[37] as there is a recognition that no one perspective represents the objective truth. Even the construction of a second-degree representation is limited to the position of the observer.[38] In this sense, representation in its entirety can be seen as pluralistic.

Within the criminal justice paradigm, second-degree representation is often the closest available account to the original event. As stated, the investigating officer would rely on, and access, second-degree representation in order to put together background information necessary for building the legal case for the criminal trial. From this perspective, second-degree representation is an indispensable building block for the case under investigation. However, it is important to

34 Perpetrator disempowerment is further discussed in the Chapter 6.

35 Patriarchal dysfunction is discussed in Chapter 6.

36 For a similar conceptual framework applied to international criminal justice, see Mark Findlay and Sylvia Ntube Ngane, 'Sham of the Moral Court?' (Sydney Law School Research Paper No. 11/10, 1 February 2011) http://ssrn.com/abstract=1753319, 7.

37 Pierre Bourdieu and Loïc J D Wacquant, *An Invitation to Reflexive Sociology* (University of Chicago Press, 1992) 36–37 40, 44.

38 Ibid 41.

recognise that reliance on second-degree representation alone seldom provides a complete picture, as it is a step removed from the actual event. But where there is no self-representation, such as in murder-suicide cases, investigators have to rely on first- or second-degree representations. The reliance on this form of social enquiry, in particular second-degree representation, can uncover the social and interactive forces around the perpetrator within a limited objective reality that is represented through the observer's eyes.

If second-degree representation is limited in its objectivity to the extent that it is subjectively dependent on the observer, third-degree representation, being two steps removed from the centre, will have even less objectivity, but the court is an exception. Building on Chapter 4, where the legitimating and unmasking functions of the court were highlighted, the polemic of facts *represented* as truth is further elaborated here. The court, when dealing with selective representations, treats them as disputed or undisputed fact. Facts are then legitimised as *truth* through the rational method of the law, such as drawing inferences inductively from relevant evidence.[39] Another way to conceptualise third-degree representation is as a representative of the legal voice, since, as it will be argued below, most of the media reporting on a case is dependent on the legal narrative in court. As such, third-degree representation easily becomes the foundation for subsequent reporting and dissemination of information to the rest of society. When examining the locality of third-degree representations, it being farthest away from the actual event, it logically follows that any claims to represent the 'truth' of the actual event, in spite of its objectivity, are questionable.[40] Representations in this outermost circle may include hearsay, rumour or gossip.[41] These representations also include reports based on second-degree representations and second-hand knowledge. Third-degree representation would consist of accounts repeated by another from people within the circles of first- and second-degree representations.

For example, in New South Wales, the *Evidence Act 1995* governs the admissibility of evidence. At the trial, the prosecutor and defence counsel take turns to examine and cross-examine witnesses over their police statements. Often, if not almost always, only selected portions of the statements are used for questioning. Because of the adversarial nature of the trial process, the complete story is seldom told or heard in court. Only what are deemed 'facts' are presented,

39 William Twining, *Rethinking Evidence: Exploratory Essays* (Blackwell, 1990) 35–80, 76; and see also Donald Nicolson, 'Truth, Reason and Justice: Epistemology and Politics in Evidence Discourse' (1994) 57(5) *Modern Law Review* 726–744, 727. The distinction between truth and fact, and the contentious subject of objective 'truth', were discussed at the end of Chapter 4.

40 Ibid.

41 Hearsay also has a technical meaning in law, which is: the testimony of an individual based on the reports of others and not from direct personal knowledge; and in legal proceedings, the general rule is that hearsay evidence is not admissible, subject to a number of exceptions.

which means not all 'facts' are presented but rather selected segments chosen for the purposes of cross-examination and examination. Most of these statements would have come from first- and second-degree representations. If the accused does not take the stand to be cross-examined (since he or she may elect to remain silent, or may be deceased), there will only be a representation through his or her solicitor, and, even so, such a legal representation will constitute second-degree representation. That being the case, an argument can be persuasively made that any claims to representing the whole 'truth' within this circle must be treated with caution. The reality is that versions of 'fact' represented within and outside institutions such as the court are often maintained and legitimated even though they belong to third-degree representation. The court can do this through applying the law to rational fact-finding,[42] a process that creates for some audiences the 'truth' and for others a way of giving selected representations more authority, or draining them of authority.

The primary purpose of this process is to inform and influence the wider audience as receivers of this meaning through the print and digital media. The meanings of these official representations, as will be shown later in this chapter in the section on media representation, are then presented as representative of official fact to the audience as a result of its legitimation from the courts through the judicial narrative. This and the following discussions develop the point on the symbiotic relationship between the media and the court made in Chapter 4. It was argued there that the emergent media representation at third degree lacks intimacy, and this is reflected in some of its rather limited representation of the official facts. While media reporting, being at the third-degree representation, may appear to have some authority in this sense, this is generally downplayed in favour of its adherence to digesting and producing information that is readable and attractive to the susceptible audience. As such, the meanings of these official representations tend to be diluted and are, or can be, generally treated by some audiences as representing 'truth', and by others as stories, gossip and information, depending on the constitution of the audience.[43]

So far, using modelling as an analytical lens, this book has argued that representation is a multidimensional creature of social construction, and this is played out specifically in filicide cases. In all this, certain representations can be seen as taking precedence over others. This is possible because of a particular social audience, such as the court and the media, which gives legitimate authority to these representations. The audience is seen as a significant social, interactive force that sustains representations and gives meaning to otherwise meaningless social categories. As Becker points out,[44] in symbolic interactionism the audience is the key to understanding society's applied 'labels', including its representations.

42 Ibid.
43 Brent Davis and Kym Dossetor, *(Mis)perceptions of Crime in Australia*, Trends and Issues in Crime and Criminal Justice No. 396(2010) 1–6, 5.
44 Above n 16.

The following section examines, with reference to the stories, the constitution of the audience in representation and the ways in which meanings and representations are transmitted and received by the audience. It concludes with the relevance of Girard's theory of mimesis and mimetic conflict to the cases, and its significance in shaping the meanings given by social actors to perpetrator, conflict and event representations. Mimesis is relevant to filicide representation because it bridges the gap between the construction of representation, such as dissimulation (as discussed above), and the creation of the conditions for violence in the family. This argument places the audience as central to the construction of representation. Located at the heart of the theorising to follow is the focus on interactive meaning, in particular on the way social interaction by certain types of authority figures and audiences shapes particular social meanings and representations.

The audience and the receivership of meaning

The context of the audience in this section refers to persons to whom the representation is presented, and on whom it impacts. The audience that receives the meaning of a particular representation consists of those with whom the perpetrator has a relationship. The degree of intimacy the audience has with the perpetrator varies. In some respects, the perpetrators are an audience to themselves; that is, they behave this way not only to act to the audience in second- and third-degree representation but also partly to convince themselves and to act, or perform, to themselves.[45] This is evident in cases such as those of Horace Faulkner, Jubilee Soprano, Mark and Libby, Danny Burrow and Jack Drummond.[46]

Generally, this chapter theorises that audiences can be categorised based on the degree of relatedness to the perpetrator, and this theoretical conceptualisation is based on Model 1. This categorisation proposes to break down the standing of the audience relative to its proximity to the killing. This allows the observer, investigator or reader to pinpoint the importance of a particular testimony. It also indicates to them the nature of such testimony, and the significance to attach to that account. More importantly, the breakdown reveals the perspectival nature of representation, which is seen in this book as critical to interpretations

45 Erving Goffman, *The Presentation of Self in Everyday Life* (Penguin, first published 1959, 1990 ed) 28.

46 For example, Brody Kitaro, Horace Faulkner, Saskia Burrow, Mark and Melanie were their own audiences in the killing of the children. For Brody, this is evident in the way he presented to the intervention team. For Horace, he wore a number of masks to convince himself of different social roles. For Saskia, she was the audience for her own projections. For Mark, this is evident in the audio-recordings of the murder-suicide and in his presentation to the police. For Melanie, her internalisations convinced her that she was not the perfect mother.

of risk. This observation, discussed more fully in Chapter 7 – that there is a positive and interactive relationship between representation and risk – suggests that some of the case study features of risk are less than visible. This is to say that some indicators of child endangerment that are perceived by some as risky will not be conceptualised in the same way by others, depending on the constitution of the audience. There are several audiences, which can be divided into several categories: the *original* audience, consisting of perpetrators and victims; the *primary* audience, consisting of persons within first-degree representation, such as family; the *secondary* audience, consisting of state actors and agency workers; the *tertiary* audience, consisting of persons within third-degree representation, such as lawyers, judges and the media; and finally, the *remote* audience, consisting of unrelated individuals, such as the general public, including news readers and television audiences.

The division of the audiences in this way impacts on the receivership of perpetrator and event representations, and this is significant to the interpretation of risk. The audience interprets, re-shapes, denies and confirms meaning based on the representations it observes. A representation of risk observed and interpreted as risk by one category of the audience may be rejected by another who does not have a similar relationship, degree or physical distance to the perpetrator or event. When Angeline Soprano's parents, for example, reported their fears to DOCS, DOCS did not receive the same meaning that the parents represented and so did not respond; and when Saskia Burrow's sister reported seeing bruises on Danny to DOCS, DOCS did not take the representation seriously and did not respond. In the first instance, Iris, Papadino and Rosaline Soprano probably expected that, after having reported to DOCS, DOCS would do something constructive about their concerns. Instead, Rosaline was told that DOCS could not help because there was insufficient information and it was 'still early days'.[47] Any reasonable person, in the legal and non-legal sense, would think that DOCS would at least monitor the situation. In the Burrow case study, West said that when DOCS had done nothing about the report he thought that the report was untrue.[48] This shows that, where the audience denies the representation of the perpetrator or event, its representation or belief loses legitimacy and arguably turns into rumour or gossip.

In the context of specific audiences, the power of the audience to legitimate a version of events is articulated most clearly by the function of the criminal justice system. In the Soprano case, the audience for Brody was Brody, Angeline and Jubilee, who functioned as the primary audience for Brody's delusions and for whom Brody wore the mask of Jesus. Angeline's family constituted the secondary audience, whose voices were carried across to the tertiary and remote audiences through the medium of legal narrative of the background facts. This set of facts then become legitimated through what Berger and Luckmann call

47 Ch 1: Jubilee Soprano.
48 Ch 1: Danny Burrow.

the kinship legitimation process[49] and, following that process, institutionalised and integrated within the criminal justice system before being transmitted to the remote audience and henceforth embedded within Manichaean categories and the confines of social and filicidal classifications – as sacrificial and hence good, or deviant, parent symbols. At the point of institutionalisation, a version of 'truth' is already constructed through the earlier legitimating process; this often happens when there is only one version, as opposed to multiple versions, of 'truth' put forth.

Where there are multiple contested versions of the 'fact', as occurred in Greta Sheng's case, it may be persuasively argued that, in the criminal justice system, only one version of 'fact' emerges and gains authority at the end of the criminal trial. This preference usually entails a rejection of the subjective voice of the perpetrator in favour of the evidence demonstrated at the trial by the prosecution and defence teams. But, as argued in Chapter 4, this objective factual version cannot be said to be representative of the events at the time because of the distance from, and degree of relatedness from, the centre in Models 1 and 2, even though it might be more believable. If this is the case, the purpose of the law's quest to ascertain a legitimate version of events as 'truth' for the remote audience must be questioned since competing explanations might be argued to be just as valid. A way of understanding this purpose is to look at the wider purpose of representation, which this chapter addresses in its final section. It is important to recognise the primary and secondary audiences as giving crucial voices to the victim and giving meaning to the representation of the victim and the killing. The media, for example, sees itself as giving a 'voice' to certain representations, as demonstrated by the Drummond case.[50] The focus of the media and the angle their reporting took indicated that the media saw itself as giving voice to other parents in situations similar to Melanie's.

Regardless, the legitimation of, and search for, some resemblance of truth amid multiple representations in child killing remains an important phenomenon. This is necessary to giving some meaning to an otherwise meaningless and inexplicable act of killing. In today's context, the utility dimension[51] present in early cultural Western and non-Western representations of child killing can no longer be justified. The socio-legal representation of the child in Western society was evolving even before major milestones in the law, such as the *United Nations Convention on the Rights of the Child* (1990), were reached. This has been made possible because of the needs of the audience to attach significance and meaning to the child, whereas before a child's place in society was less prominent.

49 Berger and Luckmann's kinship legitimation process is further discussed in the next section.

50 The reader will recall in the Drummond case that the media portrayed Melanie Drummond as a tragic heroine, and reinterpreted the killing in this light. The media's focus on this angle of the story drew readers' sympathies for Melanie and her circumstances.

51 Martin Daly and Margo Wilson, *Homicide* (Aldine De Gruyter, 1988) 37.

Society attaches different meanings and interactions to different representations. Meanings are often communicated by means of a coherent blend of shared symbols employed by social actors for audiences.[52] 'Good' and 'bad' labels are desirable and undesirable social labels conditioned by society to be pre-fixed on a particular identity. What are the standards for a good parent? These are standards set by society through various mediums, such as religious tenets, the law – the legal construction of parent roles,[53] child protection laws[54] – the commercialisation of the family,[55] and media images and reports on deviant versus good parents.[56] The stories of Hannah Bromley and Greta Sheng – as well as that of Khyra Ishaq in the United Kingdom[57] – reveal the law to be the final authority on the benchmark for what is deemed in society gross criminal negligence where parenting standards are concerned. The legal denunciation of such conduct, contained in court judgments, is relayed to the rest of society through the media by way of daily news reports (third-degree representations), from which the possibility of social and moral condemnation or praise arises.

The legitimation of the meaning of a filicide representation – of being a good or bad parent, what it means to be grossly criminally negligent parent and so on – has been objectified by the media and institutionalised and integrated into society by the courts. There are two ways in which meanings are legitimated. The

52 David Downes and Paul Rock, *Understanding Deviance* (Oxford University Press, 2003) 179.

53 For example, Capello Steppenwolf, Jack Drummond, Greta Sheng, Danny Burrow and Hannah Bromley. For a critique of the general construction of the 'normal' family by the British courts in a child residence decision, see S B Boyd, 'What Is a "Normal" Family?' (1992) 55(2) *Modern Law Review* 269–278, 272–275. For the construction of 'ideal' family in the Australian context, see *Re L* [1983] FLC 91–353, 78, 363–367. For the construction of parental role stereotypes in the Australian context, see *McMillan v Jackson* [1995] FLC 92–610; and S Berns, 'Living Under the Shadow of Rousseau: The Role of Gender Ideologies in Custody and Access Decisions' (1991) 10 *University of Tasmania Law Review* 233–255, 237, 239.

54 Above, n 2.

55 For example, childhood commercialisation is an ongoing concern; see the Family and Parenting Institute Briefing Paper (United Kingdom), *Commercialisation and Sexualisation of Childhood* (June 2011) www.familyandparenting.org/Resources/FPI/Documents/Commercialisation%20and%20sexualisation%20briefing%20-%20FINAL%20VERSION%20(3).pdf.

56 For an example of how the good mother representation is applied in the media, see Georgina Robinson, 'Woman and Baby Found Dead in Home', *Sydney Morning Herald* (online), 31 January 2011 www.smh.com.au/nsw/woman-and-baby-found-dead-in-home-20110131-1aapo.html. Also see the critique of Drummond case study for the media and legal representation of good versus bad mothers.

57 Caroline Gammell and Lucy Cockcroft, 'Starved girl Khyra Ishaq Failed by Social Services', *Telegraph* (online), 25 February 2010 www.telegraph.co.uk/news/uknews/crime/7318878/Starved-girl-Khyra-Ishaq-failed-by-social-services.html; and Lucy Cockcroft, 'How Khyra Ishaq Starved While Surrounded by Food', *Telegraph* (online) 25 February 2010 www.telegraph.co.uk/news/uknews/crime/ 7316744/How-Khyra-Ishaq-starved-while-surrounded-by-food.html.

first is through a process of legitimation, and the second is through mimesis,[58] a process in which meaning is given by one actor to a perceived undesirable action by another, thus creating a situation of conflict between the two actors. Both of these social processes focus on the audience as central to the construction of meaning in everyday life, including the meanings of representation, risk and violence, all of which are fundamental elements in filicide cases. The following paragraphs discuss how some of these meanings are sustained through legitimating instruments in society for the wider audience, and for perpetrators, who are sometimes an audience for themselves.

The first process is elucidated by Berger and Luckmann, who argue that the process of legitimation 'produces new meanings that serve to integrate the meanings already attached to disparate institutional processes'.[59] They argue that there are four levels at which legitimation can be accomplished, which are: first kinship legitimation through the family, such as an adult telling a child 'this is how things are done';[60] second, theoretical propositions in rudimentary form, such as proverbs and moral maxims; third, explicit theories by which an institutional sector is legitimated in terms of a differentiated body of knowledge, such as the law as a discourse and sphere of knowledge, or science as an epistemological foundation for knowledge; and, last, symbolic universes, which are 'bodies of theoretical tradition that integrate different provinces of meaning and encompass the institutional order in a symbolic totality',[61] such as representations and dreams.[62] All levels of legitimation proposed by Berger and Luckmann are relevant to understanding filicide representations, but the most applicable for this chapter is 'symbolic universes'.

Although Berger and Luckmann categorise legends and folktales under the second level, I would argue that myths and representations are unlike folktales and instead create a filter between the realms of the symbolic and the real. The reason for this is that they are 'provinces of meaning detached from everyday life and endowed with a peculiar reality of their own'.[63] In the realm of the symbolic, the meanings of objective and mythological symbols are subjectively assimilated by the receiver and hence they give each individual a unique significance because of their general frame of reference, which provides the framework for binding

58 René Girard, *Violence and the Sacred* (Patrick Gregory trans, Johns Hopkins University Press, 1977) 143–168, 146. See also René Girard, *A Theater of Envy: William Shakespeare* (St. Augustine's Press, 2004) 3–4.

59 Peter Berger and Thomas Luckmann, *The Social Construction of Reality: A Treatise in the Sociology of Knowledge* (Doubleday, 1966) 85. Generally, myths differ from folktales though the terms are used interchangeably, see G S Kirk, *Myth: Its Meaning and Functions in Ancient and Other Cultures* (Cambridge University Press, 1970) ch 1.

60 Ibid 87.

61 Ibid 88. They argue that symbolic processes are processes of signification that refer to realities other than those of everyday experiences.

62 Above n 61, 87–88.

63 Ibid 89.

society in a collective fashion through a shared language,[64] and provides meaning to an otherwise meaningless imagery. Berger and Luckmann explain that this can be accomplished because 'man externalises himself [sic], he constructs the world into which he externalises himself. In the process of externalisation, he projects his own meanings into reality.'[65] This appears to support this book's argument that filicide symbolism and representations have ultimately been social constructions arising from forms of human interaction, which breathe life and meaning that are reabsorbed by receivers and creators of that representation, and this legitimating process is a reflection of humankind's ability to nurture, polarise, destroy, divide and deceive. The forms of such human interaction that prevail in social and cultural life have been those that maintain a hegemonic persuasion of power and dominance. This is done by the legitimation of dominant images of the ideal family and parent in the media,[66] the law and social and support networks,[67] over the general audience in society and even to sectors of the social milieu that may not have the means to attain that representation of parenthood.

The second of these processes, mimesis, is seen here as an aspect of representation. The term 'mimesis'[68] is used by Girard to describe the process of imitation between two social actors, the imitator and the imitated, who both possess the same desires for a common object. The competition between them has the potential to lead to conflict and violence. This is especially so when one of the actors sees the other as an obstacle to achieving his or her desire. On the one hand, the imitation is an end product and, on the other, it is a process of

64 Ibid 35–40; Roland Barthes, *Mythologies* (Hill & Wang, 1972) 11; and Pierre Bourdieu, *Language and Symbolic Power* (Polity Press, 1992) 43–65.

65 Above n 61, 96. For an example, see below n 76.

66 Thomson and Walker argue that there are enduring images of motherhood and fatherhood in Western society. Motherhood images include the image of the mother as intuitive towards her child; all-giving and all-powerful; and an image of devotion. Images of fatherhood include the image of the father as breadwinner. These images, however, are myths. The authors rely on the comparison between images of black and Chicano families and the reality in these families, and argue that the reality is that these parents share childrearing burdens. There has been an emergence in images of motherhood, fatherhood or 'new parenthood'. The 'new motherhood' stresses the wage-working mother who accomplishes everything, that is, successfully managing the delicate balance between home, children and work. The 'new fatherhood' portrays fathers as intimately and actively involved with their children and responsible for their day-to-day care. 'New parenthood' portrays both parents as sharing the full weight of raising their children and sharing equal fairness, respect and cooperation. See Linda Thompson and Alexis J Walker, 'Gender in Families: Women and Men in Marriage, Work, and Parenthood' (1989) 51(4) *Journal of Marriage and the Family* 845–871, 860. See also the Harvester judgment, which entrenched in Australia the role of the working man as breadwinner while confining women and children to the home: *Ex parte HV McKay* (*'Harvester Case'*) (1907) 2 CAR 1.

67 See Nikolas Rose, 'Beyond the Public/Private Division: Law, Power and the Family' (1987) 14(1) *Journal of Law and Society* 61–76, 65. Also see Donzelot, above n 2, 122–125.

68 Above n 60.

production that is self-reflective and self-producing on a profound level. Girard's theory on representation argues that mimesis involves not simply representations but intentions and acts of acquisition: it is possible for individuals to attempt to mimic reality through philosophical, artistic and material representations, and to mimic the desires of others. In acquiring the desirable representations of others for themselves, they engender conflict between those individuals because their desires begin to converge as common objects.[69] Girard posits that individuals learn to desire from observing mediators or models, and they process their observations into learning what the individuals themselves desire by copying or mimicking the desires of others. Such mediation of desire occurs within cultural practices, and institutions, subtly appearing not only to produce the ordinariness and authenticity of that desire,[70] but also hegemonic legitimacy. As more and more desires converge, these representations, such as the 'ideal family', become not only more desirable and more conflicted but are also transformed to represent a dominant, but arguably false, reality for some social actors. This means that such representations postulated as good and desirable eventually become conflicted because of rivalry for the same goal.[71]

Girard explains that the meaning of imitation for some individuals can sometimes be translated as an act of appropriation.[72] Take the example of a hypothetical couple, Albert and Diana. Albert decides to buy a T-shirt that Diana was wearing the day before, and he wears it in front of Diana the next day. Diana, as imitated and audience, is unhappy and tells Albert not to imitate her, which Girard says means that Albert should not appropriate *her* shirt. In doing so, Diana has associated Albert's shirt with conflict and could be said to have given meaning to Albert's shirt and his mimetic action. The audience here is Diana. The shirt now represents to Diana negative emotions associated with conflict, such as jealousy, resentment, violation and anger. If Albert refuses to remove his shirt, it logically follows that there exists the possibility that Diana will become frustrated and resort to violence.

Applying Girard's theory to the case of Danny Burrow reveals a disturbing and alternative meaning of the killing in which the perpetrator is the audience for their own actions and beliefs. The reader will recall examples of Saskia's admonishments of Danny that he was behaving in a way that was 'just like [his] father'.[73] Earlier in the book I argued that Saskia saw in Danny his absent father, George. When looking at Saskia's projection of George onto Danny,[74] it makes sense to say that Saskia believed that she and Danny held the same desire for

69 Chris Fleming, *René Girard: Violence and Mimesis* (Polity Press, 2004) 6.
70 Ibid 5.
71 Above n 58, *Violence and the Sacred*, 146–148.
72 Ibid.
73 Ch 1: Danny Burrow.
74 This is an illustration of Berger and Luckmann's argument in respect of legitimating symbols in reality: above n 59. For Saskia, Danny is the symbol of her relationship with George and the one on which she projects her own meaning.

George: Danny wanted his father and Saskia wanted her partner. According to Girard, this situation will result in eventual conflict. Even though it is natural for a child to model himself or herself on a parent, the mother or father, Saskia could not tolerate Danny unwittingly mimicking his father. In this sense, she was her own audience. When she was not able to attain the ideal family she wanted, Saskia reacted out of anger and frustration and killed Danny. This appears to suggest that mimesis, like dissimulation, when applied to the cases[75] in this study, is enacted for an audience that includes the perpetrator, and can be characterised as risky. This is because the conflict is symbolic and not easily recognised.

When looking at the way Baudrillard's simulation theory fits together with Girard's mimesis theory in the broader framework of symbolic interactionism, it could be argued that they are not incompatible. Both explanations are relevant to understanding certain forms of perpetrator representations in this book. Both theories engage in analyses that explain the motivations and triggers for the killing. Baudrillard's analysis reveals the occurrence of simulation, which explains the process by which false representations are created. Girard's mimesis theory explains the context that enables seeds of violence to be planted. Both theories are connected by representation. A false representation is created when an actor mimics his or her rival in order to attain his or her rival's desire. From this, conditions for violence are created when mimesis and dissimulation produce false representations that are represented as real for the audience. When this occurs there exists the possibility of conflict between the false representation, or the image, and the real representation, the appropriated desire.[76] It logically follows that, when the representor fails to adopt the image of the false representation, the propensity and risks for violence are increased because the representor is no longer able to attain the desires of his or her rival, which have become the representor's own desires.

The story of Horace Faulkner illustrates this theoretical proposition. With the knowledge that what lies at the heart of the Faulkner conflict was a struggle for possession and power, it becomes apparent that the mimetic conflict is produced in the competition between Horace and Melissa to see who can represent themselves as the better parent. This representation is clearly seen by the parties as crucial to their belief in ownership and entitlement to the children. Horace's conflict shows that at the heart of risk construction and interpretation is representation. Representation and the audience are shown to be central to the construction of risk in these cases. Because risk is so closely tied to representation, the conclusion that follows at the end of this chapter, and in Chapter 7, is that risk appears invisible to the extent that the representation is believed. Once Horace's masks have been dislodged, it becomes clear that his loving father

75 Capello Steppenwolf's situation is similar to that of Danny Burrow. Capello's mother, Elizabeth Kramer, said that she could not stand Capello around her because he reminded her of his violent father.

76 Girard, above n 58.

persona was masking the risk to Melissa, but this does not mean that the risk was not there. Once the layer of mimetic conflict is peeled away, the risk of child endangerment is revealed as visible when viewed in the context of Horace's desire for power over and possession and ownership of his wife and children.

It has been pointed that, in the Soprano, Faulkner and Burrow stories, risk was constructed by the external audience: in Soprano, by the parents; in Faulkner, by Horace's mother, Annette, and the Family Court; and in Burrow, by Saskia's sister, Leanne, DOCS and to a lesser extent the parents West and Janis. In two of these cases, DOCS and the Family Court as authorities were able to do something constructive about the representations of risk, but did not. Particularly in the Burrow case, when DOCS failed to act on Leanne's concerns, the meaning of risk towards the child was negated and dismissed by Saskia's father as untrue. To illustrate the significance of this, the next few paragraphs discuss the utility of modelling in interpreting risk. Central to this is the relationship between the receiving of meaning by the audience and its observations of emerging risky representations. What is highlighted is the centrality of the audience to the construction of meanings of risk and representation.

When applying this theoretical proposition to the models in Chapter 4, and especially to Model 1, it can be reasonably assumed that the risks of violence would most likely erupt within the space of the first-degree (smallest) circle and to persons within this circle. This is because the first-degree circle is the space in which there is mimetic conflict. Examples of this in the cases include Horace's and Melissa's residence battle for the children, Brody's and Angeline's desire for Angeline's money, and Saskia's and Danny's desires for George. The people within the first circle would be the first witnesses to the conflict and, sometimes, to the false representations. So persons and events within first-degree representation are important targets for the authorities because they represent windows of opportunity for unmasking to occur given the appropriate intervention technique.

Going back to Model 1, the perpetrator representation model, an argument can be made that second-degree representation is where the windows of opportunity for masking should ideally occur. Second-degree representation includes persons who are one step removed from first-degree representations and persons within the circle of first-degree representation. These persons can be the police officers investigating the crime or, in the Jubilee Soprano case study, persons in the intervention team who were close enough to the crime to have been able to prevent the killing. The representations are diffused, as they come from different persons and therefore lead to different perspectives of the same event in the second-degree (medium) circle. These differing perspectives can add to the representations in the first degree and help provide a more holistic and enriching account of the event and the perpetrator, and, one could argue, on conditions of risk. This means the conditions observed by this circle of persons could be indicative of risk of child endangerment. Because of their physical distance and degree of relatedness to the event and the perpetrator, second-degree representors, as the perpetrator's primary audience depending on their distance to the centre, are able to observe, inform on and give meaning to unusual or risky behaviours that prompt the need for authorities to be vigilant.

In the Jubilee Soprano story, the reader might notice that the versions from the immediate audience, consisting of her parents and sister, combined to give a chronological view of the progression of changes in Angeline's behaviour. Their perspectives also gave meaning to conditions they considered risky, such as the changes in Angeline's behaviour and Angeline's request to withdraw money. In other words, they gave meaning to the conditions that appeared to them as risky. If so, it could be argued that, with adequate resources, the development of risk can be charted. This includes charting communication difficulties encountered by the Soprano family in dealing with DOCS, and DOCS' delayed response in prioritising that communication and recognising the risk.

These examples suggest that representations and risks are closely linked. They are connected by the audience, in that they are given meaning by the social actors, using labels, who themselves represent such an assemblage. The construction of risk based on perpetrator and event representations demonstrated here is a significant step towards understanding the stages by which child endangerment develops. As seen, risk can be exacerbated through reactions to representations, such as in the Soprano and Mark and Libby cases. Looking across the stories, there are at least three principal features of representation that develop conditions of risk: the loving parent; the disempowered spouse/parent; and dysfunctional intervention. Moreover, the stories in this book reveal that the masking function of these representations conceals from the authorities the risk of harm to the child. One possible reason for this is that the parent perpetrator is presented as loving, which is posited as a desirable representation of parenthood in Western society. In addition to this, the media's selection of desirable images, such as the loving parent, fosters and exacerbates the development of risk through its representations. Because the loving parent image is encouraged as desirable, it is not perceived to be risky.

More importantly, on the level of the symbolic, the race to acquire desirable representations fosters certain kinds of imitations that engender conflict. To be sure, not all mimesis give birth to murderous intentions, but this does not detract from the overall argument that some instances of direct conflict are resolved using violence. The argument made is that some, if not most, of these desirable representations belong in the realm of the dominant reality. These representations go unrecognised in the audience because they are deeply embedded in, and maintained by, a social reality – including media, the law and public sentiment – constructed on deep social attitudes and beliefs, such as patriarchy, born out of centuries of social and cultural development. So, even though some of these dominant representations, such as the loving father image, are widely encouraged as desirable, in the context of family dysfunction, conflict and domination they are risky because of their embeddedness in such a reality. The media is central to the delivery of information and where most of these images are embedded, encouraged and sustained. The discussion in the following section presents some observations on the nature and pattern of interaction the media has developed with filicide cases.

Media representation

This section provides a cursory discussion on the interactive nature of media representations in some of the stories.[77] It is included here to emphasise the role of the media in authorising certain representations above others, and in massively expanding the audience. This is seen as important because of the media's selective presentation of facts, which, when looked at from the masking perspective, is pivotal in endorsing certain 'risky' representations over others. This masking facilitation means that its impact on public and official responses can be disproportionate.[78] The media, consisting of radio, digital and print newspapers, magazines and television, sits in third-degree representation and is therefore significantly removed from the original source. The media's main purpose is to capture people's attention and tell a story, and as such the stories are represented in ways that are peculiar to the media.

The media reporting of a filicide case usually goes through three distinct phases. In the first stage, pre-trial, the focus is on the victim's death and/or manner of death and the progress of the police investigations. The reporting of details arising from the police investigation is usually delivered in a piecemeal fashion, with bits of information disseminated as the investigation progresses. This pattern of reporting could be characterised as the 'titillating' factor in media reporting.[79] The second phase is the trial stage or when the case reaches the court. Here, the reporting is largely selective, descriptive and factual. The media's sources of information are mainly the police and the courts.[80] This is reflected in the style of reporting, which is often a direct import of the legal narration from the parties' legal representations in the court made by the perpetrators' lawyers, the perpetrators' own representations, where available, and the judge's comments. In this phase, the focus is on the perpetrator and his or her legal representation. The third phase, observed throughout the reporting of the case, is characterised by 'finger pointing' and agenda setting.[81] Particularly in cases where the family has a history with DOCS and that association becomes known, the media focus

77 There are collected data consisting of media reports in four cases in Chapter 1. These cases are: Jubilee Soprano, Capello Steppenwolf, Hannah Bromley and Jack Drummond.

78 For examples of media impact, see Don Weatherburn and David Indermaur, 'Public Perceptions of Crime Trends in New South Wales and Western Australia' (*Crime and Justice Bulletin* no. 80, New South Wales Bureau of Crime Statistics and Research, 2004) http://search.informit.com.au/documentSummary;dn=913747370468508;res=IELHSS 7; Don Weatherburn, 'Riots, Policing and Social Disadvantage: Learning from the Riots in Macquarie Fields and Redfern' (2006) 18(1) *Current Issues in Criminal Justice* 20–31, 23.

79 An example of piecemeal reporting is evident in this media report: Robinson, above n 56.

80 Michael Teece and Toni Makkai, 'Print Media Reporting on Drugs and Crime 1995–1998' (July 2000) *Australian Institute of Criminology Trends & Issues in Crime and Criminal Justice No. 158* 1–6, 3–4.

81 For example, the Bromley, Steppenwolf, Soprano and Drummond stories. For the media's role as an agenda setter, see R Surette, 'News from Nowhere, Policy to

is usually on DOCS and whether DOCS has reneged on its responsibility to protect the children or intervene to save them.

An overall observation of the nature of news reporting is that it is temporal. With the exception of famous cases such as the Chamberlain case in 1980 and the Folbigg case in 2001 in Australia,[82] which received news coverage whenever a new development occurred, most child-killing news in my fieldwork tended to focus on a reported few cases over a short span of time. Once the perpetrator is sentenced and the court case ends, and unless there is a further appeal, the news coverage normally also dies. The few cases that maintain media attention are usually those that are deemed newsworthy and that reflect at least one or more of the following eight news values: immediacy, dramatisation, personalisation, simplification, titillation, conventionalism, structured access and novelty.[83] Child-killing cases by their nature easily satisfy at least four of these factors; for example in the Sheng story, these were immediacy, dramatisation, titillation and novelty. It is debatable whether news reports in Australia based on these values end up presenting a distorted representation of the killing rather than representing the actual picture or contextual layers in the killing.[84] This book's observation on the media reporting in these stories suggests that a holistic representation is seldom possible unless the killing is one that is overtly shocking, such as that of Hannah Bromley, where the media coverage was more extensive and descriptive than in others such as Jubilee Soprano. The story of Jack Drummond also reveals the power of the media to shape public perception and add another layer of construction to factual narrative. It is not difficult to arrive at the conclusion that media representations of child killing are more of a hindrance than an aid to understanding the deeper complexities of this phenomenon.

These observations suggest that the media adds significance and authority to the representations it prefers to broadcast. In particular, media reporting of filicide cases sifts the official from the unofficial account, and imbues certain representations with an authorised and authorising purpose. Media reporting is

Follow: Media and the Social Construction of Three Strikes and You're Out' in D Shichor and D Sechrest (eds), *Three Strikes and You're Out: Vengeance as Public Policy* (Sage, 1996) 180.

82 Matthew Benns, *When the Bough Breaks: The True Story of Child Killer Kathleen Folbigg* (Bantam, 2003); and Lindy Chamberlain, *Through My Eyes: The Autobiography of Lindy Chamberlain-Creighton* (East Street Publications, rev ed, 2004) 122–242, 239. Also see Katherine Biber, 'The Archival Turn in Law: The Papers of Lindy Chamberlain in the National Library of Australia' (2017) 39 *Sydney Law Review* 277–301.

83 Steve Chibnall, *Law and Order News: An Analysis of Crime Reporting in the British Press* (Tavistock, 1977) 23–43; and Hennessey Hayes and Tim Prenzler, *An Introduction to Crime and Criminology* (Pearson Education Australia, 2nd ed, 2009) 5.

84 Moira Peelo, Brian Francis, Keith Soothill, Jayn Pearson, Elizabeth Ackerley, 'Newspaper Reporting and the Public Construction of Homicide' (2004) 44 *British Journal of Criminology* 256–274, 274. While the study may not be applicable to the Australian context, its findings are relevant to the nature of media representations. For distortion in the Australian context, see Teece and Makkai, above n 80, 6.

an important symbolic signifier and interactor, and, as an agency of the law with respect to its selective reporting of cases, it is one of the few central tenets in Western society next to the law and public sentiment that play a key role in constructing, legitimating and sustaining representations to promote cultural coherence and a sense of order.[85]

The purpose of representation

Symbolic power of the good parent representation

In the context of parenting behaviours, the 'good parent' representation has a unique appeal in society. Its appeal is founded on its symbolism reflecting a perceived desirable level of social order, culture, class, status and/or respectability. For this reason, a misrepresentation and misappropriation of the good parent image has the propensity to negatively affect the efficiency of state intervention. Wilczynski[86] suggests the appearance and presentation of a good and respectable family background, which at first sight presents no obvious risk factors, typically allows parent perpetrators to pass undetected through the criminal justice, social and medical systems. It is not until some harm has already been done to the child that the misrepresentation is picked up by the criminal justice and child protection systems. For example, in the Jack Drummond case, the difficulties Melanie had been facing early on had been signs that things were not going smoothly for her, in the marriage and in the home, but she was able to represent herself and the family as going well. So these signs were masked and did not appear sufficiently serious to alert those around her to the possibility of child endangerment, and she was thus able to bypass early detection by the system. This is the first illustration of the power of the good parent symbol.

The second illustration is the effect of the symbol on sentencing outcomes.[87] Reading into the Drummond story, it can be observed that the media and legal constructions of Melanie's representation as the good mother led to this being a strong symbol in the public domain to the extent that it overpowered the image of the death of the child.[88] The familial, legal and media representations

85 Richard V. Ericson and Kevin D Haggerty, *Policing the Risk Society* (University of Toronto Press, 1997) 59.

86 Ania Wilczynski, 'Risk Factors for Parental Child Homicide: Results of an English Study' (1995) 7(2) *Current Issues in Criminal Justice* 193–222, 221; and also the conference presentation of Amanda Stephens, 'Truth and Uncertainty in "Shaken Baby Syndrome" cases: Law vs. Science?' (Paper presented at the University of Sydney Postgraduate Law Students Conference: Law, Life and Death, University of Sydney, 31 October 2008).

87 In Greta Sheng's case, for example, Caitlin Sheng was represented as a 'good, caring, moral person' in mitigation against the imposition of a full-time custodial sentence. See report 'Media-GS2', *The Australian*, New South Wales, 2 July 2009.

88 For example, the media reports tended to portray Melanie as a victim of her disabled child, the marriage and the system rather than as a perpetrator. For a sympathetic

of Melanie as the good mother who was on a crusade for her son's needs was, I would argue, responsible for the imposition of a non-custodial sentence in the form of a good behaviour bond.[89] To what extent the sentence was a result of 'trial by media' is unknown, but the media's role should not be discounted.[90] It may be persuasively argued that the leniency of Melanie's sentence was a custodial pardon in comparison to what would normally be a severe penalty for manslaughter or even murder. Undoubtedly criminal sanctions can be imposed to reflect the severity of moral culpability in child killing[91] and to enforce a particular morality.[92] The imposition of a non-custodial sentence for the crime of manslaughter therefore suggests that Melanie's moral culpability had been diminished, and this was as a result of mitigating factors in her favour: the prospect of her rehabilitation, her prevailing mental illness, her existing familial commitments and, as argued, the representation of her as a good mother. (This, by the way, is not meant as a value judgment either way on this outcome, but rather as an observation about the power of symbolic representation.) For French and Kayess,[93] on the other hand, it was Jack's victim characteristics and the court's representation of Jack as the Other that resulted in mitigating the severity of Melanie's offence.

Melanie Drummond is not the only example of the power of the good parent symbol in filicide.[94] In the Sutton case,[95] the deceased's parents killed

---

reinterpretation of the killing, which was mainly portrayed as a tragedy, see Ch 1: Jack Drummond.

89 This argument was also canvassed by French and Kayess, above n 11, 63–65, where they highlight that Jack's victim characteristics had strongly influenced the court's approach in addition to the court's reliance on Melanie's mental illness, frank admissions, early plea of guilt, and consequent diminished responsibility for the offence.

90 For example, Janine Albury Thompson, who strangled her autistic daughter in 1997, was charged with murder but convicted of manslaughter and sentenced to four years' imprisonment. This led to a public outcry and her sentence was reduced on appeal to 18 months. Two other examples are the cases of Lindy Chamberlain and Myra Hindley. In both of these cases, the trials were referred to as the 'trial of the century'. See Lindy Chamberlain, above n 82; and Jean Ritchie, *Myra Hindley: Inside the Mind of a Murderess* (Bay Books, 1988) 107.

91 For example, see the court judgment in *R v Horace Faulkner*, Supreme Court, New South Wales, 2004, Supreme Court No. HF1, [41] and [42], where Justice Grove cited *R v Hull* [1997] SASC 6087 *per* Justice Lander. And in Hannah Bromley's case judgment: *R v Georgina and Quentin Bromley*, Supreme Court, New South Wales, 2009, Supreme Court No. GQHB, [179].

92 Richard G Fox, 'New Crimes or New Responses? Future Directions in Australian Criminal Law' (2002) 28(1) *Monash University Law Review* 103–125, 124.

93 French and Kayess, above n 11.

94 Mercy killing is also known as altruistic filicide, which is when the parent perceives the killing to be in the child's best interests: Ania Wilczynski, *Child Homicide* (Oxford University Press, 1997), 55.

95 *R v Raymond Douglas Sutton*; *R v Margaret Ellen Sutton* [2007] NSWSC 295. See also *R v Li* [2000] NSWSC 1088, in which a mother pleaded guilty to manslaughter.

their disabled son of 29 years. The parents pleaded guilty to manslaughter and were both sentenced to a five-year good behaviour bond. The sentencing judge found, based on expert evidence, that these parent perpetrators suffered an abnormality of mind and as such needed treatment and rehabilitation as opposed to a custodial sentence, the conditions of which would only add to their health risks.[96] The judgment in this case was sympathetic to the parents' plight and, as in the Drummond case, the deceased was constructed by the court as the Other.[97]

Even though the victim in the Sutton case was an adult, it could be argued that the deceased's status is equivalent to that of a child because of the deceased's relationship of dependence on the parents. And, even though the Drummond and Sutton cases contained extenuating circumstances,[98] both the outcomes suggest that mercy killing is less serious an offence than other types of child killing.[99] The 'good parent' who kills a disabled child is represented in a favourable light as compared with a 'bad parent' who kills their children in a child residence dispute. As French and Kayess point out, both cases appeared to be 'activated by the latent belief that the "burden" and "suffering" caused by a child with disability *ipso facto* diminishes the culpability of parents for that child's murder'.[100] This also implies that the courts afforded a sympathetic interpretation to the perpetrator's actions, an interpretation easily reached when juxtaposed against the construction of the victim as the repulsive[101] Other. Taking a slightly different approach from French and Kayess, I argue that the decisions in these cases supported the symbol of the good parent at the expense of the value of human life of intellectually disabled children. Throughout both judgments, the court emphasised and stressed repeatedly the past loving actions of the offenders.[102] The parents' actions were described as 'one born of love',[103] and they were represented as having 'unchallenged good character'.[104] The purpose of such an emphatic pronouncement appears to be to maintain a clear division between the good and the bad parent symbols, and in doing so venerate the good parent rather than the value of the life of the child with disability. This harks back to

96 Ibid [36], [39].

97 As in the Drummond story, the court extensively interrogated the nature and degree of the deceased's disabilities and constructed the deceased as a living tragedy, as other than human and as a source of profound grief, shame and burden to the parents: French and Kayess, above n 11, 57–84, 65.

98 Both cases involved a child with profound disabilities. The parents suffered emotionally and were depressed at the time. The Drummond story was characterised by the lack of support services and respite. In the Sutton story, the parents had support services. The extenuating circumstances were the difficulties associated with the medical and physical care of their son, the deceased.

99 *R v Melanie Drummond*, Court of Criminal Appeal, above n 11 [34].

100 French and Kayess, above n 11, 67.

101 Ibid 66.

102 Ibid.

103 Above n 97, [42].

104 *R v Melanie Drummond*, New South Wales District Court, above n 10, [85].

both pre-Christian and early Medieval times, where destruction of the demonic and/or abnormal child was common practice in certain Western societies and non-Western societies.[105]

The reader will recall mothers who killed their children out of poverty for utility reasons were morally punished: their killings were explained with reference to demonic intervention and they were accused of witchcraft and stigmatised as witches.[106] In spite of changing social conditions in England, deformed children continued to be treated differently from normal children because they carried a separate status as a 'non-person'[107] or, one could argue, the venal Other. It appears that this representation of a child with a disability – embodying utility but more so morality dimensions – has not changed much, in spite of the development of human rights protections in the current climate. The prevalence of this representation of the disabled child as 'less worthy' in some sections of our social milieu still exists,[108] one could argue, as a social indicator acknowledging the child's marginalised status in society.

The marginalisation of the child with a disability is evident in the sentencing outcomes of the Sutton and Drummond cases, with the courts appearing to favour the symbol of the good parent. This conceals from the audience the place of the marginal child. Looking at the Steppenwolf, Drummond and Sutton judgments, all of which involved the killing of a child by a parent, the courts appeared to draw a distinction between cases in which children were killed as a result of marital disputes and those in which children were killed as a result of altruism, that is, mercy killing. In other words, the courts differentiated the context of the killing. There appears though to be no justification for this differentiation. The only apparent reason for such a differentiation is the overwhelming prevalence of the good parent symbol in the mercy-killing cases. In other words, the legal construction of the parent perpetrator representation, alongside the construction of the victim as the Other, mitigated the severity of the killing. In the Drummond and Sutton cases the parents were constructed as good parents, while in the Steppenwolf case the parent was represented as deviant. The children in the former cases were constructed as problematic, while the child in the latter

105 Catherine Damme, 'Infanticide: The Worth of an Infant Under the Law' (1978) 22 *Medical History* 1–24, 2–9. For further references, see below n 108–114.

106 Louise Jackson, 'Witches, Wives and Mothers: Witchcraft Persecution and Women's Confessions in Seventeenth-Century England' (1995) 4(1) *Women's History Review* 63–84, 75–77.

107 Damme, above n 105, 7, 22–23. Damme points out that in the United States many obstetricians admit to delivering infants so severely deformed that they took no measures to sustain the infant's life. This highlights yet another example of such separate status.

108 For a recent debate on the killing of disabled children, see Sarah-Kate Templeton, 'Doctors: Let Us Kill Disabled Babies', *The Times* (online), 5 November 2006 www.timesonline.co.uk/tol/news/uk/article625477.ece. For arguments justifying the killing of disabled infants, see Peter Singer, *Practical Ethics* (Cambridge University Press, 2nd ed, 1993) 175–217.

was seen as normal. From this perspective, it could be argued that the sentencing in mercy-killing cases illustrates the extent of the power of the good parent symbol, which appears to overpower the meaning given to the value of the life of a child with a disability.

This argument may be unusual but this is not that say that there are no competing explanations for the courts' sympathetic treatment of the perpetrators in the Drummond and Sutton cases. Could the courts have judged the perpetrators as lacking the intention to hurt others? Or is the status of the child with a disability less than that of the child without a disability? The comparison of these stories with cases in the era during which child destruction was common practice for the weaker child suggests that there still exists less than equal recognition between the two. The cases suggest that the child with disability is still criticised as problematic.

Another rationale for the court's sentencing could be its sympathetic view on these perpetrators. These perpetrators were constructed in a way that appealed to ordinary parents. Their struggles were characterised as normal because ordinary parents would struggle with these same problems. The killing too was represented as something any normal parent would have been compelled to do if they could not cope. Both the court and the media placed great emphasis on the attempts by the parent to care for the child in these two cases. This is in contrast to the Hannah Bromley story where Hannah too was a disabled child, but the parents did not try to care for her and were therefore represented by the court as bad parents. The sympathetic view of the parent perpetrator harks back to the technique of sympathetic reinterpretation of the killing. The purpose is to give acceptable meaning to an otherwise unacceptable act of violence.

The meaning given to the act of violence is important, because it informs the purpose of the court and reaffirms the power and effect of judicial representation, which affects individual lives; at the same time, judicial representation gives meaning to the law. In terms of the effect of the law on individual lives, the most visible effect lies in sentencing. This is most evident in the two cases of mercy killing discussed in this book. The effect of judicial acknowledgement of the good parent representation in mercy-killing cases is, one could argue, to preserve the symbol of the good parent in this category of cases. In this process, this image or representation is painted over the moral culpability of the perpetrators, and the severity of the act, the killing, is thus glossed over. In these cases the courts held that punishment is unnecessary and inappropriate because the perpetrators had suffered enough. This outcome can be contrasted with other cases of child killing not involving a child with a disability.

Justice Barr of the Supreme Court in the Sutton case said: 'it seems to me that nothing that the court can do by way of sentence can add to the offenders' suffering. The need for further punishment is spent.'[109] He went on to highlight

109 Above n 95, [38].

the importance of the perpetrators' rehabilitation by stating that 'a custodial sentence would be cruel because it would separate [the parent perpetrators] and deny them the full benefits of the treatment to which they are entitled'.[110] There is nothing in this sentence that suggests there is a need for deterrence, whereas in non-mercy-killing cases the element of deterrence is clear and unequivocal. This leads to a question: What kind of message should a sentence in child-killing cases send to the wider audience? For example, should punishment be aimed at deterrence, denunciation or rehabilitation, or all of these? Arguably, the sentences for child killing ought to 'mirror something of the symbolic vision of those who impose it'.[111]

With the exception of the Sutton and Drummond stories, the symbolic vision for parent perpetrators in child killing is not that of rehabilitation. In cases where the children were not intellectually disabled, the penalty is 'severe punishment'.[112] For example, in the Steppenwolf case the prosecution submitted:

> This is a case where aspects of general deterrence are important. Many persons are involved in marital disputes and many of those disputes often become heated and some unfortunately become violent. Too often, sadly, *children become pawns in those marital disputes*. That is bad enough but those who do become involved in marital disputes must clearly understand that they cannot visit violence upon their children for any reason whatsoever, but in particular for the purpose of upsetting or punishing their spouse. Such action, it should be understood, will attract a very severe punishment. The community ought to be able to expect that the courts will be quick to protect the defenceless, particularly children.[113] (Emphasis added)

The sentencing judge appeared to agree with the prosecution's submissions, saying:

> She acted in breach of a position of trust and authority in respect of a victim who was her own son. [Capello] was entitled to love, protection and nurture but instead she took away his very life.[114]
>
> In a matter involving the murder of a young child, general deterrence, denouncing the offender's conduct and making her accountable for her actions are particularly important.[115]

110 Ibid [42].
111 Downes and Rock, above n 52, 187.
112 Ch 1: Capello Steppenwolf.
113 The prosecution cited *R v Horace Faulkner*, above n 91, [41] and [42], where Justice Grove cited *R v Hull* [1997] SASC 6087 *per* Justice Lander.
114 *R v Kramer*, Supreme Court, New South Wales, 2009, Supreme Court No. EK1, [87].
115 Ibid [99].

The courts' reasoning in the sentencing outcomes of these cases appears to draw a distinction between parents who kill out of anger and revenge, and parents who kill for altruistic reasons and who showed evidence of abnormality of mind not amounting to legal insanity. The distinction appears to be based on two factors: perpetrator motive, and the extenuating circumstances of having a child with a disability and/or abnormality of mind. The court's reasoning in the Sutton case, if applied to the Faulkner story, would suggest that punishment had been 'spent' for Horace (who killed believing he was saving the children) because he had suffered enough. And there was no contention that Horace did suffer: he suffered under his delusion of persecution, believing his ex-wife was taking the children away from him. However, the decisions in the Sutton and Drummond cases imply that Horace's suffering cannot be compared with the Suttons' or the Drummonds', whose suffering directly related to sacrifice and caring for the children. This again goes back to the image of the parent as having qualities of devotion and sacrifice.

When looking across the cases discussed here, it is significant that desirable qualities of parenthood are consistently enforced by the courts in two ways: through their judicial reinterpretation of the act of violence, and through sentencing. Notwithstanding this, both non-mercy-killing cases and mercy-killing cases reveal that the children are pawns used by parent perpetrators who feel they are entitled to use violence on their children to express their anger or frustration or to expiate their guilt and depression. In spite of this, the conclusion one could draw here is that, after the dysfunctional layers are peeled away, the good, sacrificial parent perpetrator representations are praised, but there are few of these in the cases of child killing.

Governing purpose of the bad parent representation

There are two ways in which the bad parent representation can be used to govern. The first is the governance of society by making an example of the deviant perpetrator. The second is the governance of the individual through the processes of labelling. In the first, the court makes an example of the deviant perpetrator by interpreting the deviance in accordance with the bad parent representation, or by the imposition of the mask of the bad parent on the perpetrator,[116] or simply by unmasking the parent perpetrator.[117] The employment

116 The story of Greta Sheng is an example of the imposition of the mask of the bad parent. However, this is not to say that Gerald Sheng was a good parent. Instead, the imposition of the mask of bad parent is seen from the perpetrator's viewpoint. Gerald and Caitlin Sheng had maintained that they were not guilty and did their best to treat their child. From the start, they did not believe the prosecutorial construction of themselves as 'bad' parents: Ch 2: Greta Sheng; and see report 'Media-GS1', *Daily Telegraph*, New South Wales, 14 August 2009; report 'Media-GS1a', *Sydney Morning Herald*, New South Wales, 13 August 2009.

117 Horace Faulkner is an example of unmasking by the court.

of the mask in the criminal justice context and in this particular argument can be justified by looking at the mask's ability to reconstitute appearance. It has already been noted that representation is unlike masking.[118] However, as with labelling, there are some overlapping conceptualisations between representation and masking. One example of such an overlap is the ability of both to refashion the object's original existence and appearance. Girard highlights this point, as well as the argument that the purpose of the representation, or mask, is to bridge the dissimilarities between individual cases because it can replace, hide or substitute the human face. Girard says this can be achieved because:

> The mask mixes man and beast, god and inanimate object . . . Masks juxtapose beings and objects separated by differences. They are beyond differences; they do not merely defy differences or efface them, but they incorporate and rearrange them in original fashion. In short, they are another aspect of the monstrous double.[119]

What Girard means is that the mask or representation allows society to be able to grapple with the complexity and horrific acts of the deviant Other without having to see the human face behind the act of killing. He argues that the mask is:

> the point where all differences, all monstrosities are concentrated, and from which a new order will emerge. There is no point in trying to determine the 'nature' of masks, because it is in their nature not to have a nature but to encompass all natures.[120]

This is to say that representations through the use of symbols are about generalising the particular[121] – the individual – from which control and regulation can begin to reshape and refashion individual identity and govern individual attitudes and behaviour. From this view, it can be understood that the upholding of the symbolism of the good parent is crucial in order for the court to be able to justify the imposition of the non-custodial sentence – the purpose of which is to ensure the Other as beast is hidden. This has the opposite effect in Greek tragedies, where 'masks disappear when the monsters once again assume human forms'.[122] This opposite effect in reality is evident in mercy-killing cases, where the good parent representation is used to conceal the monstrosity of the killing

118 A dissimilarity is that masks are used to *represent* the representation. This said, it is incorrect to assume that representation and masking are only about concealment. See Goffman, above n 45, 30.

119 Girard, above n 58, *Violence and the Sacred*, 167.

120 Ibid 168.

121 Moscovici argues that the purpose of all representations is to make something unfamiliar, or unfamiliarity itself familiar, by anchoring and objectification through which the unfamiliar is given a place in the familiar world: Moscovici, above n 6, 11.

122 Girard, above n 58 *Violence and the Sacred*, 146–148.

and to re-represent the unacceptable violence of the killing by replacing it with a mask depicting a human face.

The evidence of this power of governance on society is also seen in the cases of Greta Sheng and Hannah Bromley, where the court stressed the utility of making the perpetrators an example to the rest of society.[123] For example, in the Bromley case the sentencing judge cited Chief Justice Wood[124] in *R v Wilkinson*:

> The need for a significant element of deterrence in cases such as the present is obvious, given the inability of young children to fend for themselves and given the difficulties experienced by outsiders, including DOCS staff, in protecting children who are at risk as the result of activities of neglect occurring within the privacy of their own homes. *The message which needs to be given to the prisoner and to any other parent or carer who stands by and allows an infant to be seriously hurt, or who, as in the present case, ignores obvious signs demanding immediate attention or other intervention for the protection of the child, is that such conduct is not accepted by the community and it will attract significant punishment under the law.*
>
> Carers and parents carry a very heavy responsibility to ensure, when children are hurt or sick, that they are taken promptly for medical attention, or that other steps are taken to remove them from risk. Parents – and this is of particular relevance to the present case – are also expected to maintain the degree of fortitude of mind and will of reasonable persons in their shoes in fulfilling that duty.[125] (Emphasis added)

This judicial denunciation uses the parent perpetrators as examples for the audience and in order to govern future similar offending behaviours. Another way in which this power is exercised is when the alleged parent perpetrator is incarcerated pending trial. For example, in the Steppenwolf story the perpetrator, Elizabeth, was placed in protective custody.[126] Protective custody was needed because society's responses, including the responses of prisoners to the nature of child killing, are usually hostile and can be life-threatening.[127] Such responses are sometimes provoked by the media's reporting of the case once it has entered the criminal justice system.[128] In this context, the public response can be seen as an

123 *R v Gerald Sheng*; *R v Caitlin Sheng*, Supreme Court, New South Wales, 2009, Supreme Court No. SHG13, [153], [154], [160]. In Hannah Bromley, the court cited the judgment of Greta Sheng to emphasise the need for deterrence.

124 Supreme Court of New South Wales, 9 April 1998, Unreported judgment.

125 *R v Georgina and Quentin Bromley*, Supreme Court, New South Wales, 2009, Supreme Court No. GQHB, [179].

126 Report 'Media-15', *Herald Sun*, Victoria, 22 October 2007.

127 Report 'Media-14', *The Age*, New South Wales, 21 October 2007; *R v Horace Faulkner*, Supreme Court, above n 91, [67].

128 In the Capello Steppenwolf story, after Elizabeth Kramer's identity was made known in the media it was reported that the public were hostile towards her. They called her names and called for violent punishment to be inflicted on her.

indication of how the media uses a bad parent representation to warn audiences of the repercussions of deviance associated with child killing. The public response also reveals the representation and status of children is such that they are seen as society's most innocent and vulnerable.

The reader will recall that a similar technique was used in the myths of Medea and Heracles, in which the horror of child killing was expressed by the chorus. Mythology is relevant to the analysis here because it reveals the 'art' of masking. The use of the chorus is a common technique in the morality plays of Euripides and Seneca. Its purpose was to represent an objective third-party, or outside, view on the moral dilemma unfolding between the actors. For instance, it can represent objective morality or the collective conscience of the audience or societal opinion in that era.[129] This is to say that the chorus, like the court or public sentiment, reminds the audience of what is beneath the masks. The effect of the chorus in the plays can also be likened to the effect of media representation. As the parallel suggests, they have the power to shape public perception, to unmask and to add an additional layer of interpretation to the moral conundrum.

The second way in which the bad parent representation is used to govern is exemplified by the power of representation to affect self-perception. While the relationship between representation and self-perception can be positive, it is the impact of the negative self-perception that this book is interested in. The consequent effect after the application of a deviant label, particularly the bad parent label, is significant for the individual. The power of a representation should not be underestimated. While representation can sometimes involve the application of a label, representation as a concept is wider than labelling theory. Labelling theory explores the interaction between the applications of rules, and hence labels, to individuals and the consequences of applying such a label.[130] Representation in this book, however, seeks to explain the interactions between different social forces that can involve having to apply a label or wear a mask. That said, there are overlapping ideas between labelling theory and this book's conceptualisation of representation. A label and a representation share similar attributes in that they are about the language of role and role-playing,[131] and also they embody the subject with a particular image and meaning that is detached from the subject's own image. For example, representations of gender in advertising often depict women either as sexy or as maternal, thus consciously and subconsciously confining women to particular categories by denying them the opportunity to be realised in a holistic manner.[132] To illustrate this argument, Edwin Schur explains: 'Response is to the label, not the individual; and

129 Donald Mastronarde (ed), *Euripides: Medea* (Cambridge University Press, 2002) 11–12; Harry Hine, *Seneca: Medea* (Aris & Phillips, 2000) 19–21, 122.
130 Downes and Rock, above n 52, 181–187.
131 Ibid 192.
132 Susan Goodwin and Joanne Finkelstein, *The Sociological Bent: Inside Metro Culture* (Thomson, 2005) 43.

the label is difficult to shed because the individual's other attributes or current accomplishments are overshadowed by it.'[133] For women, this has been the issue of control and regulation because of the construction of certain romanticised and idealised notions of the family in Western cultures.[134] The idealised notions built around good and bad mother representations affect not just women in society in general but also women inmates in prison.[135] For example, Schram's study of mothers in prison confirmed the suggestion that mother stereotypes and representations that exist outside of prison, in society, also exist inside the prison. Additionally, such stereotyping negatively affects the treatment of, and attitudes towards, women in prison. Schram questions whether stereotypes of incarcerated women are a form of social control. Her study found that there was indeed a relationship of control between correctional officers and the incarcerated women, particularly those with children. Apart from the officers' position of power, such a relationship tended to exert social control in terms of negative attitudes towards these women.[136] As such, the contention that stereotyping functions to maintain social control is supported and, in addition, the proposition in labelling theory that 'the deviant is one to whom the label has successfully been applied; deviant behaviour is behaviour that people so label'[137] also appears to support such an argument. The question of whether such labelling prompts further offending was not addressed in Schram's study.

The notion that stereotyping and labelling can affect a person's self-perception has been generally accepted,[138] but the consequences of such labelling, particularly where labelling is relevant as a social interactive presence in homicide, are under-researched. The cases in my fieldwork suggest that, in a familial setting, parent perpetrators often feel strongly that they have been unable to live up to the good parent image. The mention of 'good' and 'bad' frequently crops up in the cases in the contexts in which the perpetrators view and describe themselves. This self-labelling is prevalent in the cases, where it often takes the form of perpetrator self-reproach, and in the cases below it can even be seen to be a catalyst in the prelude to the killing.

One prominent example of this is Danny Burrow, in which the mother perpetrator had, before the killing, perceived herself as a failure during the birth of her second child. Such feelings arose when she felt acutely that her children

133 Schur, above n 5, 32.

134 A Beckerman, 'Women in Prison: The Conflict between Confinement and Parental Rights' (1991) 18 *Social Justice* 171–183, 172; Lisa Maher, 'Punishment and Welfare: Crack Cocaine and the Regulation of Mothering' (1992) 3 *Women and Criminal Justice* 35–70, 39.

135 Pamela J Schram, 'An Exploratory Study: Stereotypes about Mothers in Prison' (1999) 27(5) *Journal of Criminal Justice* 411–426, 412.

136 Ibid 423.

137 Above n 1.

138 Downes and Rock, above n 52, 186.

were rejecting her in favour of a temporary carer. She expressed the following remarks[139] at various points in time prior to the killing:

> That I thought I was a failure. I failed motherhood. Failed to get help for myself and Danny.[140]
>
> That I am a bad mother. That I should kill myself.[141]
>
> They [the children] are not happy with me. I hated myself.[142]

Melanie Drummond also described a similar negative presence before the killing: 'I realised I was not this perfect mum anymore and I could not live with that.'[143] Such perpetrator statements are powerful representations, if not examples of internalisations of the negative label. Their self-conceptualisations and self-reproach are about their failure to attain the standard of the positive label of the good parent, and this may have a propensity to mould or terminate relationships. These findings suggest that the purpose of idealised notions of the good and bad parent symbols have been to reproach, monitor and govern the Self, and as an example to others it sends out a message of what not to do. Because of the power of emotions among public responses to the deviant parent image, the parent perpetrator may sometimes go to extreme lengths to maintain, appropriate and even mimic the good parent label. For example, this was done in the Mark and Libby story. Mark had, on a number of occasions, presented himself to the authorities as the 'good' parent, and in so doing engendered conflict over the children in the ongoing child residence proceedings. This supports the argument that a representation, mask or label, when applied in the appropriate context, can either command respect, power and control or provoke abhorrence, particularly when it is employed in the context of filicide, and can shape the court's conceptualisation of the killing and the culpability of the parent.

Symbolic implications overshadowing Western perceptions of parenthood

Representation, therefore, has a dual purpose: it has the power of governance both inside and outside the Subject. The power of representation to govern social relations within the familial space lies not only in the use of parent symbolisms, particularly the image of the idealised parent;[144] Rose argues that

139 This data gives insight into self-labelling and different angles of self-representation.
140 Report from Dr Tijuana ('SB5') taken on 23 November 2001 in New South Wales, prison X, 14.
141 Ibid.
142 Ibid.
143 Report 'MD4' taken from Melanie Drummond in New South Wales on 8 January 2004 at police station A.
144 Donzelot, above n 2.

idealised notions of the family have been used as an ideological mechanism for governance purposes, such as for reproduction of a docile labour force or adherence to the general patriarchal structures in Western society.[145] Specifically, he argues that the image of the family as a creation of love, which is represented as a site of self-realisation for mothers, is nothing more than a *mask*:

> The function of this familial ideology was to mask the realities of family life, and to preserve a social institution that provided vital economic functions for capitalism: reproduction of the labour force, socialisation of children, exploitation of unpaid domestic labour of women, compensation to men for the alienating nature of their work and so forth.[146]

To be sure, this view is now contestable given that women's status in the home, especially regarding child-caring, is increasingly recognised by governments and in the workplace,[147] but this does not detract from the overall argument that such an ideology exists and that it has the capacity to mask underlying dysfunctionality and relationships within the family. The progressive social changes to women's status in the home have been normative.[148] The parents in these stories, especially the mothers,[149] reveal that there exists in them a strong need to define their parenting with reference to an idealised notion of what the good parent represents.[150] These parents internalise the labels of good and bad parent that are built from their reconstruction of the idealised image or symbol of the Universal Mother. This is the case particularly for the women in the cases who see themselves as the children's primary protector and caregiver; the symbol of motherhood masks any change to their status in the home.

145 Rose, above n 2, 124.
146 Ibid.
147 For example, the Australian Government's Paid Parental Leave Scheme, of 2011, provides financial entitlements for the child's primary caregiver, especially for the birth mother, who is eligible to receive financial assistance provided he or she meets the eligibility criteria.
148 Smart gives two legal examples of the extent of governance in family life, and the normative standards applied by the courts to the representations of a mother in divorce. In the first case, *Re SM (A Minor) (Natural Father: Access)* [1991] 2 FLR 333 (UK), the mother was represented as a good mother working in the interests of the child. The court decided that she was allowed to form a fresh relationship and have a clean break. In the second case, *Re R (A Minor) (Contact)* [1993] 2 FLR 762 (UK), the mother was represented in the same way but was constructed by the court as working to damage the welfare of the child. The court decided that she could not have a clean break and labelled her hostile for not recognising the true interests of the child. Smart argues that this move destabilised the child's existing family. See Carol Smart, 'Wishful Thinking and Harmful Tinkering? Sociological Reflections on Family Policy' in Cheryl Albers (ed), *Sociology of Families* (Pine Forge Press, 1999) 474–487, 483–484.
149 This comes across most strongly among the women in the cases, for example, Melanie Drummond, Angeline Soprano and Melissa Faulkner.
150 Donzelot, above n 2.

The fathers in the Faulkner, Bromley and Mark and Libby stories were concerned with fatherhood representation as much as, if not more than, the mothers in these stories were. Their statements throughout the cases reveal that they perceive the outward representation of their part in and responsibility for the killing and care of the children as important to them. For example, Paul, Horace and Mark reacted violently to the possibility that they might lose their children to their partners. Quentin Bromley tried to reposition his responsibility to Hannah by casting blame on Georgina during the trial, and later, in retrospect, tried to recast himself as a wayward father.[151] These examples show representation to be central to the construction of parenthood, and to these parents' own governance of their behaviour based on their perceptions of fatherhood.

Conclusion

The purpose of this chapter has been to highlight the utility of using modelling to understand and analyse different contexts of representation. Representation in child killing is clearly a multidimensional phenomenon that is not easily understood. Applying the models to the cases reveals this phenomenon to be multilayered and heavily contextualised by events surrounding the perpetrator. It also reveals the different social and interactive forces that participate in giving meaning to these events and the perpetrator's actions, including actions producing risks of child endangerment. The audience is central in this process of social construction of meaning, and its role in this cannot be ignored. What this indicates is a positive relationship between representation and the construction of risk; risk is constructed based on selected representations. Representations, such as the loving parent, elude risk detection because, as has been argued, they are deeply embedded and nurtured in society as acceptable.

The question whether representations should be regulated has been explored. Representations seen as risky or not must be regulated according to the interests, safety and well-being of the child. As representation is central to risk construction, parenting behaviours that are constructed and represented as unhealthy (such as those in the Sheng and Steppenwolf cases) and seen by society as risky are increasingly governed through their representations in the media, the law and public sentiment. The ultimate purpose of this is to enable the social governance of parents who will in the future govern themselves.[152] This means that representation is used to coerce people to conform to the norm by socially constructing them through a variety of means, such as labelling, stigmatising and shaming, and the manipulation of the loving parent representation. As such a representation is one that has been dominant in encouraging appropriate parenting behaviour, it is not constructed as risky. Perhaps it is a matter of recognising that some

151 Report 'MEDIA-HB3', *The Monthly*, New South Wales, February 2010, 37; and report 'MEDIA-HB31', *Sydney Morning Herald*, 27 May 2009.
152 Nikolas Rose, above n 2, 102.

representations, such as the loving parent, have to be unmasked in order to reveal the violence they conceal.

This chapter has also examined the techniques of labelling and sympathetic reinterpretation, which are argued as pivotal to representing the perpetrator and the killing. These techniques give meaning to an otherwise meaningless act of violence, which creates for the audience a particular representation that can be easily associated with the violence. The faces of these representations have been maintained in textual references of the media, reflecting public sentiment and legitimated in law by the courts. This demonstrates governance of parenting by those in the third-degree representation, such as the media, the law and public sentiment.

In these cases, masking and representation relate directly to the adult, and this raises concerns and questions about the place of the child in all of this, considering the focus of first-degree representations are usually on the dysfunctional parents. Sadly, the voice of the child in the storytelling is rarely heard. Even when scrutiny is applied to the state or its agents, the representation of the child only 'comes alive' after death. The only time the audience sees and hears the child is at third-degree representation, after his or her life has been brutally taken. This discussion is brought to bear in Chapter 6, which examines one of the interactions, between the loving father representation and state intervention, that produced risk to the child; and in Chapter 7, where the principal features of risk and the conditions that develop risk are examined. Chapter 7 concludes by questioning the significance of the child's voice in all of this, arguing that, amid webs of misrepresentation, failed protective intervention and distracting symbolisms, we must not forget the importance of 'seeing' the child, but only after unmasking the layers of representation that conceal the risks of violence to the child.

6 Masculine representations

Loving fathers? Failed representations leading to risk[1]

Introduction

In the previous chapters, different contexts of representation, and their interaction, were discussed as a means of understanding risk. It was argued that child killing is the product of various social interactions which can work against the safety of the child. Principal among these interactions are failed representation and false symbols. This chapter examines one of the interactions that produce risk of endangerment to the child, bridging the earlier discussions on the theorising of representation and the consequences of endangerment to the child, by selecting and examining the significant variant of patriarchy as mirrored in state obligation and leading to the risks inherent in dysfunctional intervention. In this chapter, certain representations, such as the loving father, are seen as impacting on intervention. The misunderstanding of the potential riskiness of this representation is seen as leading to consequences of endangerment for the child. The chapter portrays the pervasive ideology of the loving father as part of the wider patriarchal interpretation of the father and the family. The first section examines patriarchal

1 A modified version of this chapter has been published as a journal article, see: Janice Sim, 'Loving Fathers? Implications of State Intervention' 28(2) *University of Tasmania Law Review* 242–264. At the time of publication in 2009, section 23 of the CYP Act had not been amended. Pursuant to Justice Wood's recommendations following the Wood Inquiry, the CYP Act revisions came into effect on 2 December 2010. As such, this chapter has been revised to incorporate these changes. The chapter also references two recent research reports that were not available at the time the article was published: J Cashmore, P Parkinson, R Weston, R Patulny, G Redmond, L Qu, J Baxter, M Rajkovic, T Sitek and I Katz, *Shared Care Parenting Arrangements Since the 2006 Family Law Reforms: Report to the Australian Government Attorney-General's Department* (Research report, University of Sydney, Australia Institute of Family Studies and Social Policy Research Centre, University of New South Wales, May 2010); and D Bagshaw, T Brown, S Wendt, A Campbell, E McInnes, T Beth, B Batagol, A Sifris, D Tyson, J Baker and P Fernandez Arias, *Family Violence and Family Law in Australia: The Experiences and Views of Children and Adults from Families Who Separated Post-1995 and Post-2006* (Research report, Monash University, University of South Australia and James Cook University, April 2010). Both reports are available online: www.ag.gov.au/www/agd/agd.nsf/Page/Families_Family RelationshipServicesOverviewofPrograms_ResearchProjectsonSharedCareParenting andFamilyViolence.

interpretations of family relations in terms of mirroring the state's exercise of responsibility. The discussion examines failure of state intervention in the context of the state's interaction with the family. This failure is conceptualised as a form of patriarchal dysfunction which exacerbates dysfunctional conditions of risk and endangerment to the child. Conceding that analysis involving the interaction of various representations and symbols produces risk, the simple causal connection between patriarchy and risky intervention decisions is revealed in this chapter.

Patriarchy

Patriarchy is an authoritarian, classed, hierarchical social system founded on male dominance in which the keys of authority, definition and control are in male hands. In the twenty-first century, even after the rise of feminist consciousness, this system still prevails in both overt and covert forms, particularly in institutions such as the family, the state and its bureaucratic institutions – law enforcement and the military. In some areas, such as the workforce, education, the arts and public life, women's consciousness has taken on a topical and prominent place in society; nevertheless, as Summers[2] points out, even there patriarchy maintains influence. That being so, the institutional representation of the state, particularly where it intersects with the private, has not changed significantly over the past century and continues to preserve a pervasive masculine ideology.

Broadly in the context of filicide,[3] attention is drawn to the parallel cases of failed state intervention[4] and families in which the male assumed right to authority and ownership have collapsed. Two main themes emerge from this context: the state of dysfunction and the masculine representation of the intervention in the family crisis. Three stories have been selected to illustrate these main themes, within which the sub-themes of patriarchal dysfunction, communication and male disempowerment as a source and indicator of dysfunction, and how such perceived disempowerment affects child safety, are discussed.[5] It is within these

2 Anne Summers, *The End of Equality: Work, Babies and Women's Choices in 21st-Century Australia* (Random House Australia, 2003) ch 8. See also Joyce Dougherty, 'Women's Violence Against Their Children: A Feminist Perspective' (1993) 4(2) *Women and Criminal Justice* 91–114, 95–98.

3 Filicide is defined as 'custodial or non-custodial parents (or step-parents) killing their child(ren)' in J Mouzos and C Rushforth, *Family Homicide in Australia* (Research report, Australian Institute of Criminology Trends and Issues in Criminal Justice No. 255, Canberra: Australian Institute of Criminology, 2003) 2.

4 In this book, state intervention refers to intervention by agencies of the state apparatus and agents, such as the police, community services, health workers and the courts. The data is drawn from my study of 40 filicide cases between 2000 and 2007 that were categorised as 'assault' in the National Coroners Information System. All identifiers in the cases have been changed.

5 The themes in this chapter are informed by the information arising from my study of 40 filicide cases, in addition to the wealth of other materials on filicide. The representation of the cases has been stripped down for the purposes of anonymity and to highlight the central argument of the book.

contexts that the reader is drawn into the complex interplay between power and disempowerment, and the communication rift that is symptomatic of a deeper problem.

The reader may well recall that at the beginning of the book it was mentioned that the majority of child deaths, as a result of abuse, neglect, murder or other suspicious circumstances, were at the time of death known to the state,[6] or the parents (one or both) had previously been involved with a professional (social or medical) agency.[7] More than half of the cases in the original coronial sample were known to the state at the time of death, and more than half of these incidents of violence involved male perpetrators. In most of these cases, the family could be described as conforming to a nuclear family model such that there had been one male role model and one female role model in the children's lives, whether they were the biological or de facto parent or de facto partner. Only in a handful of cases (5 per cent) was the nuclear model incomplete, consisting of a single parent household. A broad assessment of relationship status in the stories shows that in most the family structure had been patriarchal.[8] In the stories to follow, not only were the families interacting with state agencies at the time of the child's death, but the tenacity in the male's assumed right to, and reassertion of, ownership and control of his wife and children was observed to be dysfunctional in a way that impacts on the child's safety and well-being. Crucial to this is the misrepresentation of the father as loving, and state agents' misunderstanding of this misleading representation. As was suggested in Chapter 5, because of the pervasiveness of the loving father symbol, which is widely accepted and even encouraged, risks to the child are masked.

This chapter commences with a theoretical conceptualisation of dysfunction and its applicability in the law. Over the rest of this chapter three of the stories will be examined in order to illustrate some of the dysfunctional conditions within what could be called a 'state of dysfunction', such as a persistent and progressive deterioration in marital communications. In the first case study (Isabel and Paul), a parallel is drawn between the gendered representation of the state and nature of patriarchy in the nuclear family structure. The central argument in this discussion is that the replacement of a dysfunctional parent with another equally dysfunctional 'parent' model, the state apparatus, can have the adverse consequence of augmenting female disempowerment. The state response to the

6 New South Wales Ombudsman, *Report of Reviewable Deaths in 2005 Volume 2: Child Deaths* (New South Wales Ombudsman, 2006) 7. Out of the 117 reviewable child deaths in 2005, 33 children died as a result of abuse or neglect or suspicious circumstances, out of which 25 children were known to child protection services within three years of their deaths.

7 Ania Wilczynski, 'Prior Agency Contact and Physical Abuse in Cases of Child Homicide' (1997) 27 *British Journal of Social Work* 241–253, 243.

8 Not all instances of state intervention and patriarchy are dysfunctional. By examining cases where state intervention has failed, I am seeking insights into the complexities surrounding family conflicts.

dysfunction, and some implications of the recent mandatory arrest law[9] in New South Wales, are then discussed. The second case study (Melissa and Horace) is then introduced as an illustration of my argument that family functionality is heavily dependent on the state of power relations; the chapter will look specifically here at the impact of the loss of marital power on the male parent and his ensuing response. In the third study (Mark and Libby), the point made is that child endangerment was not always apparent during the preceding incidents of intimate partner violence where the male perpetrator assumed the dominant status. The risks to the child were hidden because the violence was masked by a representation of affective ties between parent and child in addition to the emphasis on shared parenting even when there had been allegations of child endangerment. In practice, state intervention often does not recognise that the violence between the parents[10] poses serious risks to the safety of the child, despite domestic violence being recognised as child abuse. This position is suggested as both deceptive and dangerous in that it conceals the unexposed nature of the danger to the child. The chapter concludes on a note of caution that state intervention needs to adopt functional approaches towards understanding and addressing the problem of the real question of safety, instead of maintaining the patriarchal dialogue on law and order.

The state of dysfunction

Conceptualising what dysfunction is and what it represents is not easy. This section begins with a narrow theoretical conceptualisation of dysfunction in a family in which there are children, and then proceeds to a broader ambit where it can be understood that dysfunction ends. Dysfunction in a family is framed by the idea that there are certain basic conditions for child safety that, if not met, will render a particular situation to be dysfunctional. The state of dysfunction can develop from a cluster of risk factors pertinent to the family or from a stand-alone malignant condition that places a child in the family in danger. A starting point might be to define functionality. In the familial context, the promotion of safety, support and welfare of children and young persons, including the care and protection of children from harm, abuse and neglect, is the Government's foremost responsibility towards the family, as found under the CYP Act (NSW).[11] This responsibility can be interpreted as requiring all families with children to maintain a basic level of functionality, that is, the safety of children. The criterion of safety as a priority consideration and benchmark for functionality is by no

9 *Crimes (Domestic and Personal Violence) Act 2007* (NSW).

10 The term 'parents' used in this chapter reflects an essential focus of the dysfunction in the family; in this context it is intended to be gender neutral. In certain contexts, the gendered language of 'mothers' and 'fathers' might be more appropriate but for ease of reference the term 'parents' specifically refers to the mother and father or persons undertaking parenting capacity.

11 Sections 8 and 9(a) CYP Act.

means unreasonable or unusual. Consideration of safety has taken precedence in the mental health approach[12] towards domestic violence. It has been included in a number of clinical frameworks, such as those of the St George Domestic Violence Counselling Service and Adolescent Mental Health Service, whose model of practice is called the 'safety intervention model'[13] and focuses on and prioritises the safety of children by addressing practical strategies in terms of planning and alternative accommodation. Setting safety as the benchmark for functionality in the family recognises the importance of the basic right to be free from violence for all members in the family, especially women and children, whose places traditionally have been confined in terms of status and space.

One approach towards setting the benchmark for functionality might be to conceptualise dysfunction as falling short of this benchmark, where safety is an issue and children are at risk of *significant* harm. Section 23 of the CYP Act sets out at least seven circumstances in which a child is deemed 'at risk of *significant* harm'.[14] The word 'significant' was not used in the Act prior to the *Report of the*

12 For example, see the approaches taken by: Partnerships Against Domestic Violence, *Practice Standards for Working with Children and Young People Who Have Lived with Domestic Violence* (Brisbane: Family, Youth and Community Care, 1999); L Laing, *Children, Young People and Domestic Violence* (Issue Paper 2, Australian Domestic and Family Violence Clearinghouse Sydney, 2000); and New South Wales Health, *Domestic Violence Policy and Procedures for Identifying and Responding to Domestic Violence* (NSW Department of Health, 2003).

13 B Cooley and C Frazer, 'Children and Domestic Violence: A System of Safety in Clinical Practice' (2006) 29(4) *Australian Social Work* 462–473, 464, 466, 469, 471. The St George 'safety intervention model' is one example of the nationwide approach to child protection. The focus on child safety has developed across most Australian jurisdictions through government crisis intervention programs and initiatives addressing domestic violence. Examples are: the Queensland Government Department of Communities Child Safety Services, *Child Safety Practice Manual* www.communities.qld.gov.au/childsafety/child-safety-practice-manual; Victorian Government Department of Planning and Community Development, *Women's Safety* (9 September 2010) www.dpcd.vic.gov.au/women/womens-safety; Victorian Government Office of the Child Safety Commissioner, *Child Safety Policy* (State Government of Victoria Child Safety Commissioner, September 2010) www.ocsc.vic.gov.au/downloads/ocsc-child-safety-policy-september-2010.pdf; South Australian Department of Families and Communities, *Keeping Them Safe reform program* (March 2010) www.dfc.sa.gov.au/pub/default.aspx?tabid=283, which aims at long-term reform of their child protection services and systems; Western Australia Department of Child Protection, *Adoption of Signs of Safety as the Department for Child Protection's Child Protection Practice Framework* (Background paper, Department of Child Protection, 20 June 2008) www.dcp.wa.gov.au. Organisation/Documents/Signsof SafetyBackgroundPaper.pdf, which details collaborative approaches community-wide and interagency; and the Tasmanian Government's Social Policy Initiative, *Safe at Home* (4 September 2009) www.safeathome.tas.gov.au, which stresses a safety-first approach in police handling of domestic violence.

14 This inserted section might have come about partly as a result of Hannah Bromley's case, where the non-attendance of the children had been an issue of concern. This was an issue that was also flagged by report 'HB4' as a factor that, when read in the context of the family's child protection history, should have prompted the progression

Special Commission into Child Protection in New South Wales ('Wood Inquiry'), but it was inserted with the intention of improving the focus, and efficiency, of intervention on urgent and serious cases.[15] 'Significant harm' means harm that is 'imminent'[16] and is 'not minor or trivial and may reasonably be expected to produce a substantial and demonstrably adverse impact on the child or young person's safety, welfare or well-being'.[17] The section also refers to existing 'current concerns' for 'the safety, welfare or well-being of the child or young person' that result from the 'presence' of one of the seven circumstances and that raise concerns 'to a significant extent'. In other words, the risk of harm provision in the CYP Act is now imbued with an additional layer of urgency and immediacy, because it now reflects serious ('not minor') and grave ('not trivial') harms. This suggests, as was pointed out in Chapter 2, that there are at least two levels of child endangerment harm. The intended impact of this amendment is intervention. This is elaborated upon in the NSW Interagency Guidelines, which state that reporting a risk of significant harm means 'the concern is sufficiently serious to warrant a response by a statutory authority (such as NSW Police Force or Community Services) irrespective of the family's consent'.[18] It seems clear that this insertion is intended to put the emphasis on the *seriousness* of the harmful circumstance, particularly those set out in section 23 of the CYP Act, and on *intervention*.[19]

Section 23 is broad in scope, covering for example physical, psychological, educational and medical needs; physical and sexual abuse; physical and psychological harms; and harms resulting from domestic violence. One possible criticism of using the law to set the standard of functionality and safety is that there is a

---

of the risk assessment: Ch 1: Hannah Bromley. When this chapter was accepted for publication in 2009, the changes to section 23 were not in place; the changes were made on 2 December 2010.

15 Because suspected risk of harm cases are increasing annually and DOCS does not have sufficient resources to cope with this demand, the reports are being accessed as less urgent generally and children and young people end up receiving little subsequent attention. For example, a report of neglect is more likely to receive greater DOCS attention than one concerning domestic violence. Also, too many reports are being made that do not warrant the exercise of DOCS' statutory powers. See The Hon. James Wood AO QC, *Report of the Special Commission of Inquiry into Child Protection Services in New South Wales: Executive Summary and Recommendations* (State of NSW through the Special Commission of Inquiry into Child Protection Services in NSW, November 2008) ii–iii.

16 Ibid xvi. The Wood Inquiry also recommended that if the risk of harm is not significantly serious it should be referred to an early intervention program or a referral service to link the family with the most appropriate local service.

17 New South Wales Government, *Child Wellbeing and Child Protection – The NSW Interagency Guidelines* www.community.nsw.gov.au/kts/guidelines/reporting/framework.htm.

18 Ibid.

19 This chapter focuses on the conceptualisation of the state of dysfunction while Chapter 7 discusses the implications of the insertion 'significant' to risk of harm in the context of the risk discourse.

danger in stigmatising unconventional family lifestyles, and inadvertently placing children within the 'risk' paradigm that would target these families before any harm has occurred. If that is already being done, it does not appear to have been applied strictly in the cases being analysed in my study. If it were a matter for the court to decide, the emphasis[20] on the best interest of the child would not be incongruent with section 23 if the phrase 'current concerns' is judicially interpreted to mean a genuine one, as this would temper the danger of stigmatisation. Although limited to child protection, delimiting the concept of functionality at a standard of minimum safety is advantageous for two reasons. First, it establishes a minimum standard of safety expected of families towards children and does so in accordance with the objectives in the present law; and second, it provides a working definition in terms of identifying and apprehending child endangerment and a framework for early intervention to better assist families that are approaching dysfunction.

Another approach towards conceptualising functionality for child safety is to recognise that the conceptual scope of dysfunction in the family is wider than the narrow ambit of child protection. In situations of family conflict and divorce or separation, dysfunction might be conceptualised as a rupture of the marital relationship. Certainly not all conflicts have the propensity to cause child endangerment. What the additional burden is that propels a parent undergoing the period of separation stress to harm or even kill his or her child is the key question here. Having a conceptually rich approach where the safety of the children is a central issue will allow some flexibility around the conventional parent stereotype – the 'mad' or 'bad' parent perpetrator. Some common indicators of family dysfunction (though by no means all) are mental illness, substance abuse and domestic violence. Moving away from a conceptualisation of dysfunction within these fixed categories will broaden our understanding of the complexities in family relationships. In the context of a patriarchal family structure, children can be at risk where there is domestic violence,[21] and the risk does not lessen just because the violence appears to be contained between the parents. From this perspective, it can be said that domestic violence is a form of patriarchal dysfunction. It will be argued below that in some instances the point at which dysfunction has taken hold of the parent perpetrator is not always easy to pinpoint, nor is the law operative or adaptive enough to respond to the dysfunction.

In the three stories to be examined, the reader might consider patriarchal dysfunction in terms of male disempowerment or empowerment, depending on how the reader chooses to see it. Based on analyses of these three particular stories, a position is taken to interpret the male perpetrator as being disempowered in the course of the marital separation. His disempowerment evolves as part of

20 *Jocums & Schlick and Ors* [2008] FamCA 1066, [48]. For a critical reflection on judicial determination of 'best interest' for the child in child residence disputes, see Robert H Mnookin, 'Child-Custody Adjudication: Judicial Functions in the Face of Indeterminacy' (1975) 39 *Law and Contemporary Problems* 226–293, 291.

21 Or where there was no evidence of domestic violence between parent and child.

the marital rupture to the extent that he can go no further except to internalise his loss of power, turning that power into a form of dysfunctional empowerment that emerges into a disproportionate response to the crisis. It will be argued that this process of internalisation prompts the male to wear a 'cloak'[22] hiding his disempowerment, which is as much a function of patriarchal family ideology as is male empowerment. In the stories it is possible to observe a progressive deterioration in marital communication and eventual loss of marital power – felt most acutely by Paul and Horace.

Male disempowerment, or dysfunctional empowerment, and deterioration of marital communication are crucial factors in the development of the state of dysfunction. The other parallel insight that I hope the reader will reflect upon is the masculine representation of the state apparatus in its capacity as *in loco parentis*, or substitute 'parent', or guardian, in the crisis. This position, it will be argued, sometimes exacerbates the existing patriarchal dysfunction in a manner that either replaces the paternalistic imbalance or does not recognise or deal with the dysfunctional impact of violent or dangerous paternalism. A dysfunctional state intervention or no intervention at all, when family dysfunction warrants it, may also increase the risks for children that the state of dysfunction in such a family represents. These are the two main themes this chapter will develop.

Masculine representation

In a relationship of conflict, or after separation, domestic violence is mainly, and more often, perpetrated by men against women.[23] It is a critical catalyst provoking child endangerment. Where the perpetrator is unable to reach out to the partner, he may displace his aggression onto the child.[24] A previous history of violence has been shown, in a study by Wallace,[25] to exist among the majority of the male-perpetrated child killings more so than among the female cohort. From a child protection standpoint, the main condition of the state of dysfunction, putting children at risk of harm, is the precursor to violence, and it commonly begins with the absence of effective communication (at least in the eyes of the male)

22 The theoretical context of the cloak metaphor is discussed in the third section of this chapter with reference to the Mark and Libby case study.

23 Laing, above n 12. According to the National Homicide Monitoring Program, female homicide offenders are twice as likely as males to be charged with killing an intimate partner or family member, but male offenders murder intimates in greater numbers: J Dearden and W Jones, *Homicide in Australia: 2006–2007 National Homicide Monitoring Program Annual Report* (Research report, Australian Institute of Criminology Monitoring Reports 01, 2008) 12. It is not uncommon that incidents of domestic violence end in a homicide: Ruth Pollard, 'Despite Her Cries for Help, Evelina Was Left to Die', *Sydney Morning Herald* (online), 24 November 2008 www.smh.com.au/news/national/despite-all-her-cries-for-help-evelina-was-left-to-die/2008/11/23/1227375062487.html.

24 Ania Wilczynski, *Child Homicide* (Oxford University Press, 1997) 45–46.

25 Alison Wallace, *Homicide: The Social Reality* (New South Wales Bureau of Crime Statistics and Research, 1986) 115.

and is then followed by a disproportionate male response. This discussion harks back to the short study of Paul and Isabel in Chapter 2. The reader may recall that the sequence of events in that study showed at least two noteworthy communication failures that were a prelude to the violence. The first was the family's brush with external intervention while reporting the violence, and the second was Paul's assault on Isabel.

In the domestic violence context, many victims feel unable to simply leave the relationship of conflict for fear of reprisal, fear of the perpetrator, fear for their safety and their children's safety, and inability to face the overwhelming sense of helplessness[26] and loneliness. Their state of living in fear inhibits any decision that could address the violence. Even though Isabel, for example, was given a choice of how she wanted to handle the AVO breach, she was unable to make that choice: 'When I reported the breach the two officers that attended offered me a choice whether to report the breach officially or not. I should not have been offered a choice.'[27] When the state intervenes to help the family in crisis, it enters in the capacity of *in loco parentis*. That means the state assumes guardianship or parental responsibilities; its main concern is the safety of the child where there is no one suitable to care for the child.[28] The onus on the state apparatus is great when it comes to handling family crises, especially in domestic violence situations. It was Isabel's view at the time that the police officers did not completely understand what was happening:

> I felt there was general reluctance by male officers to find out what was really going on in my first two calls. Throughout this whole incident, I never once spoke to a DVLO [domestic violence liaison officer] even after contact with police, and I was unaware of this position. I was not referred to her.[29]

This lack of effective communication was compounded by the state's display of its inadequate understanding of the domestic violence complex, causing its

26 Lenore Walker, *The Battered Woman Syndrome* (Springer, 1984) 42–70. In domestic violence literature, the construct 'battered woman syndrome', proposed by Walker, which includes the concept of learned helplessness, is controversial in Australia and has been questioned: J Stubbs, 'Battered Woman Syndrome: An Advance for Women or Further Evidence of the Legal System's Inability to Comprehend Women's Experience?' (1991) 3(2) *Current Issues in Criminal Justice* 267–270, 269–270; P W Easteal, 'Battered Woman Syndrome: Misunderstood?' (1992) 3(3) *Current Issues in Criminal Justice* 356–359; and Julie Stubbs, 'The (Un)reasonable Battered Woman? A Response to Esteal' (1992) 3(3) *Current Issues in Criminal Justice* 359–361. For an alternative perspective on the construct that refutes Walker's concept of learned helplessness, see Edward W Gondolf and Ellen R Fisher, *Battered Women as Survivors: An Alternative to Treating Learned Helplessness* (Lexington Books, 1988).

27 This statement is taken from a DOCS case work manager at the coronial inquest hearing: report 'P4', Coroner Court, Westmead, New South Wales, 11–15 July 2005, Coroner Report File No. PPP.

28 Section 49 CYP Act.

29 Above n 27.

functionality to be in question and, arguably, augmenting the disempowerment felt by Isabel. The DOCS casework manager said:

> If she's saying she actually wanted to stay in that place and that would be her decision that I would certainly think it was hers to make that she was taking whatever other course of action. I couldn't see much more that we would have been able to offer it if she was saying she's not stuck there. If she was saying she was stuck there and needed some other resource then we could probably offer that assistance. She contacted the police, there is a domestic violence liaison officer and that was the appropriate course of action.[30]

The two main themes that arise here are the patriarchal dysfunction of the state apparatus and the family, and the overwhelming masculine[31] representation in response to the conflict. Not only was the official representation of the state male in character, its responses, such as its reluctance to investigate further into the background of Isabel's circumstances and its assumption that she had spoken with a DVLO, were arguably inadequate and dysfunctional. The paternalistic authoritarian response from the state constructing the boundaries of permissive individual behaviour within the family was based on conventional social roles. This reinforced on the family the order in the state that is premised on the system of male domination in the public realm,[32] whereas if the concept of functionality had been applied, the state of dysfunction would have been recognised at the time of the DOCS notification, because safety of the children would have fallen short of the standard set out in section 23(d).

The Wood Inquiry[33] was set up precisely to investigate the effectiveness of child protection services in New South Wales. The inquiry could be characterised as a knee-jerk response to the furore over the string of child deaths in 2008. Its findings on the lack of state resources prompted a similar knee-jerk law and order – masculine – response.[34] The response was to toughen the law responding to violence with violence, by implementing new police powers aimed at tackling breaches of AVOs in domestic violence situations, a problem[35] that had been brought centre stage by the reporting of the spate of family homicides in 2008. The present police powers were not in force at the time of the Isabel and Paul

30 Ibid.

31 For the purposes of this chapter, the police response to domestic violence is constructed as masculine. This construction is a model interpretation. It is, however, not the only interpretation.

32 Gerda Lerner, *The Creation of Patriarchy* (Oxford University Press, 1986) 217.

33 Above n 15.

34 Louise Hall, 'New Powers for Police in Domestic Violence Cases', *Sydney Morning Herald* (online), 28 November 2008 www.smh.com.au/news/national/new-powers-for-police-in-domestic-violencecases/2008/11/27/1227491735577.html.

35 C Humphreys, *Domestic Violence and Child Protection: Challenging Directions for Practice* (Issue Paper 13, Australian Domestic and Family Violence Clearinghouse, Sydney, 2007) 3. In 2006–2007, 43 per cent of homicides between intimates had

case study. In retrospect, some justifications can be seen for the new police powers and how they might have assisted the outcome of this case.

The new police powers broaden police officers' discretion when handling domestic violence (although there is some disagreement[36] on this). In the recent past, police officers had discretion to caution a perpetrator. This position was not too distant from a similar patriarchal response in the eighteenth century. Then, the authorities were instructed not to interfere in domestic conflicts unless there was likely to be a serious assault.[37] In contrast, it is now 'mandatory' as a matter of policy that they arrest and charge all alleged perpetrators, even when they have committed no offence.[38] With this approach, the erratic and selective ways the police had been enforcing AVOs would be minimised. The present intervention will remove from the victim the burden to press charges, shifting the responsibility away from the individual back to the state. Taking away the burden, as well as bypassing the inhibition of fear and helplessness, might empower the victim's position in the conflict, but structurally it is merely replacing one form of male control – a dysfunctional one – with another perhaps more functional but similarly less communicative one.

Throughout the Isabel and Paul case study, there were examples of interventions that could have assisted the outcome of the crisis but did not – for instance, the police's failure to make available their DVLO to Isabel; their failure to apprehend Paul in a timely manner, that is, soon after his last assault on Isabel; and the position in the crisis of DOCS, which appeared to take a detached approach in its assessment of the children's safety. The point here is not to speculate on blame or what could have been done; the circumstances of conflict canvassed in this case study are not unique. Rather, the focus is on the intersection between dysfunctional patriarchy and dysfunctional state intervention, as can be seen in other stories in this book[39] in which there was untimely intervention and

---

prior domestic violence history involving police intervention: Dearden and Jones, above n 23, 15. For prevalence of domestic violence in filicide cases between 1989 and 2002, see Mouzos and Rushforth, above n 3, 3–4.

36 Some police claim that their discretion is limited or removed by pro-arrest and mandatory arrest policies because they are under increased pressure to arrest all parties who may be perpetrators, see M Chesney-Lind, 'Criminalizing Victimization: The Unintended Consequences of Pro-Arrest Politics for Girls and Women' (2002) 2 *Criminology & Public Policy* 81–90, 82–83, 86.

37 See the *NSW Handbook for Police and Police Magistrates* (1905), cited in Judith Allen, 'The Invention of the Pathological Family: A Historical Study of Family Violence in NSW' in C O'Donnell and J Craney (eds), *Family Violence in Australia* (Longman Cheshire, 1982) ch 1. Stubbs points out the historical failure of the courts to understand women's life experiences, which were often distorted or not heard by the legal system. In particular, legal rules and standards of reasonableness applied to battered women tended to reflect male rather than female life experiences, and they subject these women to a number of damaging stereotypes. See Julie Stubbs (ed) *Women, Male Violence and the Law* (Federation Press, 1994) 192–193.

38 Section 88(b) of the *Crimes (Domestic and Personal Violence) Act 2007*.

39 Ch 1: Jubilee Soprano.

ineffective communication, with child endangerment as a result. This intersection is made dysfunctional by unhelpful interventions in which the outcome of the conflict is not, but should be, assisted by state intervention. Where a familial conflict calls for effective state intervention and that intervention fails to protect a child, this failing mirrors that of the patriarchal dysfunction in the family. This should not be the case. The representation of the state here is as masculine and paternal, and in fulfilling its statutory child protection obligations in familial conflict situations the state apparatus is, in effect, being substituted for the parental failing (or dysfunction). In order for that intervention to be functional, state intervention has to be timely and adequate. The primary role of the state under the CYP Act[40] is to assume absolute guardianship (or parental) care responsibilities for children deemed in need of care and protection. This clearly did not occur in the case of Paul and Isabel's children. In other words, the ersatz parent – the state, in its replacement of the dysfunctional parent – needs to have both eyes on the safety of the children if it is to maintain its principal obligations. The following section examines whether this can be achieved in light of the recent police powers in New South Wales addressing domestic violence.

Mirroring the state and the 'Father': 'mandatory' intervention

This section examines the state's response to domestic violence, to the extent that it is mirrored in a form of masculine representation, the 'Father' archetype, whose solution is to meet violence with violence. The question is whether this response is effective in reducing domestic violence in the long term. At face value, the implications of the new police domestic violence powers are that even though they are designed to protect women, in reality they might be further denied and even stripped of their voices. On a deeper level, the police powers represent a new form of patriarchal control. On the one hand, the mandatory arrest of the person breaching an AVO treats the breach as an offence,[41] as opposed to not treating it as an offence (such as an act violating a court order against geographic and telephone contact) because it is considered less serious by the victim. On the other hand, this development could be interpreted as a reaffirmation of the patriarchal view of women as incapable of autonomy and self-determination, weak, inferior in rational thought and emotionally unstable.[42] The appropriate affirmative step by the police, if effectively communicated, can help reify decades of dysfunctional patriarchy. At the very least, this legislative initiative represents a positive step towards acknowledging the violence instead

40 Sections 15, 16 and 49.

41 Section 14 of the *Crimes (Domestic and Personal Violence) Act 2007* (NSW); previously, section 562I *Crimes Act 1900* (repealed).

42 Simone de Beauvoir, *The Second Sex* (Vintage, 1997) 16–29, ch 3. See also Ania Wilczynski, 'Images of Women Who Kill Their Infants: The Mad and the Bad' (1991) 2(2) *Women & Criminal Justice* 71–88, 72.

of brushing it under the carpet as if the violence had been normalised as part of a familial 'subculture' or as if it did not exist.

On whether mandatory arrest laws are an appropriate strategy and an effective step towards better communication, and whether they actually effect a reduction in the incidence of male violence, the results from a US study[43] suggest that the level of intimate partner homicides increased in states implementing mandatory arrest laws. While this increase cannot be said to be analogous to an increase in the level of domestic violence, it suggests that victims are less likely to contact the police to report the perpetrator, resulting in an escalation of domestic violence and a nullification of any intended deterrent effect of arrest on the perpetrator.[44] The results also suggest that, when the arrest laws do not rely on reporting by family members but instead on reporting by third parties or outsiders, these laws reduce harm to the protected individuals and, in particular, effect a possible reduction in child homicides.[45]

Whether the arrest and detention of male perpetrators is going to be effective in the long term on the issue of child safety and reducing domestic violence is questionable, particularly if the perpetrator penalises the victim(s) with harsher abuse after the arrest.[46] If the male perpetrator is the breadwinner, removing him would inadvertently have an adverse impact on the family. Findings from several other US studies also suggest an increase in violence towards the victim among groups of lower socio-economic background, particularly if the perpetrator is unemployed or has a prior criminal record, and only a short-term deterrent effect in the other group that was employed or married.[47] Another unexpected

43 Radha Iyengar, 'Does the Certainty of Arrest Reduce Domestic Violence? Evidence from Mandatory and Recommended Arrest Laws' (Working Paper 13186, National Bureau of Economic Research, 2007) www.nber.org/papers/w13186. See also: J C Campbell, Daniel Webster, Jane Koziol-McLain, Carolyn Block, Doris Campbell, Anna Curry, Faye Gary, Nancy Glass, Judith McFarlane, Carolyn Sachs, Phyllis Sharps, Yvonne Ulrich, Susan A Wilt, Jennifer Manganello, Xiao Xu, Janet Schollenberger, Victoria Frye and Kathryn Laughon, 'Risk Factors for Femicide in Abusive Relationships: Results from a Multi-Site Control Study' (2003) 93(7) *American Journal of Public Health* 1089–1097, 1090.

44 Iyengar, ibid 17.

45 Ibid 16.

46 Iyengar, above n 43.

47 L G Mills, 'Mandatory Arrest and Prosecution Policies for Domestic Violence: A Critical Literature Review and the Case for More Research to Test Victim Empowerment Approaches' (1998) 25(3) *Criminal Justice and Behaviour* 306–318, 310. See also Lawrence W Sherman, Janell D Schmidt, Dennis P Rogan, Douglas A Smith, Patrick R Gartin, Ellen G Cohn, Dean J Collins and Anthony R Bacich, 'The Variable Effects of Arrest on Criminal Careers: The Milwaukee Domestic Violence Experiment' (1992) 83 *Journal of Criminal Law and Criminology* 137–169; and Lawrence W Sherman, 'Attacking Crime: Policing and Crime Control' in M Tonry and N Morris (eds), *Modern Policing* (University of Chicago, 1992). For a later finding, see Lawrence W Sherman, 'Policing for Crime Prevention' in L W Sherman *et al*, *Preventing Crime: What Works, What Doesn't, and What's Promising* (National Institute of Justice, 1997). For the Australian context, see Stubbs, above n 37, 4.

consequence of the arrest of the male perpetrator is the rise in the number of dual arrests of both parties to the conflict.[48] This has been noted among Indigenous women in Australia who report domestic violence and are not uncommonly arrested in the process of police attending a domestic violence complaint if it is found they have an outstanding warrant.[49] Needless to say, the arrest of the victim not only impacts on the safety of the children but also that of the victim herself, who may feel betrayed by the police and may become more afraid to defend herself and more vulnerable to manipulation by the perpetrator.[50] In other words, she becomes more disempowered.

While more research is needed, it is highly likely that arrest laws will have some impact on the functionality of the family. In spite of the mandatory arrest laws, there have been complementary police strategies[51] developed towards better handling of crises.[52] Additional research could be done to determine whether these approaches complement or minimise the impact of mandatory arrest laws, whose deterrent effects as solutions to the problem in the long term are uncertain. The question is whether mandatory intervention, which can be compared with the male's belief in his power, control and authority, reflects a holistic appreciation of child safety, or does such a response exacerbate risks of endangerment to the child by its failure to understand other resultant interactions such as the impact of arrest on remaining family members or the impact on the safety of the child following the release of the perpetrator?

A form of male disempowerment

This section examines the power relationships surrounding violence in order to understand how disproportionate responses are brought about. In the Isabel

48 Rochelle Braaf, 'Arresting Policies: Implications of Pro and Mandatory Arrest Policies for Victims of Domestic and Family Violence' (Paper presented at the Australian Institute of Family Studies conference, Melbourne, 9–11 July 2008) www.aifs.gov.au/institute/afrc10/#b.

49 See C Chan and C Cuneen, *Evaluation of the Implementation of NSW Police Service Aboriginal Strategic Plan, Commissioned by the NSW Police Service and NSW Ombudsman* (University of Sydney, Institute of Criminology, 2000) 372 and 377 for the report's recommendation (recommendation 38) on addressing the problem.

50 Braaf, above n 48, 4.

51 For example, the Victorian Police's reform of its Code of Practice has adopted an integrative, safety-first approach, notwithstanding its pro-arrest policy towards responding to domestic violence, while the UK's Metropolitan police have adopted a risk assessment model of intervention that advocates intensive training, risk assessment, standard operating procedures and a strong communication strategy and strong pro-arrest stance. See Victoria Police, *Code of Practice for the Investigation of Family Violence: Supporting an Integrative Response to Family Violence in Australia* (Victoria Police, 2006) 4, 7, 29, 31 www.police.vic.gov.au/files/documents/464_FV_COP.pdf.

52 G Campbell, 'Working Together for a Safer London', presentation by the Metropolitan Police New Scotland Yard at the 'Better Policing, Better Outcomes: Changing Police Culture to Prevent Domestic Violence and Homicide' (Paper presented at the forum at the University of New South Wales, 9 December 2008).

and Paul case study, in both instances of violence but particularly in the second, Paul began his demands by threatening Isabel with a knife, and both times Isabel managed to calm him by talking. Paul's style of communication – talking down to Isabel in an authoritative, ordering and demanding fashion – indicates a corresponding diminution of, or possibly a failing attempt to maintain, his marital authority.

Research[53] suggests that the 'husband demand/wife withdraw' interaction pattern is related to a corresponding overwhelmingly disproportionate violent response. This is because the demanding role is associated with a perceived loss of marital power by the male in a patriarchal familial framework, and in order to compensate for this the male may see it as his right to resort to physical violence. From this perspective, male disempowerment enacted in this manner supports the argument that excessive paternalism aggravates the disempowerment of women and children and their respective positions in the family. As a natural and negative consequence, such disempowerment often leads to an increase in risk factors pre-empting child endangerment. The reader may recall that, in both the Horace Faulkner and Paul and Isabel stories, the perpetrators had lost their jobs before or at the time of the dysfunction. The loss of economic and marital power are threatening for the man when faced with the potential 'loss' of his children and family, and loss of control over his children, wife and family. In this context, the loss of power corresponds to and coincides with a disproportionate and usually violent response, especially where the male feels acutely that he is going to lose his children.

This contention is demonstrated by the Faulkner case study. At the time of the breakdown in marital communications, Melissa described her inability to communicate with her husband prior to him taking their children's lives: '[W]henever I tell him something how I feel he doesn't listen, he always walks off the room once I talk about us, our situation and the children.'[54] When Horace failed to convince Melissa to resurrect their marriage, he turned angry and started to verbally threaten her:

> I love the children more than you. You don't deserve to have them. Don't tell me I haven't warned you. I told you you would never take the children away from me. You're going to be left behind and you only have yourself to blame.[55]

As with many retaliation-motivated killings[56] – characterised by a history of severe marital conflict, possessiveness and sexual jealousy, and commonly

53 J C Babcock, J Waltz, N S Jacobson and J M Gottman, 'Power and Violence: The Relation Between Communication Patterns, Power Discrepancies, and Domestic Violence' (1993) 61(1) *Journal of Consulting and Clinical Psychology* 40–50, 47.

54 Ch 1: Horace Faulkner.

55 Ibid.

56 Above n 24, 45.

perpetrated by men[57] – the risk triggers in Horace and Melissa's marital breakdown are not uncommon. Horace's desire to punish Melissa for her new life and their eventual marriage breakdown outstripped his love for the children. Unable to have his way and his demands met – that Melissa not leave the country with the children and that they reconcile their relationship – he displaced his aggression onto the children, and the only way he felt he could communicate his position in the conflict and reassert his diminishing marital authority and power in the relationship was to physically take away from Melissa what she fought so hard for – the children. Clearly, though, such fathers think of their children as property, as pawns in their moves to gain power. However, at no time did either Melissa or Isabel fear for the safety of the children because their partners had consistently been loving fathers. In her affidavit in support for her AVO application in 1997, Melissa said:

> [Horace] then grabbed me by the arm and threw me out the door, left with the kids in the car, I tried to stop him by sitting in front of the car but he threw me out. I am fearful as he can get violent based on past experience. I am not fearful for my children as he loves his children. I wish to get a DVO to stop him harassing, threatening and assaulting me.[58]

The mask of the loving father: the invisibility cloak over dysfunction[59]

There is no doubt that child residence proceedings are traumatic for all parties involved. Some parties agree to mutual separation but many couples separate on acrimonious terms. In the filicide literature,[60] the rupture of the marital relationship is often seen as the precipitating factor associated with the disproportionate male response and the subsequent killing. In some instances, there are no apparent prior warning signs before the killing takes place. What seems at first sight to be part and parcel of the relationship breakdown can, and has, turned out to be a walking time bomb waiting to explode. The Mark and Libby case study demonstrates the lack of obvious risk factors that would alert authorities to child endangerment in the situation of the parent who is characterised as a loving father. It is as though there is an 'invisibility cloak' covering the dysfunctional parent – this cloak of 'loving parent' is worn by the father on the outside as a mask that conceals his true intentions and hides the nature

57 Martin Daly and Margo Wilson, *Homicide* (Aldine De Gruyter, 1988) 213–219.

58 Ch 1: Horace Faulkner.

59 This conceptualisation is a work in progress that is matched against my empirical research in the wider context of representation.

60 Above n 24, 45. Also see J D Marleau, Bernard Poulin, Thierry Webanck, Renée Roy and Line Laporte, 'Paternal Filicide: A Study of 10 Men' (1999) 44 *Canadian Journal of Psychiatry* 57–63; D Bourget and P Gagne, 'Paternal Filicide in Quebec' (2005) 33 *Journal of the American Academy of Psychiatry and Law* 354–360.

of the underlying dysfunction. The cloak shifts the gaze away from and conceals the dysfunction by reinventing the image of the exemplary parent and consequently the represented image resists state intervention. The invisibility cloak can be likened to a veil that functions as a divide between the private and public faces. It can be theorised that this veil is an aspect of the patriarchal familial form that reveals the lingering deeply held belief that men have the right to own and control their wife and children.[61] The veil constructs and maintains the cloak in a space that has neither private nor public elements: this is the space of the social realm.[62] The question is therefore of how one pierces this space to expose to public gaze that which is hidden.

The reader will remember that in the Mark and Libby study, in Chapter 2, the children were killed while in the perpetrator father's care. This was in spite of Mark, the perpetrator, presenting the children at the police station in accordance with a court order. Prior to this, however, Libby had tried to apply for an AVO, but from the perspective of the police at the time of her application she did not appear to have any fears for the children's safety. Although she clearly had safety concerns during the child residence proceedings, as she did not report physical violence towards her or the children, the endangerment to the children and underlying state of dysfunction in the family was not apparent. The husband demand/wife withdraw interaction pattern, though, would have indicated that a corresponding disproportionate violence response arising from Mark's threat to Libby would have placed the children at risk of harm. The difficulty in taking action in the legal realm was that there were no incidents of physical violence at the time, except for the ongoing acrimonious relations as a result of the contentious child residence proceedings. The following excerpt shows how Mark felt about the processes of separation and the Family Court. Following that is a critical discussion on the recent amendment to the *Family Law Act 1975* (Cth) and its present emphasis on shared parenting.

Like Horace, Mark was unprepared to tolerate the pressures of going to court. This was how he narrated his experience of dealing with the pressure of interacting with the state, and with reference to his increasing lack of marital authority:

> This is just a quick little message for you, just to let you know how unfair and biased the system seems to be. I haven't been right through the system. I've only been trying to deal with this for three and a half months and I'm at my wit's end with it. I've been put through nothing but punishment and abuse and treated like a common criminal. And for what? I was a good husband, a good father and a good worker. I did all the right things that a father's supposed to do . . . My children mean everything to me. They were

61 Above n 32, 24, 213. See also Carolyn Harris Johnson, *Come with Daddy: Child Murder-Suicide after Family Breakdown* (University of Western Australia Press, 2005) 129–130.

62 Hannah Arendt, *The Human Condition* (University of Chicago Press, 1958) 28.

> my life and my life is non-existent anymore. I'm expected just to sit back and watch it all take place around me and I, I'm sorry but I just could not do that. I cannot bear with it anymore. I've put up with nothing but torture and abuse and punishment. . . . yet I did everything to the best of my ability. I provided the best I possibly could. I was the best father I could be. I was the best worker and husband I could be and yet for some people it just isn't enough.[63]

The recent amendment[64] to the *Family Law Act 1975* in 2006 and its current emphasis on shared parenting has been interpreted by some judges as requiring equal time even when domestic violence has been raised. This means that contact orders are now given to both parents, whereas previously they were seldom granted to fathers. In awarding greater contact between fathers and children, the courts have awarded contact (including unsupervised contact) in circumstances of alleged and uncorroborated, or poor evidence of, domestic violence.[65] While the courts have an obligation to take note of domestic violence allegations in the family, they do not have an investigative function and often have to rely on child protection reports, if any. If none are forthcoming at the time the matter is being heard, perhaps due to a fear of reprisal from the perpetrator, lack of inter-agency cooperation or lack of information-sharing[66] between state agencies, the dysfunction of the family is camouflaged and this might accentuate the crisis and exacerbate the likelihood of child endangerment. The Wood Inquiry noted that the communication discrepancy in the legal system is seen in the inconsistent and unbalanced representations by legal and state representatives in the Children's Court and that this has contributed to the lack of available, fair and up-to-date evidence before the Court.[67]

In our society there still exists a level of common sense attachment held for the parent–child bond, and rightly so. However, while giving priority to the focus on shared parenting, the aims of which are to balance contact with the children between both parents, there is also the risk of child endangerment when the propensity to violence is masked and cloaked with the invisible protection afforded by the unquestioned protective status given to the observed loving

63 Report 'ML5', taken from New South Wales Coroner Office P on 11 January 2009.

64 *Family Law Amendment (Shared Parental Responsibility) Act 2006* (Cth).

65 Lawrie Moloney, Bruce Smyth and Ruth Weston, *Allegations of Family Violence and Child Abuse in Family Law Children's Proceedings: A Pre-Reform Exploratory Study* (Research Report No 15, Melbourne: Australian Institute of Family Studies, 2007) www.aifs.gov.au/institute/pubs/resreport15/main.html. This study was conducted in Victoria and South Australia, and its findings are not representative of all Family Court decisions in Australia. The purpose of citing this study is to show the potential implications of contact orders.

66 Above n 15, iv.

67 Ibid.

emotional bond between parent and child. The common sense attachment for the parent–child relationship was reflected in the Children's Court's attitude pre-2006. This was at a time when Mark became increasingly uncooperative and non-communicative with Libby, and when Libby was beginning to fear for her children's safety. The Court felt that its decision had to be bound by the best interest of the child principle:

> The most important one is the safety of the children but it doesn't – it can be just as harmful for the children to have police go in and remove them from their father's home. And I mean, I don't know what the position of the mother is, whether she could be up there tonight or whether it means she has got to collect them tomorrow or the following day so it means that somebody has got to care for them. And that, as you know, can have an extremely adverse impact on children.[68]

Exactly when the state of dysfunction began in this case is difficult to ascertain. The dysfunction criteria under section 23 of the CYP Act would not apply in this case unless section 23(e) were amended to read:

> a parent or other caregiver has behaved in such a way towards the child, young person or [insert 'other parent'] that the child or young person has suffered or is at risk of suffering serious [insert 'physical'] and psychological harm.

These insertions, however, would open the floodgates to questions on what types of behaviour would be within the boundaries of acceptable parental conduct within the family. The insertions might even be viewed as an encroachment on the family space, particularly where an argument might be made by legal practitioners that such behaviours are typical and even normal given the state of acrimonious relations between the parties where child residence is a hotly contested issue, and where the loving father symbolism is used and applied liberally to achieve self-interested ends.

As pointed out, what exactly the straw is that breaks the camel's back is the crux of this conundrum. In spite of the fact that an increasing number of filicide circumstances suggest that emotional bonds in a dysfunctional patriarchy can become fatal for the child, the bottom line appears to be that, as long as parents appear to care for the children, the state cannot predict risk of harm to them and there is nothing the state or anyone can do to avert child endangerment.

68 Report 'ML2', taken from New South Wales Coroner Office P on 12 November 2008. Also see Mnookin, above n 20, for the complexity and indeterminacy inherent in judicial determinations of 'best interest' for the child when attempting to resolve residence disputes.

Interacting dysfunction

The 'invisibility cloak' phenomenon (encompassing elements such as patriarchal dysfunction, the 'loving parent' representation, and an expectation of equality in residence disputes) is an important form of dysfunction, but it is not the only form of dysfunction that places the child at risk of endangerment. The conceptualisation of the state of dysfunction may also include conditions such as untreated mental illness (Jubilee Soprano), familial violence (Danny Burrow, Capello Steppenwolf) and lack of trust in state agents (Hannah Bromley), which will be discussed in Chapter 7. Dysfunctional intervention by the state in these cases arose not only because of prevailing symbols of patriarchy, but also because of the interactions with dysfunctional behaviours and representations of those behaviours, such as the loving father. As seen in the Mark and Libby, Horace Faulkner and Paul and Isabel stories, these fathers' representation as loving misled family members as to their intentions to endanger the children and use them as pawns, as tools for revenge, against their ex-spouses.

These are not isolated factors of risk, and certainly dysfunctional state intervention is not a stand-alone factor that leads to child endangerment and killing; these factors are in fact part of an ongoing and interactive process by which risky representations mislead and overlap with decisions made about risk to the child. As argued in Chapters 3, 4 and 5, risk is concealed and created by layers of dysfunction, which collectively interact with representation. Even when the intention of law enforcement is to neutralise risk by removing the perpetrator from the family, it must be asked whether such a violent response exacerbates risk by perpetuating a cycle of violent reprisals. This and the next chapter suggest that it is worth looking more closely at the subtle interactions between law enforcement and the conditions of risk for the child within the state of dysfunction. This would involve addressing the layers of dysfunctional interactions that may have been socially embedded in the family and community. Instead of merely tackling one dysfunction, addressing the interaction between dysfunctionalities can produce a more holistic understanding of and response to risky conditions for the child. Interaction of dysfunctionalities is therefore discussed in Chapter 7, which looks at the conditions of risk that create opportunities for child endangerment and pervert the course of law enforcement with regard to ensuring the safety of children and the actionability of their rights and protections.

Conclusion

While it is not always possible to identify and apprehend all instances of child endangerment, particularly in cases where fathers exhibit close loving and emotional ties towards their children and where the risks are hidden, it is possible to set a minimum standard of safety in families and explore the conditions from which dysfunction arises. A clear indicator of impending child endangerment is the presence of domestic violence in a household, as might be the presence of other risky interactions such as the failure to seek adequate treatment for mental illness (seen in Jubilee Soprano).[69] The presence of domestic violence constitutes sufficient evidence that there is risk of serious psychological harm towards the child.[70] Accepting this evidence as part of the approach towards canvassing policies addressing domestic violence is crucial to timely and effective external intervention.

On the other hand, a lack of domestic violence does not mean that the child is free from harm. The intersection between state apparatus and the family plays an important role in dictating the path of the displaced parent towards or away from violent behaviour to children in his or her care as a consequence of domestic breakdown. There is a need to understand how in such cases the contextual dysfunction in the family arose, and even more so how it is interpreted (or misinterpreted) by intervening state agencies. Perhaps the trigger for the disproportionate male response is symptomatic of a wider communicative failure on all fronts, but perhaps it is also the case that, when faced with the prospect of an increasing collapse of power over the children and family, the male who is entrenched in the patriarchal framework believes he has the right to respond with possessive violence. This seems to be the cornerstone for understanding why filicide happens among fathers who appear loving but who believe themselves to have been displaced from the family, and as such confuse love and devotion with obsession and retaliatory violence, as much against their estranged partners as against their child victims.

The irony that state intervention that is intended to prevent child endangerment has the propensity to exacerbate the conflict is not lost here. This is the paradox of state intervention – it aims to and has an absolute duty to prevent child endangerment, but when it comes down to the practical handling of crises (as exemplified in the stories examined in this book), it may well exacerbate the problem. The mirroring of state intervention of a particular form of masculine representation reveals the disturbing conclusion that the loving father representation can be misunderstood. What this reflects is an inadequate understanding of the deeper complexities of the family and of male violence, their representations, interactions and distorted symbolism. What is important is the right approach to cultivating the appropriate type of state response structured towards addressing dysfunction. The disintegration of patriarchal control over the family seems to be the initial catalyst setting the backdrop for child endangerment. One suggestion is for state responses to instil and empower a healthy response[71] to conflict,

69 Even though mental illness was not discussed in this chapter, it is, like domestic violence, examined as a condition of risk in Chapter 7.

70 Laing, above n 12, 4.

71 New South Wales Government, *Keep Them Safe Evaluation Framework* (25 July 2011) www.keepthemsafe.nsw.gov.au/keep_them_safe_evaluation_framework and the Australian Government Department of Families, Housing, Community Services and Indigenous Affairs, *Protecting Children Is Everyone's Business: National Framework*

whether or not that is achievable. In any case, a more in-depth and comparative analysis of interactive representation, symbolism and consequent decision-making needs to be undertaken in order to further explore the relationship between risk factors for child safety, the impact of domestic violence and external intervention measures.

The understandings of patriarchal interpretation and interaction discussed in this chapter constitute one of the recurrent influential conditions on the safety of the child. Chapter 7 deals more broadly with a dynamic interpretation of risk that builds on this more limited and directly causal connection between patriarchy and dysfunctional intervention and identifies a network of other conditions that can be thought of as risky and from which singular or multiple risk factors may emerge. It can be conclusively said that the failings of critical agents responsible for the child's safety and welfare need to be addressed in the context of a richer understanding of representations, symbols and risk. As has been argued, representation and risk are inextricably bound. It is thus essential to recognise misleading and misdiagnosed representations and to re-acknowledge that some dominant representations and symbols that are deeply embedded in symbols of Western society, such as the father-dominated nuclear family, can be misconstrued and hence can exacerbate risk to the child.

---

for Protecting Australia's Children 2009–2020 www.fahcsia.gov.au/sa/families/pubs/framework_protecting_children/Documents/child_protection_framework.pdf; these initiatives formulate a long-term nationwide plan for support and early intervention services to focus on child well-being and safety as key priorities.

7 Risky representations

Introduction

This final chapter endeavours to draw together the connections between representation and risk in the context of child killing. The analysis to follow builds on the previous chapter's discussion of the failures of state intervention as exacerbating risks of harm to the child. In Chapter 2, this failure was conceptualised as symbolic violence. Chapter 6 examined the false representations of the 'loving father', masked in masculinity and patriarchal power imbalance, to reveal how the consequences of stereotypical representations of symbolic violence can produce real risks for the safety of the child, chief among these being the outcome of non-intervention. It is now essential to more critically theorise the manner in which interactive representations of violence, modelled as they are in Chapters 4 and 5, produce risks to child safety even where the law and the state prioritise the rights and protections of children. The crux of this concluding argument is that recurrent risk to child safety will be minimised if, along with centring the protective interests of the child, those who share responsibility for child safety, or sometimes are central to child endangerment, are more circumspect about the symbolic representation of violence and neglect.

Very broadly, though, risk in this chapter is pitched against the current international and national legal regimes ensuring the rights of the child. International law on the rights of children is enshrined in the United Nations Convention on Rights of the Child (20 November 1989) ('UNCROC'), which Australia is a party to and has ratified but has yet to fully incorporate into domestic law. This said, Australia's national framework on child protection, the *National Framework for Protecting Australia's Children 2009–2020*, is committed to, and reflects, the best interest of the child principle envisioned by the UNCROC.[1] Section 60CA of the *Family Law Act 1975* (Cth) upholds the best

1 Council of Australian Governments, *Protecting Children Is Everyone's Business: National Framework for Protecting Australia's Children 2009–2020* (Australian Government, Canberra, 2009) 12 www.coag.gov.au/coag_meeting_outcomes/2009-04-30/docs/child_protection_framework.pdf. See also the *Family Law Amendment (Shared Parental Responsibility) Act 2006* (Cth), Schedule 5; *B v B: Family Law Reform Act 1995* (1997) FLC 92-755; and the Hon Diana Bryant, Chief Justice, Family Court

interest of the child principle, and sections 60CC to 60CG contain a number of matters, including views of the child, capacity of the child's parents and risk of family violence, which the court must consider in determining the best interest of the child in the context of resolving disputes.

This pre-eminent focus on the 'best interest' (though a contested term)[2] of the child is applied across both national and international contexts in the areas of child protection and resolution of family disputes. Both contexts reflect a child-centred approach that is driven by existing domestic and international legislation. This said, the cases in this book have clearly identified failures in protective policy and organisational practicalities, such as interagency cooperation, and have raised the issue of the exacerbation of risk arising out of the nature of certain representations and symbolic interactions. For example, the representation of the loving parent when imbued with a patriarchal obsession to reassert power and control over the child is not recognised as a cultural or ideological force that poses a risk to the child, but is masked and modified as symbolic love and care rather than incipient, possessive and endangering violence. Chapter 2 critically reviewed some dominant symbols, such as love and discipline, which interactively produce distorted representations of endangerment and as such mask violent risks to the child. The book has argued that representation, distorted and confused as it becomes when interacting with false symbols (particularly of parental relationships), is at the heart of risk interpretation and construction, misinterpretation and neglect. Arising from this understanding and the reconsideration of representation it requires, there is an urgent need for recognition of such 'risky' representations within the existing socio-legal discourses around the protection of children, through deconstructing the interactive processes at work to create distorted symbols and masked meanings.

Deconstructing representation and risk

Let us commence the interrogation of the consequences for risk from distorted representation by examining the expressive function of legal/rights protections, which position child protection at the heart of familial relations. With such a

of Australia, 'Care and Protection of Children: Australia and New Zealand Experience' (Paper delivered at the 4th World Congress on Family Law and Children's Rights, Cape Town, South Africa, 20–23 March 2005) www.childjustice.org/index.php?searchword=diana+bryant&ordering=&searchphrase=all&Itemid=1&option=com_search. In the wider context of child protection, Australia is a signatory to the *Hague Convention on the Civil Aspects of International Child Abduction* (25 October 1980) and has implemented the Family Law (Child Abduction Convention) Regulations 1986 (Cth) as well as the *Hague Convention on Jurisdiction, Applicable Law, Recognition, Enforcement and Cooperation in Respect of Parental Responsibility and Measures for the Protection of Children* (19 October 1996), which entered into force in Australia through its implementation of the Family Law (Child Protection Convention) Regulations 2003 (Cth).

2 Robert H Mnookin, 'Child-Custody Adjudication: Judicial Functions in the Face of Indeterminacy' (1975) 39 *Law and Contemporary Problems* 226–293, 291.

powerful legal and policy position, how can it be that representations of familial violence, for instance, become symbolised so far from the objectives in the law? And, with such meaning mismanagement, how can recurrent and possibly tragically predictable risk scenarios for children be generated with such disturbing regularity? If it is not simply a consequence of family dysfunction and agency neglect, how might child killing be prevented through a realistic appreciation of the interactive forces at work that create the ranges and levels of distorted representation and symbolic meaning-creation modelled in Chapters 4 and 5?

The examination begins with a discussion of the national framework in relation to child protection and family law. This is followed by a brief summary of the legalistic approach, which has developed in the international context mandating legal intervention to protect children from cruelty and neglect.[3] The discussion then draws together disparate threads of observations on risk that consolidate the book's argument concerning the formative influence of interactive and symbolic representation. The discussion of *representation to risk* reiterates some of the principal risk scenarios in the cases. In this way, risk is intentionally context-specific in terms of its degree and imminence for the child, but at the same time capable of universalisation because it is exacerbated by common processes of false representation and symbolic masking. Wilczynski's categorisation of risk is then discussed to set the literature backdrop for the critical observations to follow. Against what could be seen as a limited risk analysis in the literature, it is argued that the book's approach offers a more dynamic way of examining how recurrent and predictable meanings of violence and child endangerment are interpreted and negotiated through processes of symbolic interaction in representation formation. From here, the discussion develops into a consideration of six conditions that exacerbate risk to the child. The chapter concludes with a statement on the need to return the child to a real and actual position of prominence and visibility, which is so tragically and consistently lacking in the cases. This is in order that the representations and decisions that are made about the child are more accurate, and the child may be less vulnerable to abuses and misrepresentations. The book argues the pressing need for a clearer understanding of the way in which a risky phenomenon in its critical stages can be understood, and through that an understanding of how to reduce recurrent risk. Additionally, it is argued, more critical reflection at a policy level needs to be directed at options that empower the community's role in child protection, in line with national and international developments in children's rights.

Children's rights

The pre-eminent development in children rights has been the best interest of the child principle, which has been applied to the areas of domestic child protection

3 Alister Lamont and Leah Bromfield, 'History of Child Protection Services' (National Child Protection Clearinghouse Resource Sheet, Australian Institute of Family Studies, October 2010) 1–23, 1.

and family law. However, the cases in this book, such as those of Mark and Libby, Danny Burrow, Hannah Bromley, Jack Drummond and Horace Faulkner, indicate that the focus of policing and intervention has been on the parent, and not the child. This is in spite of section 23 of the CYP Act, which stipulates that the focus of child protection must be on the child's safety and well-being. It seems less than clear that section 23 of the CYP Act was properly applied in these cases. If it had been, a reasonable observer would have identified indications of risk arising out of the compromise of children's right to safety in these families. Upon closer examination of the children's representation in these cases, the children's interests, including their physical presences,[4] were not visible, and hence not central. Additionally, the children's rights to safety and well-being were not legally prominent or actioned in a way that the language of rights provisions and protective legislation envisages.

The child-centred approach, driven by child protection and family law legislation, including the UNCROC, particularly in these cases of child killing, appears to be only a normative aspiration. It is argued here that the social and legal place and positioning of the child in these cases are concealed and diminished. By the interaction of certain symbols and representations of themes, such as good parenting and family location, in the eyes of those responsible for actioning rights and ensuring protection, the child moves out of the central focus in favour of other interpretative and interactive considerations, such as demonstrated in my earlier discussions of the 'loving father' phenomenon. If the child-centred approach were taken seriously, one would see the positioning of the child within structures of representation always as prominent and significant. However, the contrary is the norm in these cases, where the child is manifestly absent and his or her social place in the family and in society is symbolically and physically marginalised. Because of this negation, the child, through misrepresentation, is cast behind rather than at the forefront and this leads to the creation of risk. Unless this dilemma between normative rights and protections,[5] and marginalisation and inaction in practice, is addressed, the risk of child endangerment in similar type situations continues to remain high.

It is clear from the recent research by the Australian Government that, where children are capable of forming views, they value them being taken into

4 Peter Reder, Sylvia Duncan and Moira Gray, *Beyond Blame: Child Abuse Tragedies Revisited* (Routledge, 1993) 125–127. Reder, Duncan and Gray also point out the importance of sighting the child and making visible the child's experience. They argue that it is necessary for caseworker assessments of risk to be based on an interactional model that takes into account families and networks.

5 For example in *B v B: Family Law Reform Act 1995* (1997) FLC 92-755, [10.57], the Full Court acknowledged the growing emphasis on children's rights in family jurisprudence. However, it held that children's rights created under section 60B of the *Family Law Act* were not legally enforceable, as they were seen as arising from an inherent conflict between the child's best interests on the one hand and the self-determination of the child on the other, against a backdrop of age, maturity and vulnerability to pressures.

consideration. Children tend to fare better when they are involved in the decision-making processes regarding their care arrangements. In the context of shared care parenting arrangements, Australian Government research reports: 'Children consistently reported that they would like to be involved in the decision-making about their care arrangement, and not surprisingly children tended to be more satisfied with arrangements when they felt that their views had been taken into account.'[6] In other words, the representation of children is an important consideration in all decisions made by the state and the family, such as by the judge in the court or the child protection officer, and between the parents, where such decisions concern their welfare and well-being. It is pointed out in the report that children benefit from the involvement of both parents after separation, in the absence of safety concerns and high conflict.[7] This suggests that, where there are issues of conflict and safety concerns, children's representation about parenting arrangements have to be treated with caution, particularly where they may be used by either parent as pawns to wield power and control over each other, for example, in the Mark and Libby case study, discussed in Chapters 2 and 6, it was alleged by Mark that the child, Mary, expressed a wish to live with him. In Chapter 6, it was pointed out that the court decision prior to Libby's application for a recovery order considered the adverse impact of removal on the children (Mary and her siblings). This seems to suggest that, where there are allegations of inter-parental violence and veiled threats, the child may be oblivious to endangerment risks concealed by distorted representations of, and by, the parent.

Notwithstanding this, children's views are important. However, equally as important are their physical and social representations in the family. This is not to discard their views on parenting arrangements even when there is conflict and violence. Rather, throughout this book and as demonstrated by the cases, it has been observed that representation of the children's safety and social and physical status in the family has been absent. This is because the issue of the children's safety lacked prominence in the sense that the children were concealed by misleading, distorted or false representations of the parent. In some cases, where the issue of safety was visible, the safety concerns were not addressed as a matter of priority. This suggests that there needs to be a broader repositioning of the child in the family and his or her right to safety in particular, for the child, including the considerations regarding the parent and in decisions made about intervention and care arrangements, to become more prominent.

Within the context of the human rights framework, it appears clear that children have a right to safety and protection. Yet some of the conditions that impinge on this right have not been recognised, especially by parents and state

6 J Cashmore, P Parkinson, R Weston, R Patulny, G Redmond, L Qu, J Baxter, MRajkovic, T Sitek and I Katz, *Shared Care Parenting Arrangements Since the 2006 Family Law Reforms: Report to the Australian Government Attorney-General's Department* (Social Policy Research Centre, University of New South Wales, 2010), 142.

7 Ibid 143–144.

agents. As agents of the child's rights to safety and protection, the parents and state agents have a duty under the CYP Act and the *Family Law Act 1975* (Cth) to ensure the conditions of safety structured around the child are in place, to minimise risks of endangerment. Such a duty, social and legal, puts the child in a position of prominence in the family and community. There is less of a chance for risks to the child to be masked, as the central positioning of the child in this visible space ensures that the parents and state agents responsible for the child's safety and protection are accountable to the community and the child. Socially, it is about recognising the child as a separate and distinct individual rather than as 'property' with which the parent can do as he or she pleases. The following section offers a broad examination of international developments on the legal prominence of the child. The purpose of this section is to contextualise the discussion of conditions of risk to follow. Of critical importance is the recognition that child protection in recent developments is set against the framework of risk identification and management. The progressive developments in the law, from recognising the effects of physical and emotional abuse and neglect to identifying the family as the locus for intervention, set the context in which the book's conceptualisation of dysfunctional families and neglectful states emerges. In the past, before the UNCROC, these situational factors of risk would not have disempowered the actionability of children's rights, but this has since changed, and the following section introduces the framework within which imminent change can emerge, or perhaps be forestalled.

National and international developments and the legal mandate to intervene

Historically, the best interest of the child principle has not always prevailed nationally and internationally. The concept of providing protection for children did not exist throughout most of the nineteenth century.[8] Contrary to this, the patriarchal ideology that women and children could be 'owned' in the social sense is now considered inconsistent with the principles of human rights as they apply to children in a central social position of domestic interest. Having said this, it has been argued throughout this book that there are remnants of this ideology lingering in families in which the male still believes in his right to treat his wife and children as he pleases. The fact that the belief that children are not separate from their parents still exists is troubling. It is even more troubling that in the past, according to Lamont and Bromfield: 'Governments took the position that children were the property of parents who had the right to treat their child any way they saw fit.'[9] This statement resonates with much of the book's articulation of the concept of ownership of children in the social sense. In the cases, some of the parents still believed the child was theirs to do with as they

8 Above n 3.
9 Ibid.

pleased. The fact that this was once a legitimately entrenched position taken by governments makes the symbol of ownership of the child by the parent all the more significant, because of its embeddedness in social consciousness. Lamont and Bromfield point out that it was only in the late nineteenth century that the first manifestation of child protection services with a legal mandate to intervene to protect children from abuse and neglect came about, with developments internationally in the United States and United Kingdom through charitable and philanthropic endeavours.[10] Australia soon followed suit, with child protection laws developed in each state and territory. The powers to make orders to protect the welfare of children that became vested in the Supreme Courts of the states and territories included the *parens patriae* jurisdiction, which literally means 'parent of the country',[11] harking back to patriarchal ideology. The mid-twentieth century in Australia saw developments in child welfare and the re-emergence of institutionalised care.[12] This was followed, in Australia and also the United States, by the implementation of mandatory reporting laws requiring all health and welfare professionals to report suspicious cases of child abuse and neglect.[13] The 1990s and the dawn of the twenty-first century saw the development of a legal framework as a response to allegations of child abuse and neglect.[14] The adoption of the interventionist model over the minimalist model in developing state intervention responses necessarily meant a greater reflection of the notion of children's rights.[15] This model assumes that state agents, such as social workers and judges, are capable of making sound and appropriate judgments and decisions that provide better outcomes for children.[16] This also means that the state has a legal duty to act *in locus parentis* with respect to the child's protection, safety and well-being.

There was also a growing recognition of the different forms of child maltreatment and the effects of violence on children.[17] The current regime in Australia and elsewhere predominantly recognises the harmful short- and long-term implications of family violence.[18] As argued in Chapter 2, the locus of violence in the family and its representation as hidden, 'behind closed doors', are profoundly symbolic on many levels. The symbol of the family as outside of public gaze; the symbol of the child as 'property' that is not distinct from the

10 Ibid.
11 Australian Law Reform Commission, *Family Violence: A National Legal Response*, Australian Law Reform Commission Report No. 114, October 2010.
12 Above n 3.
13 Ibid 2–3.
14 Ibid 3–4.
15 Above n 11, 171.
16 Ibid 172. See also Australian Law Reform Commission and Human Rights and Equal Opportunity Commission, *Seen and Heard: Priority for Children in the Legal Process* (Australian Law Reform Commission Report 84, 1997) [3.7] www.alrc.gov.au/publications/report-84.
17 Above n 3, 5–6.
18 Ibid.

parent; the symbol of power and control of the parent over the child – all are indicative of the need to address the visibility, social and legal positioning of the child within these frames of thought. Indeed the child's views and wishes can be taken into account in respect of a report of which he or she is a subject, and when considering investigations and assessments following a report of risk of harm.[19] However, in spite of these protectionist developments, the prevalence of familial violence, particularly its hidden nature, means that outdated beliefs about the child as a dependent entity persist.

There are in existence two different but operative legal systems in Australia that are focused on bringing the child to prominence and on protecting children: the state and territory systems of child protection, and the federal family law system.[20] Higgins and Kaspiew point out that a number of problems with these two systems exist, including complaints about systemic inadequacies (e.g. overloaded systems); insufficient resources; highly proceduralised and forensic risk assessments; and risk-adverse decision-making as a result of high levels of public scrutiny.[21] In Chapters 3 and 5,[22] it was noted that the law has facilitative and expressive functions. The facilitative function, in the context of child protection, attempts to pre-empt risk of harm to the child. The expressive function, on the other hand, is concerned with punishment and social governance through the court, which legitimates standards of parenting behaviour. In the context of child protection, both functions operate conjunctively and disjunctively in the sense that the system tries to prevent risk, which is a forward-looking endeavour, while at the same time operating retrospectively on the family in instances where the dispute is brought to the court.

Higgins and Kaspiew argue that this overlap in functions in the sphere of child protection causes a 'jurisdictional gap'[23] which translates into lack of interagency cooperation and sharing of information, which are the same deficiencies identified by the Wood Inquiry. What this means is that there is a systemic gap that the parent can exploit. For example, the parent can employ representations such as the loving parent to mislead. The differing roles of the two systems also mean that there will be operational discretion with regard to the decision to intervene and this would require an application, and interpretation, of the best interest of the child principle in different jurisdictions.[24] In the same breath, the

19 Sections 30 and 31 of the CYP Act.

20 Daryl Higgins and Rae Kaspiew, 'Child Protection and Family Law . . . Joining the Dots' (National Child Protection Clearinghouse Issues Paper No. 34, May 2011) 1–24, 1.

21 Ibid 4.

22 The law's dual functions were discussed in Chapters 3 and 5. See also Bronwen Morgan and Karen Yeung, *An Introduction to Law and Regulation* (Cambridge University Press, 2009) 5–6.

23 Above n 20, 14.

24 For example, under section 36 of the CYP Act, the Director-General must have regard to a number of considerations regarding the principles of intervention when deciding the appropriate response to a report of harm concerning a child or young

parent can engage in 'forum shopping',[25] such that the parent operates different representations in two different systems to achieve his or her end. For example, as Higgins and Kaspiew argue:

> The mandate of child protection authorities is to intervene to protect children only when a parent is neither willing nor able to protect the child from harm. In contrast, the task of the federal law system that deals with parenting disputes is to resolve disputes between parents who are separated over what arrangements are in the best interest of their children.[26]

A simple example of this is the case study of Mark and Libby. When the authorities were called to ascertain the safety of the children, Mark presented himself at the police station as the loving and caring parent. However, the reader will recall that there was a pending application in the Family Court to resolve the children's care. Mark alleged that he did not attend the Family Court because he could not find legal representation in time for the hearing. It could be argued that the fact that Mark chose not to engage with the Family Court is an indication of his disregard for the system. His post-suicide soliloquy attests to this distorted representation. This case study reveals that the parent was able to represent himself in different ways to different parts of the system, utilising appropriate representations such as the loving parent for his or her means, and that this was done in a way that masked the risks of endangerment to the child.

This story also brings into question the adequacy of the law as facilitative when dealing with pre-emptive risks of endangerment. Such a scenario questions whether there are adequate rights of protection for the child in the law. Moreover, the case study also calls attention to the meanings of 'clean and well cared for'

---

person. One of the ways in which the Family Court of Australia has tried to ameliorate the impact of the divided system of child protection is through the Magellan Project, which first commenced as a pilot in the late 1990s. The Project brings together a team of judges and counsellors, and legal aid is available for a child representative to be present in every case to ensure state agents' cooperation and information exchange. See Daryl Higgins and Rae Kaspiew, '"Mind the Gap . . .": Protecting Children in Family Law Cases' (2008) 22(3) *Australian Journal of Family Law* 235–258. On 19 July 2011, the Family Violence Best Practice Principles were launched. The Best Practice Principles were developed by the Family Court of Australia and Federal Magistrates Court of Australia to guide legal practitioners and decision makers when dealing with protecting children from harm and violence. The Best Practice Principles take into account the best interest of the child principle and the principles guiding the Magellan case management system for the disposition of cases involving allegations of serious physical abuse to children. See Family Court of Australia and Federal Magistrates Court of Australia, *Family Violence Best Practice Principles* www.familylawcourts. gov.au/wps/wcm/connect/FLC/Home/Publications/Family+Law+Courts+publications/fv_best_practice_for_flc.

25 Above n 20, 15.

26 Higgins and Kaspiew, above n 24, 277.

children. Does this representation mean that there are no risks of harm? Given the nature of familial violence as hidden and layered, in the sense that it is concealed within degrees of representation, it seems tenuous and arrogant to assume that because the children are presentable there are no safety concerns. This assumption indicates the central role of representation in constructions about risk. It also alludes to the discussion about operational discretion when considering the importance of symbols and representation of parents and children, which appear more powerful than the acknowledgement of the children's rights. This suggests that representation and symbols of the parent and child trump children's rights and child protection laws, and create risk. In this understanding, an analysis of risk that moves beyond structural or institutional prediction is offered as one that is enhanced through the challenge to go behind representations and symbols, which are interacting in order to unbalance any risk matrix, and that takes risk factors at face value.

Risk

Risk has been discussed in this book in terms of the intersection between social representations, distracting symbolisms and failed protective intervention, not in the conventional manner of risk analysis. This narrow frame of risk analysis stresses one theme, which has emerged from the analysis of the cases: risk and violence can be masked and therefore misrepresented or distorted. People who are closely connected to a child at risk, such as family members and child protection and social workers, may exacerbate risk because of their inability to see past the misrepresentations of risk and violence or, if they do perceive the risks, may not be listened to because authorities have perceived only the distorted representations. For example, some family members do not see the risk to the child because they are not presented with the complete picture or representation of the situation.[27] As shown in Chapters 2, 4, 5 and 6, this issue – the inability to appreciate risky representations – also applied to social workers in the Steppenwolf, Bromley and Burrow cases. In these cases, I have argued, social and community workers did not detect the risks to the child because the child was not in a prominent position of visibility to begin with. With respect to risk being masked, it has been shown that risks of child endangerment can be masked by false and misleading representations of the loving parent, the symbols of love and discipline and disingenuous language such as the communications by the parent and social worker in the Burrow case. Sometimes, confused interpretations bring about interaction exposing children to risk that is recurrent and preventable. Every angle of this contention is illustrated by the Bromley and Faulkner cases.

27 Such as occurred in the following cases: West and Janis in the case of Danny Burrow case; Melissa in the Faulkner case; and Melanie and David Drummond in the Drummond case.

There are sometimes other family members who note the existing risks to the child, such as Saskia Burrow's sister Carrie, and Libby in the Mark and Libby case. Yet the ability to observe risks is not limited to family members. Community members are often well placed to observe risks to the child based on common sense and intuition, such as occurred in the Bromley case, where the neighbour was concerned about the boarded-up window, and in the Burrow case, where Evans' mother, Susanna, observed and commented on Saskia's treatment of Danny. Community members tend to fall under second-degree representation, and this was seen in Chapter 4 to be the ideal position from which to assess risk and to intervene. For example, Angeline's parents, Iris and Papadino, were able to 'see' the development of risks to Jubilee Soprano, their granddaughter, as second-degree representors. Second-degree representors such as some family and community members and neighbours often have the requisite physical and emotional distance from the perpetrator and victim, and yet the necessary depth of intimacy, to penetrate invisible or masked risk, because they are able to form quasi-close relationships with the family on a regular basis. By contrast, outside observers at third-degree representation, such as social workers, may not be well apprised of domestic conflicts because of lack of trust between the parent and the social worker, such as occurred in the Bromley case. While there may be some social workers who are able to form strong, trusting relationships with families to enable effective intervention, the evidence of this is not seen in these cases. Lack of trust as a condition of risk will be further discussed in the following section. Suffice to say for now that lack of trust between the family and the state is one of the conditions that can exacerbate risks of child endangerment. This condition of risk is brought about by interactions between the symbol of the family, the parent and the state against the backdrop of a long colonial history of the state in Australia removing children from their families.

It is important to highlight that risk, as positioned in this book, is context-specific to the cases in terms of degrees of representation and imminence of endangerment to the child, and at the same time it is universal in the way it is exacerbated by misrepresentation or distorted through masking. Some family members at first-degree representation, such as Angeline Soprano and David Drummond, were not able to recognise the risk to the child because they were too closely connected to the perpetrator. The observation that risk is more visible to some categories of persons than others suggests that the nature of risk is perspectival, in that risk is ascertained or constructed based on certain representations and the positioning of these representations. So risk and representation are inextricably linked. Because risk is representational, it is dependent on the same physical and social factors that structure social representations, such as emotional and physical distance, proximity, time and social interaction. In this sense, the construction of risk revolves around interpretation and meaning-making. It is crucial, therefore, to look closely at some of the conditions in which risk in the cases developed.

The conditions of risk, as demonstrated in the cases, are created through the stages in which child endangerment develops, stages that are essentially decisions based on interactive relationships in which the child is a 'bit player'. This means that at different stages of child endangerment it is possible, over time, to discern the condition which enabled the danger to the child to develop. In some cases, such as Drummond, Sheng, Faulkner and Bromley, the state of dysfunction developed over a prolonged period. In as the case of Steppenwolf, the condition, or conditions, of developing risk were less obvious but were nevertheless present. Another example is seen in Hannah Bromley's case study, where there was a duty on state agents to protect the child under section 23 of the CYP Act, but, because Hannah had been relegated to a submissive and silent position by misleading representations made by her father to social workers, the risks of harm to her were exacerbated by the absence of her physical presence in the family and the failure to intervene.

In the following section, the broad context of risk in child protection is discussed. This is followed by discussion of the conditions of risk observed in the cases in regard to the book's predominant theme, representation. In particular, the focus is on the conditions of risk, and the facade of 'invisibility', which enable child endangerment to develop.

The context of risk in child protection and the law

There are different approaches to the applicability of risk. In the legal discourse, risk is generally defined as high likelihood of foreseeable harm, in civil cases. Sometimes, the courts draw distinctions between types of risks, such as general and specific risk.[28] The principle function of civil law is to control and manage risk.[29] This is most evident in insurance contracts, where risk is framed around management of loss in hazardous events. This framework is said to discipline householders by imposing certain coercive contractual conditions.[30] While civil and criminal legal discourses place risk in terms of reasonable forseeability retrospectively in order to ascertain liability, the criminal justice and policing systems approach risk prospectively, with a forward-looking view to neutralising risk. In this sense, risk is about 'communication rules, formats and technologies used to manage dangers'.[31] In these contexts, risk is about managing foreseeable dangers such as hazards and individual deviances. With respect to individual deviances, management of risk can entail surveillance and the re-categorisation of people who are perceived by the 'authorities' as being in a position to create opportunities for disorder.[32] Nevertheless, underpinning such a conceptualisation of risk is a managerial framework maintained by an ideology of danger steeped

28 *State of New South Wales (Department of Education and Training) v Maurice O'Sullivan* [2005] NSWIRComm 198, [30]–[40].

29 Richard V Ericson and Kevin D Haggerty, *Policing the Risk Society* (University of Toronto Press, 1997) 51.

30 Ibid 50.

31 Ibid 17.

32 Ibid.

in a desire for regulation, compliance and control, and based on the acquisition of knowledge and representations.[33] In the context of child protection under the CYP Act, the approach to risk can be seen, in particular, in the use of parent responsibility contracts to manage risks within the family.[34] Evident in this form of social governance, as was discussed in Chapter 5, is the regulation of, and focus on, certain types of parenting behaviours to manage risk.

In the child protection discourse, risk has been developed around the idea of 'recognisable potential for harm', which is explained as 'not a mere theoretical or possible risk' but 'an unacceptable risk, a real risk, a likelihood of harm or a recognisable potential having regard to the need to jointly protect children and employees and to preserve reasonable civil rights'.[35] In the CYP Act, following the Wood Inquiry, the threshold for reporting risk of harm under section 23 was amended to 'risk of significant harm'. This is a higher threshold than before. Section 23 now sets out seven (previously six) circumstances that are legally designated as potential breeding grounds for child endangerment. These seven circumstances delineate the situations in which a child or young person is deemed at risk of significant harm. In Chapter 6, these circumstances were referred to as the 'state of dysfunction', which is defined as a condition developed from a cluster of risk factors in which basic conditions of child safety are not met. The situations also include circumstances of violence as inaction, defined in section 23(2) as 'a single act or omission or a series of acts or omissions',[36] as discussed in Chapter 2. The cases discussed in Chapter 2 that are pertinent to violence as inaction are Sheng and Bromley. In regard to these cases it was suggested that the parental inaction of not providing appropriate care, treatment and education for children was a risk factor that put the children at risk of significant harm. In these cases, the deceased children's interests took a backseat to the parents' interests. It appears obvious now that, had the children's needs been prioritised, their deaths may not have occurred.

Under the new section 23, reporting a risk of significant harm may bring about state intervention as a consequence. The New South Wales Interagency Guidelines website states that 'the concern is sufficiently serious to warrant a response by a statutory authority (such as NSW Police Force or Community

33 For example, the New South Wales Department of Community Services, *Children Services Directorate: Strategic Compliance Monitoring and Enforcement Framework* (New South Wales Department of Community Services, 2008) 5, 14 www.community.nsw.gov.au/docswr/_assets/main/documents/childcare_monitoring_framework.pdf.

34 As was discussed in Chapter 5, n 3. Also see section 38A CYP Act; and Nikolas Rose, *Governing the Soul: The Shaping of the Private Self* (Routledge, 1990) xi, 121–122.

35 *Commission for Children and Young People v V* [2002] NSWSC 949, [17]. The court held that the meaning of risk under section 9(4) of the now repealed *Child Protection (Prohibited Employment) Act 1998* (NSW) was still valid. See also *HL v Commission for Children and Young People* [2008] NSWADT 323, [20], which cited Haylen J in *Commissioner for Children and Young People v V* at [22]; and *R v Commission for Children and Young People* [2002] NSWIRComm 101, 104.

36 Section 23(2) CYP Act.

Services) irrespective of the family's consent'. This amendment has added a layer of urgency and immediacy to the response to risk. The guarantee of state intervention in section 23 appears to give prominence to the child's safety and well-being. This could imply operational discretion as to the decision to penalise the parent perpetrator(s) or remove the child from the family. It is questionable whether child removal in this particular sense will indeed protect and empower the child, or whether it will further conceal the child by replacing its family with a dysfunctional carer. It is also unclear to what extent section 23 impacts on some of the risks of child endangerment identified from the cases in this book. The higher threshold of 'significant harm' excludes risks that may be invisible or do not fall within one of the circumstances listed in section 23. Particularly where the risks are not perceived as sufficiently serious to warrant intervention, such as those that are concealed by the loving parent representation, the discretion to make decisions in favour of protecting the child under the legal framework may be less effective and its absence may lead to further embedding the risk.

In the following section, risk is explained and dealt with through analysis of the cases and their conditions. The discussion will refer to Chapters 4 and 5 and the analysis of cases through the models of representation. The voices of representation and the ways in which they articulate and express risk are given prominence. The case of Horace Faulkner, as discussed in Chapter 5, suggests that the motives of a loving parent are not always clear, even to the children. This indicates that risks in filicide have to be closely examined in the contexts in which they emerge, and the following discussion will illuminate some of these conditions. The understanding on risk in the following section deals with the interactions between state agents and emerging representations and symbols of the family, the parent and child. The legal protections afforded to the child are seen as relying on the operational discretion of state agents and their decision-making processes, which are distracted and diffused by prevailing symbols such as love or discipline and representations such as the loving parent. It is pointed out that risk emerges from these interactions not from the law or from actionable responses by state agents but from discretionary inaction and misleading symbols of the parent. These then require a critical place within any dynamic taxonomy that charts child endangerment.

Risks in filicide

Risk of filicide has been extensively documented by Wilczynski in her study of 48 filicide case files referred to the Director of Public Prosecutions (London) in 1984.[37] Based on this sample, Wilczynski outlined a comprehensive risk

37 Ania Wilczynski, 'Risk Factors for Parental Child Homicide: Results of an English Study' (1995) 7(2) *Current Issues in Criminal Justice* 193–222, 193.

taxonomy that includes categories such as: demographic features;[38] social characteristics;[39] psychiatric characteristics;[40] victim characteristics;[41] situational features;[42] prior family conflict and maltreatment;[43] family history;[44] and prior

38 Ibid 195–198. In this category, Wilczynski includes sub-categories pertaining to relationship to victim; sex of perpetrator; class; ethnicity; and age. Her findings are that the majority of child victims of homicide under 15 years were killed by parents or parent-substitutes (survey period between 1989 and 1992), and perpetrators were more likely to be female (53.3 per cent) than male (though this carries no significance given that there were only 48 cases). But other studies show similar proportions of men and women. Three-quarters of the offenders in her study were not in paid employment, being either engaged in sole or primary domestic duties, unemployed or students, and this was more common among women than men. Most of the offenders in her study were Caucasians, although some studies report ethnic minorities are over-represented among filicide offenders. In the age sub-categories, she argues that filicide offenders tend to be young. Men tended to cluster in middle age groups between 22 and 34 years old compared to women, who were more evenly distributed, with the average age of 27.4 years, while the average for men was 25.9 years.

39 Ibid 198–203. In this category, Wilczynski highlights sub-categories of childcare responsibilities; lack of sleep; marital status; marital status at victim's birth; presence of non-supportive partner; source of income; financial problems; accommodation problems; lack of preparation for parenting; social support; education; criminal convictions; and current pregnancy.

40 Ibid 203–206. In this category, sub-categories of prior psychiatric treatment; prior suicide attempts; prior symptoms of depression; diagnosis of mental disorder; and substance abuse were identified.

41 Ibid 206–210. Victim characteristics contain sub-categories such as number of victims; sex; age; sibling rank; surviving siblings; ethnicity; victim perceived as difficult to care for; victim's behaviour as precipitant for the killing and difficult birth.

42 Ibid 210–213. In this category, sub-categories relate to location of the offence; delay in seeking assistance; notification to authorities; denial by perpetrator; method of killing; violence towards others at the time of filicide; and suicidal behaviour at the time of filicide. Wilczynski's findings pertinent to this book are: the police play a largely reactive role in discovering crime and, because of this, all (93.7) the deaths were notified to official agencies due to actions of the suspect or their families, friends or neighbours. In 66 per cent of cases, the suspects themselves triggered the notification process. Denial is a typical feature among perpetrators. Almost half (46.8 per cent) explicitly denied criminal involvement in the child's death to the police. This was more common among men than women. In addition, the findings confirm that filicide sometimes takes place in the context of violence towards others, and it was common for offenders to express suicidal impulses or exhibit suicidal behaviours at the time of the killing.

43 Ibid 213–215. In this category, sub-categories such as relationship problems; domestic violence; prior violence to the victim; and other maltreatment were identified. Many offenders in Wilczynski's study display relationship and domestic violence problems. Sexual abuse of the victim was found to be rare in filicide cases, but emotional abuse was found to be present in 23.1 per cent of cases.

44 Ibid 215. In this category, the sub-categories are problems in childhood history; family criminality; and family psychiatric history.

agency contact.[45] From this, Wilczynski portrays the typical filicide parent, who, she argues, will have these three definitive characteristics: numerous problems; a negative perception of their situation; and a lack of social and personal resources with which to cope with their difficulties.[46] According to Wilczynski, however, the crime of filicide cannot be attributed to one individual social, psychiatric or situational factor.[47] Instead, filicide usually occurs when there is a clustering of these various factors. This has also been the observation in this book. Additionally, there is usually one overriding factor among the cluster of factors within the state of dysfunction that acts as the 'straw that breaks the camel's back'. As such, risk assessment must not only address whether risk factors are present, how many factors there are and whether the factors present an accumulation of risk, but also how they interact with each other.[48] This analysis suggests that filicide must be understood from an interactionist perspective and within a protectionist framework in which the position of the child is at the forefront of any risk analysis and subsequent intervention.

It is noteworthy that Wilczynski's approach does not factor in the influence of representation, which relies on these static indicators. The central argument of this book has been the relevance of representation in constructions about risk. It is suggested that the book's approach is more dynamic because it looks for ways in which the meanings of violence and endangerment are interpreted and negotiated. For example, the social framings of representation discussed in Chapters 4 and 5 indicate some of the characteristics of risky contexts, such as physical proximity and degrees of formalisation of relationships. These two factors are central to the contextual features of risk in the next section, which examines lack of trust, family violence, family breakdown, and the representation of the loving parent. However, this is not to say that Wilczynski's risk factors are not relevant. These contexts are seen as interactional and producing risk. In particular, the conditions of risk provide the basic foundation for stand-alone risk factors, such as those identified by Wilczynski, to remain undetected and for subsequent endangerment to materialise.

Conditions of risk[49] *developing child endangerment*

In stories such as Bromley and Burrow, some risk factors were obvious and

45 Ibid. Wilczynski found that filicidal parents have often been seen by a range of professional agencies before the child's death. This parallels an observation in the previous chapter, that out of the 117 reviewable child deaths in 2005 in New South Wales, 33 children died as a result of abuse or neglect or suspicious circumstances, out of which 25 children were known to child protection services within three years of their deaths. See New South Wales Ombudsman, *Report of Reviewable Deaths in 2005 Volume 2: Child Deaths* (New South Wales Ombudsman, 2006) 7.

46 Ibid 217.

47 Ibid 218.

48 Ibid.

49 The discussion on 'conditions of risk' in this section merits some explanation. Its use of risk terminology differs from other approaches in this area, particularly where the

identifiable. In the Bromley case, obvious risk factors were the non-attendance of the children at school, the unhygienic conditions of the family home, the refusal of the parents to allow DOCS to see the children, the family's previous history with DOCS, and the parents' disengagement with social and support services with respect to Hannah. In the Burrow story, the risk factors were the emotional, psychological and physical violence towards Danny. In these two stories, the risks were masked by parental misrepresentation, poor communication and poor interagency cooperation, which, I have argued, amounted to failure of intervention. It was argued in Chapter 4 that intervention sits at second- or third-degree representation, because of its emotional and physical proximity to the family. It was pointed out that the physical distance between state agencies and the family can be a barrier to understanding risk representations. The failure to bridge this distance can lead to misrepresentations of risk and to poor intervention. Failure to intervene also allows risk conditions to persist, and this leads to greater risk of child endangerment.

While distance may be a barrier to recognising risk, it logically follows that risk should be easily recognised at first-degree representation. However, this was shown not to be the case, because some perpetrators conceal the risks to the child with the dominant representation of the loving parent. In cases such as Sheng and Drummond, the risk factors, even though present, were masked by the parents' loving representation. In the Sheng case the continued refusal by the parents to seek the appropriate treatment for Greta, and in the Drummond case Melanie's depression and the lack of social support for the family, were masked and not recognised as risks. In these cases the attention was on the parents, who were represented as caring and loving. These observations prompt the question: should these be classified by authorities as risk factors? These conditions, though, are also ordinary, everyday factors and decisions that many parents face in the course of parenthood. Clearly, it is not one single factor but an accumulation of and the intersection of risk factors in a particular context that trigger the situation of risk.

---

differences relate to the nature and context specificity of risk, which is perceived as a 'condition' developing endangerment as opposed to a series of, or accumulation of, factors that precede an adverse event. In particular, risk in child protection assumes risk can be predicted, managed and prevented, in which case risk is constructed and measured in terms of factors that, when taken together, present an overall assessment that determines the probability of a number of scenarios, mainly endangerment, abuse, neglect and maltreatment. See Julia Krane and Linda Davies, 'Mothering and Child Protection Practice: Rethinking Risk Assessment' (2000) 5 *Child and Family Social Work* 35–45, 37; Stan Houston and Huw Griffiths, 'Reflections on Risk in Child Protection: Is It Time for a Shift in Paradigms?' (2000) 5 *Child and Family Social Work* 1–10, 6; and Peter Reder and Sylvia Duncan, 'Closure, Covert Warnings and Escalating Child Abuse' (1995) 19(12) *Child Abuse & Neglect* 1517–1521, 1520. On the other hand, the interpretation of risk offered here is context specific and places emphasis on interactional relationships, symbols and representations within, and surrounding, the family.

In spite of the fact that, in the majority of the stories, the risk factors present did not signal the endangerment to the child, it is important to contextualise these risk factors and to see them as emerging from a 'condition', because this would focus the risk analysis on the interplay and interaction of risk factors. As such, there are conditions of risk emerging from these stories that merit discussion, as they sit apart from Wilczynski's risk taxonomy. Here, risks of harm to the child are seen to develop from certain general but critical social conditions in the family and their interaction with the state. As noted already, these conditions are lack of trust between the family and state services; domestic violence; the loving parent representation; and family breakdown, including child residence disputes and marital separation; all of these, emerging from the interactionist methodology, situate risk among social interactional contexts involving representation and symbols rather than non-interactional influences.

The following taxonomy of risk conditions in child endangerment is offered as a non-exclusive scheme that considers different types of risk factors as well as varying levels of risk. This scheme moves beyond the more formalist, institutional, static risk assessment approaches previously used, by considering the interactive and deceptive contexts of pre-filicide.

Lack of trust

Lack of trust between the parent and state agents, such as DOCS, as stated earlier, can exacerbate risks of endangerment to the child. On a symbolic level, the misperception and distrust can be conceptualised as stemming from Australia's colonial history, which saw the state as the remover of children from families, especially within Indigenous communities. This symbol of the state has given rise to a widely negative perception that is deeply embedded in culture and history. It is therefore possible to argue that the historical interactions between the state and the family have led to the prevalence of distrust, and this has created a condition in which the child is placed at risk of endangerment. Implied within this symbolic representation is the inadequate interpretation of existing representations fostering distrust. For example, the representation of the state, as part of the minimalist approach to child protection, saw children removed from the family at a time when children were still thought of as the 'property of their father'.[50] The other end of the spectrum, which saw the state directly intervening in families and child removal, further embedded a profound distrust that entrenched the position of the state at third-degree representation. This is to say that the physical and emotional distance of the state from the family, in particular the child, creates risk for the simple reason that the state is too far removed to adequately interpret misleading perpetrator representations and risk. Such a profound and symbolic sense of distrust creates a condition in which the possibility of endangerment is left open and unaddressed; it is this, among other

50 Above n 15.

factors such as poor communication and social isolation, that leads to rupture of relations between parents and state agents.

Simply put, the condition of distrust between the parent and the agency can be risky for the child. This is also a condition that contains a number of other issues, such as domestic violence or disengagement from support services particularly where help and support are needed. The lack of engagement and lack of trust in state agency can become a condition in which risk of child endangerment develops progressively, because it forces the parent to disengage with support services, which exist primarily to assist them. The disengagement can also result in failures to disclose domestic violence because of the stigma and fears that the children might be removed. In some of the cases, such as Bromley and Burrow, social workers appeared too readily assured of the children's safety. In the case of Drummond, social workers focused on the parents' needs and coping strategies to deal with the existing familial conflict, but neglected to address the consequences of the failure of those strategies. In a recent study by Stanley *et al.* on social service interventions with children and families in domestic violence incidents in the United Kingdom,[51] it was found that social workers were reluctant to engage with male perpetrators and there was an overall preoccupation with women as carers, similar to findings in previous research. In the Drummond case, it was Melanie who was engaged with social services, which tried to empower her to leave the family while David attended anger management classes. Both interventions in the Drummond case were focused on the parents and were directed at empowering them to cope with the situation. However, Jack's care requirements and school placements were not sufficiently addressed by external intervention, and this could be seen as negatively impacting on the parents' capacity to cope.

The implications from the Stanley *et al.* study seem to be that social services need to pursue a long-term engagement with families, because building trust is necessary if not crucial in order for intervention to tackle long-standing issues such as domestic violence.[52] The cases in this book also attest that intermittent interventions do not work. In Australia, building trust between state agencies and families is a challenge, particularly if the agency's image is negatively associated with child removal for socio-historical reasons. This negative perception acts as a barrier and impediment to effective state intervention. In Chapter 4, it was argued that lack of trust is usually evidenced through the perpetrator's style of representing the killing. Some perpetrators do this by referring to previous experiences with state intervention, which they perceive as negative. A number of cases demonstrated this, such as Mark and Libby, Steppenwolf and Bromley.

51 Nick Stanley, Pam Miller, Helen Richardson, Foster and Gill Thomson, 'A Stop-Start Response: Social Services' Interventions with Children and Families Notified following Domestic Violence Incidents' (2011) 41 *British Journal of Social Work* 296–313, 310.

52 Ibid 297, 311.

The perpetrators in these cases felt they were misrepresented by the system, and this further fostered their distrust and social isolation. Distrust in this context is a barrier to effective communication and willingness to receive assistance or engage with services, which must be addressed in order for intervention to work and for parents to be helped out of isolating circumstances.

Family violence

The next critical condition in which risk of harm to the child develops is family violence. The prevalence of family violence in filicide cases needs to be recognised, since risks to children are highest when the violence occurs in the context of other problems.[53] For example, it was pointed out in Chapter 6 that more than half of the book's 40 coronial cases analysed involved incidents of violence either between parents or between parent and child. In some of these cases, it was pointed out that the male perpetrators often used violence as a last resort to respond to a conflict that they perceived as deadlocked.[54] In Chapter 6, it was suggested that male perpetrators saw themselves as disempowered parties in the conflict. Violence is often used by these perpetrators as a means to an end; they resort to violence to make themselves heard by their partners and in the system.[55] The National Child Protection Clearinghouse ('NCPC') points to research that suggests that inter-parental violence is exacerbated by relationship separation,[56] which is discussed below as a condition in which risks of child endangerment are likely to develop. Additionally, in the cases involving male perpetrators, such as Faulkner, Mark and Libby, Drummond and Paul and Isabel, there were interactions as a result of false symbols of functional male authority and ownership over the family, which were allowed to fester amid other dysfunctional conditions such as the male's veiled threats of violence to the partner.

Male violence has been heavily theorised in the domestic violence literature,[57] and it is recognised as a condition that predisposes the child to risk. Section 23

53 Above n 51, 300.
54 Christine Alder and Ken Polk, 'Masculinity and Child Homicide' (1996) 36(3) *British Journal of Criminology* 396–411, 408.
55 For example in the Mark and Libby case study.
56 Above n 20, 2.
57 See above n 54. See also Women's Coalition Against Family Violence, *Blood on Whose Hands? The Killing of Women and Children in Domestic Homicides* (Federation Press, 1994); Carolyn Harris Johnson, *Come With Daddy: Child Murder-Suicide After Family Breakdown* (University of Western Australia Press, 2005); Lenore Walker, *The Battered Woman Syndrome* (Springer, 1984); Julie Stubbs (ed) *Women, Male Violence and the Law* (Federation Press, 1994); and D Bagshaw, T Brown, S Wendt, A Campbell, E McInnes, T Beth, B Batagol, A Sifris, D Tyson, J Baker and P Fernandez Arias, *Family Violence and Family Law in Australia: The Experiences and Views of Children and Adults from Families Who Separated Post-1995 and Post-2006* (Research report, Monash University, University of South Australia and James Cook University, April 2010) 3.

of the CYP Act recognises the important ramifications of violence used on children and witnessed by them.[58] In Chapter 6, it was posited that masculine violence emerges from feelings of male disempowerment and the male's failure to reassert his belief in his right to control, ownership and authority over his wife and children. However, it was also pointed out that this understanding does not represent all expressions of male violence. Alder and Polk, for instance, argue that male perpetrators have different identities, emotions and objectives;[59] there are perpetrators who have no previous record of using violence and there are those who regularly use violence.[60] Their study concludes that male perpetrators who use violence use it in the context of complex and sometimes contradictory reasons with regard to their own perceptions of themselves and their situation.[61] There are also perpetrators, in this book's cases, who used violence to establish their authority in relation to the children but would reject the use of violence against the children in public; Alder and Polk make a similar observation in the scenarios they studies.[62] Alder and Polk in their conclusion argue that male violence is complex and multi-layered in terms of the male's understandings of himself in relation to his wife and children, children in their care and the wider audiences.[63]

In the female perpetrator cohort, such as the Burrow and Steppenwolf cases, the threats of violence were made towards, and indeed physical violence was used on, the child but the violence was masked behind the symbol of parental discipline. The abuse was masked because the state, in its role as *in loco parentis*, did not know at the time that its intervention was dysfunctional; this exacerbated the abuse and placed the child in a situation of danger. Also seen in the Bromley case study is the symbol of the rejected child imprisoned behind closed doors in a family where the other children were cared for. In none of these cases were the dominant symbols recognised as risky, because if had they been questioned against the backdrop of risk factors that were clearly present they may have led to questioning of the visibility of the children and their safety.

Untreated mental illness

In Chapter 6, it was argued that the state of dysfunction in the family is a condition in which the basic safety conditions of the child are not met. Needless to say, within this condition sits a host of other risky conditions. Conditions of

58 Nancy VerSteegh and Clare Dalton, 'Report From the Wingspread Conference on Domestic Violence and Family Courts' (2008) 46(3) *Family Court Review* 454–475, 456.

59 Above n 54; and see Christine Alder and Ken Polk, *Child Victims of Homicide* (Cambridge University Press, 2001), 88.

60 Ibid.

61 Ibid.

62 Ibid.

63 Ibid.

risk pointed out in the conclusion of Chapter 6 include drug and alcohol abuse and addiction, mental illness and treatment and rehabilitation issues. For example, in the Soprano case, the delayed treatment of Brody's illness and its interaction with failed state intervention contributed to Jubilee's death. Similarly, in the Drummond case the perpetrator faced difficulties parenting while being treated for ongoing depression. In these contexts, even though the risk appears manageable at first glance, it is dependent on the perpetrators' successful completion of treatment and their continued engagement with support services. Failure to do so puts the child at considerable risk of harm, particularly where there could be other ongoing interactions impacting on the child's safety, such as domestic violence and abuse.

Family breakdown, child residence disputes, marital separation

It was observed in the cases that family breakdown, marital separation and child residence disputes play a part in exacerbating the risks to the child. These are life-changing and traumatising events for the parties involved, and for the child. There is no doubt that there is a great deal of trauma involved in breakdowns and separation, especially for the party opposing the separation. This observation is confirmed by the NCPC's research on inter-parental violence, as mentioned above. For one party, the breakdown is usually accompanied by feelings of disempowerment, which result from treatment by the other spouse or 'the system'. This could suggest that some of the approaches taken to resolve separation proceedings and child residence disputes need re-examination. In many of the cases where this kind of acrimonious separation occurred, the children were the objects of violence, leading to their deaths.

Recent research such as the Shared Parenting Report highlights that in separations where there are no safety concerns the quality of the parent relationship with the child, not the amount of time the parent has with the child, is an important factor.[64] However, in light of the revelation in the Alder and Polk study and the discussion in Chapter 6, it is possible that fathers who have never resorted to violence before may turn to using violence as a response to marital separation and child residence disputes. It appears that, for some of these fathers, separation and dispute over the child's residence represent a threat to their perception of meanings of family and parenthood.[65] I have also argued that for these male perpetrators the threat is made worse by their failure to reassert control and power over their wives and children and their beliefs that they had a right to do so. This harks back to the conditions of familial violence and dysfunctional patriarchy, which can be seen as overlapping conditions that may indicate the presence of risk of harm to the child. This said, there may

64 Above n 6.

65 Some examples are the cases of Horace Faulkner, Mark and Libby and Paul and Isabel, discussed in Chapters 2 and 6.

be instances in which such conditions exist but do not lead to filicide. These conditions need to be considered in light of cumulative risk factors as well as alongside false symbols and representations.

Loving parent representation

The theme of the loving parent emerges in the context of failed state intervention in a number of cases. The appearance of the loving parent sits within a nest of other risk conditions, such as an acrimonious child residence dispute, marital separation and mental illness. While this may not necessarily be conceptualised as a risk factor, it is certainly one of the conditions which acts as a barrier to state intervention, because the appearance of this representation masks the risks to the child. The loving parent representation was likened in Chapter 6 to an 'invisibility cloak' which conceals from the authorities the risks of child endangerment and the state of dysfunction in the family. It was suggested in Chapter 5 that the loving parent representation is able to do this because it is a dominant representation in Western society. It is a condition that can foster child endangerment because of its ability to mask risks of harm to the child.

As pointed out above, the loving parent representation in the Paul and Isabel, Faulkner and Drummond cases, to list but a few, is a theme that keeps emerging from the data. In these cases, the representation masked the risks to the child through its ability to convince others that the children were not at risk. It is noteworthy, however, that not all loving parent representations are risky. It is necessary to be mindful of the context in which this representation sits, which is within interactions between family violence, mental illness and child abuse. This condition certainly does not stand alone, but neither do many of the risk factors. Instead, as has been suggested throughout this book, it is the social interactions within these conditions that produce risk to the child, and it is important if not paramount to recognise these conditions for what they can become.

Patriarchal dysfunction: ownership and duty

An observation was made in Chapter 6 that in many of the cases the male assumed right to reassertion of authority and ownership in the family had collapsed, and this had created a condition of risk to the child. In this condition, there is also present a cluster of sub-conditions, such as communication breakdown and a belief by the male that he has been disempowered, which affect child safety in the family. It was argued that this condition exists on two levels: between father and family, and between state and family. The state's response in intervention was conceptualised as masculine because of its non-committal response and impassive listening to the representations by the receiving partner/spouse regarding long-standing issues of domestic violence and threat made by the perpetrator. Chapter 6 argued that in the cases the state response parallels the male perpetrator's response to the conflict. The chapter went on to suggest that some of the laws, such as mandatory arrest, simply mirror this masculine context because of the way violence is met with violence, and may pose more problems rather than resolving violence.

The tenacity of reassertion of patriarchal ownership by the male is also evidenced by some perpetrators who laid blame on the criminal justice system rather than accept responsibility for the family breakdown, leading to the collapse of their ownership of and duty towards the children. These fathers have been acculturated with a belief that they have a right to ownership of their wives and children. Even though such an ideology has been challenged by the human rights framework and the best interest of the child principle, these challenges appear to be normative in families where patriarchal ideology continues to persist in violent ways.

How can such a condition be recognised? It is important to see it among other conditions indicative of assertion of patriarchal ideology, such as the loving parent representation, the symbol of the disempowered parent and the marital breakdown or child residence dispute situation. For example, in the Faulkner case study, all of these indicators of risk were present. Additional indicators were Horace's mental instability, allegations of violence and his constant threats towards Melissa about taking the children from her. Here, the symbol of the parent who believes they are disempowered stands out. Another troubling feature of this case is the use of the children as pawns in the parents' fight, and the parents' ability to manipulate the legal system for their own ends. This harks back to the discussions on the symbol of parental ownership, in the social sense, over children. As argued, this symbol has been used by parents as a mechanism for justifying their misuse of power and their abuse and control of their children.

The central observation in this chapter is that the interaction and influence of certain representations and symbols, when acting together in specific contexts such as those identified above, produce specific risky conclusions and consequences for the child. Consider the case of Hannah Bromley, in which there were allegations of neglect, representations of a dysfunctional home situation, one rejected child amid other non-rejected children, and distrust of the state. Had social workers gone the 'extra mile' to insist on physically seeing Hannah, they may well have immediately recognised her faltering health and taken action to remove her from the family. To do this, state agents would have to have been aware of the misrepresentations of symbols that are indicated by some of these concerns: allegations of the unseen child,[66] the father's distrust of the state and allegations of the dysfunctional state of the family's home.

What is suggested here is an interactionist approach towards child protection that is holistic and aware of representations and symbols of risk. Such an approach looks out for representations, conditions and indicators of risk, and turns risky conditions into opportunities for effective and positive intervention to produce outcomes of safety for the child. In addition, the taxonomy above does not just

66 Above n 4.

provide a list of influential factors but shows how through the interaction of flawed or misunderstood representations and symbols these factors are missed, or their 'riskiness' becomes distracted and defused. The missed opportunities for intervention can have fatal consequences for the children in the cases, but the most comprehensive and sincere strategy for intervention, if implemented correctly, can see these repeatable conditions as preventable.

Conclusion

This book has argued for a greater recognition of the central positioning and visibility of the child in the family and community, which is in line with national and international developments on children's rights and their interests. Having said this, the cases have shown that legal and rights protections can be compromised where their application depends on the operational discretion of the parties who the child relies on for protection. Illustrating this point, the book modelled case study data to show the degrees of formalisation with regard to relationships and distance. This analysis had the intention of revealing how the interaction of representations and symbols was masking the decentred position of the child and hence leading to risky interpretations of critical relationships of child endangerment. It was argued that these social framings dictate the ways certain representations are understood and the context of intervention. With state intervention failing in these cases, it is important to understand the nature of state intervention and its determination, and it is also important to improve perceptions of representations crucial to the decisions of these agencies and other individuals responsible for actioning the rights and protections of vulnerable children. This richer understanding of what lies beneath crucial representations and symbols within the critical stages leading up to the death of the child should make possible the forging of more positive interactions for producing safer outcomes for the child.

As far as the cases suggest, the representations of the parent and positioning of the child against other tragically recurrent and easily identifiable conditions of risk are the keys to uncovering risk. This was established through the cases, as modelled and theorised in Chapters 4 and 5. In Chapter 6, a variant causal demonstration (between patriarchal representation mirrored in state agency responsibility leading to dysfunctional state intervention and child endangerment) reveals that, with fatal consequences, representation can mask more than reveal.

The theme of representation has been posited as central to the construction of risk, and to the interpretation of symbols, which can endanger rather than ensure child safety. The analysis has identified representation as contributing to risk, both where key agencies and individuals fail to adequately interrogate the real nature of crucial representations and symbols, and where the interactions between these representations and symbols are misconstrued to the detriment of safe contextual conditions for the child in danger. This suggests that social representation, and the crucial interaction of false representation and distorted symbols, such as obsessive parental devotion and sacrificial violence, can function to contextualise and indicate risk rather than safety. These inappropriate constructions of social representation undermine rather than strengthen the foundations for social cohesion in environments where child safety would otherwise be ensured. Failure to appreciate the capacity of representations, and their interactions, further confuses understandings of key symbols such as state, family, child and parent, and this means that crucial situations and relationships responsible for the rights and protections of the child may be transformed into arenas of risk.

It was also argued in this book that representation can be likened to a mask, or an invisibility cloak, that conceals or wraps around risk in order to exhibit new dimensions. In this 'new dimensional' sense the mask overrides otherwise consistent understandings and conjures up alternative representations that might confuse and confound signs of risk and danger. The challenge then is to unmask and uncloak, or at the very least to see the mask for what it is at the facilitative stages of law enforcement, and to unwrap the cloak against the interests and actors who enwrap alternative and logical representations of risk.

Understanding the ways in which dominant representations can be understood differently allows for a more meaningful interrogation of these and other cases of filicide. As argued throughout the book, the interactions between the loving parent and conditions of child endangerment can be significant, recurring and containable predicators of risk. From a proactive perspective, this book urges policy makers to rethink risk assessment – moving away from the formal and proceduralised rituals to an interactionist and holistic approach that empowers child protection through revealing and re-centring the child, and showing conditions of child endangerment, when they arise, for what they really are.

Appendix

Fieldwork templates

Table A.1 Sample coronial template

Nature of document	*Autopsy report*
Source	
Deceased	
Deceased's age	
Siblings	
Manner of death	
Cause of death	
Previous incidents of abuse	
Implications for parties involved	
Key issues in death	
Impact on investigation	

Table A.2 Sample coronial template

Nature of document	*Police report of death to coroner*
Nature of document	
Parties	
Relationship status	
Circumstances at time of death	
Parties' statements	

Table A.3 Sample DPP statements template

Nature of document	
Source	
Deposing witnesses	
Parties' background	
Issues in death	
Third parties' statements about family	
Agency representation of the crisis	
Parties' statements	
Representation of death	

Table A.4 Sample DPP file template

Source and nature of document	
Victim	
Offender's crime:	
Lawyers:	
Chronology:	
Defence case:	
Offender's plea and proceedings:	
Sentence:	
Dysfunctional family context:	
Offender's background:	
Offender's medical history:	
Previous history of violence:	
Nature of violence:	
Forensic/psychiatric assessment of offender:	
Psychiatrists, doctors:	
Offender characteristics, representations:	
Third parties' statements about family:	
Third parties' statements about the offender:	
Third party legal proceedings, e.g. custody:	
Offender's statement:	
Prison custody assessment:	
Agency (DOCS, health, housing, etc.) representation of the crisis and intervention:	
The prosecutorial representation/ submissions:	
Legal build-up, opinions:	
Case law:	
Witness list:	
Judgment:	
Representation of death:	
Thoughts/notes:	

Bibliography

Articles/ books/reports

Ackerley, Elizabeth, 'Newspaper Reporting and the Public Construction of Homicide' (2004) 44 *British Journal of Criminology* 256

Adams, Michele A, 'Framing Contests in Child Custody Disputes: Parental Alienation Syndrome, Child Abuse, Gender, and Father's Rights' (2006–2007) 40 *Family Law Quarterly* 315

Adamson, Walter L, *Hegemony and Revolution: A Study of Antonio Gramsci's Political and Cultural Theory* (University of California Press, 1980)

Adinkrah, Mensah, 'Maternal Infanticides in Fiji' (2000) 24(12) *Child Abuse & Neglect* 1543

Adinkrah, Mensah, 'Men Who Kill Their Own Children: Paternal Filicide Incidents in Contemporary Fiji' (2003) 27 *Child Abuse & Neglect* 557

Agamben, Giorgio, *Means Without Ends: Notes on Politics* (Vincenzo Binetti and Cesare Casarino trans, University of Minnesota Press, 2000)

Agamben, Giorgio, David Kishik and Stefan Pedatella, *Nudities* (Stanford University Press, 2010)

Alder, Christine and Ken Polk, *Child Victims of Homicide* (Cambridge University Press, 2001)

Alder, Christine and Ken Polk, 'Masculinity and Child Homicide' (1996) 36(3) *British Journal of Criminology* 396

Alder, Jeffrey S, ' "I Loved Joe, But I Had to Shoot Him": Homicide by Women in Turn-of-the-Century Chicago' (2001–2002) 92(3–4) *Journal of Criminal Law & Criminology* 867

Alexander, Jeffrey C, 'The Celebrity-Icon' (2010) 4(3) *Cultural Sociology* 323

Allatt, Patricia, 'Stereotyping: Familism in the Law' in Bob Fryer and Alan Hunt (eds), *Law, State and Society* (Routledge, 1981)

Allen, Irving Lewis, 'Talking About Media Experiences: Everyday Life as Popular Culture' (1982) 16(3) *Journal of Popular Culture* 106

Allen, Judith, 'The Invention of the Pathological Family: A Historical Study of Family Violence in NSW' in C O'Donnell and J Craney (eds), *Family Violence in Australia* (Longman Cheshire, 1982)

Allen, Judith, 'The "Masculinity" of Criminality and Criminology: Interrogating Some Impasses' in Mark Findlay and Russell Hogg (eds), *Understanding Crime and Criminal Justice* (Law Book Company, 1988)

Anonymous, 'Chelmsford – Friday, March 10. Charge of Murder – Acquittal on the Ground of Puerperal Insanity' (1848) *Journal of Psychological Medicine* 1, 478

Appel, Jacob M, 'When Infanticide Isn't Murder', *Huffington Post* (online) 8 September 2009 www.huffingtonpost.com/jacob-m-appel/when-infanticide-isnt-mur_b_279703.html

Appignanesi, Lisa, *Mad, Bad and Sad: A History of Women and the Mind Doctors from 1800 to the Present* (Virago, 2008)

Arendt, Hannah, *The Human Condition* (University of Chicago Press, 1958)

Aristotle, *Politics*, Book 7 (Aeterna Press, 2015)

Armstrong, Nancy and Leonard Tennenhouse (eds), *The Violence of Representation: Literature and the History of Violence* (Routledge, 1989)

Arnot, M L, 'The Murder of Thomas Sandles: Meaning of a Mid-Nineteenth-Century Infanticide' in Mark Jackson (ed), *Infanticide: Historical Perspectives on Child Murder and Concealment, 1550–2000* (Ashgate, 2002)

Aubert, Vilhelm, *Elements of Sociology* (Heinemann Educational, 1967)

Australian Government Department of Families, Housing, Community Services and Indigenous Affairs, *Protecting Children Is Everyone's Business: National Framework for Protecting Australia's Children 2009–2020* www.dss.gov.au/our-responsibilities/families-and-children/publications-articles/protecting-children-is-everyones-business

Australia Law Reform Commission, *Family Violence: A National Legal Response*, Australian Law Reform Commission Report No. 114, October 2010

Australian Law Reform Commission and Human Rights and Equal Opportunity Commission, *Seen and Heard: Priority for Children in the Legal Process* (Australian Law Reform Commission Report 84, 1997) www.alrc.gov.au/publications/report-84

Ayres, Susan, 'Newfound Religion: Mothers, God, and Infanticide' (2006) 33 *Fordham Urban Law Journal* 335

Babcock, J C, J Waltz, N S Jacobson and J M Gottman, 'Power and Violence: The Relation Between Communication Patterns, Power Discrepancies, and Domestic Violence' (1993) 61(1) *Journal of Consulting and Clinical Psychology* 40

Bacon, Wendy and Robyn Lansdowne, 'Women Homicide Offenders and Police Interrogation' in Mark Findlay, Sandra J Egger and Jeff Sutton (eds), *Issues in Criminal Justice Administration* (George Allen & Unwin, 1983)

Bagshaw, D, T Brown, S Wendt, A Campbell, E McInnes, T Beth, B Batagol, A Sifris, D Tyson, J Baker and P Fernandez Arias, *Family Violence and Family Law in Australia: The Experiences and Views of Children and Adults from Families Who Separated Post-1995 and Post-2006* (Research report, Monash University, University of South Australia and James Cook University, April 2010)

Balkin, Jack M, 'Deconstruction's Legal Career' (2005) 27(2) *Cardozo Law Review* 719

Balkin, Jack M, 'Deconstructive Practice and Legal Theory' (1987) 96 *Yale Law Journal* 743

Barlow, Shirley, A (ed), *Euripides: Heracles* (Aris & Phillips, 1996)

Barthes, Roland, *Mythologies* (Hill & Wang, 1972)

Bastian, Michelle, 'Inventing Nature: Re-Writing Time and Agency in a More-than-Human World' (2009) 47 *Australian Humanities Review* 99

Baudrillard, Jean, *Simulacra and Simulation, The Body, in Theory* (University of Michigan Press, 1994)

Becker, Howard Saul, 'Labelling Theory Reconsidered' in Paul Rock and M McIntosh (eds), *Deviance and Social Reaction* (Tavistock, 1974)

Becker, Howard Saul, *Outsiders: Studies in the Sociology of Deviance* (Free Press of Glencoe, 1963)

Becker, Howard, *Tricks of the Trade: How to Think about Your Research While You're Doing It* (University of Chicago Press, 1998)

Beckerman, A, 'Women in Prison: The Conflict Between Confinement and Parental Rights' (1991) 18 *Social Justice* 171

Behlmer, George K, 'Deadly Motherhood: Infanticide and Medical Opinion in Mid-Victorian England' (1979) (October) *Journal of the History of Medicine* 403

Benjamin, Walter, *Illuminations* (Harry Zohns trans, Schocken Books, 1st ed, 1986)

Benn, Melissa, *Madonna and Child: Towards a New Politics of Motherhood* (Jonathan Cape, 1998)

Benns, Matthew, *When the Bough Breaks: The True Story of Child Killer Kathleen Folbigg* (Bantam, 2003)

Berns, S, 'Living Under the Shadow of Rousseau: The Role of Gender Ideologies in Custody and Access Decisions' (1991) 10 *University of Tasmania Law Review* 233

Bentley, Amelia, 'Mother Gets Life Sentence for Killing Children', *Sydney Morning Herald* (online), 24 November 2010 www.smh.com.au/queensland/mother-gets-life-sentence-for-killing-children-20100224-p2yo.html

Berger, Peter L and Thomas Luckmann, *The Social Construction of Reality: A Treatise in the Sociology of Knowledge* (Doubleday, 1966)

Bessant, Judith and Richard Hil, 'Parenting on Trial: State Wards' and Governments' Accountability in Australia' (1998) 26(2) *Journal of Criminal Justice* 145

Bessant, Judith and Rob Watts, 'History, Myth Making and Young People in a Time of Change' (1998) 49 *Family Matters* 5

Biber, Katherine, 'The Archival Turn in Law: The Papers of Lindy Chamberlain in the National Library of Australia' (2017) 39 *Sydney Law Review* 277

Birch, Helen (ed), *Moving Targets: Women, Murder and Representation* (Virago Press, 1993)

Bluglass, Robert, 'Infanticide' (1990) 2(8) *The Psychiatrist* 139

Bluglass, Robert, 'Infanticide and Filicide' in Robert Bluglass and Paul Bowden (eds), *Principles and Practice of Forensic Psychiatry* (Churchill Livingstone, 1990)

Bond, George C and Angela Gilliam (eds), *Social Construction of the Past: Representation as Power* (Routledge, 1994)

Bouma, Gary D, *The Research Process* (Oxford University Press, 4th ed, 2000)

Bourdieu, Pierre, *Homo Academicvs* (Peter Collier trans, Stanford University Press, 1988)

Bourdieu, Pierre, *Language and Symbolic Power* (Harvard University Press, 1991)

Bourdieu, Pierre, *Masculine Domination* (Stanford University Press, 2001)

Bourdieu, Pierre, *Outline of a Theory of Practice* (Cambridge University Press, 1977)

Bourdieu, Pierre, *Pascalian Meditations* (Polity Press, 2000)

Bourdieu, Pierre and Loïc J D Wacquant, *An Invitation to Reflexive Sociology* (University of Chicago Press, 1992)

Bourget, Dominique and Pierre Gagne, 'Paternal Filicide in Quebec' (2005) 33 *Journal of the American Academy of Psychiatry and the Law* 354

Bourget, Dominique, Jennifer Grace and Laurie Whitehurst, 'A Review of Maternal and Paternal Filicide' (2007) 35 *Journal of the American Academy of Psychiatry and the Law* 74

Boyd, John D, *The Function of Mimesis and its Decline* (Fordham University Press, 1980)

Boyd, S B, 'What Is a "Normal" Family?' (1992) 55(2) *Modern Law Review* 269

Braaf, Rochelle, 'Arresting Policies: Implications of Pro and Mandatory Arrest Policies for Victims of Domestic and Family Violence' (Paper presented at the Australian Institute of Family Studies conference, Melbourne, 9–11 July 2008) http://citeseerx.ist.psu.edu/viewdoc/download?doi=10.1.1.498.6097&rep=rep1&type=pdf

Braithwaite, John, *Crime, Shame and Reintegration* (Cambridge University Press, 1989)

Bronfen, Elisabeth, *Over Her Dead Body: Death, Femininity and the Aesthetic* (Manchester University Press, 1992)

Bronitt, Simon and Bernadette McSherry, *Principles of Criminal Law* (Lawbook, 2nd ed, 2005)

Brown, Melanie, 'The Portrayal of Violence in the Media: Impacts and Implications for Policy' (Australian Institute of Criminology, 1996)

Bryant, Diana, Chief Justice, Family Court of Australia, 'Care and Protection of Children: Australia and New Zealand Experience' (Paper delivered at the 4th World Congress on Family Law and Children's Rights, Cape Town, South Africa, 20–23 March 2005)

Butler Committee (UK), *Report of the Committee on Mentally Abnormal Offenders, Cmnd 6244* (London: HMSO, 1975)

Butterfield, Jessica, 'Blue Mourning: Postpartum Psychosis and the Criminal Insanity Defense, Waking to the Reality of Women Who Kill Their Children' (2006) 39 *John Marshall Law Review* 515

Campbell, G, 'Working Together for a Safer London' (Presentation by the Metropolitan Police New Scotland Yard at the University of New South Wales, 9 December 2008)

Campbell, J C, Daniel Webster, Jane Koziol-McLain, Carolyn Block, Doris Campbell, Anna Curry, Faye Gary, Nancy Glass, Judith McFarlane, Carolyn Sachs, Phyllis Sharps, Yvonne Ulrich, Susan A Wilt, Jennifer Manganello, Xiao Xu, Janet Schollenberger, Victoria Frye and Kathryn Laughon, 'Risk Factors for Femicide in Abusive Relationships: Results from a Multi-Site Control Study' (2003) 93(7) *American Journal of Public Health* 1089

Campbell, Joseph, *Myths To Live By* (Penguin, first published 1972, 1993 ed)

Campion, John F, James M Cravens and Fred Covan, 'A Study of Filicidal Men' (1988) 145(9) *American Journal of Psychiatry* 1141

Carnagey, Nicholas L, Craig A Anderson and Brad J Bushman, 'The Effect of Video Game Violence on Physiological Desensitization to Real-Life Violence' (2007) 43 *Journal of Experimental Social Psychology* 489

Carrington, Kerry, *Who Killed Leigh Leigh? A Story of Shame and Mateship in an Australian Town* (Random House, 1998)

Cashmore, J, P Parkinson, R Weston, R Patulny, G Redmond, L Qu, J Baxter, M Rajkovic, T Sitek and I Katz, *Shared Care Parenting Arrangements Since the 2006 Family Law Reforms: Report to the Australian Government Attorney-General's Department* (Research report, University of Sydney, Australia Institute of Family Studies and Social Policy Research Centre, University of New South Wales, May 2010)

Cavanagh, Kate, R Emerson Dobash and Russell P Dobash, 'The Murder of Children by Fathers in the Context of Child Abuse' (2007) 31 *Child Abuse & Neglect* 731

Chagnon, Napoleon A, *Yanomamo: The Fierce People* (Holt, Rinehart & Winston, 1983)

Chan, C and C Cuneen, *Evaluation of the Implementation of NSW Police Service Aboriginal Strategic Plan, Commissioned by the NSW Police Service and NSW Ombudsman* (University of Sydney, Institute of Criminology, 2000)

Chamberlain, Lindy, *Through My Eyes: The Autobiography of Lindy Chamberlain-Creighton* (East Street Publications, rev ed, 2004)

Charon, Joel M, *Symbolic Interactionism: An Introduction, an Interpretation, an Integration* (Pearson Education, 9th ed, 2007)

Chesney-Lind, M, 'Criminalizing Victimization: The Unintended Consequences of Pro-Arrest Politics for Girls and Women' (2002) 2 *Criminology & Public Policy* 81

Chew, Kenneth S Y, Richard McCleary, Maricres A Lew and Johnson C Wang, 'The Epidemiology of Child Homicide in California, 1981 through 1990' (1999) 3 *Homicide Studies* 151

Chibnall, Steve, *Law and Order News: An Analysis of Crime Reporting in the British Press* (Tavistock, 1977)

Christoffel, Katherine K, Nora Keating Anzinger and Mary Amari, 'Homicide in Childhood: Distinguishable Patterns of Risk Related to Developmental Levels of Victims' (1983) 4(2) *American Journal of Forensic Medicine and Pathology* 129

Christoffel, Katherine K and Kiang Liu, 'Homicide Death Rates in Childhood in 23 Developed Countries: U.S. Rates Atypically High' (1983) 7 *Child Abuse & Neglect* 339

Clair, Robert N St, *The Sociology of Knowledge as a Model for Language Theory: Language as Social Science* (Edwin Mellen Press, 2006)

Clements, Luke and Janet Read (eds), *Disabled People and the Right to Life: The Protection and Violation of Disabled People's Most Basic Human Rights* (Routledge, 2008)

Cockcroft, Lucy, 'How Khyra Ishaq Starved While Surrounded by Food', *Telegraph* (online) 25 February 2010 www.telegraph.co.uk/news/uknews/crime/7316744/How-Khyra-Ishaq-starved-while-surrounded-by-food.html

Cohen, Stanley, 'Criminology and the Sociology of Deviance in Britain' in Paul Rock and Mary McIntosh (eds), *Deviance and Social Control* (Tavistock, 1974)

Collier, Richard, *Masculinity, Law and the Family* (Routledge, 1995)

Congreve, William, *The Mourning Bride: A Tragedy* (Dodo Press, 2008)

Connell, R W, *Gender and Power: Society, the Person and Sexual Politics* (Allen & Unwin, 1987)

Connell, R W, *Masculinities* (University of California Press, 2nd ed, 2005)

Connell, R W, 'The State, Gender, and Sexual Politics' (1990) 19 *Theory and Society* 507

Cooley, B and C Frazer, 'Children and Domestic Violence: A System of Safety in Clinical Practice' (2006) 29(4) *Australian Social Work* 462

Council of Australian Governments, *Protecting Children Is Everyone's Business: National Framework for Protecting Australia's Children 2009–2020* (Australian Government, Canberra, 2009)

Criminal Law Revision Committee (UK), *Offences Against the Person*, *Cmnd. 7844* (Fourteenth Report, Criminal Law Revision Committee, 1980)

Crittenden, Patricia M and Susan E Craig, 'Developmental Trends in the Nature of Child Homicide' (1990) 5(2) *Journal of Interpersonal Violence* 202

Daly, Martin and Margo Wilson, *Homicide* (Aldine De Gruyter, 1988)

Damme, Catherine, 'Infanticide: The Worth of an Infant Under the Law' (1978) 22 *Medical History* 1

Davies, M, *Asking the Law Question* (Law Book, 1994)

Davis, Brent and Kym Dossetor, '(Mis)perceptions of Crime in Australia' 396 (2010) *Trends and Issues in Crime and Criminal Justice* 1

De Beauvoir, Simone, *The Second Sex* (Vintage, 1997)

D'Orban, P T, 'Women Who Kill Their Children' (1979) 134 *British Journal of Psychiatry* 560

Dearden, J and W Jones, *Homicide in Australia: 2006–2007 National Homicide Monitoring Program Annual Report* (Research Report, Australian Institute of Criminology Monitoring Reports 02, 2008)

De Silva, Suresh and Kim Oates, 'Child Homicide: The Extreme of Child Abuse' (1993) 158 *Medical Journal of Australia* 300

Denzin, Norman K, *Symbolic Interactionism and Cultural Studies: The Politics of Interpretation, Twentieth-Century Social Theory* (Blackwell, 1992)

Denzin, Norman K and Yvonna S Lincoln, *Strategies of Qualitative Inquiry* (Sage, 1998)

Denzin, Norman K and Yvonna S Lincoln, *The Sage Handbook of Qualitative Research* (Sage, 4th ed, 2011)

Dickinson, J R and J A Sharpe, 'Infanticide in Early Modern England: The Court of Great Sessions at Chester, 1650–1800' in Mark Jason (ed), *Infanticide: Historical Perspectives on Child Murder and Concealment, 1550–2000* (Ashgate, 2002)

Digby, Anne, 'Women's Biological Straightjacket' in Susan Mendus and Jane Rendall (eds), *Sexuality and Subordination: Interdisciplinary Studies in Gender in the Nineteenth Century* (Routledge, 1989)

Divale, W T and M Harris, 'Population, Warfare and the Male Supremacist Complex' (1976) 78(3) *American Anthropologist* 521

Donnelly, Hugh, Stephen Cumines and Ania Wilczynski, 'Sentenced Homicides in NSW 1990–1993: A Legal and Sociological Study' (Judicial Commission of NSW, 1995)

Donzelot, Jacques, *The Policing of Families* (Pantheon Books, 1st American ed, 1979)

Dougherty, Joyce, 'Women's Violence Against Their Children: A Feminist Perspective' (1993) 4(2) *Women and Criminal Justice* 91

Douglas, Mary, *Natural Symbols: Explorations in Cosmology* (Cresset Press, 1970)

Downes, David and Paul Rock, *Understanding Deviance* (Oxford University Press, 2003)

Durkheim, Emile, *The Rules of Sociological Method* (Free Press of Glencoe, 1962)

Easteal, P W, 'Battered Woman Syndrome: Misunderstood?' (1992) 3(3) *Current Issues in Criminal Justice* 356

Edwards, Susan S M, 'Neither Bad nor Mad: The Female Violent Offender Reassessed' (1986) 9(1) *Women's Studies International Forum* 79

Eekalaar, J, 'The Emergence of Children's Rights' in H D Krause (ed), *Child Law* (Dartmouth Publishing, 1992)

Eliade, Mircea, *Myth and Reality* (William R Trask trans, Harper & Row, 1963)

Eliade, Mircea, *Myths, Dreams and Mysteries: The Encounter Between Contemporary Faiths and Archaic Realities* (Philip Mairet trans, Harper & Row, first published 1957, 1960) [trans of: *Mythes, Rêves et Mystères* (first published 1960)]

Ellinger, E P and K J Keith, 'Legal Research: Techniques and Ideas' 10 (1979) *Victoria University of Wellington Law Review* 1

Elliot, Alistair, *Euripides: Medea* (Chameleon Press, 1992)

Elshtain, Jean Bethke (ed), *The Family in Political Thought* (University of Massachusetts Press, 1982)

Emery, John L, Enid F Gilbert and Frederick Zugibe, 'Three Crib Deaths, A Babyminder and Probable Infanticide' (1988) 28(3) *Medicine, Science and the Law* 205

Esteal, W, 'Battered Woman Syndrome: Misunderstood?' (1992) 3(3) *Current Issues in Criminal Justice* 356

Ericson, Richard Victor and Kevin D Haggerty, *Policing the Risk Society* (University of Toronto Press, 1997)

Euripides, *Heracles and Other Plays* (John Davie trans, Penguin Books, 1963)

Euripides, *Medea* (online) (E P Coleridge trans, ebooks@Adelaide, last updated 28 August 2010) at Ebooks@Adelaide http://ebooks.adelaide.edu.au/e/euripides/medea

Euripides, *Medea and Other Plays* (Philip Vallacott trans, Penguin Books, 1963)

Ewing, Charles Patrick, *Fatal Families: The Dynamics of Intrafamilial Homicide* (Sage, 1997)

Family and Parenting Institute Briefing Paper (United Kingdom), *Commercialisation and Sexualisation of Childhood* (June 2011) www.gov.uk/government/publications/letting-children-be-children-report-of-an-independent-review-of-the-commercialisation-and-sexualisation-of-childhood

Faubion, J D (ed), *Michel Foucault: Power: Essential works of Foucault 1954–1984, volume 3* (Penguin, 1994)

Findlay, Mark, 'The Ambiguity of Accountability: Deaths in Custody and the Regulation of Police Power' (1994) 6(2) *Current Issues in Criminal Justice* 234

Findlay, Mark and Sylvia Ntube Ngane, 'Sham of the Moral Court?' (Sydney Law School Research Paper No. 11/10, 1 February 2011) http://ssrn.com/abstract=1753319

Findlay, Mark, Uglješa Zvekic and United Nations Interregional Crime and Justice Research Institute, *Alternative Policing Styles: Cross-Cultural Perspectives* (Kluwer Law and Taxation, 1993)

Fison, Lorimer and A W Howitt, *Kamilaroi and Kurnai: Group-Marriage and Relationship, and Marriage by Elopement* (Anthropological Publications, 1967)

Fitzpatrick, Peter, *The Mythology of Modern Law* (Routledge, 1992)

Fleming, Chris, *René Girard: Violence and Mimesis, Key Contemporary Thinkers* (Polity Press, 2004)

Foucault, Michel, *Discipline and Punish: The Birth of the Prison* (Alan Sheridan trans, Penguin Books, 1977) [trans of: *Surveiller et punir: Naissance de la prison* (first published 1975)]

Foucault, Michel, *Madness and Civilization: A History of Insanity in the Age of Reason* (Richard Howard trans, Tavistock, 1965)

Foucault, Michel, *The History of Sexuality, Volume 1: An Introduction* (Penguin, 1981)

Fox, Richard G, 'New Crimes or New Responses? Future Directions in Australian Criminal Law' (2002) 28(1) *Monash University Law Review* 103

Frazer, James George, *The Golden Bough: A New Abridgement* (Oxford University Press, first published 1994, 2009 ed)

Freeman, M D A, 'Freedom and the Welfare State: Child-Rearing, Parental Autonomy and State Intervention' (1983) *Journal of Social Welfare Law* 70

Freeman, M D A, 'Towards a Critical Theory of Family Law' (1985) 38 *Current Legal Problems* 153

French, Phillip and Rosemary Kayess, 'Deadly Currents Beneath Calm Waters: Persons with Disability and the Right to Life in Australia' in Luke Clements and Janet Read (eds), *Disabled People and the Right to Life: The Protection and Violation of Disabled People's Most Basic Human Rights* (Routledge, 2008)

Friedman, Susan Hatters, Sarah McCue Horwitz and Phillip J Resnick, 'Child Murder by Mothers: A Critical Analysis of the Current State of Knowledge and a Research Agenda' (2005) 162(9) *American Journal of Psychiatry* 1578

Gammell, Caroline and Lucy Cockcroft, 'Starved Girl Khyra Ishaq Failed by Social Services', *Telegraph* (online), 25 February 2010 www.telegraph.co.uk/news/uknews/crime/7318878/Starved-girl-Khyra-Ishaq-failed-by-social-services.html

Ganem, Natasha M and Robert Agnew, 'Parenthood and Adult Criminal Offending: The Importance of Relationship Quality' (2007) 35 *Journal of Criminal Justice* 630

Gardner, Christine Anne, 'Postpartum Depression Defense: Are Mothers Getting Away With Murder?' (1990) 24 *New England Law Review* 953

Garland, David, 'Frameworks of Inquiry in the Sociology of Punishment' (1980) 41(1) *British Journal of Sociology* 1

Garland, David, 'Perspectives on Punishment' (1991) 14 *Crime and Justice* 115

Garland, David, *Punishment and Modern Society: A Study in Social Theory* (University of Chicago Press, 1900)

Garland, David and Peter Young (eds), *The Power to Punish: Contemporary Penality and Social Analysis* (Humanities Press, 1983)

George, S M, 'Female Infanticide in Tamil Nadu, India: From Recognition Back to Denial?' (1997) 5(10) *Reproductive Health Matters* 124

Geyer-Kordesch, J., 'Infanticide and the Erotic Plot: A Feminist Reading of Eighteenth-Century Crime' in M Jackson (ed), *Infanticide: Historical Perspectives on Child Murder and Concealment, 1550–2000* (Ashgate, 2002)

Girard, René, *A Theater of Envy: William Shakespeare*, Carthage reprint (St. Augustine's Press, 2004)

Girard, René, *The Scapegoat* (Johns Hopkins University Press, 1986)

Girard, René, *Violence and the Sacred* (Johns Hopkins University Press, 1977)

Girard, René and Mark Rogin Anspach, *Oedipus Unbound: Selected Writings on Rivalry And Desire* (Stanford University Press, 2004)

Girard, René and Robert Doran, *Mimesis and Theory: Essays on Literature and Criticism, 1953–2005, Cultural Memory in the Present* (Stanford University Press, 2008)

Girard, René, Jean-Michel Oughourlian and Guy Lefort, *Things Hidden Since the Foundation of the World* (Stanford University Press, 1987)

Goetting, Ann, 'When Parents Kill Their Young Children: Detroit 1982–1986' (1988) 3(4) *Journal of Family Violence* 339

Goffman, Erving, *Asylums: Essays on the Social Situation of Mental Patients and Other Inmates* (Anchor Books, 1st ed, 1961)

Goffman, Erving, *Frame Analysis* (Harvard University Press, 1974)

Goffman, Erving, 'The Interaction Order' (1983) 48 *American Sociological Review* 1

Goffman, Erving, *The Presentation of Self in Everyday Life* (Penguin, first published 1959, 1990 ed)

Gold, Penny Schine, *The Lady and the Virgin: Image, Attitude and Experience in Twelfth-Century France* (University of Chicago Press, 1985)

Golsan, Richard Joseph, *René Girard and Myth: An Introduction*, *Theorists of Myth* (Garland, 1993)

Gondolf, Edward W and Ellen R Fisher, *Battered Women as Survivors: An Alternative to Treating Learned Helplessness* (Lexington Books, 1988)

Goode, Eric and Nachman Ben-Yehuda, 'Moral Panics: An Introduction' in *Moral Panics: The Social Construction of Deviance* (Blackwell, 1994)

Goodrich, Peter, *Languages of Law: From Logics to Memory to Nomadic Masks* (Weidenfeld & Nicolson, 1990)

Goodwin, Sarah McKim Webster and Elisabeth Bronfen, *Death and Representation*, Parallax (Johns Hopkins University Press, 1993)

Goodwin, Susan and Joanne Finkelstein, *The Sociological Bent: Inside Metro Culture* (Thomson, 2005)

Gordon, A, 'Murder Most Foul', *Daily Telegraph Mirror* (Australia), 24 July 1995

Gordon, C (ed), *Michel Foucault: Power/Knowledge: Selected Interviews and Other Writings, 1972–1977* (Harvester Press, 1980)

Grant, R, 'Mother of All Crimes', *Sydney Morning Herald* (New South Wales), 11 March 1995

Haimes, E, 'Embodied Spaces, Social Places and Bourdieu: Locating and Dislocating the Child in Family Relationships' (2003) 9(1) *Body & Society* 11

Halder, Peter, 'Myth-Understood' (Spring 1994) 5(1) *Law and Critique* 113

Hall, Louise, 'New Powers for Police in Domestic Violence Cases', *Sydney Morning Herald* (online), 28 November 2008 www.smh.com.au/news/national/new-powers-for-police-in-domestic-violence-cases/2008/11/27/1227491735577.html

Hall, Timothy, *Wanted: A Casebook of Unsolved Crimes of Violence in Australia* (Angus & Robertson, 1976)

Hanawalt, Barbara, 'The Female Felon in Fourteenth-Century England' (1974) 5 *Viator* 253

Hanneman, R and S Patrick, 'On the Uses of Computer-Assisted Simulation Modeling in the Social Sciences' (1997) 2(2) *Sociological Research Online* www.socresonline.org.uk/2/2/5.html

Hargrave, D R and D P Warner, 'A Study of Child Homicide Over Two Decades' (1992) 32(3) *Medicine, Science and the Law* 247

Hasche, A, 'Sex Discrimination in Child Custody Determinations' (1989) 3 *Australian Journal of Family Law* 218

Hayes, Hennessey and Tim Prenzler, *An Introduction to Crime and Criminology* (Pearson Education Australia, 2009)

Heidensohn, F, *Women and Crime* (Macmillan, 1985)

Helmholz, R H, 'Infanticide in the Province of Canterbury during the Fifteenth Century' (1975) 2 *History of Childhood Quarterly* 379

Hénaff, Marcel, 'Lévi-Strauss and the Question of Symbolism' in Boris Wiseman (ed), *The Cambridge Companion to Lévi-Strauss* (Cambridge, 2009)

Higgins, Daryl and Rae Kaspiew, 'Child Protection and Family Law . . . Joining the Dots' (National Child Protection Clearinghouse Issues Paper No. 34, May 2011)

Higgins, Daryl and Rae Kaspiew, '"Mind the Gap . . .": Protecting Children in Family Law Cases' (2008) 22(3) *Australian Journal of Family Law* 235

Hine, H M (ed), *Seneca: Medea* (Aris & Phillips, 2000)

Hippocrates, *On the Sacred Disease* (Francis Adams trans, Internet Classics Archive) http://classics.mit.edu//Hippocrates/sacred.html

Hoffer, Peter C and N E H Hull, *Murdering Mothers: Infanticide in England and New England 1558–1803* (New York University Press, 1981)

Hoffman, Eva, 'Home as Concentration Camp', *New York Times* (online), 17 October 1999 www.nytimes.com/books/99/10/17/reviews/991017.17hoffmat.html

Holub, Renate, *Antonio Gramsci: Beyond Marxism and Postmodernism* (Routledge, 1992)

Hopwood, John S, 'Child Murder and Insanity' (1927) 73 *Journal of Mental Science* 95

Houston, Stan and Huw Griffiths, 'Reflections on Risk in Child Protection: Is It Time for a Shift in Paradigms?' (2000) 5 *Child and Family Social Work* 1

Huckerby, Jayne, 'Women Who Kill Their Children: Case Study and Conclusions Concerning the Differences in the Fall From Maternal Grace by Khoua Her and Andrea Yates' (2003) 10(147) *Duke Journal of Gender Law & Policy* 149

Humphreys, C, *Domestic Violence and Child Protection: Challenging Directions for Practice* (Issue Paper 13, Australian Domestic and Family Violence Clearinghouse Sydney, 2007)

Hunt, A, 'Postmodernism and Critical Criminology' in B D McLean and D Milovanovic (eds), *New Directions in Critical Criminology* (Collective Press, 1991)

Hunter, William, 'On the Uncertainty of the Signs of Murder, in the Case of Bastard Children' (1784) 6 *Medical Observations and Inquiries by a Society of Physicians in London* 266

Husain, Arshad and Anasseril Daniel, 'A Comparative Study of Filicidal and Abusive Mothers' (1984) 29 *Canadian Journal of Psychiatry* 596

Hutchinson, Terry, *Researching and Writing in Law* (Lawbook, 2nd ed, 2006)

Hyde, Alan, *Bodies of Law* (Princeton University Press, 1997)

Iyengar, Radha, 'Does the Certainty of Arrest Reduce Domestic Violence? Evidence from Mandatory and Recommended Arrest Laws' (Working Paper 13186, National Bureau of Economic Research, 2007) www.nber.org/papers/w13186

Jackson, Louise, 'Witches, Wives and Mothers: Witchcraft Persecution and Women's Confessions in Seventeenth-century England' (1995) 4(1) *Women's History Review* 63

Jackson, Mark, 'Infanticide: Historical Perspectives' (1996) 146(6736) *New Law Journal* 416

Jackson, Mark (ed), *Infanticide: Historical Perspectives on Child Murder and Concealment 1550–2000* (Ashgate, 2002)

Jackson, Mark, *Newborn Child Murder: Women, Illegitimacy, and the Courts in Eighteenth-Century England* (Manchester University Press, 1996)

Jacobs, J W, 'Euripides' Medea: A Psychodynamic Model of Severe Divorce Pathology' (1988) 42(2) *American Journal of Psychotherapy* 308

Jarrell, Randall, 'On Preparing to Read Kipling' in E Gilbert (ed), *Kipling and the Critics* (New York University Press, 1963)

Jason, Janine, 'Centers for Disease Control and the Epidemiology of Violence' (1984) 8 *Child Abuse & Neglect* 279

Jensen, Vickie and Jill DuDeck-Biondo, 'Mothers in Jail: Gender, Social Control, and the Construction of Parenthood Behind Bars' in Stacy Lee Burns (ed), *Ethnographies of Law and Social Control* (Emerald, 2005)

Johnson, Carolyn Harris, *Come With Daddy: Child Murder-Suicide After Family Breakdown* (University of Western Australia Press, 2005)

Johnson, Carolyn Harris, 'Familicide and Family Law: A Study of Filicide-Suicide Following Separation' (2006) 44 *Family Court Review* 448

Jones, Ann, *Women Who Kill* (Holt, Rinehart & Winston, 1980)

Jung, Carl, *Aspects of the Masculine* (R F C Hull trans, Routledge, 2003 [first published 1989])

Kaplun, David and Robert Reich, 'The Murdered Child and His Killers' (1976) 133(7) *American Journal of Psychiatry* 809

Karam, Joe, *David and Goliath: The Bain Family Murders* (Reed Books, 1997)

Kavanagh, Thomas M, *The Limits of Theory* (Stanford University Press, 1989)

Kellum, Barbara A, 'Infanticide in England in the Later Middle Ages' (1974) 1(3) *History of Childhood Quarterly* 367

Kemshall, Hazel, *Understanding Risk in Criminal Justice* (Open University Press, 2003)

Kenny, Mary, 'The Best Mothers Don't Have to Be Clever', *Telegraph* (online) (UK), 1 June 2009 www.telegraph.co.uk/comment/personal-view/5419796/The-best-mothers-dont-have-to-be-clever.html

Kevelson, Roberta, *The Law as a System of Signs* (Plenum Press, 1988)

King, Roy D and Emma Wincup (eds), *Doing Research on Crime and Justice* (Oxford University Press, 2000)

Kirk, G S, *Myth: Its Meaning and Functions in Ancient and Other Cultures* (Cambridge University Press, 1970)

Kitsuse, John, 'Societal Reaction to Deviant Behaviour: Problems of Theory and Method' (1962) *Social Problems* 247

Koch, Andrew M, *Knowledge and Social Construction* (Lexington Books, 2005)

Kramer, Kirsten Johnson and William D Watson, 'The Insanities of Reproduction: Medico-Legal Knowledge and the Development of Infanticide Law' (2006) 15(2) *Social and Legal Studies* 237

Krane, Julia and Linda Davies, 'Mothering and Child Protection Practice: Rethinking Risk Assessment' (2000) 5 *Child and Family Social Work* 35

Krause, Harry D (ed), *Child Law: Parent, Child and State* (Dartmouth Publishing, 1992)

Krishnaswamy, S, 'A Note on Female Infanticide: An Anthropological Inquiry' (1984) 45(3) *Indian Journal of Social Work* 297

Kunz, Jenifer and Stephen J Bahr, 'A Profile of Parental Homicide Against Children' (1996) 11(4) *Journal of Family Violence* 347

Laclau, Ernesto, and Chantal Mouffe, 'Post-Marxism without Apologies' (1987) 166 *New Left Review* 79

Laing, L, *Children, Young People and Domestic Violence* (Issue Paper 2, Australian Domestic and Family Violence Clearinghouse Sydney, 2000)

Lamont, Alister and Leah Bromfield, 'History of Child Protection Services' (National Child Protection Clearinghouse Resource Sheet, Australian Institute of Family Studies, October 2010)

Langer, William L, 'Infanticide: A Historical Survey' (1974) 1(3) *History of Childhood Quarterly* 353

Lansdowne, Robyn and Wendy Bacon, 'Women Homicide Offenders and Police Interrogation' in Mark Findlay, Sandra J Egger and Jeff Sutton (eds), *Issues in Criminal Justice Administration* (George Allen & Unwin, 1983) 53

Lansdowne, Robyn and Wendy Bacon, *Women Homicide Offenders in NSW: Feminist Legal Action Group Report* (Feminist Legal Action Group, 1982)

Laster, Kathy, 'Infanticide and Feminist Criminology: "Strong" or "Weak" Women?' (1990) 2 *Criminology Australia* 14

Lee, James Z and Wang Feng, *One Quarter of Humanity: Malthusian Mythology and Chinese Realities, 1700–2000* (Harvard University Press, 1999)

Lemert, Edwin M, *Social Pathology: A Systematic Approach to the Theory of Sociopathic Behaviour* (McGraw-Hill, 1951)

Lerner, Gerda, *The Creation of Feminist Consciousness: From the Middle Ages to Eighteen-Seventy* (Oxford University Press, 1993)

Lerner, Gerda, *The Creation of Patriarchy* (Oxford University Press, 1986)

Leveillee, Suzanne, Jacques D Marleau and Myriam Dube, 'Filicide: A Comparison by Sex and Presence or Absence of Self-destructive Behaviour' (2007) 22 *Journal of Family Violence* 287

Li, Lillian M, 'Life and Death in a Chinese Famine: Infanticide as a Demographic Consequence of the 1935 Yellow River Flood' (1991) 33(3)(July) *Comparative Studies in Society and History* 466

Little, Craig B, *Deviance and Control: Theory, Research, and Social Policy* (Peacock, 3rd ed, 1995)

Lock, Joan, 'Carers Who Kill Are Nothing New' (1995) 145(6699) *New Law Journal* 870

Lowenstein, Ludwig F, 'Infanticide: A Crime of Desperation' (1997) 21(2) *The Criminologist* 81

McCallum, David, 'Coercive Normalization and Family Policing: The Limits of the "Psy-Complex" in Australian Penal Systems' (2007) 16(1) *Social and Legal Studies* 113

McKee, Geoffrey R, *Why Mothers Kill: A Forensic Psychologist Casebook* (Oxford University Press, 2006)

McKenna, R William and J Claude Evans (eds), *Derrida and Phenomenology* (Dordrecht; Boston: Kluwer Academic, 1995)

McKeon, M, 'Historicizing Patriarchy: The Emergence of Gender Difference in England, 1660–1760' (1995) 28(3) *Eighteenth-Century Studies* 295

MacKinnon, C A, 'Feminism, Marxism, Method, and the State: Toward Feminist Jurisprudence' (1983) 8(4) *Signs* 635

MacKinnon, C A, *Towards a Feminist Theory of the State* (Harvard University Press, 1989)

Maher, Lisa, 'Punishment and Welfare: Crack Cocaine and the Regulation of Mothering' (1992) 3 *Women and Criminal Justice* 35

Maier-Katkin, Daniel, 'A Rationale for Infanticide Laws' (December 1993) *Criminal Law Review* 903

Manning, Peter, 'Theorizing Policing: The Drama and Myth of Crime Control in the NYPD' (2001) 5(3) *Theoretical Criminology* 315

Marland, Hilary, 'Getting Away with Murder? Puerperal Insanity, Infanticide and the Defence Plea' in M Jackson (ed), *Infanticide: Historical Perspectives on Child Murder and Concealment, 1550–2000* (Ashgate, 2002)

Marland, Hilary, 'Under the Shadow of Maternity: Birth, Death and Puerperal Insanity in Victorian Britain' (2012) 23(1) *History of Psychiatry* 78

Marleau, Jacques D, Bernard Poulin, Thierry Webanck, Renée Royand and Line Laporte, 'Paternal Filicide: A Study of 10 Men' (1999) 44 *Canadian Journal of Psychiatry* 57

Mastronarde, Donald (ed), *Euripides: Medea* (Cambridge University Press, 2002)

Mead, George Herbert, *Mind, Self & Society from the Standpoint of a Social Behaviorist* (University of Chicago Press, 1934)

Meagher, Robert Emmet, *Herakles Gone Mad: Rethinking Heroism in an Age of Endless War* (Olive Branch Press, 2006)

Mills, L G, 'Mandatory Arrest and Prosecution Policies for Domestic Violence: A Critical Literature Review and the Case for More Research to Test Victim Empowerment Approaches' (1998) 25(3) *Criminal Justice and Behaviour* 306

Milner, L S, *Hardness of Heart/Hardness of Life: The Stain of Human Infanticide* (University Press of America, 2000)

Mirk, John, *Instructions for Parish Priests* (Lund: Gleerup, 1974)

Mnookin, R H, 'Child-Custody Adjudication: Judicial Functions in the Face of Indeterminacy' (1975) 39 *Law and Contemporary Problems* 226

Moloney, Lawrie, Bruce Smyth and Ruth Weston, *Allegations of Family Violence and Child Abuse in Family Law Children's Proceedings: A Pre-Reform Exploratory Study* (Research Report No 15, Melbourne: Australian Institute of Family Studies, 2007) https://aifs.gov.au/publications/allegations-family-violence-and-child-abuse-family-law-childrens-proceedi

Morgan, Bronwen and Karen Yeung, *An Introduction to Law and Regulation* (Cambridge University Press, 2009)

Morgan, Jenny, *Who Kills Whom and Why: Looking Beyond Legal Categories* (Victoria Law Reform Commission, 2002)

Morris, Allison and Ania Wilczynski, 'Parents Who Kill Their Children' (January 1993) *Criminal Law Review* 31

Moscovici, Serge, *Social Representations: Explorations in Social Psychology* (New York University Press, 2001)

Moseley, Kathryn L, 'The History of Infanticide in Western Society' (1986) 1 *Issues in Law and Medicine* 345

Mouzos, Jenny, *Homicidal Encounters: A Study of Homicide in Australia 1989–1999*, Australian Institute of Criminology Research and Public Policy Series No. 28 (Australian Institute of Criminology, 2000)

Mouzos, Jenny and C Rushforth, *Family Homicide in Australia* (Research report, Australian Institute of Criminology Trends and Issues in Criminal Justice No. 255, Canberra: Australia Institute of Criminology, 2003)

Muncie, John (ed), 'The Beatles and the Spectacle of Youth' in Ian Inglis (ed) *The Beatles, Popular Music and Society: A Thousand Voices* (Palgrave Macmillan, 2000)

Myers, Steven A, 'The Child Slayer: A 25-Year Survey of Homicides Involving Preadolescent Victims' (1967) 17 *Archives of General Psychiatry* 211

Nash, Kate (ed), *Readings in Political Sociology* (Blackwell 2000)

New South Wales Child Death Review Team, *Annual Report 2009* (New South Wales Child Death Review Team, 2010) www.ombo.nsw.gov.au/news-and-publications/publications/annual-reports/nsw-child-death-review

New South Wales Child Death Review Team, *The Fatal Assault of Children and Young People* (New South Wales Commission for Children and Young People, 2002) www.parliament.nsw.gov.au/committees/inquiries/Pages/inquiry-details.aspx?pk=1698#tab-reports

New South Wales Department of Community Services, *Children Services Directorate: Strategic Compliance Monitoring and Enforcement Framework* (New South Wales Department of Community Services, 2008) www.opengov.nsw.gov.au/download/11982

New South Wales Health, *Domestic Violence Policy and Procedures for Identifying and Responding to Domestic Violence* (New South Wales Department of Health, 2003)

New South Wales Law Reform Commission, *Partial Defences to Murder: Provocation and Infanticide Report 83* (New South Wales Law Reform Commission, 1997)

New South Wales Ombudsman, *Report of Reviewable Deaths in 2005 Volume 2: Child Deaths* (New South Wales Ombudsman, 2006)

New South Wales Ombudsman, *Report of Reviewable Deaths in 2006 Volume 2: Child Deaths* (New South Wales Ombudsman, 2007)

New South Wales Ombudsman, *Reviewable Deaths Annual Report 2003–2004: An Overview* (New South Wales Ombudsman, 2004)

Nicolson, Donald, 'Truth, Reason and Justice: Epistemology and Politics in Evidence Discourse' (1994) 57(5) *The Modern Law Review* 726

Nielssen, Olav, Matthew Large, Bruce Westmore and Steven Lackersteen, 'Child Homicide in New South Wales from 1991 to 2005' (2009) 190(1) *Medical Journal of Australia* 7

Oberman, Michelle, 'Mothers Who Kill: Coming to Terms with Modern American Infanticide' (2004) 8 *DePaul Journal of Health Care Law* 3

Oberman, Michelle, 'Understanding Infanticide in Context: Mothers Who Kill 1870–1930 and Today' (2002) 92 *Journal of Criminal Law & Criminology* 707

O'Donovan, Katherine, *Sexual Divisions in Law* (Weidenfeld & Nicolson, 1985)

O'Donovan, Katherine, 'The Medicalisation of Infanticide' (1984) *Criminal Law Review* 259

O'Malley, Pat, *Crime and Risk* (Sage, 2010)

Oxford English Dictionary of Current English (Oxford University Press, 1996)

Pagelow, M D, *Family Violence* (Praeger, 1984)

Pakrasi, Kanti B, *Female Infanticide in India* (Calcutta, Editions Indian, 1970)

Papadopoulou, Thalia, *Heracles and Euripidean Tragedy* (Cambridge University Press, 2005)

Parker, Elizabeth and Frances Good, 'Infanticide' (1981) 5(2–3) *Law and Human Behaviour* 237

Parshley, H M (ed), *Simone de Beauvoir: The Second Sex* (Vintage, 1997)

Partnerships Against Domestic Violence, *Practice Standards for Working with Children and Young People Who Have Lived with Domestic Violence* (Brisbane: Family, Youth and Community Care, 1999)

Pattullo, P, *Judging Women* (National Council for Civil Liberties, 1983)

Peelo, Moira, Brian Francis, Keith Soothill, Jayn Pearson and Elizabeth Ackerley, 'Newspaper Reporting and the Public Construction of Homicide' (2004) 44 *British Journal of Criminology* 256

Pollard, Ruth, 'Despite Her Cries for Help, Evelina Was Left to Die', *Sydney Morning Herald* (online), 24 November 2008 www.smh.com.au/news/national/despite-all-her-cries-for-help-evelina-was-left-to-die/2008/11/23/1227375062487.html

Pollock, Griselda, *Vision and Difference: Femininity, Feminism, and Histories of Art* (Routledge, 1988)

Pomeroy, Sarah B, *Goddesses, Whores, Wives, and Slaves: Women in Classical Antiquity* (Schocken Books, 1975)

Powell, Barry B, *Classical Myths* (Pearson Education, 5th ed, 2007)

Preston, James, *Mother Worship: Theme and Variations* (University of North Carolina Press, 1982)

Rabin, D, 'Bodies of Evidence, States of Mind: Infanticide, Emotion and Sensibility in Eighteenth-Century England' in M Jackson (ed), *Infanticide: Historical Perspectives on Child Murder and Concealment, 1550–2000* (Ashgate, 2002)

Rao, Nandini, 'Interpreting Silences: Symbol and History in the Case of Ram Janmabhoomi/Babri Masjid' in George Clement Bond and Angela Gilliam (eds), *Social Construction of the Past: Representations as Power* (Routledge, 1994)

Rapaport, Elizabeth, 'Mad Women and Desperate Girls: Infanticide and Child Murder in Law and Myth' (2006) XXXIII *Fordham Urban Law Journal* 527

Reder, Peter and Sylvia Duncan, 'Closure, Covert Warnings and Escalating Child Abuse' (1995) 19(12) *Child Abuse & Neglect* 1517

Reder, Peter and Sylvia Duncan, 'Conflictual Relationships and Risks of Child Abuse' (1999) 6 *Journal of Child Centred Practice* 127

Reder, Peter and Sylvia Duncan, *Lost Innocents: A Follow-Up Study of Fatal Child Abuse* (Routledge, 1999)

Reder, Peter, Sylvia Duncan and Moira Gray, *Beyond Blame: Child Abuse Tragedies Revisited* (Routledge, 1993)

Reece, Laura E, 'Mothers Who Kill: Postpartum Disorders and Criminal Infanticide' (1991) 38 *UCLA Law Review* 699

Resnick, Phillip J, 'Child Murder by Parents: A Psychiatric Review of Filicide' (1969) 126(3) *American Journal of Psychiatry* 325

Resnick, Phillip J, 'Murder of the Newborn: A Psychiatric Review of Neonaticide' (1970) 126(10) *American Journal of Psychiatry* 1414

Rhodes, R A W 'The New Governance: Governing Without Government' (1996) XLIV *Political Studies* 652

Ritchie, Jean, *Myra Hindley: Inside the Mind of a Murderess* (Bay Books, 1988)

Robinson, Georgina, 'Woman and Baby Found Dead in Home', *Sydney Morning Herald* (online), 31 January 2011 www.smh.com.au/nsw/woman-and-baby-found-dead-in-home-20110131-1aapo.html

Ronald, N Giere, 'How Models Are Used to Represent Reality' (2004) 71(5) *Philosophy of Science* 742 www.jstor.org/stable/10.1086/425063

Rorty, Richard, *Contingency, Irony and Solidarity* (Cambridge University Press, 1989)

Rose, Nikolas S, 'Beyond the Public/Private Division: Law, Power and the Family' (1987) 14(1) *Journal of Law and Society* 61

Rose, Nikolas S, *Governing the Soul: The Shaping of the Private Self* (Routledge, 1990)

Rose, Nikolas S, *Powers of Freedom: Reframing Political Thought* (Cambridge University Press, 1999)

Rutherford, Leslie and Sheila Bone (eds), *Osborn's Concise Law Dictionary* (Sweet & Maxwell, 8th ed, 1993)

Sampson, Rana, John E Eckand, Jessica Dunham, 'Super Controllers and Crime Prevention: A Routine Activity Explanation of Crime Prevention Success and Failure' (2010) 23(1) *Security Journal* 37

Scheff, Thomas J, *Being Mentally Ill: A Sociological Theory* (Aldine, 2nd ed, 1984)

Schmitt, Carl, *The Leviathan in the State Theory of Thomas Hobbes: Meaning and Failure of a Political Symbol* (George Schwab and Erna Hilfstein trans, University of Chicago Press, 2008) [trans of: *Leviathan in der Staatslehre des Thomas Hobbes* (first published 1938)]

Schram, Pamela J, 'An Exploratory Study: Stereotypes About Mothers in Prison' (1999) 25(5) *Journal of Criminal Justice* 411

Schur, Edwin M, *Labeling Deviant Behavior: Its Sociological Implications* (Harper & Row Monograph Series in Sociology, 1971)

Schur, Edwin M, *Labeling Women Deviant: Gender, Stigma, and Social Control* (McGraw-Hill, 1983)

Schwartz, Lita Linzer and Natalie K Isser, *Child Homicide: Parents Who Kill* (Taylor & Francis, CRC Press, 2007)

Scott, P D, 'Parents Who Kill Their Children' (1973) 13(2) *Medicine, Science, and the Law* 120

Scraton, Phil, *Law, Order and the Authoritarian State: Readings in Critical Criminology* (Open University Press, 1987)

Seaborne, Davis D, 'Child Killing in English Law' (1937) 1 *Modern Law Review* 203

Shaw, B D, 'The Family in Late Antiquity: The Experience of Augustine' (1987) 115 *Past and Present* 3

Shengold, Leonard, *Soul Murder Revisited: Thoughts about Therapy, Hate, Love and Memory* (Yale University Press, 1999)

Sherman, Lawrence W, 'Attacking Crime: Policing and Crime Control' in M Tonry and N Morris (eds), *Modern Policing* (University of Chicago, 1992)

Sherman, Lawrence W, 'Policing for Crime Prevention' in L W Sherman *et al*, *Preventing Crime: What Works, What Doesn't, and What's Promising* (National Institute of Justice, 1997)

Sherman, Lawrence W, Janell D Schmidt, Dennis P Rogan, Douglas A Smith, Patrick R Gartin, Ellen G Cohn, Dean J Collins and Anthony R Bacich, 'The Variable Effects of Arrest on Criminal Careers: The Milwaukee Domestic Violence Experiment' (1992) 83 *Journal of Criminal Law and Criminology* 137

Shoemaker, Donald J, *Theories of Delinquency: An Examination of Explanations of Delinquent Behaviour* (Oxford University Press, 2005)

Silverman, Robert and Leslie Kennedy, 'Women Who Kill Their Children' (1988) 3(2) *Violence and Victims* 113

Silverman, Robert A and Marc Riedel, 'Murdered Children: A Comparison of Racial Differences Across Two Jurisdictions' (1990) 18 *Journal of Criminal Justice* 401

Singer, Peter, *Practical Ethics* (Cambridge University Press, 2nd ed, 1993)

Sim, Janice, 'Loving Fathers? Implications of State Intervention' (2009) 28(2) *University of Tasmania Law Review* 242

Smart, Carol, 'Disruptive Bodies and Unruly Sex: The Regulation of Reproduction and Sexuality in the Nineteenth Century' in Carol Smart (ed), *Regulating Womanhood: Historical Essays on Marriage, Motherhood and Sexuality* (Routledge, 1992)

Smart, Carol, *Law, Crime and Sexuality* (Sage, 1995)
Smart, Carol, 'Wishful Thinking and Harmful Tinkering? Sociological Reflections on Family Policy' in Cheryl Albers (ed), *Sociology of Families* (Pine Forge Press, 1999)
Smithey, Martha, 'Infant Homcide: Victim/Offender Relationship and Causes of Death' (1998) 13(3) *Journal of Family Violence* 285
Social Policy Research Centre, Report for the Australian Government, Attorney-General's Department, *Shared Care Parenting Arrangement since the 2006 Family Law Reforms* (May 2010)
Somander, K H Lis and Lennart M Rammer, 'Intra-and-Extrafamilial Child Homicide in Sweden 1971–1980' (1991) 15 *Child Abuse & Neglect* 45
South Australian Department of Families and Communities, *Keeping Them Safe Reform Program* (Adelaide, Department of Families and Communities, 2004)
Spinelli, Margaret G, 'A Systematic Investigation of 16 Cases of Neonaticide' (2001) 158(5) *American Journal of Psychiatry* 811
Spinelli, Margaret G, 'Maternal Infanticide Associated with Mental Illness: Prevention and the Promise of Saved Lives' (2004) 161(9) *American Journal of Psychiatry* 1548
Stanley, Nick, Pam Miller, Helen Richardson-Foster and Gill Thomson, 'A Stop–Start Response: Social Services' Interventions with Children and Families Notified following Domestic Violence Incidents' (2011) 41 *British Journal of Social Work* 296
Stanton, Josephine and Alexander Simpson, 'Filicide: A Review' (2002) 25 *International Journal of Law and Psychiatry* 1
Stephens, Amanda, 'Truth and Uncertainty in "Shaken Baby Syndrome" cases: Law vs Science?' (Paper presented at the University of Sydney Postgraduate Law Students Conference: Law, Life and Death, University of Sydney, 31 October 2008).
Stern, Edward, 'The Medea Complex: The Mother's Homicidal Wishes to Her Child' (1948) 94(395) *Journal of Mental Science* 321
Strang, Heather, 'Child Abuse Homicides in Australia: Incidence, Circumstances, Prevention and Control' in D Chappell and S Egger (eds), *Australian Violence: Contemporary Perspectives II* (Australian Institute of Criminology, 1995)
Strang, Heather, 'Children as Victims of Homicide' (Australian Institute of Criminology, March 1996)
Street, John, 'Celebrity Politicians: Popular Culture and Political Representation' (2004) 6 *British Journal of Politics and International Relations* 435
Stubbs, Julie, 'Battered Woman Syndrome: An Advance for Women or Further Evidence of the Legal System's Inability to Comprehend Women's Experience?' (1991) 3(2) *Current Issues in Criminal Justice* 267
Stubbs, Julie, 'The (Un)reasonable Battered Woman? A Response to Esteal' (1992) 3(3) *Current Issues in Criminal Justice* 359
Stubbs, Julie (ed), *Women, Male Violence and the Law* (Federation Press, 1994)
Sullivan, Mark, '"More Popular than Jesus": The Beatles and the Religious Far Right' (1987) 6(3) *Popular Music* 313
Summers, Anne, *Damned Whores and God's Police* (Penguin, 2nd ed, 2002)
Summers, Anne, *The End of Equality: Work, Babies and Women's Choices in 21st-Century Australia* (Random House, 2003)
Surette, R, 'News from Nowhere, Policy to Follow: Media and the Social Construction of Three Strikes and You're Out' in D Shichor and D Sechrest (eds), *Three Strikes and You're Out: Vengeance as Public Policy* (Sage, 1996)
Sutherland, Edwin, *White Collar Crime* (Holt, Rinehart & Winston, 1961)
Synnott, Anthony, *The Body Social: Symbolism, Self and Society* (Routledge, 1993)

Teece, Michael and Toni Makkai, 'Print Media Reporting on Drugs and Crime 1995–1998' (July 2000) *Australian Institute of Criminology Trends & Issues in Crime and Criminal Justice No. 158*

Templeton, Sarah Kate, 'Doctors: Let Us Kill Disabled Babies', *The Times* (online), 5 November 2006 www.thetimes.co.uk/article/doctors-let-us-kill-disabled-babies-frghsq88919

Teubner, Gunther, *Law as an Autopoietic System* (Blackwell, 1993)

Tindale, N B, 'The Pitjandjara' in M G Bicchieri (ed), *Hunters and Gatherers Today* (Holt McDougal, 1972)

Thompson, Linda and Alexis J Walker, 'Gender in Families: Women and Men in Marriage, Work and Parenthood' (1989) 51(4) *Journal of Marriage and the Family* 845

Trocme, Nico and Duncan Lindsey, 'What Can Child Homicide Rates Tell Us About the Effectiveness of Child Welfare Services?' (1996) 20(3) *Child Abuse & Neglect* 171

Twining, William, *Law in Context: Enlarging a Discipline* (Clarendon Press, 1997)

Twining, William, *Rethinking Evidence: Exploratory Essays* (Blackwell, 1990)

Twining, William and David Miers, *How to Do Things with Rules: A Primer of Interpretation* (Cambridge University Press, 5th ed, 2010)

Ullman, Dana, 'Homeopathic Medicine: Europe's #1 Alternative for Doctors', *Huffington Post* (online), 3 March 2010 www.huffingtonpost.com/dana-ullman/homeopathic-medicine-euro_b_402490.html

Unnithan, N Prabha, 'The Processing of Homicide Cases with Child Victims: Systemic and Situational Contingencies' (1994) 22(1) *Journal of Criminal Justice* 41

Varsava, Jerry A, *Contingent Meanings: Postmodern Fiction, Mimesis and the Reader* (Florida State University Press, 1990)

VerSteegh, Nancy and Clare Dalton, 'Report from the Wingspread Conference on Domestic Violence and Family Courts' (2008) 46(3) *Family Court Review* 454

Victor, Jeffrey S, 'Moral Panics and the Social Construction of Deviant Behaviour: A Theory and Application to the Case of Ritual Child Abuse' (1998) 41(3) *Sociological Perspectives* 541

Victoria Police, *Code of Practice for the Investigation of Family Violence: Supporting and Integrative Response to Family Violence in Australia* (Victoria Police, 2017) www.police.vic.gov.au/content.asp?a=internetBridgingPage&Media_ID=132058

Victorian Government Department of Planning and Community Development, *Women's Safety* (9 September 2010) www.dpcd.vic.gov.au/women/womens-safety

Victorian Government Office of the Child Safety Commissioner, *Child Safety Policy* (State Government of Victoria Child Safety Commissioner, September 2010) www.justice.vic.gov.au/utility/about+the+department/child+safe+policy

Virueda, Marie and Jason Payne, *Homicide in Australia 2007–2008 National Homicide Monitoring Program (NHMP) Annual Report* (Australian Institute of Criminology Monitoring Reports No. 13, 2010)

Wagner, Anne, Tracey Summerfield and Farid Samir Benavides Vanegas (eds), *Contemporary Issues of the Semiotics of Law* (Hart, 2005)

Walker, Lenore, *The Battered Woman Syndrome* (Springer, 1984)

Wallace, Alison, *Homicide: The Social Reality* (New South Wales Bureau of Crime Statistics and Research, 1986)

Ward, Phil, *AZARIA! What the Jury Were Not Told* (Griffin Press, 1984)

Ward, Tony, 'The Sad Subject of Infanticide: Law, Medicine and Child Murder, 1860–1938' (1999) 8(2) *Social & Legal Studies* 163

Weatherburn, Don, 'Riots, Policing and Social Disadvantage: Learning from the Riots in Macquarie Fields and Redfern' (2006) 18(1) *Current Issues in Criminal Justice* 20

Weatherburn, Don and David Indermaur, 'Public Perceptions of Crime Trends in New South Wales and Western Australia' (Crime and Justice Bulletin No. 80, New South Wales Bureau of Crime Statistics and Research, 2004) http://search.informit.com.au/documentSummary;dn=913747370468508;res=IELHSS

Welldon, Estela V, *Mother, Madonna, Whore: The Idealization and Denigration of Motherhood* (Free Association Books, 1988)

Wells, Celia, 'Whose Baby Is It?' (1988) 15(4) *Journal of Law and Society* 323

Western Australia Department of Child Protection, *Adoption of Signs of Safety as the Department for Child Protection's Child Protection Practice Framework* (Background paper, Department of Child Protection, 20 June 2008) www.signsofsafety.net/organisations/department-for-child-protection/

Westman, B, 'The Female Felon in Fourteenth-Century England' (1974) *Viator V*, 9

Wilczynski, Ania, *Child Homicide* (Oxford University Press, 1997)

Wilczynski, Ania, 'Images of Women Who Kill Their Infants: The Mad and the Bad' (1991) 2(2) *Women and Criminal Justice* 71

Wilczynski, Ania, 'Mad or Bad? Child-Killers, Gender and the Courts' (1997) 37(3) *British Journal of Criminology* 419

Wilczynski, Ania, 'Preventing Child Homicide: A Report from the NSW Child Protection Council's Child Death Review Committee' (NSW Child Protection Council, 1995)

Wilczynski, Ania, 'Prior Agency Contact and Physical Abuse in Cases of Child Homicide' (1997) 27 *British Journal of Social Work* 241

Wilczynski, Ania, 'Risk Factors for Parental Child Homicide: Results of an English Study' (1995) 7 *Current Issues in Criminal Justice* 193

Wilczynski, Ania, 'Why Do Parents Kill Their Children?' (1994) 5 *Criminology Australia* 12

Wilkey, Ian, J Pearn, G Petrie and J Nixon, 'Neonaticide, Infanticide and Child Homicide' (1982) 22(1) *Medicine, Science and the Law* 31

Williamson, Beth, *The Madonna of Humility: Development, Dissemination and Reception, c.1340–1400* (Boydell Press, 2009)

Wilson, Paul, *Murder of the Innocents: Child Killers and Their Victims* (Rigby, 1985)

Wolfgang, Marvin E, *Studies in Homicide* (Harper & Row, 1967)

Women's Coalition Against Family Violence, *Blood on Whose Hands? The Killing of Women and Children in Domestic Homicides* (Federation Press, 1994)

Wood AO QC, James, *Report of the Special Commission of Inquiry into Child Protection Services in New South Wales* (State of NSW through the Special Commission of Inquiry into Child Protection Services in NSW, November 2008)

Wygant, Amy, *Medea, Magic and Modernity in France: Stages and Histories, 1553–1797* (Ashgate, 2007)

Yarwood, David J, 'Child Homicide: Review of Statistics and Studies' (Dewar Research, June 2004)

Yin, Robert K, *Case Study Research: Design and Methods* (Sage, 3rd ed, 2003)

Young, Jock, 'Thinking Seriously About Crime' in Mike Fitzgerald, Gregor McLennan and Jennie Pawson (eds), *Crime and Society: Readings in History and Theory* (Routledge & Kegan Paul, 1981)

Young, T R and Garth Massey, 'The Dramaturgical Society: A Macro-Analytic Approach to Dramaturgical Analysis' (1978) 1(2) *Qualitative Sociology* 78

Cases[1]

B v B: Family Law Reform Act 1995 (1997) FLC 92-755
Bowman v Secular Society Ltd [1917] AC 406
Commission for Children and Young People v V [2002] NSWSC 949
Ex parte HV McKay (*'Harvester Case'*) (1907) 2 CAR 1
Gronow v Gronow (1979) 144 CLR 513
HL v Commission for Children and Young People [2008] NSWADT 323
Jocums & Schlick and Ors [2008] FamCA 1066
McMillan v Jackson [1995] FLC 92-610
Milirrpum v Nabalco Pty Ltd (1971) 17 FLR 141
O'Donoghue (1927) 20 Cr.App.R. 132
Raby [1976] FLC 90-104
R v Albury-Thomson (1998) 16 CRNZ 79
R v Cooper [2001] NSWSC 769
R v Commission for Children and Young People [2002] NSWIRComm 101
R v Folbigg [2003] NSWSC 895
R v Hoeler [2004] NSWCCA 184
R v Hull [1997] SASC 6087
R v Keli Lane [No. 17] [2010] NSWSC 1544
Re L [1983] FLC 91–353
R v Li [2000] NSWSC 1088
R v Pope [2002] NSWSC 397
R v Raymond Douglas Sutton; *R v Margaret Ellen Sutton* [2007] NSWSC 295
R v Rg [2006] NSWSC 21
R v Richards [2002] NSWSC 415
R v Sette [2000] NSWSC 648
Re R (A Minor) (Contact) [1993] 2 FLR 762 (United Kingdom)
Re SM (A Minor) (Natural Father: Access) [1991] 2 FLR 333 (United Kingdom)
State of New South Wales (Department of Education and Training) v Maurice O'Sullivan [2005] NSWIRComm 198

Legislation

Coroners Act 1980 (NSW)
Coroners Act 2009 (NSW)
Child Protection (Prohibited Employment) Act 1998 (NSW) (repealed)
Children and Young Persons (Care and Protection) Act 1998 (NSW)
Children's Court Act 1987 (NSW)
Crimes Act 1900 (NSW)
Crimes (Domestic and Personal Violence) Act 2007 (NSW)
Evidence Act 1995 (NSW)
Family Law Act 1975 (Cth)
Family Law Amendment (Shared Parental Responsibility) Act 2006 (Cth)

1 None of the fieldwork materials including newspaper reports and case law can be referenced in the bibliography to comply with human ethics undertakings to de-identify all parties.

Family Law (Child Abduction Convention) Regulations 1986 (Cth)
Family Law (Child Protection Convention) Regulations 2003 (Cth)
Hague Convention on the Civil Aspects of International Child Abduction (25 October 1980)
Hague Convention on Jurisdiction, Applicable Law, Recognition, Enforcement and Cooperation in Respect of Parental Responsibility and Measures for the Protection of Children (19 October 1996)
Infanticide Act 1922 (United Kingdom)
Infanticide Act 1938 (United Kingdom)
Queensland Criminal Code 1899
Stuart Bastardy Act of England 1623 21 Jac. I, c. 23 (England)
United Nations Convention on the Rights of the Child (20 November 1989)

Other

Australian Government Family Assistance Office, *Paid Parental Leave Scheme for Working Parents* www.familyassist.gov.au/payments/family-assistance-payments/paid-parental-leave-scheme/
Family Court of Australia and Federal Magistrates Court of Australia, *Family Violence Best Practice Principles* www.familycourt.gov.au/wps/wcm/connect/fcoaweb/family-law-matters/family-violence/family-violence-best-practice-principles/
New South Wales Government, *Child Wellbeing and Child Protection: The NSW Interagency Guidelines* www.community.nsw.gov.au/kts
New South Wales Government, *Keep Them Safe Evaluation Framework* (25 July 2011) www.keepthemsafe.nsw.gov.au/resources/?a=82819
Queensland Government Department of Communities Child Safety Services, *Child Safety Practice Manual* www.communities.qld.gov.au/childsafety/child-safety-practice-manual
Tasmanian Government's Social Policy Initiative, *Safe at Home* (4 September 2009) www.safeathome.tas.gov.au

Index

For Product Safety Concerns and Information please contact our EU representative GPSR@taylorandfrancis.com
Taylor & Francis Verlag GmbH, Kaufingerstraße 24, 80331 München, Germany

www.ingramcontent.com/pod-product-compliance
Ingram Content Group UK Ltd.
Pitfield, Milton Keynes, MK11 3LW, UK
UKHW022010180926
475701UK00003B/291
* 9 7 8 0 3 6 7 5 8 5 5 0 1 *